Women
and the
Literature
of the
Seventeenth Century

Women and the Literature of the Seventeenth Century

An Annotated Bibliography
based on Wing's *Short-title Catalogue*

Compiled by
Hilda L. Smith
and
Susan Cardinale

Bibliographies and Indexes in Women's Studies, Number 10

Greenwood Press
New York • Westport, Connecticut • London

Library of Congress Cataloging-in-Publication Data

Smith, Hilda L.
  Women and the literature of the seventeenth century : an annotated
bibliography based on Wing's Short-title catalogue / compiled by
Hilda L. Smith and Susan Cardinale.
    p. cm. — (Bibliographies and indexes in women's studies,
  ISSN 0742-6941 ; no. 10)
  Includes bibliographical references.
  ISBN 0-313-22059-X (lib. bdg. : alk. paper)
    1. Women and literature—Great Britain—History—17th century—
Bibliography.   2. English literature—17th century—Bibliography.
3. English literature—Women authors—Bibliography.   4. Women—
History—Modern period, 1600-   —Sources—Bibliography.
5. Bibliography—Early printed books—17th century.   6. English
imprints.   I. Cardinale, Susan.   II. Wing, Donald Goddard, 1904-
Short-title catalogue of books printed in England, Scotland,
Ireland, Wales, and British America, and of English books printed in
other countries, 1641-1700.   III. Title.   IV. Series.
Z2013.5.W6S6   1990
[PR113]
016.8208′09287—dc20   89-28652

British Library Cataloguing in Publication Data is available.

Library of Congress Catalog Card Number: 89-28652
ISBN: 0-313-22059-X
ISSN: 0742-6941

First published in 1990

Greenwood Press, Inc.
88 Post Road West, Westport, Connecticut 06881

Printed in the United States of America

♾™

The paper used in this book complies with the
Permanent Paper Standard issued by the National
Information Standards Organization (Z39.48-1984).

10 9 8 7 6 5 4 3 2 1

Contents

Preface

Background

This project, begun in the early seventies, was initially an effort to build upon the prodigious work of Donald Wing. His <u>Short-title Catalogue of Books Printed in England, Scotland, Ireland, Wales, and British America and of English Books Printed in other Countries 1641-1700</u> (New York: The Index Society, 1945) remains a bibliographical classic. The second edition has been expanded by the Index Committee of the Modern Language Association to include over 120,000 publications.

Unfortunately, the enormity of this project necessitated abbreviating titles. In addition, the lack of subject access to the items cited in the Wing <u>STC</u> limits its usefulness to some degree for contemporary scholars.

The well-documented difficulties of doing historical research on women during this period compound these problems. Works by women were published anonymously or pseudonymously; men signed satirical pieces as females; even serious publications by men were sometimes mistakenly attributed to women. At the least, an expansion of the short titles by and about women, and a reading of materials, especially previously unexamined ones, seemed necessary for historians of women.

Locating works for and about women proved a particularly challenging task. Many titles were truncated in the Wing <u>STC</u> before information about their pertinence to women was apparent. Or titles were not revelatory of contents at all. A wide net had to be cast so that the wheat could be separated from the chaff without considerable danger of missing obscure items.

Characteristics of the Bibliography

The bibliography is divided into two main sections. Part I includes only publications by women. Entry numbers are followed by "B" for "by." Part II includes works for and about women as well as material mistakenly attributed to women but likely written by men. Entry numbers are followed by "A" for "about."

We should note the difficulty of determining authorship of some items. Petitions by individuals were almost always written by men; however, if they are narratives, or if details are offered from a first-person perspective, we included them in Part I. After a close reading of problematic material, if we were still unsure of male or female authorship, we consulted other sources--usually library catalogs or works by other scholars like David Erskine Baker, Mary Anne O'Donnell or Patricia Higgins (see below).

or if details are offered from a first-person perspective, we included them in Part I. After a close reading of problematic material, if we were still unsure of male or female authorship, we consulted other sources--usually library catalogs or works by other scholars like David Erskine Baker, Mary Anne O'Donnell or Patricia Higgins (see below).

In Part II we have included works addressing the role of women in marriage. Because books about domestic arts and childrearing were usually written for women, they are also in the bibliography. The quantity of material published during this period necessitated narrowing the scope of Part II in some ways. For example, only those ballads, plays and novels written by men about living or historical figures are listed. (Those about women in general or fictional female characters are omitted.) Pornographic material is limited to that whose primary characters are women or whose tone is overtly misogynistic. Some publications, like La Calprenede's novel Cleopatra, are omitted, even if their titles would indicate inclusion, if their contents do not focus on women.

Items with both unique titles and distinct Wing STC numbers have separate entries; however, only one edition is listed for each title. (Only the edition examined is entered in the bibliography.) An asterisk following a Wing number indicates multiple editions. Pseudonymous works are entered under title with cross-references from the authors' pseudonyms. Anonymous publications are also under title. Entries that are out of Wing STC-number sequence are cross-referenced from the Wing entries. Cross-references in Parts I and II are to entry numbers. To suggest the tone of individual pieces, we have used quotations from many of the original documents.

Entries have been verified in the Wing STC, the British Library or Library of Congress catalogs. In cases of dubious attribution we have deferred to these sources. We have modernized spellings, so that, for example, "tryal," "dutchess" and "divil" appear in contemporary form and are alphabetized accordingly. Lengthy titles are shortened if space considerations so dictate.

An addendum notes works not read because they were unavailable or because they were discovered after the final numbering sequence had been completed. Chronological and general indexes are keyed to page numbers. The general index does not include authors because they are listed alphabetically in sequence in each section with extensive cross-references.

A final section listing female booksellers, publishers and printers follows the main bibliography. Women authors who printed their own books are omitted if they were not printers by profession. Readers should consult Morrison's Index (see below) for further information.

The following abbreviations are used throughout the bibliography:

Wing STC: Donald Wing's Short-title Catalogue of Books Printed in England, Scotland, Ireland, Wales, and British America and of English Books Printed in other Countries 1641-1700

EEB: Early English Books, 1641-1700 microfilm collection
        (University Microfilms International)

TT: The Thomason Tracts microfilm collection
        (University Microfilms International)

 *:   Multiple editions are listed in the Wing STC; however, only the edition consulted is listed.

N.I.W.: The item was not found in the Wing STC. (Most of these works are listed in the British Library or Library of Congress catalogs.)

Relationship to Other Sources

Some material has been added to the Wing STC literature. In Part I we include works that were written by women during the period but published later. Also, if we have discovered writing by women in general collections, we include it. In Part II serials like The Wandring Whore expand the Wing material. Most importantly, material collected by George Thomason (the Thomason tracts, 1640-1661)--some of it excluded from the Wing STC--augments the bibliography. References culled from other sources, primarily the British Library and the Library of Congress catalogs, are also interfiled and identified as "N.I.W." (not in Wing).

Titles filmed in the University Microfilms International collections Early English Books, 1641-1700 and The Thomason Tracts are annotated with reel and position locations. It should be noted that because the MLA Wing project has altered, added to or omitted many of the original Wing numbers in its recent edition of the Wing Short-title Catalogue, confusion may arise if a new Wing number is searched on microfilm that is keyed to the old numbers. This bibliography lists only the new numbers, so it may be necessary to consult the earlier edition of the Wing catalog while using the microfilm collections.

We have located some filmed essays, stories or plays in collections. Reel positions are listed both for these individual items and for the collections in which they appear. Sometimes only the collection is listed in the Wing STC. In such cases, the unlisted items within the collections are identified as "N.I.W." Reels and positions are listed for all editions we located on film; the index for each microfilm collection notes the edition filmed at a particular place on a given reel.

Acknowledgements

A project like this one, involving a large number of discrete works, many of which are anonymous, benefits greatly from the special skills and knowledge of others. We are grateful for the advice and assistance of librarians and staff at the following institutions: the Beinecke Library of Yale University, the Bodleian Library of Oxford University, the British Library, the Folger Shakespeare Library, the Friends Library (London), the Houghton Library of Harvard University, the Huntington Library, the Library of Congress, the McKeldin Library of the University of Maryland, the Nagoya University Library in Japan, the National Library of Medicine and the Newberry Library. In particular, we are grateful to R. K. Browne, English Language Collections of the British Library, Nati Krivatsy of the Folger Shakespeare Library, to Phil Lapsansky of the Library Company of Philadelphia, to Elizabeth Brown of the Haverford College Library Quaker Collection, to Linda Chase of the Bender Library of The American University, to Lisle Law of University Microfilms International, to the MLA Wing project at Yale University and to the Primate Research Institute of the University of Kyoto, where Susan Cardinale spent time working on this book. This work was supported in part by a Faculty Research Board Grant from the University of Maryland, College Park, and a grant form the Taft Committee, University of Cincinnati. We would also like to thank Cynthia Requardt, Gregory Smith, and Susan Hines for their assistance.

Finally, we would like to thank our families for their support and good humor.

Secondary Sources

Over the years we have worked with many sources in addition to the Wing <u>STC</u>. We will list only those which we consulted regularly during work on the present bibliography:

Baker, David Erskine. <u>Biographia Dramatica</u>. New York: AMS Press, 1966.

British Museum. Department of Printed Books. Thomason Collection. <u>Catalogue of the Pamphlets, Newspapers, and Manuscripts relating to the Civil War, the Commonwealth, and Restoration, collected by George Thomason, 1640-1661</u>. London, 1908.

Crawford, Anne and Tony Hayter, eds. <u>Europa Biographical Dictionary of British Women</u>. London: Europa Publications Ltd., 1983.

Halkett, Samuel and John Laing. <u>Dictionary of Anonymous and Pseudonymous English Literature</u>. Edinburgh: Oliver and Boyd, 1926-[62].

Higgins, Patricia. "The Reactions of Women." In <u>Politics, Religion and the English Civil War</u>, ed. Brian Manning, 179-222. New York: St. Martin's Press, 1974.

Matthews, William, comp. <u>British Autobiographies: An Annotated Bibliography of British Autobiographies Written or Published before 1951</u>. Berkeley: The University of California Press, 1955.

Morrison, Paul G. <u>Index of Printers, Publishers and Booksellers in Donald Wing's Short-title Catalogue.</u> Charlottesville: The University of Virginia Press for the Bibliographical Society of the University of Virginia, 1955.

O'Donnell, Mary Ann. <u>Aphra Behn: An Annotated Bibliography of Primary and Secondary Sources</u>. New York: Garland Press, 1986.

Smith, Joseph. <u>A Descriptive Catalogue of Friends' Books, or Books written by Members of the Society of Friends</u>. London: J. Smith, 1867.

Introduction

In the early 1970s, research was just beginning in the new women's history on seventeenth-century English women. There was little monographic literature beyond Alice Clark's The Working Life of Women in the Seventeenth Century (1919), Doris Mary Stenton's The English Woman in History (1957), Ruth Kelso's The Doctrine for the Lady of the Renaissance (1956) and Keith Thomas' pioneering essay titled "Women and the Civil War Sects" in Past and Present 13 (April 1958).

In researching English women at this time, it became clear that an annotated bibliography of works by and about women was essential for an understanding of their circumstance. Such an enterprise is predicated on the argument that, to this end, it is wise to read as broadly as possible in both types of literature for a given period. After reading nearly fifteen hundred discrete works, we are reinforced in this belief, even though many scholars have concentrated on writing about women of only one type, e.g., domestic guides, during the last two decades (1).

We began by examining items on women listed in the Thomason tracts index. As feminists, we became excited upon finding items such as parliaments of women and petitions by maids and widows. Despite our highest hopes, the vast majority of these works were misogynistic satires or scatological tales. On the other hand, the anonymous Essay in Defense of the Female Sex and Poulain de la Barre's The Woman as Good as the Man were startling and fascinating works of feminist argumentation. In addition, gynecological textbooks proved much more than descriptions of and prescriptions for women's illnesses; they also revealed general social attitudes about the distinct moral and intellectual capacities of the sexes thought to be correlated with temperature and moisture level.

Reading these materials has not always been its own reward. In fact, there were disappointments. For example, the impressiveness of the quantity of writings by Quaker women was diminished by their repetition: most were warnings, especially to citizens of particular towns or to public officials, to cease persecution or to repent. Alternatively, the Friends were admonished to lead a modest, orderly and pious life. Mystics such as Jane Lead and prophets like Eleanor Douglas wrote in nearly impenetrable prose, sometimes rendering their ideas virtually inaccessible to the modern reader.

The satirical work has also been something of a letdown. Men never seemed to tire of using feminine imagery to mock women, lambast marriage or titillate other men. Women were depicted as sexual battlements under siege, while men, their organs flaccid, languished. Other than the unique contemporary view of women as the more lustful sex, the misogynistic message seemed altogether reminiscent of other pornography in other times. Plus ca change, plus c'est la meme chose...

On the positive side, however, there was the anonymous Advice to the Maids and Women of London which urged them to trade needlework and spinning for double-entry bookkeeping in order to enhance their chances for economic security, and the tenacious Elinor James or Elizabeth Poole, who gained the ear of the General Council to speak against physical harm to Charles I. Like the Quaker women who defended women's right to speak in public and criticized hireling priests, they demonstrated the emergence of a self-confidence which was to prove essential to future generations of women.

We should say a word about the total number of publications by women. Although it was a commonplace accepted by earlier historians that women's published work was insignificant and of little value as a gauge of the intellectual character of the age, we believe that, at the least, this bibliography shows that many women did write, whether for private or public consumption. But beyond these surviving works, it is possible, even likely, that most women's ideas were not recorded, their private writings were not made public, or libraries did not consider their work worthy of preservation. So we must continue to search for their words elsewhere.

WORKS BY WOMEN

Annotating 637 titles by women has revealed a spectrum of writers that is not evident when focusing on, say, one genre of women's writing or works of a single author. It has demonstrated the importance of post-1650 activity by a critical group of women who wrote about topics of general interest (2). They clearly moved beyond the contribution of the Elizabethan scholar/author noted for her linguistic skills and translation of male authors.

The period following 1640 saw a dramatic increase in women's writings over earlier years. Patricia Crawford has noted that although they comprise only about 1.2% of the total published between 1640 and 1700, this percentage represents a doubling of their pre-Civil War rate (3). Perhaps equally significant was the range of topics they addressed and the emergence of a few well-published authors: Mary Astell; Aphra Behn; Margaret Cavendish, Duchess of Newcastle; Lady Eleanor Douglas; Margaret Fell Fox; Elinor James; Jane Lead; Mary Marsin; Mary Pix and Dorothy White. These women wrote plays, biographies, poetry, fiction and non-fiction. They explored social issues, moral philosophy, natural science, religious ideas and political theory. From Cavendish's ambivalent posture to James' brash entreaties to the king, they revealed an equally wide range of personality and intellectual perspective.

Among these prolific women, Margaret Fell Fox represents the most frequently published group of women writers of the period, the Quakers. Her work comprises 13% of the total Quaker contribution (171 titles between 1641 and 1700).* These women began writing in the early 1650s and continued to produce in volume during every decade of the century. There were forty-three Quaker titles printed during the fifties, forty-seven during the sixties, twenty-three in the following decade, twenty-eight in the 1680s and thirty during the final ten years of the seventeenth century.

Five types of Quaker documents were dominant: exhortations to remain faithful or discussion of religious doctrine (54), entreaties to repent (31), criticism of ministers or public officials (18), complaints of religious persecution (16) and reports of women's meetings (10).

Writing about doctrinal matters appeared consistently over the decades. Entreaties to repent were published primarily during the fifties and sixties (total 25),

*Analysis of documents in this introduction is based on one title per entry, rather than multiple editions of a single work.

with only six thereafter. Reports of the women's meetings did not proliferate until the last two decades of the century, as the meetings were established in a number of English counties during the late 1670s, a decade later than the general monthly and quarterly meetings (4).

Quaker women represented the interests (except for support of the women's meetings, which was opposed by a number of Quaker men) and followed the publication pattern of their brothers in the Society. Discussion by women of specific acts of persecution occurred in the greatest numbers in 1660-62, 1670-72, 1675-77 and particularly 1680-86--the periods of the most arrests for dissent and most stringent attempts at governmental control (5). When persecution abated, Quakers turned their attention to issues of faith and matters of internal governance. At these times the women also concentrated on marital issues, support of the poor and administration of their meetings.

Including this Quaker material, about 55% of writing by women concerned religion; however, this figure should be considered along with the fact of disproportionate production by a few women: Elinor James wrote nineteen pieces, Lady Eleanor Douglas published sixty-four, Dorothy White produced seventeen, Mary Marsin issued fourteen, Jane Lead penned sixteen, and Margaret Fell Fox contributed twenty-three. The twenty-two women who wrote more than five works each in fact represent about half of the total output. Religious writing usually appeared as distinct types: (1) mystical or prophetic treatises characterized by rhetorical flourishes or cryptic language, (2) warnings to repent promising future contentment or dire consequences if unheeded, and (3) tales of religious conversion. The mystic Jane Lead imagined other worlds and guided her sect, the Philadelphians, to a closer communion with God, removed from established doctrines. Her sixteen books testify to her direct experience of God, revealing eight realms of the soul and the freeing of the spirit from earthly bonds. Moreover, in A Messenger of An Universal Peace (1698), she explicitly stated that God's word is available to all "without distinction of Sex, Age or Person." In A Revelation of the Everlasting Gospel Message (1697), fearing her message was being ignored, Lead reported bias "If it be a Woman, who can therefore have no Authority, and against whom many not Unjust Prejudices do lie."

Lady Eleanor Douglas, writing in the 1640s and 1650s, authored sixty-four mostly brief prophetic pieces. Fascinated with numerology, the biblical book of Daniel and apocalyptic portions of scripture, she viewed the seventeenth century, the reign of Charles I and the date of her birth as prophetically significant. She based her predictions about the evolution of religion and politics in Great Britain in part on these dates. Many of her books, printed at her own expense, were banned, and she was eventually forced to publish them in Holland. Imprisoned in England for printing violations, she compared her incarceration to that of Daniel, warning England of the folly of ignoring her prophecies--even though she was a woman. There is little evidence that she had a following.

Fifth Monarchist mystic Anna Trapnel was a less productive writer. Her five lengthy prophetic works, including The Cry of a Stone (1654) and A Legacy for Saints (1654), a transcription of her experiences during religious trances, describe her compulsion to alert the nation to Cromwell's arrogance and the unfairness of tithes (6).

Women also wrote religious works as members of the Church of England. Elinor James' nineteen brief pieces were addressed primarily to public officials. Assuring the citizens of London in 1688 that James II might be converted to Protestantism, she stated, "God that chang'd Nebuchadnezar's Heart, can convince my Sovereign Lord, and make him more zealous for the Protestant Religion than ever he was for Rome." James produced little in the early '80s, the vast majority of her work appearing between 1688 and 1690, when she addressed the legitimacy of James II and the ascension of William and Mary. She never directed her statements to Mary II and seems not to have identified with women in royal or religious authority. Most of the other Anglican women wrote meditations or memoirs that do not express the zeal of sectarian and Quaker writings.

One of the most prominent Anglican authors was Mary Astell, who supported the right of women to a serious, advanced education and respect within marriage. She linked reason to religion and argued that, like men, women should explore scripture intellectually as well as spiritually. In A Serious Proposal to the Ladies (1694), she argued for a women's college dedicated to the pursuit of learning and good works. Astell decried the frivolous lives of leisured women and advised them to leave cards, fashion and social affairs, for charitable deeds and the life of the mind (7).

Her work was preceded by Bathsua Makin's proposal for a girls' school offering foreign language, science and mathematics and philosophy. Makin looked nostalgically to the Elizabethan period, which she considered salutary for women's learning, and noted the examples of Margaret More, Lady Jane Grey and the Queen herself. Makin could count Hannah Wolley among those sympathetic to her hope for better educational opportunities for women: In introductions to her household guides and cookbooks, Wolley admonished families for allowing their daughters' minds to lie fallow while permitting their less talented sons to attend university.

Feminist ideas during this period can be traced from the works of Margaret Cavendish, Duchess of Newcastle in the fifties and sixties to Wolley and Makin in the sixties and seventies, through Astell's work at the end of the century. Similar sentiments can be observed in the poetry of Anne Winchilsea, Sarah Fyge Egerton, Elizabeth Singer Rowe and Lady Mary Chudleigh's The Female Advocate. The Duchess of Newcastle was something of an enigma. She lamented women's lack of ability and character and believed men the stronger sex; but she also wrote angry denunciations of the limitation of women by men to the domestic sphere, of male arrogance and of women's lack of access to higher education. She questioned the burden of childbirth and wondered why women should be loyal to a government they could not empower. Cavendish asked her sisters, perhaps rhetorically, to "make frequent Assemblies, Associations, and Combinations amongst Our Sex, that we may unite in Prudent Counsels, to make ourselves as Free, Happy and Famous as Men" (8). She was a blazing feminist star, self-absorbed, who wrote in isolation. In contrast, Astell was a more consistent thinker who, though much less prolific than Newcastle, gained considerable attention with her tenable plan for a women's college.

The four others revealed more anger than Astell and less hope. Winchilsea was disappointed and incensed about ridicule of women's writing. Although she herself was noted as a wit, much of her poetry attacked flippant attitudes and their deleterious impact on women. Her interest in female friendships and nature pointed the way to an exploration of religious truth. Chudleigh focused on the family and saw wives as degraded. Encouraging women to avoid weakening their marriages, she pushed them "to be wise." Rowe wrote about female friendship as well as heterosexual relations, bringing a unique sense of humor to her poetry. The young Egerton, writing quite a strident response to Robert Gould's satirical Love given O'er (1682), called men ambitious and defended the rational powers of women.

Literary output increased dramatically as the century progressed. Although Katharine Philips, Anne Winchilsea and, to a lesser extent, Elizabeth Singer Rowe, were noted as poets during the latter part of the seventeenth century, they were eclipsed by Aphra Behn. She is remembered today primarily as a dramatist and novelist, but she also wrote poetry and translated scientific treatises. (She wrote nearly sixty volumes in total.) Aside from the fact that she supported herself with proceeds from her writing, she is of interest as a woman who wrote Restoration comedy similar to her male counterparts, full of sexual intrigue and allusion. She was also concerned about restrictions on women's education and professional prospects. In her translation of Fontenelle's A Discovery of New Worlds (1688), she praised his intention to render science comprehensible to women, but deplored his condescending tone and simplistic language. Ample evidence for her sympathy for her sex also emerges in introductions to her plays and in her clear objection to arranged marriage (9).

Finally, a word about the publications addressed to royalty: There are two anonymous poems and several by Aphra Behn (the consummate royalist) written for Mary II and others which resemble those of men in their obsequiousness and restraint (see below). But the remaining items, aside from individual petitions, are remarkable for their daring. Worthy of note are Elizabeth Hatton's broadside written to Charles I in support of Parliament; Alicia D'Anvers' poetic criticism of the French-Belgian alliance addressed to William III; and Joan Whitrowe's broadsides to William III and Mary II, accusing him of wasting time hunting and advising her to use "holy Women in former ages for your Example" and to follow a parsimonious style of life.

WORKS FOR AND ABOUT WOMEN

Several topics or themes appeared consistently over time in the nearly 1,000 items for and about women listed in Part II. They include the attempted religious conversion of women (usually away from Catholicism), discussion about the tenability of or reported instances of witchcraft, anti-Catholic texts (often utilizing derogatory female imagery), arguments about female fashion, advice to women about proper behavior and duties to their husbands, and misogynistic material. Dominant in the latter category were attacks on the mistresses of Charles II (during his reign); amusing or negative portrayals of prostitutes; mock petitions and parliaments of women. Other types of books appeared as well: cookbooks, gynecological/obstetrical guides, medicinal recipe books, testimonials, funeral sermons and biographies.

Domestic guides, including cookbooks and collections of medicines and ointments, were among the most popular type of literature published; most saw multiple editions. Works centering on religion were ubiquitous during the 1640s, especially by Puritans like Richard Braithwaite (The English Gentleman and the English Gentlewoman). (The section about women was originally printed in 1631.) Following the Restoration, men tended to link religious advice to their sisters to the dangers of attraction to Catholicism. These volumes, often penned by Anglican divines, also sometimes conveyed a political message, urging loyalty to both church and crown. They were less emotional and didactic than such books appearing during the mid-century decades.

In addition, two texts were translated from the French (the anonymous Discourse of Women, 1662, and Du Bosc's well-known L'Honnete Femme, appearing as The Accomplish'd Woman in 1656). Although Du Bosc advocated serious learning for women, the 1692 edition of this work, The Excellent Woman Described, as well as the Discourse, are notable for their emphasis on allegedly negative qualities of women--pity, cruelty, jealousy, avarice, concupiscence.

In contrast, the English authors were often sympathetic to women's lack of power and, stressing traditional values (Halifax, 1688), usually assumed women possessed a benign nature. Often they discussed female duty and deportment, giving equal attention to behavioral concerns, spiritual matters, forms for correspondence and candying and preserving (see especially Robert Codrington's 1664 edition of The Second Part of Youth's Behaviour, John Heydon's Advice to a Daughter, 1658, and Gervase Markham's The English Housewife, 1649). Aside from the usual advice to check female vanity and to be submissive even to intemperate husbands, some original thoughts were purveyed: Francis Boyle Shannon (1696) blamed arranged marriage for societal decay, while Thomas Hilder (1653) suggested that women had a duty to further the family fortune.

If such volumes were popular because they reflected dominant attitudes, the expectation that women would assume a dependent role and a compliant posture would seem to render them particularly vulnerable to aggressive husbands. But publications about wife abuse were rare, appeared randomly and seem to indicate no clear social trend; however, two works are of interest because they discussed abuse of women as a moral question.

In 1682 William Heale's 1609 edition of Apologie for Women was reissued as The Great Advocate and Oratour for Women. Heale opposed corporal discipline of women (a "custome so common to undervalue the worth of that sexe"), questioned it as a measure of masculinity and emphasized positive relations between the sexes. In 1650 Mones A. Vauts took a different position in The Husband's Authority Unvail'd. Annotating his text with biblical references, he held a husband's authority to be self-evident and explored submission and authority. Abused women--if they were virtuous--could expect to be rewarded for their forbearance in the afterlife. Vauts did take care to warn certain men against striking their wives, but only if the men were drunken or irreligious.

The disparity between these texts, the only two in this bibliography focusing on the issue, renders discussion of the extent of abuse problematic. It may be more fruitful to look for accounts of women like Anne Wentworth (1677-79), whose testimonials to nearly two decades of abuse hint at the longevity of violence toward women in English society that Heale alluded to early in the century.

Pornographic literature has been viewed as another indicator of malevolent attitudes toward women. The number of such works reached their zenith at the Restoration and in the last two decades of the century (10). Misogyny was predictably present in these works; however, there seems to be no evidence at present that misogynistic themes became more acute or strident as a function of the frequency of publication of pornographic work. It is therefore difficult to gauge any change in attitudes toward women which might be reflected in this literature.

Unfortunately it is difficult to tease apart the possibly misogynistic versus satirical intent of many of these writers. For example, a piece that is primarily an anti-Catholic diatribe includes this description of the Duchess of Portsmouth, a mistress of Charles II: "Portsmouth, that Pocky-Bitch,/A Damn'd Papistical-Drab,/An ugly deformed Witch,/Eaten up with the Mange and Scab." Similarly, The Batechellor's Answer to the Maids Complaint (1675) addresses the nature of marriage; yet its tone and sentiments reveal its anti-woman bias: "To be tyed for term of life like a monkey by the loyns to a bedpost with the same woman" is unthinkable. Ultimately one wonders if the attitude toward marriage or religion, or the image of women portrayed in such satires, was salient.

In any case, seventeen works of satire appeared during the 1640s, with seven specifically of a sexual nature. The 1650s produced seven general and six sexual satires, while there were only five combined during the 1660s. In the 1670s, eleven combined appeared, while eight were published during the 1680s. During the '90s five general and nine sexual satires were printed.

These figures may be misleading, however, for several reasons. We did not count certain publications that were marginal if their subject matter, rather than satirical intent, seemed paramount (attacks on prostitution and the Parliament are examples).   In addition, (as noted in the <u>Preface</u>) we include only those pornographic works which focused on women or which were pointedly misogynistic. Finally, we counted only titles, rather than editions, so that we have weighed equally a work published once and one issued several times.

Partially in response to this flow of pornographic material and sexual satire, there appeared eleven defenses of women. Two appeared by 1650; the remaining volumes were published during the last three decades of the seventeenth century. Only works by Agrippa von Nettlesheim, Poulain de la Barre, Samuel Torshell and Nahum Tate were signed. Of the total, the only treatise comparable to those of feminist women was by Poulain de la Barre, a Frenchman. Employing a Cartesian model to argue the intellectual equality of the sexes, he described the evolution of sex roles and favored women's education for public activity. The others merely protested satires of women, posited biblical or classical female role models or praised women for their modesty, beauty and sweet natures.

Publications that also had a steady audience were gynecological textbooks, funeral sermons, religious essays and meditations. Witchcraft was another topic which held lasting interest over sixty years. There were thirty-five works about witches, including transcripts or descriptions of trials, averaging around five per decade, with the largest number printed during the 1650s.

Although funeral sermons are in some ways almost formulaic in their descriptions of the piety and virtue of the deceased, they do provide some information about upper class women, particularly regarding their education and charitable works. Elizabeth Scott of Kent (d. 1659) was an especially generous person, giving gifts to poor scholars and donating one fifth of her annual income to charity. (She is one of several women whose writings are included in their eulogies or collections of deathbed testimonials: "I was born a child of wrath, and an heir of hell...Yet I did duties in a formal way, and was very confident.")

William Gouge's sermon preached at the funeral of Margaret Ducke was perhaps unintentionally revealing of her psychological state: The wife of a prominent physician, she is described as meek and perhaps obsessively reclusive. Today we might call her agoraphobic. (See also John Hart's description of Mrs. Drake's decade-long depression in <u>Trodden Down Strength</u>, 1647, possibly caused by a forced marriage, exacerbated by post-partum hormonal imbalance and characterized by nightmares, listlessness and manic episodes. One might also question the mental state of the celebrated Sarah Wight, described in Henry Jessey's popular <u>The Exceeding Riches of Grace...viz, Mrs. Sarah Wight, lately hopeless and restless</u>, 1647. Although she survived her seventy-day trance, she engaged in head-banging, expressions of anger and even attempted suicide.)

In distinction, Susanna Perwick (d. 1661), apparently a talented musician who died prematurely at twenty-four, had mastered harmony, calligraphy, cookery and accountancy. She was a generous woman who had been tutored by eminent musicians and was a good conversationalist to boot. Similarly Anne Baynard, who died in 1697, was characterized in a sermon by John Prude as a "subtle Disputant" in the "hard and knotty argument of metaphysical learning."

Equally remarkable is John Collings' double funeral sermon, occasioned by the deaths of two sisters. Frances Hobart of Norfolk, a widow, was responsible for reducing the debt left by her husband by 6000 pounds. Her sister Katharine Couten, however, was not so fortunate. Her poignant life was marked by the deaths of many children, the ruin of her husband's estate, his escape to Italy and a final confining illness. Another exception to the quotidian sermon is Timothy Rogers' memorial (1697) about Elizabeth Dunton, the wife of publisher John Dunton. Rogers unabashedly champions women's education and mentions feminists such as Mary Astell.

Altogether there were seventy-five funeral sermons for women, the overwhelming majority of which either totally ignored the deceased or described traditional feminine activities and traits. On average they appeared ten per decade, except for the nineties, when their number doubled.

There were several female figures, aside from royalty, who were the subject of controversy, gossip or general interest during this period. Pope Joan, the focus of five publications (1663-1689), was a legendary fictitious figure who had received attention earlier in the century. She was reputed to have studied in Athens and ascended to the papacy through deception, only to become impregnated by an aide. Discussion about her revolved around the "papist" threat and the veracity of her story. Refuting her existence, one author focused on her sexuality, denigrating her through association with the "Whores of Rome."

Another celebrated figure was Mary Carleton, "The German Princess," tried as a bigamist and thief. The nearly twenty publications about her are generally clustered in 1663, the year of her first trial, and 1673, her execution date. Like Pope Joan, Carleton was a clever character who allegedly dressed as a man and assumed a distinctly male persona. Of course, like Pope Joan, her challenge to the sexual status quo guaranteed her demise in disgrace. (Carleton was executed.)

Only a few more publications appeared about Carleton than about Elizabeth Cellier, a midwife who was implicated in the Meal-tub Plot. (The Plot, 1679-80, was a spurious Presbyterian plot to counter the Popish Plot, which backfired and further discredited Catholics.) Material read about Cellier comprise 33% of the total publications about women during the first year of her fame (1680). This percentage is especially interesting in view of her fairly minor role in the Plot. Much of the writing critical of Cellier focuses on her profession--a likely topic, given the well-documented attempts during this period by physicians to discredit or control midwifery. (See works by Cellier, Jane Sharp and Nicholas Culpeper in defense of the skilled and important role of midwives in childbirth and, in distinction, Peter Chamberlen's earlier A Voice in Rama, in which he proposed state regulation of the profession.)

Other midwives gained notoriety as well. Aside from Cellier and Hester Shaw, who was forced to rebut a challenge to her reputation by a minister in the "plain style of a weak woman," another midwife was celebrated for a totally different reason. Mary Hobry was a French woman who was repeatedly physically abused by her alcoholic husband. In desperation she strangled him one night, then dismembered his body. This event was reported unsympathetically in several publications in 1687 and 1688, including a poem by Elkanah Settle in which he compared her to Medea.

The remaining publications about female criminals (other than accused witches, prostitutes and religious dissenters) appeared almost exclusively in the last three decades of the century. Among the cases reported, two women were executed for harboring enemies (Alicia Lisle and Elizabeth Gaunt, coincidentally both in 1685); two were servants who turned against their masters (Charity Philpot and Margaret Clark in 1681 and 1680, respectively); two were accused of fraud or bribery (Anne Price and Mary Butler, 1680 and 1700); two were thieves (Mary Frith, known also as "Moll Cutpurse," and Margaret Martel in 1662 and 1697) and one killed her husband in a jealous rage (Elizabeth Lillyman in 1675). The remaining cases concern women accused of infanticide (Abigail Hill, Mary Goodenough, Elizabeth Howard and an anonymous woman from Durham). Stories of female crime were usually sensationalist and often depicted a penitent, but dignified outsider presented as an example to her sex. A secondary theme was sometimes the threat of Catholic criminals to Protestants.

Like the single incident of a woman supposedly arrested for buggery (Mary Higgs in 1677), reported cases of infanticide must be viewed with skepticism. They are often found in publications recounting "strange" or "terrible" news, many of which are classified in the General Index as "bizarre tales." The news is usually of the tabloid variety--narratives of visions or trances, monstrous births, miraculous cures, resurrections, transvestism, excessive fasting or sleeping, calamities visited upon persons uttering oaths, or of witchcraft. These publications may have served much as tragedy apparently did in ancient Greece or as reports of grotesqueries or violence do today. Beyond this purgative function, they surely helped to popularize the notion of witchcraft (including works centering on Mother Shipton, a prophetic witch) and may have furthered the mystification of female sexuality.

Of the documents written about royal figures, several are histories of Elizabeth, Mary II; Mary, Queen of Scots, Henrietta Maria or Queen Christina of Sweden. Christina was of particular interest because of her exceptional competence and abdication following her public commitment to Catholicism. Of course, Mary, Queen of Scots was invoked as a warning of the imminence of Catholic incursion. Other items discussed Henrietta Maria's war preparations, the controversy surrounding the birth of The Old Pretender (James Frances Edward Stuart) and the prospect of joint rule by William and Mary. An anonymous broadside of 1689 (Reasons for Crowning the Prince and Princess of Orange King and Queen Joyntly) captured the essence of such discussions. The author supported the replacement of James II by a non-Stuart to avoid a dispute over a claim by the Prince of Wales and to meet the challenge presented by political instability in Europe. (He also noted the advantage of a "Vigorous and masculine administration" as "more capable to govern than a woman.")

Works written to or for female royals were typically occasional poems noting arrivals, departures, births, deaths and illnesses. The forty-odd eclogues, elegies, sermons and panegyrics published upon the sudden death of Mary II seem virtually interchangeable. They inevitably expressed the country's grief in dramatic, almost bathetic, language and lauded Mary in her maternal or wifely role. Notwithstanding occasional mention of her leadership qualities, enumeration of her womanly virtues was standard. The sentimentality that characterizes these publications was ridiculed by an anonymous poet in The Mourning Poets (1695); he called the work of most of his colleagues bombastic and pedantic and lamented the ubiquity of the elegy.

Perhaps the most important point to make about writings for and about royalty, aside from their contrast with those by women (see above), is that, like the several volumes of poetry by Oxford dons printed to honor royal women, they were obviously written for patrons or out of quest of economic advantage. Clearly most women were unable to participate in the reciprocal patronage system, so it is not surprising that the overwhelming majority of such sycophantic material was written by men.

CONCLUSION

Although we have found few commonalities in the writings of men and women during the latter half of the seventeenth century, we were often able to discover linkages. For example, Flemish visionary Antonia Bourignon's posthumously published religious treatises prompted a public debate between John Cockburn and George Gauden. Quaker Anne Docwra and apostate Francis Bugg aired their differences in several publications at the end of the century, stooping to personal attack in the process. Mary Chudleigh answered John Sprint's condescending sermon endorsing wifely subservience with a spirited rejoinder. Elizabeth Avery's brother Thomas Parker, was incensed at her audacity in publishing a book "beyond the custom of your Sex," even though he admitted that he hadn't actually seen her work. Susanna Parr, excommunicated by Exon minister Lewis Stucley after an altercation, was not, it seems the only woman he ostracized: Mary Allein was also turned out and defamed in one of Stucley's sermons. Thus one can gain insights about individual women and their works through their interchanges with men.

On the other hand, it is difficult to ascertain the personal feelings of men, especially when they wrote prescriptive guides or composed in a professional capacity. For example, ministers describing deceased women in funeral sermons felt an obligation to demonstrate their erudition, to maintain a formal posture and to offer a moral lesson to the congregation. It must have been nearly impossible for them to give a sense of immediacy and to portray realistically the person being memorialized. Similarly, men advising women about proper conduct had both to consider popular attitudes and to maintain their credibility. These constraints might well have dictated to some degree what they said. In short, what we have missed most are straightforward descriptions of male-female interactions and accounts of women's daily activities, revealing actual male attitudes.

In preparing this book, we have read a broad cross-section of literature by men and women. The tone and focus of these works are quite distinct, as noted above. The lack of much commonality between the sections may be due in part to the fact that only writings about women, and not men's other contributions, are included here. In this selection, at least, it is clear that the sexes truly sounded alike only when they wrote about the same topic--for example, a shared faith or mutual support of a particular form of government. Finally, it should be remembered that the publications by men were meant to sell. (Many could be called seventeenth-century potboilers.) This fact alone could account for the difference between the two sections of the book: Women more often wrote for personal gratification or out of dedication to a cause; thus, their work was characterized more consistently by urgency, enthusiasm and honesty.

1. Hilda Smith, Reason's Disciples: Seventeenth-Century English Feminists (Urbana: University of Illinois Press, 1982), xvi.

2. Patricia Crawford, "Women's Published Writings 1600-1700" in Women in English Society 1500-1800, Mary Prior, ed. (London and New York: Metheun, 1985) and Elaine Hobby, Virtue of Necessity: English Women's Writing 1649-88 (Ann Arbor: University of Michigan Press, 1989). These are the most important efforts to characterize and quantify women's writings during the second half of the seventeenth century.

3. Crawford, ibid., 266.

4. Richard T. Vann, The Social Development of English Quakerism 1655-1755 (Cambridge: Harvard University Press, 1969), 102. This book remains the best account of the social and institutional origins of the Society of Friends during the second half of the seventeenth century. For works focusing specifically on women, Mable Richmond Brailsford's Quaker women 1650-1690 (London: Duckworth and Co., 1915) is the classic study of the contribution of individual women to the early formation of the Society of Friends. A more recent analysis can be found in Michael J. Galgano's "Out of the Mainstream: Catholic and Quaker Women in the Restoration Northwest" in The World of William Penn, Richard S. Dunn and Mary Maples Dunn, eds. (Philadelphia: University of Pennsylvania Press, 1986).

5. Richard T. Vann, ibid., 92.

6. Phyllis Mack, "Women as Prophets during the English Civil War," Feminist Studies, 8, No. 1 (1982), 19-45. This article analyzes the contributions of sectarian women, with special emphasis on the mystical and prophetic characteristics of their religiosity.

7. Hilda Smith, ibid., and Ruth Perry, The Celebrated Mary Astell: An Early English Feminist (Chicago: The University of Chicago Press, 1986). Smith's work is a survey of feminist ideas which evolved from 1650 to 1720. Ruth Perry treats Mary Astell, the most important of these feminists, in greater depth.

8. Margaret Cavendish, Duchess of Newcastle. Orations of Divers Sorts (London, Printed by A. Maxwell, 1668), 238-240.

9. Angeline Goreau, Reconstructing Aphra: A Social Biography of Aphra Behn (New York: Dial Press, 1980). This book is a recent study of both the life and writings of Aphra Behn.

10. Roger Thompson, Unfit for Modest Ears: A Study of Pornographic, Obscene, and Bawdy Works written or published in England in the Second Half of the Seventeenth Century (London: Macmillan, 1979). This book describes publication patterns of pornographic literature during this period.

Part I

Works By Women

1B Abbott, Margaret. A Testimony against the False Teachers of this Generation.
[London? 1659.] 8 pages. A 70B.

This Quaker tract inveighs against "false prophets," especially ministers currently
preaching in England. Abbott says she was formerly under their control, but
"came to be lighted with the light of Jesus Christ." She criticizes both greedy
priests and would-be proselytizers of the Quakers.

An Account of the Travels, Sufferings and Persecutions. See 114B.

Adams, Mary. The Ranters Monster. See 753A.

2B A[dams], M[ary]. A warning to the inhabitants of England. [London], 1676.
7 pages. A 489.

This non-Quaker sectarian tract emphasizes the tension between God's
vengeance and his merciful love. Adams calls upon sinners to repent,
reminding them God has been patient through their drunkenness and
debauchery. She warns He has demonstrated His wrath on prior
occasions--through plague and fire--when sinners ignored entreaties to repent.

Admirable and notable things of note. See 334B.

3B Advice to the women and maidens of London. By one of that sex. London,
Printed for Benjamin Billingsley, 1678. 36 pages. A 664. EEB Reel 908:15.

This anonymous author advises women to cease working with lace and
needlecraft and learn to keep account books. She cautions women to "avoid
the Danger of a helpless and forlorn Condition, incident to Widows." She claims
accounting is no more difficult than needlework and shows how to keep a
ledger and to keep track of inventory.

4B [Alcoforado, Marianna d'.] Five Love-Letters from a Nun to a Cavalier. London,
Printed for R. Bentley, 1693. 112 pages. A 892*. EEB Reel 1298:7 and 1372:17.

Translated by Roger L'Estrange, this romance purports to be love letters of a nun scorned by a French army officer in Portugal. They supposedly demonstrate a "Woman may be Flesh and Blood, in a Cloyster, as well as in a Palace." She dwells on the glories of the affair and bemoans her current sequestered state.

5B [Alcoforado, Marianna d'.] Seven Portuguese Letters. Being a second part to the Five Love Letters from a Nun to a Cavalier. London, Printed for H. Brome, 1681. 78 pages. A 893*. EEB Reels 404:10, 372:11, and 1453:6.

These romantic, emotional letters continue 4B. Here the nun claims she still cares for her lover and wishes to renounce her vows and join him.

6B [Alleine, Theodosia.] The Life and Death of that Excellent Minister of Christ Mr. Joseph Alleine. London, Printed for Nevil Simmons and Thomas Sawbridge, 1677. 311 pages. A 1015*. EEB Reels 1322:10 and 1372:23.

Only a portion of this book was written by Theodosia Alleine: "A Full Narrative of [Joseph Alleine's] life." The remainder contains comments about him and excerpts from his own writings. Theodosia Alleine's contribution is a factual biography which stresses her husband's piety.

7B Allen, Hannah. Satan, His Methods and Malice Baffled. London, Printed by John Wallis, 1683. 89 pages. A 1025. EEB Reel 1734:9.

This narrative describes Allen's personal and spiritual difficulties after the death of her first husband. When she was twenty and living with an aunt and uncle, she went through a religious conversion, then married Hannibal Allen, who died eight years later. After his death she gave birth to a child. Believing she would soon die, Allen attempted suicide and survived only with the aid of ministers and friends.

[Almanack.] The Womans Almanack. See 345B.

[Almanack.] The Woman's Almanack: Or, Prognostication Forever. See 376B.

[Almanack.] Her Prognostication for...1654. See 803A.

[Almanack.] The Woman's Almanack for...1694. See 472B.

The Amours of Messalina, Late Queen of Albion. See 31A.

8B Anderdon, Mary. A Word to the World. [London, 1662.] Broadside. A 3084A. EEB Reel 1754:8.

Anderdon addresses the Episcopal people who she says are "making war against the Light." She asks for the cessation of religious persecution, claiming she is trying "to bring those back to God who have abandoned Him." Anderdon composed this piece while imprisoned in Exon Jail for her religious activism as a Quaker.

9B Anne, Queen of England. The Princess Anne of Denmark's Letter to the Queen. London, [1688]. Broadside. A 3224.

Anne tells Queen Mary she is fleeing [to Nottingham] with her husband, George, Prince of Denmark, "to avoid the Kings [James] displeasure." She says she does not wish to threaten the king's position, saying the "Prince of Orange designs [sic] the King's safety." At this time William was about to invade England. Despite Anne's assurances she reveals anti-Catholic sentiment.

10B <u>An Answer To Pereat Papa: Or, A Reply by way of Letter from a Gentlewoman to a Person of Quality; Commending to her consideration a Paper Entituled Pereat Papa; Or, Reasons why Popery should not inherit the Crown.</u> [London, 1681?] 4 pages. A 3372. EEB Reel 48:28.

This sharply argued defense of Catholic succession ridicules the pompous use of Latin by the author of <u>Pereat Papa</u>. Claiming she originally thought the pamphlet a satire, the author says she feels qualified to critique it on practical grounds, though she is ignorant of Common Law. Pragmatically she notes many Catholics have held the throne. In her own defense, she says, "'Tis a pity the World should see the Coxcomb uncorrected, and that by the hand of a Woman."

11B [Ariadne.] <u>She Ventures, and He Wins</u>. A Comedy. Written by a Young Lady. London, Printed for Hen. Rhodes, J. Harris, and Sam. Briscoe, 1696. 44 pages. S 3054. EEB Reel 511:43.

The preface indicates this play is based on a novel. The author wanted it performed abroad if it received "a favourable Reception from my own Sex" and a little encouragement from men. She apologizes for presenting it publicly and confesses she had "Inclinations for Scribbling from my childhood," manifested after the death of playwright Aphra Behn. The plot is typical of Restoration farce, with disguised players in pursuit of one another. It closes with a triple wedding.

[Astell, Mary.] <u>A Farther Essay Relating to the Female-Sex</u>. See 348A.

12B [Astell, Mary.] <u>Letters Concerning the Love of God</u>. London, Printed for Samuel Manship and Richard Wilkin, 1695. 312 pages. N 1254. EEB Reel 503:7.

Astell initiated this correspondence in 1693 with John Norris, Platonist joint editor of <u>The Athenian Mercury</u>, a magazine for women. Astell reveals she is torn between her love of God and duty to her sex. Admitting this duality, she concludes: "Fain wou'd I rescue my Sex...from that meanness of Spirit into which the Generality of 'em are sunk." She questions Norris about God as the "efficient Cause of all our Sensations" and the "sole Object of our Love." This item is listed under Norris in Wing's <u>STC</u>.

13B [Astell, Mary.] <u>A Serious Proposal To the Ladies, For the Advancement of their true and greatest Interest</u>. London, Printed for R. Wilkin, 1694. 172 pages. A 4062*. EEB Reels 9:6 and 1375:24,25.

Astell's significant essay proposes a women's college conducive to the development of the "rational" capacities. She asks upper-class women to eschew idleness for serious study and Christian service, and says her object is not "to expose, but to rectify your Failures." The college would also be a retreat from the modern world where women could develop friendships away from "the rude attempts of designing Men." Astell was the leading feminist writer of the time.

14B Astell, Mary. <u>A Serious Proposal to The Ladies: Part Two. Wherein a Method is offer'd for the Improvement of their Minds</u>. Second Edition Corrected. London, Printed for Richard Wilkin, 1697. 142 pages. A 4065A. EEB Reel 1414:49.

In part two of Astell's proposal for a women's college, she expresses irritation at the lack of female enthusiasm for her idea. She continues to criticize the degradation of women, who are expected "To Eat and to Drink and to pursue the little Impertinencies of Life." Astell's curriculum is based partially on Cartesian epistemology, with emphasis on single women, whose lives should be dedicated to "the Glory of Reforming this Prophane and Profligate Age."

[Astell, Mary.] <u>Six Familiar Essays Upon Marriage</u>. See 529B.

15B [Astell, Mary.] <u>Some Reflections upon Marriage, occasion'd by the Duke and Dutchess of Mazarin's case; which is also consider'd</u>. London, Printed for John Nutt, 1700. 98 pages. A 4067. EEB Reel 1029:10.

Astell discusses the celebrated divorce case of her acquaintance, the Duchess of Mazarin, accused of promiscuity, while her husband's more notorious liaisons were ignored. She moves from an abstract argument justifying marriage as a sacred institution, to a concrete criticism of the relations between spouses. She cites factors contributing to the decline of marriage: husbands' misuse of power, the scorn of satirists, undue emphasis on beauty and wit in women, arranged marriages, female passivity in the face of mistreatment, the sexual double standard, and the romanticization of marriage by women.

Astrea. See Aphra Behn.

16B Atkinson, Elizabeth. <u>A Breif [sic] and Plain discovery of the Labourers in mistery, Babilon generally called by the name of Quakers</u>. [London], Printed for P. L., 1669. 8 pages. A 4129A. EEB Reel 1495:3.

Atkinson was a Quaker who turned against the sect. She accuses the group of arrogance and says they should no longer call "the tower of Babel which they are building in their imaginations Mount Zion." Atkinson claims although Quakers have commendable principles, they have lately abandoned them. See also 562B and <u>Addendum</u> 8.

17B Atkinson, Elizabeth. <u>The Weapons of the People called Quakers Turn'd backward by the Shield of Truth</u>. [London], 1669. 10 pages. A 4129B.

Atkinson answers critics who have termed her impudent and arrogant for speaking in the plural. Calling herself "that Despised, Contemptible Instrument," she says they will not heed a purveyor of the light outside the group. She says Friends are content when they hear kind words, but "rage when the pillows are torn from under [their] arms."

Audley, Eleanor. See Douglas, Lady Eleanor Touchet Davies.

18B Audland, Anne (Newby). <u>A True Declaration of the Suffering of the Innocent, who is hated and persecuted without a cause. Wherein is discovered the zeale of the Magistrates and people of Banberry, persecuting and imprisoning them that are sent of the Lord.</u> London, Printed and are to be sold by Giles Calvert, 1655. 6 pages. A 4195.

This brief account by a female Quaker preacher tells how William Allen, a justice of the peace from Banbury, persecuted Quakers. See also 782A.

19B [Aulnoy, Marie Catherine Jumelle de Berneville, Comtesse d'.] <u>The Ingenious and Diverting Letters of the Lady---Travels into Spain.</u> In Three Parts. Fourth Edition. London, Printed for Samuel Crouch, 1697. 288 pages. A 4217C*, A 4223A and A 4223B.

This romance details the treatment accorded Aulnoy during her travels in Spain. First published in England in 1691, it was a hugely popular work which went through eleven editions by 1808.

20B [Aulnoy, Marie Catherine Jumelle de Berneville, Comtesse d'.] <u>The Memoirs of the Countess of Dunois...Containing withal A Modest Vindication of the Female Sex.</u> London, Printed for Tho. Cockerill, 1699. 185 pages. A 4218. EEB Reel 119:4.

Aulnoy disclaims a false memoir attributed to her and signed by St. Evremont. Although this book is alleged to be her legitimate autobiography, the facts of her life seem embellished. The lengthy convoluted tale depicts Aulnoy as coaxed into involvement in romantic intrigues by her parents and the nuns who taught her. The early influence of romantic literature is also noted. The so-called "vindication" is not a defense of women, but a statement about Aulnoy's own adventures. Use of this word may indicate the currency of feminist- style writings.

21B [Aulnoy, Marie Catherine Jumelle de Berneville, Comtesse d'.] <u>Memoirs of the Court of France.</u> In Two Parts. London, Printed for R. Bentley and T. Benett, 1692. 160 pages. A 4218A*. EEB Reel 80:4.

Aulnoy's novel supposedly relates the affairs of the Duke of Maine as well as the marriages and liaisons of other illegitimate royal children in France.

22B [Aulnoy, Marie Catherine Jumelle de Berneville, Comtesse d'.] <u>The Novels of Elizabeth, Queen of England, containing the history of Queen Ann of Bullen.</u> Two Vols. London, Printed for Marc Pardoe, 1680-81. 135 pages. A 4221*. EEB Reel 9:13 and 14.

In this romantic description of the Henrican court, Aulnoy assumes a Catholic perspective in depicting the passion of Henry VIII for Anne Boleyn and the romantic intrigues of the English court. She faults Henry's lust and defends Catherine of Aragon.

23B [Aulnoy, Marie Catherine Jumelle de Berneville, Comtesse d'.] <u>The Present Court of Spain: or the Modern Gallantry of the Spanish Nobility unfolded in several histories.</u> [Translated by J. P.] London, Printed for H. Rhodes and J. Harris, 1693. 379 pages. A 4223*. EEB Reel 1626:31.

This romance consists primarily of stories of Spanish court life.

24B Avery, Elizabeth. <u>Scripture-Prophecies Opened...which do attend the second</u> <u>coming of Christ</u>. London, Printed for Giles Calvert, 1647. 46 pages. A 4272. EEB Reel 445:3 and TT Reel 65:E.413(4).

Avery was a Fifth Monarchist millenarian. Her views were based largely on readings of Daniel and Revelations. These three letters discuss the resurrection of the dead and how the heavens and earth are to be dissolved. They include extensive commentaries from scripture. See also 687A.

25B [B., J.] <u>Severall petitions presented to the honourable Houses of Parliament</u> <u>now Assembled. The humble Petition of many thousands of Courtiers...concerning</u> <u>the staying of the Queenes intended voyage into Holland</u>. London, Printed for John Wright, 1641. [February 1641] 3 pages. B 124. EEB Reel 250:E.135(31) and TT Reel 24:E.135(31).

Women fear Henrietta Maria's departure will interrupt trade. They think she may be leaving because of the "unpublisht printing of many licentious and scandalous Pamphlets...wounding her sacred Majestie." They suggest punishment for the pamphleteers and, in support of the queen, point to the heir she produced for the country. She is encouraged to remain in England. Although the author is listed as J. B. in the Wing <u>STC</u>, these initials do not appear on the document.

26B Barker, Jane. <u>Poetical Recreations: Consisting of Original Poems</u>. London, Printed for Benjamin Crayle, 1688. 109 pages. B 770. EEB Reel 52:3.

This is the first of a two-part book of poetry addressing popular contemporary subjects such as friendship, young love, and false lovers. Only one poem, "A Virgin Life," which praises spinsterhood, presents feminist views of the period. Barker, a respectable and modest female poet whose work is similar to Katherine Philips', went to France as a Jacobite sympathizer. She apparently never married and expressed a distaste for matrimony.

27B Barwick, Grace. <u>To all present Rulers, whether Parliament or whomsoever, of</u> <u>England</u>. London, Printed for M. W., 1659. 4 pages. B 1007A.

Quaker Barwick's husband Robert served under General John Lambert. This document includes letters to Parliament, speaking against hireling priests and prophets; to Lambert, warning the army to fear and trust the Lord; and to Friends, reminding them to remember God's cause and "remove the oppression of Tithes."

28B Bastwick, Susanna. <u>To the High Court of Parliament of the Commonwealth of</u> <u>England, Scotland, and Ireland</u>. [London, 1654.] Broadside. B 1073. EEB Reel 1646:11 and TT Reel 246: 669.f.19(28).

A physician's widow asks Parliament for aid. Her deceased husband, who had appealed from exile in Sicily in 1640, lost his livelihood and fortune because he supported Parliament. Bastwick asks for assistance for her family in lieu of the funds never granted her husband.

29B [Bateman, Susanna.] I [sic] matter not how I appear to Man. London, [1656]. 8 pages. B 1097.

In this Quaker tract Bateman warns the English they cannot hide from God. She claims the nation has lost its faith and cannot continue in its current course. She says the evil will be discovered "by the Light; therefore it is vain to get coverings." This lyrical piece is written in a prophetic voice.

30B Bathurst, Elizabeth [Anne]. An expostulatory appeal to the Professors of Christianity. [London, 1680?] 7 pages. B 1135A. EEB Reel 166:6.

Although this is ostensibly a Quaker entreaty to unite with Christ, it is primarily a defense of Bathurst's right to present her view of God's message. (She claims in 1678, when she called for universal repentance, her congregation discouraged her.) Bathurst says her faith led her to "go about from one Watch-man of the Night to another, inquiring after my Souls Beloved" (Christ). She could not find inspiration in scripture.

31B Bathurst, Elizabeth [Anne]. The Sayings of Women... spoken...in several Places of the Scriptures. London, Printed by T. Sowle, 1683. [27] pages. B 1135B.

Bathurst claims her purpose is "to shew how the Lord poured out his spirit...not only on the male, but also on the female." She includes dialogues between women and Christ, concluding: "That as Male and Female are made one in Christ Jesus, so Women receive an Office in the Truth as well as Men... and must give an account of their stewardship to their Lord, as well as the men."

32B Bathurst, Elizabeth [Anne]. Truth Vindicated. London, Printed and sold by T. Sowle, [1695]. 225 pages. B 1135C*. EEB Reels 1274:10, 1246:4 and 1348:28.

Bathurst defends the Quaker faith against its detractors and explains how the Society of Friends has found the truth and the light. Introductory comments by her father indicate she died prematurely after revealing a quick mind and an interest in religion. Her views of original sin, free will and other doctrinal matters are presented.

33B Bathurst, Elizabeth [Anne]. Truth's Vindication, Or, A gentle stroke to wipe off the Foul Aspertions cast upon the People of God call'd QUAKERS. London, Printed and sold by T. Sowle, 1679. 225 pages. B 1137*.

This publication is the same as 32B.

34B Bayly, Mary Fisher (joint author). False Prophets and their False Preachers Described. [London, 1652.] 8 pages. A 894BA. EEB Reel 302:9.

This Quaker tract criticizes "false prophets" and corrupt preachers. It warns against pride, covetousness, drunkenness, lying, swearing, and oppression. A special caveat goes to "lovers of pleasures more than lovers of God." Although this work is listed under Thomas Aldam in the Wing STC, it is co-authored by six persons, including Bayly, Jane Holmes and Elizabeth Hooten, prisoners at York castle.

35B Bayly, Mary Fisher.   "Mary Bayly's Testimony Concerning her Deceased Husband." In William Bayly. Collection of the Several Wrightings [sic] of. [London], 1676. [2] pages. B 1517. EEB Reel 166:10.

Bayly hesitates to comment on her husband's death, thinking it presumptuous to infer meaning from the Lord's actions. She vows to accept the death and "not to murmur against the Lord." This brief and rather meek commentary is filled with scriptural allusions.

36B Beck, Margaret. The Reward of Oppression, Tyranny and Injustice, committed by the late Kings and Queens of England and others, by the unlawful Entry, and unlawful Deteiner of the Dutchie Lands of Lancaster. London, [1655.] 4 pages. B 1648*. EEB Reel 1195:8.

This appeal is addressed to Oliver Cromwell, Lord Protector over the earlier royal appropriation of the duchy of Lancaster, allegedly kept from its rightful owner, Beck's husband. Beck tells of the difficulty of supporting herself and her son as a seamstress. She says he received eighty pounds upon his father's death, but the family has never recovered the duchy lands. A lengthy genealogical account of land ownership is appended. The issue is whether the land had been granted to a female when a male heir was living.

Beckwith, Elizabeth. See 87A.

37B Behn, Aphra.   Abdelazer, or the Moor's Revenge.   London, Printed for J. Magnes and R. Bentley, 1677. 71 pages. B 1715*.
EEB Reels 167:5 and 1324:3.

Aphra Behn, a major dramatist and novelist, lived between 1640 and 1689. She is probably the first British woman to earn her living by writing. In this drama, after sacking Fez and killing its king, King Philip of Spain takes as his prisoner the orphaned Moorish prince Abdelazer. The boy, Eleazar, becomes an outstanding general in the Spanish military. Wishing to avenge his father's death, he becomes lover to the passionate Queen Isabella, his step-mother. A series of intrigues follows, resulting in several murders, incarcerations and an insurrection. The play is an adaptation of Lusts Dominion; or The Lascivious Queen.

38B Behn, Aphra. "Adventures of the Black Lady." In All the Histories and Novels. London, Printed for Samuel Briscoe, 1698. [10] pages. Item: N.I.W. Collections: B 1711*, B 1712*.   EEB Reels 82:9 and 1454:5.

This story is about Bellamora, a young woman who arrives in London from Hampshire looking for Madam Brightly. She is an orphan and, although pregnant, refuses to marry Fondlove, the father of her child. She is afraid he will hate her if she agrees to the match. Bellamora seeks assistance from Madam Brightly, not knowing she is Fondlove's sister. He finally convinces her to marry him for the sake of the child.

39B [Behn, Aphra.] Aesop's Fables. [With Francis Barlow.] Three Parts. London, Printed by H. Hills Jun. for Francis Barlow, 1687. A 703. EEB Reel 339:28.

Behn's rendition of these classic fables in verse accompanies the engravings of Francis Barlow. Many of her allusions are to contemporary politics, society or literature. Excerpt: "Women do oft those heights of glory reach/Which even the schools have wanted power to teach."

40B Behn, Aphra, trans. "Agnes de Castro, or the Force of Generous Love." [By Jean Baptiste de Brilhac]. In The Histories and Novels of the late Ingenious Mrs. Behn. Second Vol. London, Printed for Samuel Briscoe, 1696. 38 pages. Item: B 4693A. Collections: B 1711*, B 1712*, B 1766A. EEB Reels 82:9, 121:5 and 1454:5.

This translation of Agnes de Castro, Nouvelle Portugaise (1688) tells of the beautiful Ines, daughter of Pedro Fernandez de Castro, Major Domo to Alphonso XI of Castille. Ines falls in love with the Infante Don Pedro, betrothed to another. After her death, Ines and Pedro are secretly wed. When the king learns of their union, he has Ines murdered in Pedro's absence. Pedro, greatly aggrieved, vows revenge against his father Alphonso IV of Portugal, and precipitates a civil war.

41B Behn, Aphra. All The Histories and Novels written by the late ingenious Mrs. Behn, entire in one volume. Third Edition. London, Printed for Samuel Briscoe, 1698. [544] pages. B 1712*. EEB Reel 1454:5.

This collection, edited by Charles Gildon, contains the following titles: Oroonoko, The History of the Nun, Adventures of the Black Lady, The Fair Jilt, Agnes de Castro, The Lovers Watch, The Ladies Looking-Glass, The Lucky Mistake, Memoirs on the Court of the King of Bantam and The Life and Memoirs. See individual titles for descriptions.

42B Behn, Aphra. The Amorous Prince or The Curious Husband. London, Printed by J. M. for Thomas Dring, 1671. 82 pages. B 1717.

Behn's second play revolves around the wooing of two women by Prince Ferdinand, son of the Duke of Florence. The action includes impersonations, duels and murder attempts. The major and minor plots are based on Don Quixote, IX and Davenport's City Night-cap.

Behn, Aphra. The Amours of Philander and Silvia. See 62B.

43B Behn, Aphra. The City Heiress; or, Sir Timothy Treat-all. London, Printed for D. Brown, T. Benskin and H. Rhodes, 1682. 61 pages. B 1719*. EEB Reel 270:7.

Behn's comedy features gay blade Tom Wilding, who seeks revenge for his disinheritance by his uncle. Wilding involves two heiresses in a plot to entrap his uncle. The play is adapted from Massinger's The Guardian and Middleton's A Mad World My Masters. It is a Tory attack on Whigs--Shraftesbury in particular.

44B Behn, Aphra. A Congratulatory Poem to her Most Sacred Majesty. London, Printed for William Canning, 1688. 7 pages. B 1721*. EEB Reels 445:31 and 783:13.

This poem honors the pregnancy of Mary of Modena, which eventuated in the birth of James Francis Edward. Excerpt: "Like the first sacred Infant, this will come with Promise laden from the Blessed Womb/To call the wandring scatter'd Nations home."

45B Behn, Aphra. A Congratulatory Poem to her Sacred Majesty Queen Mary Upon her Arrival in England. London, Printed by R. E. for R. Bentley and William Canning, 1689. 6 pages. B 1723. EEB Reel 167:6.

Behn wrote this poem while residing in the country outside London (her "long retreat"). The baroque pindaric welcomes Mary II to the throne. Behn intimates her succession will herald the end of civil strife. Behn was clearly pleased that the Stuart line would be continued.

46B Behn, Aphra. A Congratulatory poem to the King's most sacred Majesty on the happy birth of the Prince of Wales. London, Printed for William Canning, 1688. Broadside. B 1724. EEB Reel 1301:14.

This exuberant self-confident poem honors the birth of the Old Pretender, son to James II and Mary of Modena. It was written only days before William of Orange was invited by several members of Parliament to take the throne with Mary, Princess of Orange.

[Behn, Aphra.] The Counterfeit Bridegroom. See 589A.

47B [Behn, Aphra.] The Debauchee: Or, The Credulous Cuckold. London, Printed for John Amery, 1677. 63 pages. B 4869. EEB Reel 484:15.

Although the Wing STC lists this comedy under Richard Brome, it is attributed to Behn by Hargreaves, Montagu Summers, and others. The main characters are Lord Loveless (gallant to Mrs. Saleware), Sir Oliver Thrivewell, George Careless, Mr. Saleall, Lady Thrivewell, Clara (her sister) and Mrs. Crostill, a young widow in love with Careless.

48B Behn, Aphra, trans. A Discovery of New Worlds. By Bernard Le Bovier de Fontenelle. London, Printed for William Canning, 1688. 158 pages. Item: F 1412*. Collections: B 1711A, B 1714. EEB Reels 857:25 and 1787:8.

This work by Fontenelle, a French scientist and man of letters, is prefaced by 52B. Based primarily on Bishop John Wilkins' The Discovery of a World in the Moone, it centers on Descartes' theory of vortexes, refuted by Newton's Principia. It is a series of dialogues meant to simplify the Copernican system, mainly for women.

49B Behn, Aphra. "The Dumb Virgin." In Histories, Novels and Translations. Second Vol. London, Printed by W[illiam] O[nley] for S[amuel] B[riscoe] and sold by M. Brown, 1700. 34 pages. Item: N.I.W. Collections: B 1711A, B 1714. EEB Reels 857:25 and 857:25.

This novella, set in Venice, was posthumously published. Its protagonists are Rinaldo, a senator, and his family. Rinaldo's wife and son are attacked by Turkish pirates at sea. The son is kidnapped and presumed dead. The wife later bears a deformed but brilliant daughter and a beautiful but dumb one.

When the two grow up, the son returns to Venice and seduces the silent sister Maria, then mistakenly kills Rinaldo. Only later does he learn he has made love to his sister and murdered his father. Belvideera, the deformed sister, survives everyone and becomes a recluse.

50B Behn, Aphra. The Dutch Lover. London, Printed for Thomas Dring, 1673. 98 pages. B 1726. EEB Reel 445:32.

In this drama, Don Ambrosio rears his adopted son Silvio along with his own children. The major theme is the ill-conceived notion of the arranged marriage. The plot makes use of concealed identities, low comedy and chance meetings. The source for the play is Don Fenise, a novel of intrigue supposedly translated from the Spanish.

51B Behn, Aphra. The Emperor of the Moon. London, Printed by R. Holt for Joseph Knight and Francis Saunders, 1687. 67 pages. B 1727*. EEB Reel 203:4.

The protagonist in this comedy is the alchemist and astrologer, Doctor Baliardo. The action revolves around the courtships of his daughter Elaria and his niece Bellemante. The story, adapted from the Italian commedia dell'arte, is based on the French farce Arlequin Empereur dans la Lune.

52B Behn, Aphra. "Essay on Translation and Translated Prose." In Histories, Novels and Translations. Second Vol. London, Printed by W[illiam] O[nley] for S[amuel] B[riscoe] and sold by M. Brown, 1700. 20 pages. Item: N.I.W. Collections: B 1711A, B 1714. EEB Reels 857:25 and 1787:8.

Behn discusses translating and her rendering of 48B. She lauds Fontenelle's introduction of a female character, but criticizes her depiction as inconsistent and unrealistic. Behn suggests his notion of other inhabited worlds may offend the theological precepts of some; however, she says "the Scripture was not design'd to teach us astronomy, no more than Geometry or Chronology."

53B Behn, Aphra. "The Fair Jilt; or The Amours of Prince Tarquin and Miranda." In The Histories and Novels of the late ingenious Mrs. Behn. Second Vol. London, Printed for S. Briscoe, 1696. 178 pages. Item: B 1729. EEB Reels 121:5 and 445:33. Collections: B 1711*, B 1712*, B 1766A. EEB Reels 82:9, 121:5 and 1454:5.

This novel is about a beautiful, well-educated, orphaned heiress in a religious order in Antwerp. Miranda, is vain, egocentric, and predatory. She loves a young priest, Father Henrick, who rejects her. In retaliation she defames his character, then causes the downfall of a young page she had enlisted to murder her sister Alcidiana. The theme is the contrast between reality and appearance.

54B Behn, Aphra. The False Count; or A New Way to Play an Old Game. London, Printed by M. Flesher for Jacob Tonson, 1682. 65 pages. B 1730*. EEB Reels 203:5 and 1195:9.

Julia is forced to marry jealous old Francisco, a merchant in league with Don Carlos, the governor of Cadiz. Francisco's daughter, Isabella, is betrothed to Antonio, but considers him inferior. Antonio woos her to gain access to Julia's sister Clare, who loves him. Meanwhile Don Carlos feigns courtship of Clare in an attempt to see the closely guarded Julia. In the end, Francisco is shamed into surrendering his wife, and Antonio and Clare marry. The source for this play is A. Montfleury's Ecole des Jaloux.

55B Behn, Aphra. The Feign'd Curtezans. Or A Nights Intrigue. London, Printed for Jacob Tonson, 1679. 71 pages. B 1733. EEB Reel 203:6.

In this comedy Count Morosini's nieces Cornelia and Marcella flee Viterbo and pose as courtesans in Rome to avoid arranged marriages. Two English travellers, Galliard and Fillamour, hear of their beauty and resolve to meet them. Characters disguise themselves, misunderstandings abound, and identities are mistaken. Finally Octavio, formerly contracted to marry Marcella, agrees to allow Fillamour to claim her; Galliard wins Cornelia; and Laura is united with Julio.

56B Behn, Aphra. The Forc'd Marriage; or The Jealous Bridegroom. London, Printed by H. L. and R. B. for James Magnus, 1671. 89 pages. Item: B 1734*. EEB Reels 446:1 and 857:28.

Erminia, the daughter of retiring General Orguilius, is promised to his successor Alcippus. But she secretly pledges her love to the king's son Philander. After some dramatic and tragic events, the parents see the injustice of arranged marriages, Alcippus no longer desires Erminia, and she and Philander are united. As a moral criticism of forced marriage, this play is reminiscent of Beaumont-Fletcher romances, especially The Maid's Tragedy.

57B Behn, Aphra. The Histories and Novels of the late Ingenious Mrs. Behn...Together with the Life and Memoirs of Mrs. Behn. Written by One of the Fair Sex. London, Printed for Samuel Briscoe, 1696. 416 pages. B 1711*. EEB Reels 82:9, 1454:5 and 1787:8.

For a description of individual items see the following titles by Behn: Oroonoko, The Fair Jilt, Agnes de Castro, La Montre (The Lover's Watch), The Lady's Looking-Glass, The Lucky Mistake, and Love Letters by Mrs. Behn. The Life and Memoirs of Mrs. Behn, written by a "Gentlewoman of her Acquaintance," offers biographical information--her birth in Canterbury, her early voyage to Surinam, her alleged marriage to a Dutch merchant, and her death, caused by an "unskilful physician" in 1686. She is called a woman of wit, honor, good humor and judgment.

58B Behn, Aphra. Histories, Novels and Translations, written by the most ingenious Mrs. Behn. Second Vol. London, Printed by W[illiam] O[nley] for S[amuel] B[riscoe] and sold by M. Brown, 1700. 446 pages. B 1711A. EEB Reel 857:25.

This edition of Behn's work, dedicated to Evelyn, Viscount Newark, includes The Blind Lady (see The Unfortunate Bride), The Dumb Virgin, The Wandring Beauty, The Unhappy Mistake, A Theory or System of New Inhabited Worlds, Essay on Translation and Translated Prose, and The Unfortunate Happy Lady. See individual titles for descriptions.

59B Behn, Aphra, trans. The History of Oracles, and the Cheats of the Pagan Princes. By Bernard Le Bovier de Fontenelle. London, 1688. 227 pages. F 1413*. EEB Reel 29:11.

This work is based on Anton van Dale's Latin treatise, translated into French by Fontenelle, a scientist and humanist. Fontenelle's criticism of pagan religions encourages the reader to apply his techniques to Christianity, thereby diminishing it. See also 48B.

60B Behn, Aphra. The History of the Nun: Or, the Fair Vow-Breaker. London, Printed for A. Baskerville, 1689. 148 pages. Item: B 1737. EEB Reel 121:3. Collections: B 1711*, B 1712*. EEB Reels 82:9, 1454:5, 1787:8.

This novel concerns a beautiful and talented, but evil, young nun named Isabella. She leaves the cloister to marry Henault, later reported killed in military action. When he returns to surprise her with her second husband, Villenoys, she smothers him as he sleeps. She then stitches Villenoys' coat to the sack holding Henault's body, so both drown during his attempt to dispose of it. Isabella, having broken all of her vows, is finally executed.

61B Behn, Aphra. The Lady's Looking-Glass, to Dress Herself by: or, The Whole Art of Charming. London, Printed by W. Onley for S. Briscoe, 1697. 24 pages. Item: B 1738. EEB Reel 121:4. Collections: B 1711*, B 1712*. EEB Reels 82:9, 1454:5 and 1787:8.

This sequel to 69B, Behn's adaptation of Bonnecorse's work, is told from the perspective of a looking-glass. Damon and Iris are reintroduced, and Behn uses their dialogue to argue against restrictive clothing for women and to champion garments that are "free, natural, and easie." While describing female beauty in traditional romantic language, she proposes that the corporeal extends beyond physical attributes.

[Behn, Aphra.] The Lives of Sundry notorious Villains. See 531A.

62B Behn, Aphra. Love-Letters between a Nobleman and his Sister. Three Vols. London, Printed and are to be sold by Randal Taylor, 1684. B 1740*. EEB Reels 82:10, 1195:10, 1376:17, 1495:11 and 1823:1.

This multi-volume novel, Behn's first and longest, is based on a contemporary scandal involving Forde Grey, Earl of Tankerville, Lady Mary Berkeley and her sister Henrietta. Modeled after Portuguese Letters by Alforcado, it is in turn narrative and epistolary. The parts are titled Love Letters between a Nobleman and his Sister, Letters from a Noble-man to his Sister, and The Amours of Philander and Silvia.

[Behn, Aphra.] Love Letters between Polydorus the Gothick King and Messalina, Late Queen of Albion. See 542A.

Behn, Aphra. Love-Letters from a Nobleman. See 62B.

63B Behn, Aphra. "Love-Letters by Mrs. A. Behn." In The Histories and Novels of the late ingenious Mrs. Behn. London, Printed for Samuel Briscoe, 1696. 15 pages. Item: N.I.W. Collections: B 1711*, B 1712*. EEB Reels 82:9, 1454:5 and 1787:8.

These eight letters, written by Astrea to Lycidas, are probably to Behn's lover John Hoyle. They testify to their tempestuous affair. Excerpt: "Your staunch Prudence is proof against love, and all the bank's on my side: You are so unreasonable, you wou'd have me pay where I have contracted no debt: You wou'd have me give and you, like a Miser, wou'd distribute nothing."

Behn, Aphra. The Lover's Watch. See 69B.

64B Behn, Aphra. The Lucky Chance, or An Alderman's Bargain. London, Printed by R. H. for W. Canning, 1687. 69 pages. B 1744. EEB Reel 1195:10.

Bellmour has been expelled from the country because he killed a man in a duel. Returning to London, he discovers Sir Feeble Fainwould has led his fiancee Leticia to believe Bellmour dead to marry her himself. Meetings, masquerades, dances and pranks ensue until Bellmour and his friend Gayman win their ladies. The comedy is based on Shirley's The Lady of Pleasure.

65B Behn, Aphra. "The Lucky Mistake: A New Novel." In The Histories and Novels of the late ingenious Mrs. Behn. London, Printed for R. Bentley, 1689. 112 pages. Item: B 1745. EEB Reel 1416:2. Collections: B 1711*, B 1712*. EEB Reels 82:9, 1454:5 and 1787:8.

This realistic novel has a comic theatrical ending. The story, which parallels Romeo and Juliet, is set in Orleans. It concerns a romance between Atlante and Rinaldo, carried on through meetings, letters, secret conversations and a balcony dialogue. Atlante is coveted by Count Vernole, who finally marries her sister Charlot. The style shows the influence of Madame de Lafayette.

66B Behn, Aphra, trans. [By Paul Tallement.] Lycidas: or The Lover in Fashion. London, Printed for Joseph Knight and Francis Saunders, 1688. 64 pages. T 129. EEB Reel 439:17.

This volume is a sequel to 90B. The author speaks as a man who visited the "Isle of Love" and lived there in bliss with his beloved until she became indifferent and took new lovers. Behn's poetry collection 68B is included in this edition.

67B Behn, Aphra. Memoirs on the Court of the King of Bantam. London, Printed for Samuel Briscoe, 1697. 30 pages. Item: B 1746. Collections: B 1711*, B 1712*. EEB Reels 82:9, 1454:5 and 1787:8.

This posthumously published short story supposedly took place during Christmas of 1682. It concerns heroine Philabella's attempts to secure a dowry from Would-be King so she can marry Valentine Goodland. An elaborate description of Christmas festivities is included.

68B [Behn, Aphra.] Miscellany, being a Collection of Poems by several hands. Together with Reflections on morality, or Seneca Unmasqued. London, Printed for J. Hindmarsh, 1685. 382 pages. M 2230. EEB Reel 190:11.

This collection, dedicated to Sir William Clifton, includes poems from Behn's friends, the Earls of Dorset and Rochester, Sir George Etherege, Anne Wharton, Nahum Tate, Henry Neville Payne, Henry Crispe, Mrs. Taylor, Tom Brown and

Thomas Otway. It also contains Behn's eulogy for Rochester and La Rouchefoucauld's translated maxims. The collection is also included in 66B.

69B Behn, Aphra. La Montre: or the Lover's Watch. London, Printed by R. H. for W. Canning, 1686. 243 pages. Item: B 3596. Collections: B 1711*, B 1712*. EEB Reels 82:9, 1454:5 and 1787:8.

The conceit of this piece is time passing on the hands of a clock. Behn traces the path of love through prose and poems ostensibly written by Damon and Iris. The work is an adaptation of La Montre by Balthazar de Bonnecorse. See also the sequel, 61B.

[Behn, Aphra.] A New song sung in Abdelazer. See 635A.

70B Behn, Aphra. "Oroonoko." In The Histories and Novels of the late ingenious Mrs. Behn. London, Printed for Samuel Briscoe, 1696. 101 pages. Item: B 1749. EEB Reel 54:5. Collections: B 1711*, B 1712*, B 1766A. EEB Reels 82:9, 121:5, 1454:5 and 1787:8.

This novel of ideas, the most popular of Behn's fictional works, is at once a social satire, a story of intrigue and a tale of love. In Surinam, Oroonoko, the honorable and heroic protagonist, is the last in a race of kings. He loves the beautiful Imoinda, who is pressed into service in his wicked grandfather's seraglio. After a secret marriage, Oroonoko and Imoinda share a night of love, then she is sold into slavery. He is also enslaved aboard an English ship. After a tumultuous plot, including a reunion of the lovers and a slave insurrection led by Oroonoko, he suffers a gruesome death--dismemberment and disembowelling. Behn's theme is the failure of noble ideals in a corrupt world.

71B Behn, Aphra. A pindarick on the death of our late Sovereign. London, Printed by J. Playford for Henry Playford, 1685. 5 pages. B 1750*. EEB Reels 344:11 and 1195:11.

This poem was written upon the death of Charles II following a stroke in 1685. Behn compares him to Moses and likens his brother James to Joshua. Excerpt: "Like Moses, he has led the Murm'ring Crowd, beneath the Peaceful Rule of his Almighty Wand."

72B Behn, Aphra. A pindarick poem on the happy Coronation. London, Printed by J. Playford for Henry Playford, 1685. 25 pages. B 1753. EEB Reels 446:2 and 857:29.

This lengthy baroque poem honors the ascension of James II to the throne upon the death of his brother, Charles II. A great admirer of James, Behn speaks of his bravery in battle. An elaborate description of the coronation ceremonies is also included.

73B Behn, Aphra. A pindaric poem to the Reverend Doctor Burnet, on the honour he did me of Enquiring after me and my Muse. London, Printed for B. Bentley and to be sold by Richard Baldwin, 1689. 8 pages. B 1754. EEB Reel 408:6.

Behn had just refused a commission to write a poem for King William. Here she announces Burnet will write the pindaric for the "Great Nassau" (William). Burnet eventually delivered the coronation sermon.

74B Behn, Aphra. A Poem humbly dedicated to the great Patern [sic] of Piety and Virtue Catherine Queen Dowager, on the Death of her dear Lord...King Charles II. London, Printed by J. Playford for Henry Playford, 1685. 6 pages. B 1755A. EEB Reel 835:5.

Catherine of Braganza, new widow of Charles II, is honored in this poem. The image of the pieta is invoked in a sympathetic portrait.

75B Behn, Aphra. A poem to Sir Roger L'Estrange, on his third part of the History of the Times relating to the Death of Sir Edmund Bury-Godfrey. London, Printed for Randal Taylor, 1688. 7 pages. B 1756. EEB Reel 270:8.

This poem marks the publication of a volume by L'Estrange, a prominent journalist and pamphleteer, in which he discusses the death of Sir Edmund Berry- Godfrey. He was the justice of the peace for Westminster murdered after hearing depositions from Titus Oates and Israel Tongue of the infamous Popish Plot. L'Estrange suggested Godfrey committed suicide and questioned the existence of a plot. Behn praises his truthfulness in the face of chaos.

76B Behn, Aphra. Poems upon Several Occasions. London, Printed for R. Tonson and J. Tonson, 1684. 144 pages. B 1757*. EEB Reels 525:2 and 1454:6.

This collection includes Behn's translation of 90B. It also contains poems about Monmouth, John Hoyle (Behn's lover) and others dedicated to persons identified only by initials. Some of the baroque songs are sexually explicit and may be autobiographical. There are commendatory verses by Thomas Creech, John Cooper, John Adams and possibly by John Dryden. See also 66B and 90B.

77B Behn, Aphra. A Prologue by Mrs. Behn to her new play, called Like Father Like Son. London, Printed for J. V., 1682. Broadside. B 1759. EEB Reel 1396:13.

Spoken by the actress Mrs. Butler, this prologue includes allusions to public coffers that benefit mistresses of officials. Behn says those who try to please through expensive clothing or beauty will often be outdone by those who are loyal. The epilogue to this apparently unpublished comedy was spoken by Mr. Gevan, who reminds the audience no one has been libelled, so no one should take offense.

78B Behn, Aphra. Prologue spoken by Mrs. Cook. London, Printed for Charles Tebroc [Corbet], [1684]. Broadside. B 1759A.

Behn wrote this prologue for the revision of John Fletcher's play Valentinian, by her friend, the Earl of Rochester. The speaker says women can demonstrate wit, as well as cunning, on the stage, and this play, while not serious, is a vehicle for female cleverness.

79B Behn, Aphra. Prologue to Romulus. London, Printed for Nathaniel Thompson, 1682. Broadside. B 1760. EEB Reel 1435:8.

This anti-Puritan prologue was written for Romulus and Hersilia, an anonymous play published in 1683.   Excerpt: "Ours is a Virgin Rome, long, long, before/Pious Geneva Rhetorick call'd her Whore."

[Behn, Aphra.]   The Revenge. See 89A.

80B Behn, Aphra. The Roundheads; or The Good Old Cause. London, Printed for D. Brown, T. Benskin, and H. Rhodes, 1682. 56 pages. B 1761*. EEB Reels 54:6 and 1396:14.

Generals Lambert and Fleetwood vie for power after the death of Cromwell and the demise of his son Richard.   Lord Wariston, the Council chairman, champions each alternately, depending on who offers the larger bribe.   The Council meets in a drunken comic romp. Finally the citizenry reject the Rump, the protagonists win their ladies and the Roundhead leaders are detained. The source for this farce is John Tatham's The Rump. It is a satire on the last days of the Commonwealth.

81B [Behn, Aphra.] The Rover (Part I); or The Banish't Cavaliers. London, Printed for John Amery, 1677. 83 pages. B 1763*. EEB Reels 446:3 and 1627:9.

A group of exiled English cavaliers visit Naples for the carnival.   The action revolves around their several attempts at romance. During their intrigues, near reconciliations and revelations, each meets a different fate. The source for the comedy is Killigrew's Thomaso, the Wanderer.

82B Behn, Aphra. The Rover (Part II). London, Printed for Jacob Tonson, 1681. 85 pages. B 1765. EEB Reel 446:4.

This comedy continues 81B. The plot is complicated through mistaken identity, duels in the dark, bedroom intrigue and farce. Ariadne agrees to marry the Englishman Beaumond; the two fools Blunt and Fetherfool are exposed; and hero Willmore wins the courtesan La Nuche.

83B Behn, Aphra. Sir Patient Fancy. London, Printed by E. Flesher for Richard Tonson and Jacob Tonson, 1678. 91 pages. B 1766. EEB Reel 203:7.

Sir Patient Fancy, a wealthy hypochondriacal old alderman, has married the lovely young Lucia. She takes Wittmore as a lover and claims he is courting Fancy's step-daughter Isabella, so the illicit couple can meet.   A plan to trick Fancy backfires, the lovers are united, and Fancy declares his intention to lead a life of pleasure. One protagonist in the play, Lady Knowall, may have been a caricature of Mary Astell. Moliere's La Malade Imaginaire is the inspiration for this comedy.

[Behn, Aphra.] The Ten Pleasures of Marriage. See 858A.

[Behn, Aphra].   A Theory or System of Several New-Inhabited Worlds Lately Discover'd. See 48B.

84B Behn, A[phra.] <u>To the Most Illustrious Prince Christopher Duke of Albemarle,</u> <u>on his Voyage to his Government of Jamaica</u>. London, Printed for John Newton, 1687. 9 pages. B 1768. EEB Reel 203:8.

This poem is dedicated to the second Duke of Albemarle, made the Governor General of Jamaica after he endorsed a plan for fishing on a submerged Spanish wreck. He was married to Elizabeth, the daughter of Henry, second Duke of Newcastle, to whom Behn refers in her poem. Of Elizabeth, she says "she is descended from Prince and Poet too."

85B Behn, Aphra. <u>The Town-Fopp; or Sir Timothy Tawdry</u>. London, Printed by T. N. for J. Magnes and R. Bentley, 1677. 66 pages. B 1769*. EEB Reels 446:5 and 1454:7.

Timothy Tawdry and Celinda are engaged, even though she loves Bellmour, a companion of her brother Friendlove. Bellmour is ordered to marry Diana by his uncle Plotwell, who threatens disinheritance if he refuses. Eventually Plotwell promises to annul the forced marriage, Celinda agrees to marry Bellmour, Friendlove becomes Diana's suitor, and Sir Timothy returns to his companion Betty Flauntit. The comedy is based on George Wilkins' <u>The Miseries of</u> <u>Enforced Marriage</u>.

86B Behn, Aphra. <u>Two Congratulatory Poems</u>. Second Edition. London, Printed for Will. Canning, 1688. [12] pages. B 1771. EEB Reel 1396:15.

The first poem is a congratulatory message to Queen Mary on her pregnancy. She is compared to the Virgin Mary and called the "Second Bless'd of Womankind." The second praises the birth of Mary's son. Astrological signs are said to augur well for the child's future. This son, the Old Pretender, was the unsuccessful claimant to the crown during the eighteenth century.

87B Behn, Aphra. "The Unfortunate Bride: or, The Blind Lady a Beauty." In <u>Histories, Novels and Translations by the most ingenious Mrs. Behn</u>. Second Vol. London, Printed for Samuel Briscoe, 1698. [22] pages. Item: B 1772*. EEB Reels 12:10 and 1116:9. Collection: B 1711A. EEB Reel 857:25.

This tragi-comic short novel contains a romance about Frankwit and Belvira, neighbors in Staffordshire. She goes to London after her mother dies, and he follows to woo her. After he receives his own inheritance, it quickly disappears and they separate. She marries, thinking him dead. He returns, her husband sees them together and tries to stab him. Belvira is mistakenly killed, and Frankwit kills her husband in revenge. This is more realistic than most of Behn's writings.

88B Behn, Aphra. "The Unfortunate Happy Lady. A True History." In <u>Histories,</u> <u>Novels and Translations by the most ingenious Mrs. Behn</u>. Second Vol. London, Printed for Samuel Briscoe, 1698. [40] pages. Item: N.I.W. Collections: B 1711A, B 1714. EEB Reels 857:25 and 1787:8.

This theatrical novel is set in a fashionable London brothel. William Wilding, an extravagant rake, has mortgaged his late father's estate to support his flamboyant lifestyle. He wants to avoid paying a share to his sister, Philadelphia. Instead he places her in a brothel run by Lady Beldam. When

Philadelphia perceives her brother's intent, she enlists the aid of Gracelove, her first customer. He removes her to a better situation. The second part, a narrative, finds Gracelove shipwrecked for six years. Philadelphia is married and widowed, while William has lost his fortune and reformed. When Gracelove returns, he marries Philadelphia. The theme: justice is served when deserving persons have financial security.

89B Behn, Aphra. "The Unhappy Mistake: or, the Impious Vow Punish'd." In Histories, Novels and Translations, Written by the most Ingenious Mrs. Behn. Second Vol. London, Printed by W. O. for S. B. and sold by M. Brown, 1700. 87 pages. Item: N.I.W. Collections: B 1711A, B 1714. EEB Reels 857:25 and 1787:8.

This novel is about Lucretia and Miles Hardyman, children of Sir Henry. Although Miles loves Diana, his father forbids marriage because of her meager dowry. Lucretia falls in love with Diana's brother, Lewis Constance. When Miles discovers Lewis embracing his sister Diana, he challenges him to a duel and injures him. Miles flees, unaware of the identity of his victim, who eventually marries Lucretia. Miles returns five years after his father's death to discover his sister has married, he has inherited 10,000 pounds, and Diana still awaits him.

90B Behn, Aphra, trans. "Voyage to the Isle of Love." [By Paul Tallement.] In Poems upon Several Occasions. London, Printed for R. Tonson and J. Tonson, 1684. 128 pages. Item: N.I.W. Collection: B 1757*. EEB Reels 525:2 and 1454:6.

Behn's adaptation of a fantasy by Paul Tallement, a French cleric, includes a dedication to the Earl of Salisbury, with whom some satirists suggested she was having an affair. It is romantic, sometimes erotic, songs and prose about the psychology of love. Here Aminta dies and Lysander is left alone. See also 66B.

91B Behn, Aphra. "The Wandring Beauty." In Histories, Novels and Translations by the most ingenious Mrs. Behn. London, Printed for S. Briscoe, 1698. 33 pages. Item: B 1773A*. Collections: B 1711A, B 1714. EEB Reels 857:25 and 1787:8.

This short novel is about the importance of a good marriage for a wealthy woman. Arabella Fairname's parents attempt to marry her to the rich but elderly Sir Robert Richland. She is pursued by the parson, Mr. Prayfast, who spurns her when he thinks she has no money. Lucius Lovewell, another suitor, marries her without knowing her origins. The climax sees the twin revelations of her marriage (to her parents) and her origins (to her husband). This work is a variation on both the novel of manners and the traditional romance.

92B Behn, Aphra. The Widdow-Ranter; or The History of Bacon in Virginia. London, Printed for James Knapton, 1690. 56 pages. B 1774. EEB Reel 1056:14.

This play dramatizes events surrounding Nathaniel Bacon's rebellion in Virginia. Bacon is labeled a rebel by his fellow Council members when he attacks the Indians before receiving his commission. He is romantically involved with Queen Semernia, a noble Indian maid whom he mistakenly wounds. A subplot involves the Widdow Ranter, an earthy Amazonian woman, who woos Daring, one of Bacon's lieutenants. The source for this play is a pamphlet which chronicles Bacon's story, Strange News from Virginia (1677).

[Behn, Aphra.] Woman Turned Bully. See 963A.

93B Behn, Aphra. Young Jemmy. [London], Printed for P. Brooksby, [c1681].
Broadside. B 1775.

> This poem is about the Duke of Monmouth. Excerpt: "The busie fopps of
> state/Have ruin'd his condition./For Glittering Hopes he has left the shade/His
> Peaceful Hours are gone:/By flattering Knaves and Fools Betray'd/Poor Jemmy
> is undone."

94B Behn, Aphra. The Young King: or, The Mistake. London, Printed for D. Brown,
T. Benskin and H. Rhodes, 1683. 63 pages. B 1776*. EEB Reel 121:6.

> In this drama Scythia and Dacia are at war. Prince Thersander of Scythia,
> disguised as Clemantis, courts the Dacian Princess Cleomena. She rules in
> place of her brother Orsames, held captive in an island castle. In the end, the
> truth is revealed, and both countries, united by the marriage of Thesander and
> Cleomena, make a peace. A second plot involves Prince Orsames who ends
> by marrying his cousin Olympia. The play is based on the eighth part of
> Calprenede's Cleopatra.

95B Behn, Aphra. The Younger Brother; or, The Amorous Jilt. London, Printed
for J. Harris and sold by R. Baldwin, 1696. 52 pages. B 1778. EEB Reel 203:9.

> George Marteen, younger brother of Sir Merlin, is to be matched by his father,
> Sir Rowland, with the rich old Lady Youthly. He was formerly betrothed, to
> Mirtilla (the Amorous Jilt), who married Sir Morgan Blunder while George was
> studying business abroad. Meanwhile George falls in love with Lady Youthly's
> granddaughter Teresia, his father's fiancee and object of Merlin's interest.
> Finally George and Teresia, Wellborn and Olivia, Lady Youthly and Chaplain
> Twang are mated. George's other objectives are met as well. Bremond's
> Hattige and D'Urfey's The Royalist are the sources for this comedy.

96B Bell, Susanna. The Legacy of a Dying Mother To Her Mourning Children.
Being the Experiences of Mrs. Susanna Bell, who Died March 13, 1672. London,
Printed and are to be sold by John Hancock, 1673. 62 pages. B 1802. EEB Reel
203:11 (mislabeled B 1801).

> The Epistle Dedicatory, comprising most of the text, notes Bell lived in both Old
> and New England. The author addresses her thoughts, experiences and
> qualities--sincerity, plain-heartedness, humility, charity and mercy. Bell's
> autobiography, written for her children, follows. It describes their births and
> sicknesses as well as the dangers of traveling alone.

97B [Bernard, Catherine.] The Count of Amboise; or, The Generous Lover.
London, Printed for R. Bentley and M. Magnes, 1689. 204 pages. B 1983. EEB
Reel 1030:24.

> This novel, translated by Peter Bellon and dedicated to Elizabeth Slingsby, tells
> of a man generous enough to yield his mistress to his rival. The protagonist
> is a member of the court of Francis II. Before his arranged marriage to Mlle.

de Roye takes place, she meets M. de Sansae and, thinking him her intended, falls in love with him. At the end, de Sansae is slain at Chartres.

98B [Bernard, Catherine.] The Female Prince; or, Frederick of Sicily. In Three Parts. London, Printed for H. Rodes, 1682. [244] pages. B 1984. EEB Reel 1324:4.

This romance is dedicated to the Countess of Conway and signed by "F[errand] S[pence]." Although nothing indicates female authorship, the Bernard attribution is accepted by the Library of Congress and the British Library. The plot concerns the king and queen of Italy, who wish for a son to continue their line. When a daughter is born, they conceal her sex and raise her as a boy, Prince Frederick. Intrigues revolve around her mistaken identity.

The Best Newes from York. See 330B.

99B [Bettris, Jeane.] A Lamentation for the Deceived People of the World. [London, Printed for Thomas Simmons, 1657.] 8 pages. B 2085. TT Reel 140:E.931(4).

In this typical Quaker call for repentance, Bettris addresses inhabitants of Alesbury and environs, naked sinners under God's scrutiny. She entreats their leaders to cease deceiving the people and blaspheming the Lord, reminding them truth comes "by owning the Light which comes from the Son of God."

100B Biddle, [H]ester. Oh! Wo, Wo, from the Lord. London, Printed for Thomas Simmons, 1659. 4 pages. B 2864C.

Biddle was a Quaker writer and activist converted by Francis Howgill. She traveled to Barbados and Newfoundland as a missionary, was imprisoned several times and prophesied the return of Charles II. Urging repentance, she warns here of the imminence of judgment day and charges the rulers and priests of Dartmouth with corruption.

101B Biddle, [H]ester. To the Inhabitants of the Town of Dartmouth. London, 1659. B 2864D.

This item does not exist in the collection of the Library Company of Philadelphia. It is probably a ghost of 100B.

102B Biddle, [H]ester. The Trumpet Of the Lord God Sounded forth unto these Three Nations. 24 pages. London, 1662. B 2864E.

This item is likely a ghost of 103B.

103B Biddle, [H]ester. The Trumpet of the Lord Sounded forth unto these three Nations. London, 1662. 24 pages. B 2865. EEB Reel 1119:7.

Writing from Newgate Prison, Biddle addresses British sinners, especially Londoners, warning of destruction "if they Repent not." She laments the proliferation of hireling priests, rioting, "stage-playes," ballad singing, cards, dice, taverns and the like. Biddle also refers to her former Anglican life, including years spent in Oxford.

104B Biddle, [H]ester. <u>A Warning From the Lord God of Life and Power</u>. London, Printed for Robert Wilson, 1660. 22 pages. B 2866. EEB Reel 1088:3.

This rhetorical Quaker appeal entreats Londoners to reform and turn to the Lord. (Biddle assumes His voice.) Excerpt: "O my soul is truly poured forth unto the Lord for thee." Biddle argues London should be a model and a "nursing Mother" to the nation.

105B Biddle, [H]ester. <u>Wo to the towne of Cambridge</u>. London, 166? Broadside. B 2866A.

Biddle warns Cambridge residents of the city's coming destruction resulting from sinfulness. This diatribe is more significant as an appeal for Quaker prisoners: Biddle claims God will protect them, and the city is incurring His wrath by imprisoning them.

106B Biddle, [H]ester. <u>Wo to thee city of Oxford</u>. London, [1655]. Broadside. B 2867. TT Reel 246:669.f.19(77).

This broadside is a call to repentance. Biddle is especially critical of the sins of pride, covetousness and "voluptuousness."

107B Birgitte, Saint. <u>The Most Devout Prayers of</u>. Antwerp, Printed for T. D., 1686. 22 pages. B 2959*. EEB Reel 1197:6.

In fervid, graphic language St. Birgitte addresses Jesus in fifteen prayers. She speaks mostly about His wounds from the crucifixion: "...thy face pale and wanne, thy head crowned with thorns...thy hands nailed, thy veins broken, thy bones disjoynted."

108B [Blackborow, Sarah.] <u>Herein is held forth the Gift and Good-will of God to the World</u>. London, Printed for Thomas Simmons, 1659. 8 pages. B 3063. EEB Reel 1178:2.

Blackborow, a Quaker also known as Blackbury, criticizes poor treatment of the Friends--"scoffings, scornings, and despiteful usage, imprisonments." She warns the Lord grows impatient with those who turn from Christ and the light.

109B Blackborow, Sarah. <u>The Just and Equal Ballance Discovered</u>. London, Printed for M. W., 1660. 14 pages. B 3064.

Blackborow discusses the equality in Christ of male and female. It is typical of other Quaker entreaties to seek the light. Blackborow claims religion need not be practiced in temples, and stresses "the inward parts." She also addresses preaching and testifying by women and criticizes attacks on women's right to act as Christ's "vessels."

B[lackborow, S[arah]. <u>The Oppressed Prisoners Complaint</u>. See 670A.

110B [Blackborow, Sarah.] <u>A Visit to the Spirit in Prison</u>. London, Printed for Thomas Simmons, 1658. 13 pages. B 3065.

Blackborow claims by following the "light," people can avoid certain distinctions of institutionalized religion. Her language is lyrical: "His [Christ's] breathings are sweet and his shinings are pure." She criticizes ministers who persecute, lack church affiliations or preach for money. She condemns those who "cast the children of the Lord into prison, because they cannot deny the witnesse of God in their consciences."

111B Blaithwaite, Mary. The complaint of Mary Blaithwaite Widdow; setting forth her sad condition, occasioned by the late dissolution of the Parliament, and neglect of justice ever since. [London, 1654.] 8 pages. B 3129.

Blaithwaite says her property was seized unjustly. A warrant charges she was suspected of dispersing "scandalous pamphlets." Blaithwaite's emotional plea emphasizes her state as a "distressed widow" with "fatherless children." She had apparently attended court for eighteen weeks, waiting for her petition to be read. She is beseeching the king only because Parliament is dissolved, and she is destitute.

112B Blandford, Susannah. A Small account given forth by one that hath been a traveller for 40 years in the good old way. [London], 1698. 40 pages. B 3163A.

In this autobiography, Blandford says she was born an Anglican "of good parents" but was unable to find spiritual satisfaction within the Church. Upon hearing God's message through the Quakers, "it rent the Vail, chased away my dark thoughts" and gave her an understanding of scripture. Blandford claims Quaker Edward Burroughs aided in her conversion. This work is "an encouragement to the Weary to go forward."

113B Blandford, Susannah. A Small Treatise. London, 1700. B 3163B.

During a description of Quaker tenets, Blandford maintains that vicious attacks on the Friends have not shaken her faith. She says a true Friend has "a Spirit of Pride mixed with Man's will." Her postscript concerns the Rector of Edburton George Keith and his spiritual conflicts.

114B Blaugdone, Barbara. An Account of the Travels, Sufferings, and Persecutions of Barbara Blaugdone. [London], Printed and sold by T. Sowle, 1691. 38 pages. N.I.W.

In this extraordinary saga, an itinerant Quaker preacher from Bristol describes her experiences for the "Encouragement of Friends." Blaugdone tells of numerous imprisonments throughout England and Ireland and of several fasts, including one lasting a year during which she drank only water. She tells of several close encounters with death: She was threatened by a man wielding a knife, a "Wolf-Dog," sailors who nearly tossed her overboard, a butcher who "swore he would cleave my Head in twain," and a beadle who administered a severe thrashing "till the Blood ran down my Back." Throughout Blaugdone exhibited courage.

115B Boothby, Frances. Marcelia: or The Treacherous Friend. A Tragi-comedy. London, Printed for Will. Cademan and Giles Widdowes, 1670. [94] pages. B 3742. EEB Reel 172:3.

In the prologue, Boothby speculates the theatre will empty when the audience realizes the playwright is a woman. This typical Restoration comedy is set in France, with star-crossed lovers vying for attention and the usual theatrical devices. A dialogue between two men: "'Tis better be a Dog, than a Woman's slave/ That knows not what she would, or would not have."

116B Boulbie, Judith. A Few Words to the Rulers of this Nation. [London, 1673.] [No pagination.] B 3827A.

Boulbie was a Quaker from Yorkshire. Here she warns about the urgency of repentance and the folly of drinking, gambling and feasting in lieu of prayer. She claims England has "far exceeded Sodom" in its debauchery. Boulbie says she loves her native land and cannot bear to witness its excesses.

117B Boulbie, Judith. A Testimony for Truth against all Hireling-Priests and Deceivers. [London, 1655.] 7 pages. B 3828. EEB Reel 1416:13.

Boulbie attacks priests and encourages her countrymen to turn to God before it is too late. She charges priests have used their clerical status to shield themselves, but it is inadequate to hide their faults. Boulbie warns God must be served not by the letter of scripture but in its spirit.

118B Boulbie, Judith. To all Justices of the Peace or other Magistrates to whom this may come. [London, 1667.] [No pagination.] B 3828A.

Boulbie holds God has given free will to the multitude to see if they will use it in His behalf. She says the justices of the peace have abused it by placing innocent people "in your prisons and Dungeons." She warns of the inexorable day of judgment. The author's name is spelled "Bowlbie" in this document.

119B [Bourignon, Antoinette.] An Admirable Treatise of Solid Vertue, Unknown to the Men of this Generation. London, 1699. 342 pages. B 3840. EEB Reel 345:5.

Bourignon was a Flemish visionary who favored seclusion, penance and mortification. She attacked many religious organizations and alienated others because of her harsh, autocratic personality. Her primary dictum was that religion consists in emotion rather than knowledge or practice. In 1675 she declared her allegiance to Catholicism. This massive two-part treatise was translated from the French and published posthumously. It encourages total imitation of Christ. See also 384A.

120B [Bourignon, Antoinette.] [La Lumiere du monde] The Light of the World: A most True Relation of a Pilgrimess, M. Antoinette Bourignon, Travelling towards Eternity. Three Parts. London, [Christian de Cort], 1696. Parts paginated separately: 192, 140 and 211 pages. B 3842, B 3842A. EEB Reels 1179:1 and 1276:13.

Bourignon claims she is a Christian who believes in the Apostle's Creed, the Gospels and the Old and New Testaments. She discusses attaining perfection and communion with God, conversion of the Jews, free will and predestination, the state of neonates, the fall of humankind and so on. Bourignon calls for renunciation of worldly wisdom, alleging religion has become corrupt. This volume, her magnum opus, endeared Bourignon to many Scottish Presbyterians.

121B Bradmore, Sarah. Prophecy of the Wonders. London, Printed by S. J., 1686. [No pagination.] B 4139.

Bradmore wrote this satire on astrology to edify the ignorant and to make money. She predicts the entry of whales into rivers and riots among quack doctors. Invoking Agrippa, she says we do not understand the heavens, and calls astrologers fools.

122B [Bradstreet, Anne Dudley.] Several poems compiled with great variety, Wit and Learning, full of Delight. By a Gentlewoman in New-England. The Second Edition, Corrected by the Author, and enlarged by an Addition of several other Poems found amongst her Papers after her Death. Boston, Printed by John Foster, 1678. 255 pages. B 4166. EEB Reel 759:15.

This posthumous edition of Bradstreet's work is based on 123B. It was likely edited by John Rogers, her nephew. Several testimonials appear, with the editor's assurance it was penned by a woman. There are newly added eulogies for Bradstreet (by John Morton) and her mother (by the poet). Changes to the original poems are usually word substitutions, although there are also changes in entire passages, most notably in "Dialogue between Old England and New," the "Four Monarchies" and an elegy for Philip Sidney.

123B [Bradstreet, Anne Dudley.] The Tenth Muse Lately sprung up in America. Or Severall Poems, compiled with great variety of Wit and Learning, full of delight. By a Gentlewoman in those parts. London, Printed for Stephen Bowtell, 1650. 207 pages. B 4167.

The first book of English poetry written in America was published without Bradstreet's knowledge but with the permission of her brother-in-law, John Woodbridge. There are elegies and epitaphs, poems about the four humors, seasons, elements, ages and monarchies of the world; and about old and New England. Bradstreet retained a Renaissance view remarkable for its humanism, realism and passion.

124B Bregy, Charlotte de Flecelles, Countess de. The Royal Standard of King Charles the II. London, Printed for G. Horton, 1660. 6 pages. B 4342. TT Reel 155:E.1048(5).

Countess de Bregy was a French writer who knew Louis XIV, Mazarin and the queens of England and Sweden. Here she praises Charles, noting his fine ancestry, which, the author argues, should have rendered him ruler of three kingdoms. He is called an amiable and accomplished prince.

125B Brooksop, Jone. An Invitation of Love unto the Seed of God...and a Lamentation for New England. London, Printed for Robert Wilson, [1662.] 15 pages. B 4983. EEB Reel 680:25.

Brooksop asks her audience to hearken to the Lord: "He speaks peace unto his Israel and to all them that put their trust in him." She recommends proper fear and dread of the Lord and claims it is not she who is testifying, but rather Christ who speaks through her.

126B Browning, Mary. A Catalogue of Theological, Historical and Physical books...at her shop at the corner of the Exchange, in Amsterdam. Amsterdam, [1680?] [No pagination.] B 5187A.

This catalog lists no books obviously written by women.

127B Burch, Dorothy. A Catechisme of the severall Heads of Christian Religion. London, Printed by Matthew Simmons for John Hancock, 1646. [No pagination.] B 5612.

Burch uses an interlocutory format to present her religious views. She wishes to vindicate herself and others mistreated by their Kentish minister, who has reviled her both publicly and privately. Burch discusses God, creation, salvation and other topics from a Puritan perspective, saying neither repentance, faith nor fasting can assure salvation. This is an unusually practical catechism.

128B C., W. Poems on Several Occasions. London, Printed for the author and Published by R. Taylor, 1684. 64 pages. C 162. EEB Reel 85:14.

This volume, which contains a prefatory letter by Dryden, is dedicated to the Princess of Wales. There are many poems for individual women, including Elizabeth, Viscountess of Doneraite, Lady Dowager De la Warr, Lady Hodgson, Lady Pakington, Mary Irwin and Lady Mary Chudleigh. Other poems are feminist in sentiment or are bucolic friendship poems to women.

129B [Campbel, Agnes.] Advertisement Be Agnes Campbel, relict of the Deceast Master William Guthrie, Minister of the Gospel.   [Edinburgh], 1666 [1665]. Broadside. A 608. EEB Reel 1413:3.

This notice is a disclaimer wherein Campbel charges recently published sermons allegedly by her late husband are not his work. She bases her conclusion on a comparison of published texts with her husbands's notes, and discussions with his followers. The author is not the notorious printer of the same name, widowed by Andrew Anderson in 1676.

130B [Cartwright, Johanna.] The Petition of the Jewes for the Repealing of the Act of Parliament for their banishment out of England.   [With Ebenezer Cartwright] London, Printed for George Roberts, 1649. 6 pages. C 695.

Cartwright and her son Ebenezer were freeborn of England and lived in the Jewish community in Amsterdam. They argue that since the Second Coming is near, Jews should be allowed to return to England because only the English and Dutch navies are capable of transporting them to the Holy Land. The petition was sent to General Thomas Halifax.

131B Cary (Rande), Mary. Little Horns Doom and Downfall; or, a Scripture Prophesie of King James, and King Charles. London, Printed for the Author, 1651. 48 pages. C 736. TT Reel 172:E.1274(1).

Cary was a Fifth Monarchist millenarian who apparently led no congregation, but styled herself a minister. Most of her predictions were based on scripture. This work, written seven years before publication, is dedicated to Cromwell's three daughters. Its central thesis is the importance of prophecy. Cary comments on scripture, linking it to the present and claims it predicted the Civil War and the death of Charles I.

132B Cary, (Rande), Mary. "A New and More Exact Mappe or, Description of New Jerusalems Glory when Jesus Christ and his Saints with him shall reign on earth a 1000 years." In Little Horn's Doom and Downfall. London, Printed for the Author, 1651. [276] pages. N.I.W. TT Reel 172:E.1274(1).

Cary predicts a rule of the saints, who will appropriately use the sword against evil. Satan is envisioned as bound for 1000 years during the saintly rule. Women are to be permitted to prophesy and share their husbands' property rights. The unpaginated text is directed to Parliament, the army and the people.

133B Cary (Rande), Mary. The Resurrection of the Witnesses, And Englands Fall from--The Mystical Babylon--Rome. London, Printed by D. M. for Giles Calvert, 1648. [195] pages. C 737*. TT Reel 111:E.719(2).

Cary declares the millennium is nigh in an extended exposition of Revelations 11. She attempts to relate the biblical events of this book to contemporary ones.

134B Cary (Rande), Mary.] Twelve New Proposals to the Supreme Governours of the Three Nations now assembled at Westminster concerning the Propagation of the Gospel, New modling of the Universities, Reformation of the Laws, supply of the necessities of the Poor. London, Printed by Henry Hills for R. C. and are to be sold by Giles Calvert, 1653. 13 pages. N.I.W.

Cary states she believes Parliament is not meeting often enough, nor working diligently. She presents proposals for their consideration and suggests propagation of the gospel, repeal of the tithe law ("which is a great oppression not only to the estates, but to the consciences of many good people"), expulsion of unscrupulous and idle persons from the Church, parsimonious consolidation of small parishes, augmented programs for the education of ministers, democratization of the universities, and so on.

135B Cary (Rande), M[ary.] A Word in Season to the Kingdom of England. Or, A Precious Cordiall for a distempered kingdom. London, Printed by R. W. for Giles Calvert, 1647. 12 pages. C 739. TT Reel 62:E.393(26).

Cary argues for a stronger country in this religious tract. She warns ignoring the poor is the way to ruin, and refusing to punish drunkenness, swearing and sin brings destruction. Cary also advises England's rulers not to outlaw those who would prophesy. The tone of this work is quite aggressive.

Cavendish, Margaret. See Newcastle, Margaret Cavendish, Duchess of.

136B [Cellier, Elizabeth.] An Abstract of the Tryal of Elizabeth Cellier, [and] The Humble Petition of Elizabeth Cellier. Finished, Friday, July the 2nd by Elizabeth Cellier. London, [1678.] N.I.W.

The first part of this work is a reproduction of 137B, Cellier's defense of her part in the Meal-tub Plot. The remainder is a transcript of her first trial, and it is not written by her.

[Cellier, Elizabeth]. The Ladies Answer to that Busiebody. See 497A.

[Cellier, Elizabeth.] Maddam Celliers Answer to the Popes Letter. See 553A.

137B Cellier, Elizabeth. Malice Defeated: Or, a Brief Relation of the Accusation and Deliverance of Eliz. Cellier. London, Printed for Elizabeth Cellier, 1680. [48] pages. C 1661. EEB Reel 449:14.

Elizabeth Cellier, a midwife and a protagonist in the Meal-tub Plot, was tried for treason in June of 1680 and acquitted. This is a personal defense of her innocence against charges of conspiring with the Catholic party to introduce a false prince and subvert parliamentary government. She says witnesses against her at the trial were untrustworthy and defends herself in a narrative of events leading to the accusations. See also 138B, 260A, 512A, 603A, 787A and 880A.

138B Cellier, Elizabeth. The Matchless Rogue; or, A Brief Account of the Life of Don Thomazo, The Unfortunate Son. London, Printed for Elizabeth Cellier, 1680. [2] pages. C 1662. EEB Reel 58:16.

This document, in response to either 260A or 787A, is prefaced by a caustic biography of Thomas Dangerfield ("Don Thomazo Ganderfield"), accused of complicity with Cellier in the Meal-tub Plot. He allegedly robbed his father at eleven, then pursued a life of crime after fleeing to Scotland. The tone is angry and sarcastic, in sharp contrast with Cellier's other work. See also 137B, 512A, 603A and 880A.

[Cellier, Elizabeth.] Mistriss Celliers Lamentation. See 595A.

139B Cellier, Elizabeth. "A Scheme for the Foundation of a Royal Hospital, and Raising a Revenue of Five or Six Thousand Pounds a year, by and for the Maintenance of a Corporation of skilful Midwives, of such Foundlings, or Exposed Children, as shall be admitted therein." In The Harleian Miscellany, Vol. 4 (London: White and Company, John Murray and John Harding, 1809), 142-147. Item: N.I.W.

Cellier, midwife to the royal family during the reign of James II, proposes a detailed plan for a royal hospital for foundling children administered by a corporation of midwives. They would act as overseers for the children and would teach skills and establish standards for the profession. Midwives could seek advice about difficult births from consulting physicians and experienced midwives. They could also tap a special fund for their own children. Finally, the foundlings would receive shelter and training. See also 140B.

140B Cellier, Elizabeth. To Dr.---An Answer to his Queries, concerning the Colledg of Midwives. [London, 1688.] 8 pages. C 1663. EEB Reel 1457:3.

Cellier defends her proposal to establish a corporation and school for midwives to encourage the study of anatomy and cultivation of skills needed for difficult deliveries.   She answers a physician who called her arrogant and claims doctors should control the midwifery profession. See also 139B.

[Cellier, Elizabeth.] A True Copy of a Letter of Consolation. See 889A.

141B Centlivre, Susanna. The perjur'd husband: or, The adventures of Venice. A Tragedy. London, Printed for Bennett Banbury, 1700. 40 pages. C 1671. EEB Reel 449:15.

This tragedy, signed by "Susanna Carroll," concerns the vacillating Bassino, in love with Aurelia, although he is wed to Placentia. Aurelia, untrue herself, lies to her betrothed, Alonzo, about their liaison to spare her lover. The major themes are the folly of arranged marriage, the proper role of friendship, the relation of guilt to deceit, and the duality of reason and passion. The copy examined contains the handwritten word "whore" below Centlivre's signature.

The Challenge, sent by a Young Lady. See 187A.

142B Channel, Elinor. A Message from God [By a Dumb Woman To his Highness the Lor]d Protector Together with "A Word of Advice to the Commons of England and Wales, for the Electing of a Parliament". London, Printed by Arise Evans, 1653, or as the vulgar think, 1654. 14 pages. C 1936.

Channel, an Anglican from Cranley in Surrey, awoke with a vision after a head injury which she says precluded evil thoughts. She claims the Lord beckoned to her to travel to London, "that she might express her mind to [Cromwell] and have rest in her spirit." Her message: "The Sword must be stayed. The world draweth toward an end, and the knots of peace and love must be made in all Christian lands." Channel did not see Cromwell, but the document describes her visit to London.

143B [Cheevers, Sarah.]   This is a short Relation of Some of the Cruel Sufferings...of Katherine Evans and Sarah Chevers [sic], in the Inquisition in the Isle of Malta. London, Printed for Robert Wilson, 1662. [104] pages. T 935. EEB Reel 899:30.

These documents record the three-year captivity of two Quaker women in Malta under the Inquisition. It includes prayers and songs; letters to family, friends, and the Pope's Lord Inquisitor in Malta; and a description of the city and events leading to their incarceration. Excerpt: "We did eat our bread weeping, and mingled our drink with our tears. We did write to the Inquisitor, and laid before him our innocency." After an unsuccessful rescue attempt by Daniel Baker, whose remarks appear here, the women were released through the intervention of a friend of Henrietta Maria. See also 143B, 268B and 72A.

144B Cheevers, Sarah.   To All People Upon the face of the Earth; A Sweet Salutation. [London], Printed for R. Wilson, 1663. [35] pages. C 3776A.

In this Quaker entreaty to recognize the power of the light, Cheevers refers to her joint ministry with Katherine Evans and attacks ministers who deny the light but call themselves teachers.   She also discusses the benefits of living by Quaker precepts. The piece follows and is continuously paged with 268B. See also 143B, 268B and 72A.

145B C[hidley], K[atherine.] Good Counsell, to the Petitioners for Presbyterian
Government, That They May Declare their Faith before they Build their Church.
London, [1645]. Broadside. C 3831.

Chidley was a radical sectarian, later a Leveller, from Shrewsbury, then London.
She generally favored religious toleration, but here she speaks against Scottish
Presbyterian authoritarianism and sainthood. See also 576B.

146B Chidley, Katherine. The [J]ustification of the Independent Churches of Christ.
Being an answer to Mr. Edwards his booke, which hee hath written against the
government of Christs Church. London, Printed for William Larnar, 1641. [82]
pages. C 3832. EEB Reel 256:E.174(7) and TT Reel 30:E.174(7).

Chidley declares the congregations of the saints ought to depend only upon
Christ.   She addresses [Thomas] Edwards throughout, challenging his
contention that religious toleration will breed division. She says: "We plead for
no toleration that shall disturb the peace of Churches or Townes" and
addresses details of ritual, prayer and dogma.   Finally Chidley challenges
Edwards to a debate: "But if you overcome me, your conquest will not be great,
for I am but a poore worme, and unmeete to deal with you."

147B C[hidley], K[atherine.] A New-Yeares Gift, or A Brief Exhortation to Mr.
Thomas Edwards. London, 1645. 23 pages. C 3833. EEB Reel 232:E.23(13) and
TT Reel 4:E.23(13).

Chidley addresses Edwards so "he may breake off his old sins" and begin
anew. She responds to his first book, an "insinuating, contradictory, revengeful
story."   She challenges his threat to eliminate Separatism, refuting his
arguments, defending those outside the Church of England, and claiming his
approach aids the papal hierarchy. Chidley's son was Samuel Chidley, an
expelled Puritan minister.

[Christina, Queen of Sweden.]   A Declaration of the Most High and Mighty
Princesse. See 269A.

148B [Christina, Queen of Sweden.] A Letter sent from the Queen of Sweden to
the King of France, touching the Affairs of that Kingdome, and the King of Scots.
London, Printed for G. Horton, 1652. 7 pages. C 3965.

This letter concerns military movements and the spread of the plague in the
Spanish army.

149B [Chudleigh, Mary, Lady.] The F[emale] A[dvocate]; Or, a Plea for the just
Liberty of the tender Sex, and particularly of Married Women. Being reflections on
a late rude and disingenuous discourse, delivered by Mr. John Sprint, in a sermon.
By a Lady of Quality. London, Printed for Andrew Bell, 1700. 55 pages. C 3984.

This piece is signed by "Eugenia," identified as Chudleigh by the British Library.
It replies to a wedding sermon by John Sprint endorsing wifely obedience.
Chudleigh satirically chides Sprint's awkward and insensitive description of
marriage, which he apparently perceived as rightly more indulgent of male
than female needs. She criticizes Sprint severely, "Insolent man! To preach us

gravely into slavery and chains, and then deride and banter us." See also 816A and 933A.

150B [Chudleigh, Mary, Lady.] The Female Preacher. Being An Answer to a late Rude and Scandalous Wedding-Sermon, Preach'd by Mr. John Sprint. London, Printed for H. Hills, [1699?]. 24 pages. C 3984A.

This piece is signed "Eugenia" and is the same as 149B.

151B [Clark, Frances.] A Briefe Reply to the Narration of Don Pantaleon Sa, by one of the sisters of the gentleman murthered on the New-Exchange. [London, 1653.] 7 pages. C 4439. TT Reel 111:E.724(9).

For herself and her sister, Elizabeth Worsopp, Clark petitions the "Councell of State" for justice and compensation in the allegedly unprovoked murder of their brother, Harcourt Greenway. He was attacked with a pistol by Don Pantaleon, the brother of the Portuguese ambassador. She fears he may go unpunished because of diplomatic immunity.

152B Clark, Margret. The True Confession of Margret Clark, Who Consented to the Burning of her Masters... House. London, Printed and Sold by Joseph Collier, 1680. 6 pages. C 4482. EEB Reel 87:7.

This piece centers on Clark's prison confession shortly before her execution. She said she was bribed to conspire with John Satterwait to set three fires to her master's house; here she repents her actions. Both she and her co-conspirator were Catholic, and she seeks forgiveness from Protestants. See also 941A.

[Clark, Margret.] Warning for Servants. See 941A.

153B Clark, Mary. The Great and Wonderful Success and Vertues of Clark's Compound Spirits of Scurvey-Grass. [London, 1685?] Broadside. C 4483A.

Mary Clark claims a miraculous compound developed by her husband sixteen years ago is now available only from her. She discredits other offerings as poor imitations and includes a list of agents who sell her product. Clark's curative is alleged to be effective in the treatment of scurvy, toothache, worms, lameness, hip-pain, asthma and dropsy. A list of satisfied customers is included.

154B Clayton, Anne. A Letter to the King. [London, 1660.] Broadside. C 4609.

A Quaker "handmaiden" directs this broadside to Charles II upon his restoration. She says before his return to the throne she had a vision of three spirits who predicted the event. She repeatedly notes one was a female. Clayton says the truth of the gospel can be seen only in the actions of God's followers.

Clayton, Prudence. John Clayton, Executor of Dame Mary Clayton. Appellant. Prudence Clayton, Respondent. See 486B.

155B [Clipsham, Margery and Mary Ellwood.] The Spirit that works Abomination and its Abominable Work Discovered. [London, 1685.] 8 pages. C 4716A*.

This Quaker tract warns against listening to Satan disguised as Christ. The women charge some Quakers are spreading slander. Susanna Aldrige is named along with her work Abominations in Jerusalem Discovered, critical of the women's meeting. Clipsham and Ellwood claim Aldrige's tone is bitter and her language confusing. They say she was probably led astray by a preacher identified as C. H.

156B [Cockburn, Catharine (Trotter).] Agnes de Castro. A Tragedy. London, Printed for H. Rhodes, R. Parker, and S. Briscoe, 1696. [47] pages. C 4801. EEB Reel 87:12.

This play, which takes place in Coimbra, Portugal, is dedicated to Charles, Earl of Dorset and Middlesex. The prologue by William Wycherly was written at the request of the seventeen-year-old author. The plot revolves around a triangle: The Prince of Portugal loves Agnes de Castro, dear to his wife, to whom Agnes is also devoted. The princess discovers her husband's secret but remains discreet. After some convoluted action, including a near rape, a kidnapping and a murder, the prince unsuccessfully attempts suicide.

157B [Cockburn, Catharine (Trotter).] Fatal Friendship. London, Printed for Francis Saunders, 1698. C 4802. EEB Reel 486:26.

This tragedy, written in blank verse, is about Gramont and Felicia, a poor, secretly married couple whose infant son has been kidnapped by pirates. To secure ransom money and bail for a friend, Gramont agrees to marry the wealthy widow Lamira, but refuses to consummate the marriage. No villain appears in the play, and, according to Cockburn, the characters all mean well, even though they inadvertently confound their own actions. The tale is meant "to discourage Vice, and recommend a firm unshaken Virtue" (Cockburn).

Coleman, Elizabeth. The Harlots Vail rent. See 563B.

158B Collins, An[ne]. Divine songs and meditacions. London, Printed by R. Bishop, 1653. 96 pages. C 5355. EEB Reel 177:1.

These strongly autobiographical poems, songs, discourse and meditations were written for the benefit of Christians of "disconsolate Spirits." Collins notes she has suffered a confining illness, but has remained active through her "theological enjoyments." Her focus is the vanity of earthly things and the joy of faith.

159B [Conway, Anne Finch, Viscountess.] The Principles of the Most Ancient and Modern Philosophy. Amsterdam, Printed in Latin at Amsterdam by M. Brown, 1690. [And reprinted in English in London, 1692] 168 pages. C 5989. EEB Reel 60:15.

This philosophical treatise was written by one of the most scientifically knowledgeable women of the 1600s. Compiled after Conway's death, it includes writings about physical and biological science and theology. Conway also comments on Descartes, Hobbes and Spinoza.

160B Cooke, Frances. Mrs. Cookes Meditations, Being an Humble Thanksgiving to her Heavenly Father. London, Printed by C. S., [1650?]. 16 pages. C 6008.

Cooke thanks God for her survival of a horrible storm at sea. The work is mostly religious rumination, but includes a description of Cooke's adventure and a poem she wrote about her safe delivery.

A Coppy of 1. The Letter sent by the Queenes Majestie. See 333B.

161B C[otton], P[riscilla.] A Briefe Description by way of Supposition. [London? 1659.] 4 pages. C 6473B.

In this rare example of original political theory by a woman Cotton describes a utopian community where all faiths compete fairly for followers. The state makes no attempt to suppress "heretics." It supports twelve groups on a lush island. Hospitals for the poor, places for the "dispelling of errors," and workhouses for the idle are provided. Cotton emphasizes separation of church and state and universal education, irrespective of wealth.

162B C[otton], P[riscilla]. To the Priests and People of England, we discharge our Consciences, and give them Warning. [With Mary Cole] London, Printed for Giles Calvert, 1655. 8 pages. C 6474. TT Reel 129:E.854(13).

This description of a Quaker attempt at religious conversion is interesting for its justifications for female participation in the service.

163B C[otton], P[riscilla]. A Visitation of Love unto all People. n.p., 1661. 4 pages. C 6475. EEB Reel 1400:27.

Cotton's Quaker tract calls all nations to follow Christ. She mentions Turks, Jews, papists and others. She entreats them not to worship other gods and offers assurances that Christ's return will reunite all the earth's peoples. They must renounce their "idolatry, covetousness, pride and all uncleanness."

[Cromwell, Elizabeth.] The Court and Kitchin of Elizabeth. See 236A.

Curwen, Alice. A Relation of the Labour. See 253A.

164B D'anvers, Alicia. Academia: or, the Humours of the University of Oxford. London, Printed and sold by Randal Taylor, 1691. 67 pages. D 220. EEB Reel 138:23.

This ribald, scurrilous doggerel caricatures young men at Oxford--early on as innocent and spoiled by their mothers, and later as debauched and poorly educated. It centers on a young man's naive, amusing description of the buildings and activities at Oxford.

D'anvers, Alicia. The Oxford-Act: a poem. See 676A.

165B D'anvers, Alicia. A Poem Upon his Sacred Majesty, his Voyage for Holland. London, Printed for Thomas Bever, 1691. [8] pages. D 221. EEB Reel 451:14.

In this poetic dialogue between "Belgia" (Belgium) and "Britannia" (Britain) dedicated to Queen Mary, D'anvers expresses her opposition to war and criticizes the French-Belgian alliance. She claims the two countries have made England bleed.

Davies, Eleanor. See Douglas, Eleanor Touchet Davies, Lady.

166B Davy, Sarah. <u>Heaven Realiz'd or the Holy Pleasure of daily Intimate Communion God...(Mrs. Sarah Davy) Dying about the 32 Year of her Age...The Record of My Consolations, and the Meditations of My Heart</u>. [London], Printed for Edward Calvert, 1670. 151 pages. D 444. EEB Reel 1227:16.

A woman who died at thirty-two wrote this religious autobiography. Davy describes "drinking of the Rivers of the pleasures of God," calls Christ her Bridegroom, and uses the sensual vocabulary of religious ecstasy to describe her relation with a female minister. She discusses her conversion and its effect on her life. The volume is less formulaic than others by women. A second title page announces, "This before her marriage and signed Sarah Roane, Dec. 1660."

Desjardins, Marie Catherine Hortense. <u>The Amours of the Count of Dunois</u>. See 914A.

167B [Desjardins, Marie Catherine Hortense.] <u>The Annals of Love, containing Select Histories of the Amours of Divers Princes Courts, pleasantly related</u>. London, Printed for John Starkey, 1672. 422 pages. D 1187A. EEB Reel 340:22.

This volume contains historical vignettes about courtship. Among the protagonists are Catherine of Aragon, The Fraticelles (an Italian religious order); Dulcinus, King of the Lombards; Don Pedro of Castille and Jacaya, King of the Ottoman Empire. Although the Wing <u>STC</u> lists Desjardins as author, this edition bears no attribution on the title page.

168B [Desjardins, Marie Catherine Hortense.] <u>The Disorders of love. Truly expressed in the unfortunate amours of Givry with Mademoiselle de Guise</u>. London, Printed for James Magnes and Richard Bentley, 1677. 148 pages. D 1188. EEB Reel 180:13.

Originally published under Desjardins' pseudonym "Mme. de Villedieu," this novel takes place in France. The action involves the Houses of Anglure and Guise. The hero is Givry, while the heroines are Mademoiselle de Guide and Madame de Maugiron. A typical adventure, it is set against the siege of Paris by the Duke of Parma.

169B [Desjardins, Marie Catherine Hortense.] <u>The Husband Forc'd to be Jealous, or The Good Fortune of Those Women That Have Jealous Husbands</u>. Translated by N. H. London, Printed for H. Herringman, 1668. 157 pages. D 1188A. EEB Reel 1525:20.

Set in Greece, this stock romance revolves around intrigues and actions prompted by jealousy. There is no obvious clue as to authorship in the volume.

170B [Desjardins, Marie Catherine Hortense.] Love's Journal: a romance, made of the Court of Henry the II of France. London, Printed by Thomas Ratcliff and Mary Daniel, 1671. 126 pages. D 1189.

This novel is the first part of a translation of Le Journal Amoureux, originally published in France in 1670. It recounts the struggles and romantic escapades of the young Duke Octavo, who is handsome and virtuous. The setting is France, where the duke travels to seek the aid of Henry II in vindicating his father's murder by villains he believes to be at large there.

171B [Desjardins, Marie Catherine Hortense.] The Loves of Sundry Philosophers and Other Great Men. [London], Printed by T. N. for Henry Herringman and John Starkey, 1673. 270 pages. D 1190. EEB Reel 711:5.

These stories, translated from the French, obviously embellish the love-lives of "great men"--Socrates, Julius Caesar, Cato, D'Andelot, Bussy D'Amboyse.

172B [Desjardins, Marie Catherine Hortense.] The Memoires of the Life, and Rare Adventures of Henrietta Silvia Moliere. Two Vols. London, Printed by J. C. for Wm. Cooke, 1672. 262 pages. D 1191*. EEB Reel 92:2.

Although the title page notes it was "Written by her Self," this book is actually an elaborate fiction about a beautiful and mysterious woman who, as an infant, was left to nurse, discovered by a duke, and raised in the home of a financier who pursued her. Rendered in a confessional style, it traces the heroine's travels and describes her romances.

173B [Desjardins, Marie Catherine Hortense.] The Unfortunate Heroes: or, the Adventures of ten famous men. [London], Printed by T[homas] N[ewcomb] for H. Herringman, 1679. 265 pages. D 1193. EEB Reel 711:6.

These "adventures" are romantic dramatizations of episodes from the lives of Ovid, Lentulus, Hortensius, Cepion, Horace, Virgil, Cornelius Gallus, Crassus, Agrippa and Herennius. This volume comprises the first four parts only of the original edition.

174B [Dirrecks, Geertruyde Niessen.] An Epistle to be Communicated to Friends. [n.p., 1677.] 8 pages. D 1558. EEB Reel 842:5.

Dirrecks discusses childrearing, advising parents to be good examples for their offspring, to require no more than their natural ability seems to allow, and to be patient when they "fall short of their Duty." She also discusses commerce among tradesmen "who take too much Liberty in getting and borrowing Money." Dirrecks questions the accumulation of great debt and bemoans the effect of business failures on widows, orphans, the old and weak. This is an unusually worldly and practical Quaker commentary.

175B D[ocwra], A[nne]. An Apostate-Conscience Exposed, and the Miserable Consequences thereon Disclosed for Information and Caution. London, Printed and sold by T. Sowle, 1699. 67 pages. D 1777.

Docwra, a Quaker, says charges leveled against the Friends by Francis Bugg, a "Poore Indegent Person" from Suffolk, should be addressed by a civil magistrate. She details the history of his interaction with herself and Quaker leaders, including George Fox and George Whitehead, and addresses passages from his books about the Society of Friends. See also 125A, 127A and 179B.

176B D[ocwra], A[nne]. A Brief Discovery of the Work of the Enemy. London, 1683. [No pagination.] D 1777A.

Docwra attacks male Friends who apparently attempted to influence the Society's familial policy. When some members protested their assertion of power, they were expelled from the Society. Docwra claims they lack "the Humility of Truth and true Charity" and have forsaken the light within for selfish gain.

177B D[ocwra], A[nne]. An epistle of love and Good Advice to my old friends and fellow sufferers in the late-times the old royalists and their Posterity. London, Printed for Andrew Sowle, 1683. 11 pages. D 1778. EEB Reel 350:18.

This Quaker tract is dedicated to the old royalists and anyone who has a sincere desire to seek the Lord. Docwra defends prophesying women and speaks of Paul's view of the unity of humankind.

178B D[ocwra], A[nne]. A Looking-Glass for the Recorder and Justices of the Peace, and Grand Juries for the town and county of Cambridge. [London, 1682.] 11 pages. D 1779. EEB Reel 1381:23.

Docwra asks for toleration of dissidents, citing laws for freedom of religious belief; however, she claims they do not afford rights to heretics, "but only such as have formerly been adjudged so to be by the Canonical Scriptures." Docwra says laws governing church attendance are meant for "Popish Recusants."

179B D[ocwra], A[nne]. The Second Part of an Apostate Conscience Exposed: Being an Answer to a Scurrilous Pamphlet, Dated the 11th of April 1699. Written and published by F. Bugg, intituled Jezebel Withstood. London, Printed and sold by T. Sowle, 1700. 48 pages. D 1780.

Docwra answers Francis Bugg, a former Quaker and critic of the Friends, calling him an "Apostate Quaker." She argues critics are malicious and should not be pacified. She accuses him of forgery and attempting to trick the clergy by signing his estate over to his son and then begging among the Friends. This rejoinder was written by Docwra at seventy-six. See also 175B, 125A and 127A.

180B D[ocwra], A[nne]. Spiritual Community, Vindicated amongst people of different persuasions in some things. [London, 1687.] 4 pages. D 1781. EEB Reel 1459:15.

Docwra emphasizes inner light, saying those who recognize it "have unity and spiritual community." She states the king's toleration of religious dissent manifests God's directive "which He hath put forth in the Kings heart." Docwra criticizes churches that "place the Bond of their community in their Christian liturgy." She concludes it is unchristian to seek revenge upon those who chose a variant form of worship.

181B D[ocwra], A[nne]. True Intelligence to be Read and Considered in the Light. Cambridge, 1683. Broadside. N.I.W.

This disclaimer denies the joint authorship by Docwra, George Whitehead and T. Elwood of a broadside entitled A Brief Discovery of the Enemy, but concedes existence of one of the same title written by Docwra alone (176B).

182B Dole, Dorcas. Once More a Warning to thee O England: But more particularly to the Inhabitants of the City of Bristol. [London], 1683. [17] pages. D 1834*. EEB Reels 814:9 and 1526:3.

Dole, a Quaker from Bristol, encourages repentance by those who "pretend the Scripture is your only Rule." In particular, she entreats teachers and rulers to cease religious persecution. Quoting from Ezekiel 33.8-9, she maintains her conscience is clear. Dole dates the document September 17, 1683 from Newgate Prison.

183B Dole, Dorcas. A Salutation and Seasonable Exhortation to Children. London, Printed and sold by T. Sowle, 1700. 12 pages. D 1835A*.

This piece, dated originally from Bridewell Prison in Bristol in April of 1682, is dedicated to Quaker children. Dole reminds them of their obligation to the Lord and their parents and encourages them to live by faith. This edition includes a postscript to the children who maintained the meeting while Friends were imprisoned.

184B Dole, Dorcas. A Salutation of my Endeared Love to the Faithful in all Places, That bear their Testimony for the Lord. [London], Printed for John Bringhurst, 1685. 8 pages. D 1836*.

Dole entreats Quakers to manifest their private faith publicly. Saying obedience is better than sacrifice, she offers love to those who "make a profession of the Truth" and claims "...my Soul is inlarged beyond what Ink and Paper can demonstrate." Dole dates this piece from Newgate Prison in Bristol on December 17, 1684.

Dole, Dorcas. "To you that have been Professors of the Truth of God, in the City of Bristol." See 535B.

185B [Douglas, Eleanor Touchet Davies, Lady.] Amend, Amend; Gods Kingdome is at hand: amen, amen. The Proclamation: Mene, Mene; Thine Finished (or ended;/Tekel; Thou Found Fickle, or Weak by/Them./Peres, they Peers or Parliement Mem:/Mene Tekel Upharsin/K: Parliement House. [London, 1643.] 12 pages. D 1967. EEB Reel 181:11.

First published in Amsterdam in 1633, this verse was written by a well-known female seer who foretold the execution of Charles I. Here Douglas employs a key: Belshazzar is apparently meant to be Charles. Excerpt: "When Death for One as tis no Lesse/ by Statute Law of Late:/To have two wifes at once, yet thine/Owne case or present state. /What is it but to say the truth?/The Beame doth not espie;/Rather to be plucked out then/A mote in others Eie."

186B [Douglas, Eleanor Touchet Davies, Lady.] And without proving what we say.
[London? 1648.] [8] pages. D 1968. EEB 1667:8.

Douglas criticizes the king's solicitor general, Baron Trevare, for misusing his
authority in appropriating her property during her imprisonment. Referring to
biblical sources, her own prophecies and historical events, she alleges he
mistreats other widows and is a poor advisor to the king.

187B [Douglas, Eleanor Touchet Davies, Lady.] Apocalyps, [sic] Chap. 11. Its
Accomplishment shewed from Lady Eleanor. [London? 164?] 8 pages. D 1969.
EEB Reel 937:14.

Douglas calls Babylon and Sodom examples of the "incurable Blindness
Arrogancy begets." She notes Belshazzar (Charles I) has ignored the warnings
of the prophet Daniel (herself). (Douglas identified with Daniel because her
maiden name, Eleanor Audlie, made the anagram 'Reveale O Daniel.') She
describes events between 1642 and the earthquake of 1645 and connects
England's present inertia to its resistance to earlier warnings of catastrophe.
She cites "monstrous levied Taxes devouring young and old, "Engines of war...
destroying men by Sea and Land," etc.

188B [Douglas, Eleanor Touchet Davies, Lady.]   Apocalypsis Jesu Christi.
[London?], 1644. 32 pages. D 1970.

Douglas addresses the "Reverend men of God and Judges," citing scriptural
prophets and their predictions of recent events in England. Their accuracy
supposedly confirms the validity of her own. Douglas says judgment day will
occur in 1700 and notes signs of it, e.g., the sun in the sign of cancer, the
voice of four beasts, the seventh and last seal opened in heaven, the playing
of seven trumpets.

189B [Douglas, Eleanor Touchet Davies, Lady.] The Lady Eleanor, Her Appeale.
[London], 1641. 20 pages. D 1971. EEB Reel E.72(33) and TT Reel 30:E.72(33).

Douglas signs this prophetic tract from Kensington. She invokes God's power
to destroy mighty Babylon, citing symbols which predict Judgment Day in
nineteen years and a passage from Daniel 2: "Thou sawest still that a stone
was cut without hands, which smote the Image upon the feete: That of Iron,
and Clay, and brake them in peeces." To strengthen her credibility, she alludes
to her father as a Peer of the Realm.

190B [Douglas, Eleanor Touchet Davies, Lady.] The Lady Eleanor her appeal.
n.p., 1646. 40 pages. D 1972. EEB Reel 937:15.

This work begins with the tale of a young Scottish psychic who could discern
biblical passages through closed books. Douglas claims the Book of Daniel
legitimizes her own mission to predict the future through its emphasis on the
number one, on virgins and so on. She is apparently trying to establish herself
as a seer, emphasizing her responsibility as a woman to save the world.

191B [Douglas, Eleanor Touchet Davies, Lady.] The Appearance or Presence of
the Son of Man. [n.p.], 1650. 16 pages. D 1972A.

This fragment, with extensive explanatory marginalia, cites Psalm 48. Douglas documents her reliability as a prophet, noting her predictions of Buckingham's death and judgment day. She also refers to the reputations of her and her husband's families.

192B [Douglas, Eleanor Touchet Davies, Lady.] The Arraignment. [London], 1650. 12 pages. D 1972B.

The Lady Eleanor notes impediments that prevent people from hearing the word of God and maintains they should work toward eliminating them: An offending hand should be cut off; the entire body should not be sacrificed to save a foot. Douglas dwells on the dark side of the final days, stressing the Second Coming.

193B [Douglas, Eleanor Touchet Davies, Lady.] As not unknowne. This petition or prophesie on record, presented to His Majestie in the yeare 1633. [London, 1644/5.] Broadside. D 1973. TT Reel 246:669.f.10(22)

Douglas says her petition of 1633 (text included) has been ignored. She discusses the arrest and incarceration of Archbishop Laud, noting the appropriateness of his punishment. To the Kings Most Excellent Majesty, appended, requests burial of three persons executed under Laud "shrouded in loose sheets of paper." The order of the Court of High Commission, also included, orders her appearance for publishing unlicensed books.

194B [Douglas, Eleanor Touchet Davies, Lady.] Before the Lord's second coming, of the last days to be visited, signed with the Tyrant Pharaohs overthrow. [London], 1650. 16 pages. D 1974. TT Reel 94:E.616(11).

Douglas says the overthrow of the pharaoh is a sign of Christ's return to earth. Speaking of herself as His messenger, Douglas refers to Britain as "these distracted Dominions" and recalls the wrongful execution of Charles I. She suggests the seventeenth century will see Christ's return, although the moment of the event remains unclear, even to her. Douglas bases her prediction on Daniel and Revelations.

195B [Douglas, Eleanor Touchet Davies, Lady.] The Benidiction. [sic] From the A:lmighty O:mnipotent. [London?], 1651. [3] pages. D 1975*. EEB Reel 1307:21.

A congratulatory message to Oliver Cromwell, this brief letter is confused and unclear, like much of Douglas' work. It praises Cromwell and reminds him the initials A. O. ("O" being a symbol of the sun) could be ascribed both to God and to himself; she encourages him to work for God's ends and concludes with an anagram fashioned from Cromwell: "Howl/Rome."

196B [Douglas, Eleanor Touchet Davies, Lady.] The Benediction. I have an errand to thee O Captain. n.p., 1651. Broadside. D 1976.

This item is identical to 195B.

197B [Douglas, Eleanor Touchet Davies, Lady.] Bethlehem Signifying the House of Bread: or War. [London], 1652. 12 pages. D 1978. EEB Reel 937:16.

The inspiration for this piece is Ezekiel 16: "Cause Jerusalem to know her Abomination." Douglas speaks of a widow's mite and of her two years in Bedlam prison, which she calls "Bethlehem's Hospital." She claims the presiding magistrate did not permit her a proper defense and intersperses allusions to a "beast" and "true believers" with descriptions of her arrest and accusations by Litchfield minister. She invokes her ancestors to help justify her present prophetic role.

198B [Douglas, Eleanor Touchet Davies, Lady.] The Bill of Excommunication, for abolishing henceforth the Sabbath called Sunday or First day. [n.p.], 1649. 8 pages [incomplete]. D 1979. EEB Reel 1614:14.

The Lady Eleanor discusses abolishing the sabbath, which she claims is now profaned, and suggests a new day of celebration, "Moonday." Citing historical events, she questions the authority of the Crown to establish the sabbath. In a numerological reference, she mentions Christ's rising at Easter (after three days) and the three isles of Britain. The copy examined is obviously incomplete.

199B [Douglas, Eleanor Touchet Davies, Lady.] The Blasphemous charge against her. Second Edition. [London?], 1649. 12 pages. D 1980*. EEB Reel 1422:15.

This publication concerns the illegal printing of Douglas' books of prophecy. She was fined and imprisoned until she could produce bond. While incarcerated she had no writing materials. Her anagrams and other "scandalous matter" were said to be antagonistic toward ecclesiastical officials, judges, the king and the state. She was charged specifically with having falsely pretended to receive revelations from God and selling books without a license. This document includes her petition of 1633, the order in Council, an extract from the register of the Court of High Commission, and its findings and sentence.

200B [Douglas, Eleanor Touchet Davies, Lady.] The Brides preparation. [London], 1644 [45]. [8] pages. D 1982. TT Reel 45:E.274(13).

Douglas speaks of Christ and the bride's (the city's) preparation for the Second Coming. She refers to images of the city from Revelations and the life-giving force of the menses: "and Mensura for Menses, etc. And for the tree of life/which yields it[s] monthly fruit for the healing of nations whose evill [is] incurable without it." Douglas declares sinners are to seek the "water of life," the only remedy for their condition.

201B [Douglas, Eleanor Touchet Davies, Lady.] The Crying Charge. Ezekiel 22. [London?], 1649. 8 pages. D 1982A. EEB Reel 1422:16.

This piece concerns the trial of Douglas's brother, Mervyn Touchet, Earl of Castlehaven, for sodomy and conspiracy to rape, and it includes his confession. See also 233B, 247B and 875A.

202B [Douglas, Eleanor Touchet Davies, Lady.] The Day of Judgements modell. [London], 1646. 15 pages. D 1983. TT Reel 55:E.337(23).

Douglas cites Revelations 7: "Today if yee shall heare his voice." She says the truth of Christ is veiled, as the ark was concealed and as Adam and Eve were also covered by fig leaves. She claims the number 144 signifies Christ's return--the four winds of May and the spring term of the courts. Douglas links the white judicial robes to the resurrection. She establishes connections between biblical numerology and the events of the 1640s in England.

203B [Douglas, Eleanor Touchet Davies, Lady.] The Dragons Blasphemous charge against Lady Eleanor Douglas. [n.p.], 1651. D 1984.

This item is identical to 199B.

204B [Douglas, Eleanor Touchet Davies, Lady.] Elijah the Tishbite's Supplication when Presented the likeness of Hand. [n.p.], 1650. [8] pages. D 1985. TT Reel 94:E.616(12).

Douglas requests a sign indicating the Lord's presence. She speaks of God's cleansing wrath (against the Jews) evidenced in destruction of the Tower of Babel, the flood and the plagues. Douglas expects further demonstrations of God's wrath and notes the innocent, like widows, will suffer along with the guilty. Much of the text is incoherent.

205B [Douglas, Eleanor Touchet Davies, Lady.] The Everlasting Gospel. [London?], Decem., 1649. 14 pages. D 1986. EEB Reel 937:17.

Douglas emphasizes her link with the number one: her birth in the first year of the king's reign in the first county, the daughter of the first peer, in July--the month named after the first Roman emperor. She claims the Lord of Hosts told her in 1644: "Nineteen years and a half to the Judgement, and you as the meek Virgin." Douglas recounts receiving prophecies, including some concerning the rise and demise of monarchies and plagues. She also discusses events surrounding the publication of her work in Holland.

206B [Douglas], Eleanor Touchet Davies, Lady. The Excommunication out of Paradice. [London], 1647. 16 pages. D 1987. EEB Reel 937:18.

This conciliatory and humble pamphlet, addressed to Cromwell, criticizes circumcision as an "Antichristian custom in times of ignorance." She calls it an apocalyptic sign of the demise of civilization, which she considers imminent. (Her analysis is based on her reading of Brutus' betrayal of Caesar and the events of the Ides of March.) Douglas further cites the tenure of English politicians (Buckingham, in particular) to confirm her dating. She closes by referring to the "water of life" and the "rivers of living water."

207B [Douglas, Eleanor Touchet Davies, Lady.] Ezekiel, Chap. 2. [n.p., 1647?] 24 pages. D 1988. EEB Reel 937:19.

Douglas warns of Judgment Day and cites four visions: a man looking upward, a lion's voice, a laboring ox, and a quickly flying eagle. All are supposedly clues to the appearance of a prophet or watchman. She speaks of women sleeping while their newborn infants choke and recounts a tale of a woman who slept in a hospital while her arm "lay broyling on the fire." Douglas also mentions clocks, alarms, and other mechanisms of warning and uses the image of Christ taking his bride.

208B [Douglas, Eleanor Touchet Davies, Lady.] Ezekiel the Prophet Explained as follows. [n.p., 1647?] 8 pages. D 1988A.

This item is dated April 2, 1647. Douglas claims many others have misinterpreted Ezekiel in the past; she offers her own explanation in this document.

209B [Douglas, Eleanor Touchet Davies, Lady.] For the blessed feast of Easter. [Amsterdam?], 1646. 16 pages. D 1989.

The Lady Eleanor warns of doom and offers further indications that "Babylon" will fall during the seventeenth century. Douglas alludes to Revelations and speaks of preparations for the "lamb's" wedding and the decline of the king and Parliament. She prepares for "a Reformation set forth before the End; a new Modell, a new Heaven and a new Earth, new Jerusalem prepared as a Bride to meete her Husband."

210B [Douglas, Eleanor Touchet Davies, Lady.] For the most honourable States sitting at Whitehall. London, 1649. 8 pages. D 1989A.

Douglas predicts establishment of God's temple since Charles I has been executed. Citing numerological proofs, she prophesies England's doom in a conflagration as well as the Second Coming. This confused piece is a fragment.

211B [Douglas, Eleanor Touchet Davies, Lady.] For the right noble, Sir Balthazar Gerbier Knight: From the Lady Eleanor. [n.p.], 1649. 8 pages. D 1989B.

Douglas' text is based on Isaiah 30.9-10: "This is a rebellious people, lying children, that will not hear the Law of the Lord." She says God will make prophets of all of his servants. Emphasizing the importance of spreading His message, Douglas warns of Britain's fall if it does not heed God's word.

212B [Douglas, Eleanor Touchet Davies, Lady.] For Whitsontyds last feast: The Present. [n.p.], 1645. 16 pages. D 1990.

The text derives from Acts 1, concerning the coming of Christ and the righting of wrongs in the fullness of time. Douglas limits numerological references and links Daniel's prophecies to present events.

213B [Douglas, Eleanor Touchet Davies, Lady.] [Four fragments.] [London, 1646-48.] N.I.W.

This volume, lacking a title page, contains parts of four works. It begins with a narrative of Douglas' trial and lists witnesses who testified against her, with mention of her sentence to the Gatehouse. The court declared she had published expositions of the Book of Daniel and attacks on ecclesiastical officials and judges through anagrams and other "scandalous matter." She was fined and jailed until "she enter[ed] Bond with sufficient security to write no more." She was not permitted writing materials in prison.

214B [Douglas, Eleanor Touchet Davies, Lady.]   From the Lady Eleanor, Her Blessing to her beloved daughter...Lucy, Countesse of Huntingdon. [London], 1644. 38 pages. D 1991. EEB Reel 229:E.10(1) and TT Reel 2:E.10(1).

The Lady Eleanor uses imagery from the story of Joseph and his coat of many colors to denounce the Civil War. She interprets a passage in Daniel 7 in which he sees a vision of four great beasts: a lion, a bear, a leopard and a harpy ("having great Iron Teeth and Nayls of Brasse"). Together they supposedly constitute the four British kingdoms, with Ireland represented by the harpy. Douglas includes a lengthy biblical allegory about the development of the English monarchy.

215B   [Douglas],   Eleanor   Touchet   Davies,   Lady.   The   Gatehouse Salutation...Revelations at Chap. 4...for Westminsters Cathedral... and courts of Westminster...February, 1646. [London], 1646. 7 pages. D 1991A.

In this verse pamphlet the Lady Eleanor tells of Christ's birth in a manger and concludes: "So Gates and Prison doors be no more shut/The King of Glory comes, your souls lift up." The poem is to be sung to the tune of "Magnificat."

216B [Douglas, Eleanor Touchet Davies, Lady.] Given to the Elector, Prince Charls [sic] of the Rhyne. Amsterdam [London], Printed for Frederick Stam, 1633 [1651]. 10 pages. D 1992*. EEB Reel 1307:22.

Douglas commences with a poem entitled "Babylon or Confusion."   She recounts the story of Belshazzar the King, who was feasting and drinking from golden temple vessels when he was interrupted by the hand of God. This image is a warning to the Dutch to drop charges against her. The text is based on Daniel 5.

217B [Douglas, Eleanor Touchet Davies, Lady.] Great Brittains visitation. [London], 1645. [30] pages. D 1994.

Douglas utilizes numerology, invoking the seven spirits, citing the seventeenth century, the last seven hundred years, etc. She also notes there have been twenty-four kings since the conquest, equivalent to the sum of the prophets and apostles. Douglas recalls in 1625 she learned from Daniel the Resurrection was to occur during the reign of Charles I. She describes other signs linked to it. Pagination is irregular.

218B [Douglas, Eleanor Touchet Davies, Lady.] Hells Destruction. By the Lady Eleanor Douglas. [n.p.], 1651. 16 pages. D 1995.

The imprisoned Douglas discusses the devil's power in the world of darkness and over human souls, the placement of stars in the heavens, and the injustice of her arrest. She describes conditions in her cell, concluding with the apocryphal linking of events; she closes ominously, saying God's law has been thwarted.

219B [Douglas, Eleanor Touchet Davies, Lady.] Her Appeal from the Court to the Camp. [n.p.], 1649. 8 pages. N.I.W.

This pamphlet, addressed to Lord Fairfax, is inspired by Daniel 12: "Many shall be purified, and made white, and tryed: But the wicked shall do wickedly." The Lady Eleanor tells of the five wise and five foolish virgins and mentions several other parables to illustrate Christ's return and marriage with the Church. She says the Stuarts were "justly turned out of stewardship."

220B [Douglas, Eleanor Touchet Davies, Lady.] I am the first and the last, the beginning and the ending: From the Lady Eleanor, the word of God. [London], 1644/5? 8 pages. D 1996. EEB Reel 232:E.25(4) and TT Reel 5:E.25(4).

This unfinished item has no title page. According to Thomason, it was seized while in press. It concerns the Second Coming.

221B [Douglas, Eleanor Touchet Davies, Lady.] Je Le Tien: The General Restitution. [n.p.], 1646. 46 pages. D 1996A.

Douglas says although the Second Coming cannot be predicted, one must be prepared for it. She discusses Christ's gifts of grace and forgiveness and the inability of most people to avoid damnation. She notes 490 years separated Daniel's prophecy and Christ's crucifixion, and offers numerological and scriptural analyses to support her points. Douglas also refers to early Christian heresies and speaks of Christ's pardon. She concludes: "Je E'en: Ti/I hold it."

222B [Douglas, Eleanor Touchet Davies, Lady.] The Lady Eleanor Douglas, Dowager, her Jubiles plea or appeal. [n.p., 1650?] 4 pages. D 1996B.

The imprisoned John Sowel, Knight, is called a herald, "appointed for displaying his Title...in the West Parts." Douglas links the Stuarts with the Douglases, citing familial tragedies. She refers to disarray wrought when Sowel's grandfather committed bigamy during the reign of Elizabeth. This document seems to be an attempt to elevate the Douglas family name.

223B [Douglas], Eleanor Touchet Davies, Lady. The Mystery of General Redemption. [London], 1647. 32 pages. D 1996C. EEB Reel 1422:17 (misnumbered D 1996A).

The Lady Eleanor discusses Christ's redemption of all who were cursed by Adam's original sin. She maintains God has promised "for the womans seed to vanquish the serpents power" and notes Christ's first comment was to his mother. Since everything must eventually return to its origins, she predicts humankind will revert to its prelapsarian beginnings. Douglas charges Adam fell from grace because of his own (not Eve's) frailty.

224B [Douglas, Eleanor Touchet Davies, Lady.] The New Jerusalem at Hand. [n.p.], 1649. 26 pages. D 1997. EEB Reel 1422:18.

Douglas laments the severing of the royal line with the execution of Charles I. She draws parallels between biblical incidents and internecine conflict during his reign. Douglas discusses her own family history, claiming her husband, Archibald Douglas, was the son of James I. Three of his letters (1637-39) to Dr. James Sybald, Minister of Clerkenwell, are included in the document. Most interesting perhaps is Douglas's own reference (1648) to her husband's "Divine Prophecies."

225B [Douglas, Eleanor Touchet Davies, Lady.] The New Proclamation, in answer to a Letter. London, 1649. 8 pages. D 1998. EEB Reel 1614:19.

Douglas explicates Philip 2.6 in response to a query she received. For this exercise she read both the original Greek text and its English translation. The primary focus of the biblical quotation is God's tripartite nature. Douglas attempts to explain this conundrum and reminds the questioner that Christ "did in effect affirm himself to be God."

226B [Douglas, Eleanor Touchet Davies, Lady.] Of Errors joynd with God's Word. [London?], 1645. 7 pages. D 1999. EEB Reel 1614:12.

This piece, dedicated to Parliament, is apparently a reply to King James his Divine Prophecie. Douglas discusses a prophecy about the dual ascent to heaven of darkness and light. She alludes to a verse from Daniel about a birth linking France and Spain.

227B [Douglas], Eleanor Touchet Davies, Lady. Of the General Great Days Approach. [n.p.], 1648. 20 pages. D 1999A.

The Lady Eleanor predicts the coming of Christ and calls herself His maidservant. She notes foreshadowings of the Resurrection in a particularly convoluted tract. Douglas includes many references to lives of the Old Testament prophets.

228B [Douglas, Eleanor Touchet Davies, Lady.] Of Times and Seasons their Mystery. [London?], 1651. 12 pages. D 2000. EEB Reel 1614:13.

This document, filled with Apocalyptic images, centers on tyranny and the demise of kingdoms. Douglas uses sexual and birthing images, calling Revelations, for example, "this man-childe of the woman seed." She describes particular events as comprehended by the circuit of the Zodiac.

229B [Douglas, Eleanor Touchet Davies, Lady.] A Prayer or Petition for peace. [n.p.], 1644 [49]. 16 pages. D 2001*. EEB Reel 1614:16.

Douglas says Christ is the only hope for the divided nation. He is thus linked to women: "our alone Savior Jesus Christ, made of the womans seed according to the flesh: A woman making her first witness of the resurrection." She speaks of incest in Sodom and Gomorrah and offers a prayer for forgiveness and redemption for England. Douglas supports her belief that judgment day will occur during the seventeenth century by citing a measurement of the biblical ark.

230B [Douglas, Eleanor Touchet Davies, Lady.] A Prophesie of the Last Day to be revealed in the last times; and then of the cutting off of the Church, and of the redemption out of hell. London, 1645. [8] pages. [Incomplete] D 2004. EEB Reel 1614:15.

Douglas predicts humankind will see "the cutting off the Church, and the Redemption out of Hell." She says mysteries will be then be clarified, including future events. The prophet Daniel and John the Baptist are cited. Douglas refers to numbers and passages in the Bible supporting the imminence of the world's end.

231B [Douglas, Eleanor Touchet Davies, Lady.] Reader, the heavy hour at hand. [London, 1648.] 4 pages. D 2005A.

Douglas says England should not be surprised by Christ's return because she has predicted it. She connects biblical events with the contemporary political and social situation in England. Again she says the final days are nigh.

232B [Douglas, Eleanor Touchet Davies, Lady.] The Lady Eleanor her Remonstrance to Great Britain. [London], 1648. 8 pages. [incomplete] D 2006. EEB Reel 1758:9.

The Lady Eleanor maintains Christ has chosen to absent himself from worldly affairs; she says He will return when He alone chooses to do so. Douglas employs numerology to show how the books of Daniel and Revelations portend the Second Coming soon. References to the sun and moon confirm this prophecy.

233B [Douglas, Eleanor Touchet Davies, Lady.] The Restitution of Prophecy; that Buried Talent to be revived. [n.p.], 1651. 52 pages. D 2007. EEB Reel 937:20.

This item, longer and more historically bound than most of Douglas' writings, supposedly attacks the accusers of the Earl of Castlehaven, Douglas' iniquitous brother. Douglas also lambasts academic publications ("University Excrement"), noting difficulty getting her work published. She uses numerological analysis to link Christ to the ascension of Charles I and connects contemporary with biblical events. Douglas places special emphasis on sexual imagery and scandals. See also 201B and 247B.

234B [Douglas, Eleanor Touchet Davies.] The Restitution of Reprobates. [London], 1644. 35 pages. D 2008. EEB Reel 228:E.3(4) and TT Reel 1:E.3(4).

Douglas says mercy and judgment go together and quotes scripture to support her belief that those who "speake a word against the sonne of man" will nevertheless be forgiven. She distinguishes between sufficient and efficient cause and notes scholars are unwilling to accept the total meaning of original sin. Douglas also observes forgiveness [Christ] appropriately was born of a woman [Mary]; this birth was fitting because "a woman [was] the occasion of the worlds woe and undoing." The pagination is irregular.

235B [Douglas, Eleanor Touchet Davies.] The Revelation Interpreted by the La. E. [London?], 1646. 15 pages. D 2009. EEB Reel 1614:17.

Douglas refers to a sea creature with seven heads and ten horns capped by crowns. This powerful animal (presumably Charles I) drew its strength from a dragon, namely, George Villiers, Duke of Buckingham. She links him, through numerology and scripture, to the murder of the French king in 1610. She also analogizes idolatry under Charles to worship of Babylon's golden icon.

236B [Douglas, Eleanor Touchet Davies, Lady.] Samsons Fall, presented to the House, 1642. Kings 13. London, 1642 [1649]. 16 pages. D 2010.

Douglas says Samson was "overcome by a <u>Womans importunity</u>, her inchanting notes, whereby laid in a Trance." She warns women are not to be trusted: "she to be trusted whilst a Sieve or net retains water." Douglas claims she can recall the king (either Charles I or to Christ). There are extensive biblical allusions and symbolism in this pamphlet.

237B [Douglas, Eleanor Touchet Davies, Lady.] <u>Samson's Legacie</u>. London, 1642. 24 pages. D 2011. EEB Reel 244:E.96(19) and TT Reel 17:E.96(19).

Douglas offers to bring the king to Parliament, even though she suspects her assistance will be refused. She recalls Samson's seduction by the Philistine Delilah and indirectly compares her to Henrietta Maria; she cites other biblical female figures who caused the decline of governments. Douglas also accuses the Catholic Church of undermining the king. She concludes with an entreaty to demons to depart England.

238B [Douglas, Eleanor Touchet Davies, Lady.] <u>The [Second] Co[ming of Our] Lo[rd.] Dedicat[ed to Great] Britt[ain] by the La[dy]: Eleanor.</u> London, 1645. [24] pages. D 2012. EEB Reel 1614:18.

In this pamphlet the Lady Eleanor forecasts the Second Coming in the year 1700.

239B [Douglas, Eleanor Touchet Davies, Lady.] <u>The Serpents Excommunication. In Essex where cutting down a Wood, divers of these Sprouts of the Warlike Ash, or Branches grew.</u> [8] pages. [London?], 1651. D 2012A. EEB Reel 1307:23.

This is an obscure pamphlet, mostly in verse, with biblical allusions (to Moses, the pharaoh, the serpent, Eden) and much animal imagery (snakes, frogs, lice, flies). It seems to be an analogy comparing Douglas' own imprisonment with the expulsion of the Jews from Egypt by the pharaoh. Excerpt: "Thy Twelve alloted years expir'd/So <u>Woman</u> releas'd here." There is no signature on the title page; however, it is signed at the end by "E: Do:" and by "the Lady Eleanor."

240B [Douglas, Eleanor Touchet Davies, Lady.] <u>A sign given them being entered into the day of [J]udgment To set their House in order</u>. London, 1644. [Reprinted 1649] 16 pages. D 2012AA.

In this warning to Parliament Douglas advises members to prepare for the Second Coming. She compares Charles I to Manasseh, son of Hezekiah, implicitly criticizing the king's association with Archbishop Laud. She predicts the end of the king's reign in 1655, based on astrological signs. Additions to the 1644 text made in 1649 apparently predate Charles' execution.

241B [Douglas, Eleanor Touchet Davies, Lady.] <u>Sions Lamentation Lord Henry Hastings, His Funerals blessing, by his grandmother.</u> [London? 1649.] 8 pages. D 2012B. EEB Reel 1307:25.

Douglas describes the funeral cortege of her grandson, was the first born to her daughter, Lucy Countess of Huntingdon, and one of three sons who died.

242B [Douglas, Eleanor Touchet Davies, Lady.] The Star to the Wise, 1643. London, 1643. 20 pages. D 2013. EEB Reel 241: E.76(28) and TT Reel 13:E.76(28).

The Lady Eleanor addresses the House of Commons, showing cause why her books should be licensed.

243B [Douglas, Eleanor Touchet Davies, Lady.] Strange and wonderfull prophesies by the Lady Eleanor Audeley. Who is yet alive, and lodged within White Hall. London, Printed for Robert Ibbitson, 1649. 6 pages. D 2014*. TT Reel 88:E.571(28).

This verse litany of Lady Eleanor's prophecies includes the beheading of Charles I, conversion of Whitehall into an encampment for soldiers, disembowelling and embalming of the king and the end of the monarchy forever. This is one of only a few of Douglas' pamphlets bearing a London printer's imprint. It was reprinted three times during the nineteenth century.

244B [Douglas, Eleanor Touchet Davies, Lady.] To the most honorable the High Court of Parliament assembled. My Lords; ther's a time. [n.p., 1642.] [4] pages. D 2015. EEB Reel 244:E.96(19).

Douglas offers to bring the imprisoned Charles I to Parliament again. The incarceration apparently occurred earlier in the Civil War than his later internment in 1649. Douglas also refers to the influence of Henrietta Maria, which she considers deleterious. The Lady Eleanor compares her to Delilah.

245B [Douglas, Eleanor Touchet Davies, Lady.] Tobits Book, A Lesson Appointed for Lent. [n.p.], 1652. 16 pages. D 2016. EEB Reel 1422:19.

Douglas explores legends of the Last Supper, the Tygris-Euphrates flood and the fish in Egypt. She speaks of Abraham and Sarah, Jonah and the whale, Noah's ark and the marriage of Tobias: "So finished his magnificat Tobias, that Brides incomparable Lustre or preparation: New Jerusalem precious Edifice so ravished with it." Her signature is "Tobias signifying Good, for Good-Friday."

246B [Douglas, Eleanor Touchet Davies.] Wherefore to prove the thing. [n.p., 1648.] 8 pages. D 2017. EEB Reel 1667:8.

Douglas compares the three "Judges of the Earth," "the Grave and prudent Barons of Exchequer" to the "Three in high Court of heaven." She criticizes their law, intended "to overthrow a lawful Purchase and Joynture, after injoyed so many years...the widows Estate to cut it off, by such trivial incumbrances sifted forth." (She was apparently able to remove her jointure while incarcerated.) Her estate, Englefield, was purchased by the Marquis of Winchester while she was imprisoned. This item is a fragment.

247B [Douglas, Eleanor Touchet Davies, Lady.] The word of God, to the Citie of London, from the Lady Eleanor; of the Earle of Castle-Haven: condemn'd and beheaded: April 25, 1631. [London?], 1644. [19] pages. D 2018.

Mervyn Touchet, Earl of Castlehaven, was convicted of abetting the sexual molestation of his daughter, conspiring in the rape of his wife, and of sodomy, for which he was hanged. The Lady Eleanor, his sister, accuses his wife Ann and her brother Ferdinando of conspiring against the Earl. The case is interesting as the successful conviction of a man accused of participating in the rape of his wife and daughter, based partially on his wife's testimony. See also 201B, 233B and 875A.

248B [Douglas, Lady Eleanor.] The Writ of Restitution. [London], 1648. 10 pages. D 2019. EEB Reel 1422:20.

The Lady Eleanor quotes from Psalms and Acts cautioning kings and judges to be wise and heed the prophets. She discusses the case of three people who were charged with contempt of court and acquitted. Many, she says, plead ignorance of the law "as the man laying the fault on Eve." This is an interesting example of how Douglas addresses sexual distinctions in her writings.

249B [Douglas, Eleanor Touchet Davies, Lady.] [Zach. 12. And they shall look upon him, whom they have pierced.] [London, 1649.] 8 pages. D 2020. EEB Reel 1003:2.

This pamphlet, lacking a title page, is the same as 239B.

The Dying Speeches of Several Excellent Persons, who suffered for their Zeal against Popery. See 411B.

250B Eedes, Judith. A Warning to all the Inhabitants of the Earth. London, Printed by J. B. for the author, 1659. 4 pages. E 241A. EEB Reel 415:10.

Eedes, a Quaker, directs her comments especially to magistrates and "rulers." She asks them to "cease persecuting any for matter of conscience." Her language, quite angry, contains feminine imagery: "Then paleness of face with thy hands on thy Loynes, as a woman in travail crying to be delivered, from that body of sin." Eedes warns if they do not repent, authorities will receive God's "Indignation and Wrath, Tribulation and Anguish for ever."

251B [Egerton], S[arah F[yge.] The Female Advocate: or, an Answer to a late Satyr against the Pride, Lust and Inconstancy of Woman. Written by a Lady in Vindication of her sex. London, Printed by H. C. [for] John Taylor, 1686. 24 pages. E 251A. EEB Reel 867:21.

This early feminist verse was apparently written by fourteen-year-old Sarah Fyge. It defends women's rational powers in answer to 400A. In the preface she claims "all Men are Good, and fitting for Heaven, because they are men; and women irreversibly Damn'd because they are women." Egerton claims women are superior because they are not earthly like Adam. She offers examples of heroic women and wives who sacrificed for their husbands. In distinction, she says men are ruined by ambition. See also 29A.

252B An Elegy upon the death of Mrs. A. Behn; the incomparable Astrea. By a young lady of quality. London, Printed by E. J., 1689. Broadside. E 4467A.

The author of this elegy, dated April 22 1689, refers to the poet Katherine Philips as well as Aphra Behn and warns men will now regain their advantage in the [literary] war of the sexes.   Excerpt: "What have we one? What have our crimes deserv'd?/Why this injurious Rape?/The World is widdow'd now." There is much sexual imagery in this broadside.

253B Eliza's Babes: or, the Virgins-Offering. Being Divine Poems and Meditations. London, Printed by M. S. for Laurence Blaiklock, 1652. 102 pages. E 526. EEB Reel 142:10.

Signed "By a Lady" and dedicated "To my sisters," this volume is a collection of mostly religious writings, some of which are dedicated to specific women. Example: "Now welcome sweet and pleasant Morn,/Doe you not thinke that I you scorn:/Cause with a more Oriental light,/Imbellisht is my blest spirit."

254B Elizabeth of England, Consort of Frederick I, King of Bohemia. ...Also the Declaration and Petition of the Palsgrave and the Queene his mother to Parliament for their annuall Pension...disclaiming any hand or consent in Prince Roberts actions, against the Parliament. London, Printed for I. Underhill, 1642. [6] pages. N.I.W. EEB Reel 247:E.122(12) and TT Reel 21:E.122(12).

This two-page item is appended to a letter by Henrietta Maria sent from the Hague (332B). Elizabeth and Frederick Henry disclaim approval or support of her son Prince Rupert's alleged cruelties in England. They say they have unsuccessfully attempted to dissuade him. Asking Parliament to refrain from punishing them for Rupert's actions, they request their pensions.

[Elizabeth of England, Consort of Frederick I, King of Bohemia.] A Declaration of the Queen of Bohemia. See 270A.

255B Elizabeth of England, Consort of Frederick I, King of Bohemia. The Queen of Bohemia her Desires and Propositions to the House of Commons, Sept. 24, with the House of Commons Answer to the said Desires. [London], Printed for I. White, 1642. Broadside. E 527. EEB Reel 247:E.118(40).

Elizabeth was the eldest daughter of James I and Anne of Denmark and sister to Charles I. After she was widowed by Frederick of Bohemia in 1632, she had financial problems, particularly after the onset of the English Civil War. Here she asks for a continuation of her stipend of 12,000 pounds because Charles refused to pass the bill for tonnage and poundage, and Parliament limited her payment, extracted from this levy. She claims Parliament has ordered payment, so it should not be delayed because of the actions of Prince R[upert] in England, who apparently decided not to pay her until "the present Distractions are setled in this Kingdom."

Elizabeth of England, Queen Consort of Frederick I, King of Bohemia. The Resolution of the House of Commons touching the Queene of Bohemia and the Prince Elector Palatine. See 761A.

256B Elizabeth, Queen of England. The Golden Speech of. London, Printed for Tho. Milbourne, [1659]. Broadside. E 528*.

This item is the same as 264B.

257B Elizabeth, Queen of England. Injunctions given by the Queenes Majestie. Concerning both the clergie and Laity of this Realme. [27] pages. [London], 1641. E 529. EEB Reel 183:2.

The proclamation (c1559) was meant to suppress "superstition" and to "plant true Religion, to the extirpation of all Hypocrisie, enormities and abuses." The queen outlaws charms, witchcraft, anti-Christian doctrine, prayer in non-local parish churches, interruption of sermons, printing of unlicensed books, etc. She allows an increased voice for Parliament in England's spiritual affairs and renews the breach with Rome. The Second Book of Common Prayer is restored with minor changes in response to the Marian reaction.

258B Elizabeth, Queen of England. The Last Speech and Thanks of. n.p., 1671. E 530.

This item is the same as 264B.

259B Elizabeth, Queen of England. A Letter of Advice to a friend about the currency of clipt-money...To which is annex'd the Declaration publish'd by Queen Elizabeth, upon her Reforming the Coin. London, Printed for Edward Castle, 1696. 38 pages. J 29*. EEB Reels 791:51 and 1150:30.

The queen's proclamation, covering six pages, concerns the valuation of base monies called testoons. It dates from September of 1560.

260B Elizabeth, Queen of England. A most excellent and remarkabl [sic] speech. [London], Printed for Humphrey Richardson, January 28, 1643. 6 pages. E 531. EEB Reel 142:11.

This conciliatory speech was addressed to Parliament in the seventeenth year of Elizabeth's reign. She notes the reciprocal duties of princes and subjects and presents her opinion of Parliament. She alludes to the "imbecility and unablenesse of our sex to governe such a powerfull and mighty Kingdom as this is." Among a sovereign's duties she cites public defense, the institution of good protective laws and maintenance of equality under law. She says she has never "performed any act prejudicial to the liberty, or opposite to the known lawes of the land" and emphasizes the freedom, obedience and implacability of the English.

261B Elizabeth, Queen of England. A Pattern or President [sic] for Princes to Rule by, and for Subjects to Obey By. London, Printed by William Miller, 1680. 39 pages. P 875. EEB Reel 872:39.

This publication concerns Elizabeth's troubles with Mary. It includes a 1586 Parliamentary petition recommending Mary's execution, with Elizabeth's answers and request for an alternative solution. A second request for Mary's end claimed Parliament considered banishment and rejected it. Excerpt from Elizabeth's remarks on the qualities of a leader: "... he was scarcely well furnished for Kingly Government, if he lacked Justice, Temperance, Magnanimity, or Judgment. As for the two latter, I will not boast; my Sex doth not permit it."

262B Elizabeth, Queen of England. <u>Queen Elizabeth's Opinion Concerning the</u>
<u>Transubstantiation</u>. [London], Printed for F. E., 1688. Broadside. E 532. EEB
Reel 1864:17.

This broadside alleges a priest visited Elizabeth during her detention at
Woodstock and attempted to convert her. The queen's reply in verse is surely
apocryphal; however, prayers and speeches which follow --after her safe escape
from a fire, following her ascension to the throne, after an armada defeat--may
be genuine.

263B Elizabeth, Queen of England. <u>A Speech made by Queen Elizabeth...In</u>
<u>Parliament, 1593...Concerning the Spanish Invasion</u>. [London], Printed for D. Mallet,
1688. Broadside. B 533. EEB Reel 1668:7.

Elizabeth reluctantly compares herself with "wise, noble, and virtuous Princes,"
but only with regard to particular actions. She suggests her nonimperialistic
inclinations may be unpopular, saying her "womanhood and weakness" have
been mitigating factors in her foreign policy: "I am contented to Reign over my
Own, and to Rule as a Just Princess." The queen denies she has instigated
a quarrel with Spain and maintains she will firmly defend her country against
aggression. She asks the lords lieutenant of the counties and justices of the
peace to organize for defense and enforce laws relating to war.

264B Elizabeth, Queen of England. <u>Queene Elizabeths Speech To Her Last</u>
<u>Parliament</u>. [London, 1642.] [5] pages. E 534*. EEB Reels 142:12 and
259:E.200(15); TT Reel 35:E.200(15).

This speech is Elizabeth's most famous, dating from 1601, two years before her
death. It reveals her wisdom, strength and humanity. Addressing the speaker
of the Commons, she acknowledges the gratitude of her subjects and his
advice. She considers her reign, reasserts her subservience to God and
compares ruling to taking bitter pills. Excerpt: "And though you have had and
may have many mightier and wiser Princes sitting in this Seat, yet you never
had nor shall have any that will love you better."

265B [Elson, Mary.] <u>A Tender and Christian Testimony to Young People</u>. [London,
1685.] 8 pages. E 642. EEB Reel 1440:44.

Although this item is attributed to Elson, her signature is only the first of twenty
representing the women's meeting. They remind young Quakers of the strength
of God's faith and true light and issue a caveat to young women about dress.
(Avoid colorful clothing, lace and ribbons.) Servants are encouraged to be
meek and mistresses to set good examples. Mutual support among the women
of the meeting is mentioned.

266B [Elson, Mary.] <u>A True Information of our blessed Womens Meeting</u>. London,
Printed and sold by Andrew Sowell, 1680. 5 pages. N.I.W.

This item is bound with 611B. Elson offers a brief history of the women's
meeting, which had existed for over two decades. Its purpose was designated
by George Fox as caretaker for "the Sick, the Weak, the Widdows and the
Fatherless." Women identified the poor among the faithful, and the men's
meeting provided funds for their care.

Ephelia. See Joan Philips.

267B An Essay in Defence of the Female Sex. In Which are inserted characters of a pedant, a squire, a beau, a vertuoso. Written by a Lady. London, Printed for A. Roper, E. Wilkinson, and R. Clavel, 1696. 148 pages. A 4060. EEB Reels 9:5 and 756:2.

This sprightly feminist essay argues against women's exclusion from educational institutions.   It describes male tyranny and claims men have purposely obliterated the records of women' past. The author uses a biological model to buttress her argument. She denies the essay was written by a man and says "with equal Care, by the same Models ...they will no more be able to [discern] Man's Stile from a Woman's, than they can tell whether this was written with a Goose's Quill or a Gander's." Although the Wing STC attributes it to Astell, the tone is lighter than hers, and the view of female education less revolutionary; the author is probably Judith Drake.

Eugenia. See Lady Mary Chudleigh.

268B Evans, Katherine. A Brief Discovery of God's Eternal Truth; and, A Way opened to the simplehearted. London, Printed for R. Wilson, 1663. 56 pages. E 3453. EEB Reel 416:8.

This Quaker tract was written by a missionary who was imprisoned in Malta. Evans argues those who profane Christ will be lost. She praises Christ's "pure, perfect, holy" nature and asks that His light be allowed to shine through the faithful. See also 143B and 72A.

[Evans, Katherine.]   This is a short Relation of Some of the Cruel Sufferings... of Katherine Evans and Sarah Chevers, in the Inquisition in the Isle of Malta. See 143B.

269B [Evelyn, Mary.] Mundus Muliebris: Or, The Ladies Dressing- Room Unlock'd, and her Toilette Spread. London, Printed for R. Bentley, 1690. 23 pages. E 3521*. EEB Reels 184:7 and 1652:3.

Evelyn's lengthy poetic burlesque satirizes women's vanity and criticizes them for reading romances, seeing plays and farces, and otherwise entertaining themselves.   She nostalgically regards the age of chivalry and includes a "fop-dictionary." It is intended as a guide for young gentlemen preparing to depart for university. Evelyn was the daughter of the royalist diarist John Evelyn.

270B Everard, Margaret.   An Epistle of Margaret Everard to The People called Quakers and The Ministry among them. [London], Printed for Brabazon Aylmer, 1699. 8 pages. E 3535.

With a heavy heart Everard accuses her fellow Quakers, especially the leaders, of uncharitableness.   Assuming responsibility for her own thoughts, she suggests "it is not our good Works that is the Meritorious cause of our acceptance, but God's free Love in his Son; and our good Works are the effect of God's Love in Christ." In other words, "Faith without Works is dead."

271B [Eyre, Elizabeth (Packington).] <u>A Letter from a Person of Quality in the</u> <u>North... concerning Bishop Lake's Late Delclaration Of his Dying in the Belief of the</u> <u>Doctrine of Passive Obedience as the Distinguishing Character of the Church of</u> <u>England</u>. London, Printed for Awnsham Churchill, 1689. 10 pages. E 3940. EEB Reel 379:26.

Eyre asks why churches must have distinctive doctrines; she thinks this practice leads to schisms. She suggests a dying persons's words should not be adopted as dogma: "For if dying Mens Sentiments were to be the Rule of our Faith, we should have a very uncertain Standard." Regarding obedience to the church, she says, "Yet as I am an <u>English</u> man...as I am to obey the King...subjects ought to obey without any other reserve."

272B Fairman, Lydia. <u>A Few Lines Given Forth</u>. London, Printed for Thomas Simmons, 1659. Broadside. F 257. EEB Reel 1423:14.

Fairman's Quaker tract encourages belief in the "light" which she says will promote the fear of God, the destruction of sin and acquisition of wisdom.

273B Fanshawe, Ann Harrison, Lady. "Memoirs." In <u>The Memoirs of Anne, Lady</u> <u>Halkett and Ann, Lady Fanshawe</u>. John Loftis, ed. Oxford, The Clarendon Press, 1979. [91] pages. Item: N.I.W.

Ann Harrison (1625-1680) addressed this commemorative biography of her husband to their son Richard, an infant when his father died. The account describes their married life, but contains little reflective material. Sir Richard Fanshawe was a classical scholar and ambassador to Portugal and Spain. Lady Fanshawe relates their experiences there and in Ireland and France. Although this biography was supposedly written in 1676, its detail and exact chronology indicate it was probably based on earlier journal entries.

274B Fearon, Jane. <u>Universal Redemption offered in Jesus Christ, In opposition</u> <u>to...Doctrine of Election and Reprobation</u>. [London], 1698. 54 pages. F 576A.

This work presents arguments against Calvinist and Puritan theories of predestination. Fearon, a Quaker, notes the idea that human fate is predetermined is injurious to God because it renders Him the author of sin and implies He delights in the deaths of sinners. Fearon says she is publishing her views because an Anabaptist minister prevented her from speaking in his church.

275B Featherstone, Sarah. <u>Living Testimonies Concerning the Death of the</u> <u>Righteous...Joseph Featherstone and Sarah his Daughter</u>. London, Printed for Andrew Sowle, 1689. 27 pages. F 576B.

Featherstone, a Quaker, was the widow of Joseph and the mother of Sarah. She describes her husband as righteous and enthusiastic, while Sarah is tender, harmless and obedient. The last of ten children, all of whom predeceased their father, she died of a fever at fourteen. A second document, authored by Featherstone's second husband, concerns both the child and his deceased first wife and daughter.

276B [Fell, Lydia.] A Testimony and Warning Given forth in the love of Truth.
[London? 1676.] 7 pages. F 625. EEB Reel 353:20.

This Quaker tract was penned by a daughter of Margaret Fell Fox. It is
addressed to the "Governor, Magistrates and People" of the island of Barbados.
She asks them to turn to the Lord and reminds them a number of important
women promised to repent at the time of a bad fire, but had not done so. The
Lord had sent them faithful messengers, including herself, but still they resisted
His call.

277B Fell, Sarah. The Household Account Book of Sarah Fell of Swarthmoor Hall.
Cambridge, The University Press, 1920. 597 pages. N.I.W.

This account book, kept by a daughter of Quaker Margaret Fell Fox between
1673 and 1678, lists household disbursements ("mother's account"), expenses
for the forge, shipping enterprises and the women's meeting. It is particularly
useful for its portrayal of female participation in a rural economy.   It
demonstrates women's involvement in managing financial affairs and exchanging
goods and services in the community.   Sarah Fell was one of the chief
organizers of the women's meeting in Furness. She was imprisoned briefly in
1676 for her religious activities.

278B Fell [Fox], Margaret [Askew].   A Call to the Universall Seed of God,
throughout the Whole World. [London], 1665. 17 pages. F 625A. EEB Reel
1441:64.

This tract was written by the most influential seventeenth-century female Quaker,
a millenarian, while she was in prison at Lancaster Castle. Fell retells the tale
of the Samarian at the well as an example of Christ's willingness to
communicate with a woman.   She emphasizes public areas (rather than
churches) for worship, the Second Coming, and the authority of Christ rather
than an ecclesiastical hierarchy.

279B [Fell Fox, Margaret Askew]. A Call Unto the Seed of Israel. London, Printed
for Robert Wilson, [1668?] 38 pages. F 626. EEB Reel 1331:9.

Fell tries a final time to convert the Jews who, though securing legal status
under Cromwell, did not receive a formal guarantee of freedom to worship until
1673. She argues the light is natural and does not emanate from Christ. The
work also supports Quakers abroad. Fell wrote it during her second term in
Lancaster Castle; it was eventually translated into Latin.

280B [Fell Fox, Margaret Askew.]   The Citie of London Reproved for its
Abominations. London, Printed for Robert Wilson, [1660]. Broadside. F 626A.

In a spirited broadside Fell calls for repentance of the guilty for persecuting the
just. She compares London to Sodom and Gomorrah for feasting on behalf of
Cromwell and, later, Charles II. She warns of its demise and urges turning to
God before it is too late.

281B Fell [Fox], Margaret [Askew]. Concerning ministers made by the will of man.
London, Printed in the 4th month 8th day for M. W., 1659. Broadside. F 626B.
EEB Reel 1652:14.

Fell maintains only through Christ, not man-made institutions, can one attain grace.   Christ is called "the high Priest over the household of God, whose government is on his shoulders."   During an illness, when Fell was troubled and "sinful," she claims Christ comforted her and "placed his word in my heart." Only through such direct intervention by Christ, she says, can one find salvation.

282B [Fell Fox, Margaret Askew.] The Daughter of Sion Awakened, and Putting on Strength: She is Arising, and Shaking herself out of the Dust and Putting on her Beautiful Garments. [London], 1677. 19 pages. F 627. EEB Reel 1669:24.

Fell predicts a bitter time ahead and predicts the Second Coming.   She summarizes tribulations of the biblical Hebrews and notes Christ's birth brought the light to all humankind. She says although women must bring forth children in pain, God protects them and their progeny from the "serpent's" power. Excerpt: "He hath made no difference in this work between male and female but they are all one in Christ Jesus."

283B [Fell Fox, Margaret Askew.] A declaration and an information from us the people of God called Quakers, to the present governors, the king and both houses of Parliament, and all whom it may concern. London, Printed for Thomas Simmons and Robert Wilson, 1660. 8 pages. F 628. EEB Reel 981:18.

This Quaker tract accuses the government of persecution; it is directed towards the king, Parliament and other governors of the land.   It was personally presented to the king by Fell on April 22, 1660. The purpose of the piece is also to convince the king of the Friends' innocence and peacefulness.

284B [Fell Fox, Margaret Askew.]   An Evident Demonstration to Gods Elect. [London, Printed for Thomas Simmons, 1660.] 16 pages. F 629*. EEB Reels 1592:28 and 1652:15.

Fell tries to demonstrate the necessity to "come to witnesse True Faith." She argues one's faith must be tested just as gold is tried in fire; one can survive such a test only by relying on faith in Christ. A two-page postscript signed by W. C. is appended.

285B Fell [Fox], Margaret [Askew].   False Prophets, Anticrists [sic], Deceivers, which are in the World. London, Printed for Giles Calvert, 1655. 22 pages. F 631. EEB Reel 1592:29.

Fell's first published work is a commentary on Revelations 16.13. She points to the hypocrisy of English Protestants who allegedly aided their fellows on the continent while persecuting Quakers at home.

286B [Fell Fox, Margaret Askew.] For Manasseth Ben Israel. The Call of the Jewes out of Babylon. London, Printed for Giles Calvert, 1656. 21 pages. F 632. TT Reel 131:E.868(11).

Fell encourages Menasseth to convert Jews in Holland and the Jewish community in England, just readmitted after a long period of exile. This book was translated into Dutch by William Ames. Fell comments on the Old

Testament, quoting Isaiah and emphasizing the light and repentance without mentioning Christ.

287B [Fell Fox, Margaret Askew.] A Letter Sent to the King from M. F. [London, 1666.] 8 pages. F 633. EEB Reel 960:16.

Fell's letter was delivered to the king on June 29, 1666 by Elizabeth Stubbs. She accuses him of persecuting Quakers for six years since his return to the throne and breaking his promise at the Restoration that he would not do so as long as they were peaceful. A prisoner at the time of this unsuccessful entreaty, Fell was kept under arrest for two more years.

288B [Fell Fox, Margaret Askew.] A Loving Salutation, to the Seed of Abraham Among the Jewes. London, Printed for Tho. Simmons, 1656. 37 pages. F 634*. EEB Reels 1592:30 and 31.

Fell argues only the ransomed and redeemed can return to Zion. She entreats the Jews to turn "to the light that shewes you sin and evil." Fell here assumes they already have knowledge of the light. Her focus is more positive than threatening.

289B [Fell Fox, Margaret Askew.] A Paper Concerning such as are made Ministers by the Will of Man. London, Printed for H. W., 1659. 3 pages. F 634A. EEB Reel 1383:21.

The first part of this Quaker tract, missing a title page, concerns the apparently male right to determine who will be God's ministers. Fell says all who "wear the old garment are by the children of light denied." They are said to live in "envy, debates, derision, scornes, loftiness, lightmindness" and so on. The first page is signed by M. F. [Margaret Fell], while the last two pages are signed by G. F. [George Fox].

290B [Fell Fox, Margaret Askew.] The Standard of the Lord Revealed. [London?] 1667. [132] pages. F 635.

This abstract of the Bible was written during Fell's second imprisonment in Lancaster Castle. It explains how God worked through the Jews until Christ's birth.

291B [Fell Fox, Margaret Askew.] "The Testimony of Margaret Fox concerning her late Husband George Fox; with a brief account of some of his Travels, Sufferings and Hardships Endured for the Truth's Sake." In George Fox. A Journal...or historical account of the Life...[of George Fox]. London, Printed for Thomas Northcott, 1694. [9] pages. Item: N.I.W. Collection: F 1854. EEB Reel 815:10.

These pages introduce George Fox's journal. Fell's brief biographical summary of it was written after his death. She reveals she did not see him during his final six months. He died when she was seventy-six.

292B Fell [Fox], Margaret [Askew]. A Testimonie of the Touchstone, for all Professions, and all Forms. London, Printed for Thomas Simmons, 1656. 36 pages. F 636. EEB Reel 562:21.

Fell posits religious principles for all Christians. She also attacks the current Ranter view that a person's word is infallible during possession by the Holy Spirit. Fell says this notion confuses evil with good and darkness with light.

293B [Fell Fox, Margaret Askew.] <u>This is to the Clergy who are the Men that goes [sic] about to settle Religion...according to the Church of England</u>. [London, Printed for Robert Wilson, 1660.] 8 pages. F 637. EEB Reel 1383:22.

Fell reminds bishops and presbyters of the abuses of early ecclesiastical courts and warns them not to "bring upon your selves the guilt of innocent blood." She cites religious experiences: miracles, speaking in and interpreting tongues--all valid because they emanate from Christ. Avoiding typical Quaker rhetoric, Fell assumes a political posture: "...remember that you were warned in your lifetime to keep your hands from limiting of peoples consciences."

294B [Fell Fox, Margaret Askew.] <u>This Was Given to Major Generall Harrison and the Rest</u>. London, Printed for Thomas Simmons, 1660. 7 pages. F 638.

In a rambling, flowing essay, containing only two paragraphs, Fell urges the military to "Read this in the Fear of the Lord" and reminds them God granted their powerful positions and only through Christ can they find truth and salvation.

295B [Fell Fox, Margaret Askew.] <u>To the Generall Councill of Officers of the English Army and to every member in particular</u>. [London, Printed for Thomas Simmons, 1659.] 8 pages. F 638A.

This pamphlet is essentially the same as 296B.

Fell [Fox], Margaret Askew. <u>To the General Council of Officers.</u> See 866A.

296B [Fell Fox, Margaret Askew.] <u>To the General Councel, And Officers of the Army, And to every Member in particular</u>. [London], Printed for Thomas Simmons, 1659. 8 pages. F 638C.

In a forceful, cogent piece, Fell notes the army and Council have displaced Parliament and "...may execute that which ye formerly desired after, and suffered for, and laboured for, and warred for." She argues against military conscription and, emphasizing God's strength rather than Christ's love, she advises them to rule righteously and adhere to God's will. Largely eschewing "light" imagery, Fell limns a vengeful God who has heretofore issued many warnings.

297B [Fell Fox, Margaret Askew.] <u>To the Magistrates and People of England where this may come</u>. [London], 1664. Broadside. F 638D.

Fell asks why the Quakers are being imprisoned for worshipping Christ and obeying His commands. She charges the magistrates would likewise imprison Christ and the apostles if they had the opportunity. Fell wrote this piece while imprisoned in Lancaster Castle.

298B [Fell Fox, Margaret Askew.] <u>A Touch-stone, or a Perfect Tryal by the Scriptures, of all the Priests, Bishops and Ministers...unto which is Annexed, Women's Speaking Justified</u>. London, 1667. 94 pages. F 639. EEB Reel 761:24.

Fell wrote this tract while in prison in Lancaster Castle. It explains her distrust of the bishops' counsel to the king. She accuses the clergy of intolerance, persecution, keeping the people in ignorance, and reliance on the Old Testament and education, rather than divine inspiration. Womens Speaking Justified (301B) is bound separately.

299B F[ell Fox], M[argaret Askew.] A True Testimony from the people of God. London, Printed for Robert Wilson, 1660. 28 pages. F 640. EEB Reel 1592:32.

In this tract, laced with biblical references, Fell cites the chief difference between Quakers and other religious groups: Others comprehend the words, but the Quakers grasp the spirit of Christ and the Apostles. She says God's throne and scepter reside within.

300B F[ell Fox], M[argaret.] Two General Epistles to the Flock of God. [Lancaster, 1664.] 6 pages. F 641. EEB Reel 1149:10.

This work is directed to Quakers scattered abroad. It says no matter how great the distance separating them, they are still "in the Unity of this Faith, and Fellowship of this Gospel." She beseeches them to stand firm in the liberty God has granted.

301B [Fell Fox, Margaret Askew.] Womens Speaking Justified, Proved and Allowed of by the Scriptures. London, 1666. 19 pages. F 642*. EEB Reel 1423:16.

Perhaps Fell's most important treatise, this work defends women's right to speak and preach against the opposition of ministers and others. Fell suggests limiting the testimony of "whoring women," "tatle- tales" and those who "usurp authority over the man."

302B Fiennes, Celia. The Journeys of Celia Fiennes. London, The Cresset Press, 1949 [1698]. N.I.W.

First published in 1888 under the title Through England on a Side Saddle in the Time of William and Mary, this volume contains the comments and observations of an aristocratic woman who traveled on horseback in near solitude through England. Much of Fiennes' account concerns her 'great journey' in 1698 to Newcastle and Cornwall. While naive and priggish at times, she was also energetic and outspoken. Fiennes observed cloth manufacturing, field crops, mining, orchards, the grounds and interiors of country houses and other cultural and industrial activities. She suggested that women improve their minds and make their lives "pleasant and comfortable as well as profitable."

303B [Fisher, Abigail.] An Epistle in the Love of God to Friends, with a Little Chiefly to their...Children. London, Printed and sold by T. Sowle, 1696. 20 pages. F 984A.

Fisher reminds fellow Quakers they are witnesses to the power and word of God. She encourages them to place service to Christ before all else and exhorts the young to be chary of temptation and to honor and obey their parents: Fisher advises a simple way of life.

304B [Fisher, Abigail.] A few lines in true Love to such that frequent the meetings of the people called Quakers. London, Printed by T. Sowle, 1694. 8 pages. F 984B*.

Fisher addresses Quakers attending meetings who do not appreciate the testimony of the truth. She asks: "Why do you love to hear? Do you not desire to be of that number that quakes and trembles at the Word of the Lord?" She argues for total receptivity to change through love of God and truth. Fisher writes lyrically with little attention to paragraph form.

305B [Fisher, Abigail.] Salutation of True Love to all Faithful Friends, Brethren and Sisters. London, Printed for Thomas Northcott, 1690. 20 pages. F 986. EEB Reel 1615:26.

Fisher offers tenderness to younger Quakers and their children, whom she calls "natural branches of such who have been grafted into the true Vine." She describes herself as a younger sister and says God will plead with those who deny rights to the Quakers. Fisher also claims the work and travel of the Friends in the service of Christ have not been in vain.

306B [Fletcher, Elizabeth.] A few words in season to all the Inhabitants of the Earth. London, Printed and are to be sold by Robert Wilson, 1660. 8 pages. F 1328. EEB Reel 982:11.

This Quaker tract employs a good bit of light imagery. Fletcher accuses her audience of pride, covetousness, blasphemy, drunkenness, adultery and lust. She says: "This is a Warning from the Lord to warne you before his Wrath break forth upon you."

307B [Forster, Mary.] A Declaration of the Bountifull Loving- Kindness of the Lord, Manifested to his Hand-maid Mary Haris. London, Printed and sold by T. Sowle, 1693. 12 pages. F 1603A*. EEB Reels 692:6 and 1284:13.

Forster tells of a beautiful young Quaker woman who "still lived in the Customs and Fashions of this Evil World." She fell ill and was cured only when she repented and begged for mercy. She became more deeply religious as she weakened and died committed to the Quaker faith. Forster relates this tale for the comfort and strength of those "of a fearful heart."

308B Forster, Mary, ed. A Guide to the Blind Pointed to, Or, a true testimony to the light within. 89 pages. London, 1671. F 1608.

This volume was written by Thomas Forster and edited by Mary Forster.

309B Forster, Mary. Some Seasonable Considerations to the Young Men and Women. Who in this Day of Tryal are made willing to offer up themselves, Estates or Liberty. London, Printed and sold by Andrew Sowle, 1684. [12] pages. F 1604. EEB Reel 692:7.

Forster speaks in favor of free assembly and serious commitment to religion and against personal prejudice and fancy dress (except for lace). She likens God to a husband and religious dedication to marriage. Forster also encourages verbal discretion, quoting James: "Whosoever seemeth to be Religious, and bridleth not his Tongue, that mans Religion is vain."

310B [Forster, Mary.] These several Papers was [sic] sent to the Parliament the twentieth day of the fifth Month, 1659. [London], Printed for Mary Westwood, 1659. 72 pages. F 1605. EEB Reel 316:24.

This document includes a list of Quaker women who defended their right to submit a petition. They say: "But let such know, that this is the work of the Lord at this day, even by weak means."

Fox, Margaret Fell. See Fell [Fox], Margaret Askew.

311B Freke, Elizabeth. Mrs. Elizabeth Freke Her Diary, 1671 to 1714. Mary Carbery, ed. Cork, Guy and Company, 1913. 143 pages. N.I.W.

Freke recorded events occurring between 1671 and 1714 in this diary. In County Cork she was tutored in botany, geography, cookery, brewing remedies, needlework and stitchery. Her marriage was opposed by her father; her courtship lasted seven years. Freke relates the misfortunes of her married life in Ireland and speaks of domestic tasks, family affairs, quarrels and troubles. She includes inventories of household goods and discusses health, home medicine and her social life. Throughout she laments her lot. Freke's difficulties were complicated by moves to and from her husband's home and by his alleged extravagance.

312B [Friends, Society of. London Yearly Meeting of Women Friends.] A Living Testimony from the power and spirit of our Lord Jesus Christ in our faithful Womens meeting and Christian socity [sic]. [London, 1685]. 8 pages. L 2598A. EEB Reel 767:10.

The Quaker women's meeting commits itself to work and service--"To help Families that are Poor, and have Children" and to visit the sick. Aged women are asked to teach younger members discretion, virtue, love and religion. They are to be treated as mothers, younger women as sisters, and widows are to be honored. Signatories are Mary Forster, Mary Elson, Anne Travice, Ruth Crowch, Susannah Dew and Mary Plumstead.

313B Friends, Society of. York Yearly Meeting of Women Friends. Testimony for the Lord, and his Truth. Given forth by the Women Friends, at their Yearly Meeting at York. [London, 1692.] 8 pages. F 2239B.

This distinctively gentle piece is addressed to Friends and "tender Sisters." They are encouraged to avoid vain customs and fancy clothing, set examples for children and servants, and provide for the widowed and fatherless. The authors hope the next yearly meeting will include women from other regions. Among the signatories are Catharine Whitton, Judith Boulbie, Elizabeth Sedman, Frances Taylor, Mary Waite, Elizabeth Beckwith and Mary Lindley.

314B Friends, Society of. York Yearly Meeting of Women Friends. From our Women's Yearly Meeting held at York. [London, 1698.] 7 pages. F 2239C.

The women of York claim the power of God is made manifest in their meetings. Special recognition is accorded love and good works, while a warning is issued against overindulgence in food and apparel. The women are advised to control their children well. Fear that the early female Quaker preachers and protesters will not be replaced is evident in this report.

315B Friends, Society of. York Yearly Meeting of Women Friends. From our Women's Meeting dated from York. [London, 1696.] 8 pages. F 2242A.

The women discuss successes of the monthly meetings in York and elsewhere. They are advised to avoid feasting and celebration on festive occasions lest they forget those who sacrificed for religious toleration. Mothers are told they must be models for their children. Military language emphasizes the general exhortation: "Put on the Breastplate of righteousness, the Helmet of Salvation, and take the Sword of the Spirit." A concluding statement encourages a strict, even harsh, approach to childrearing.

316B Gargill, Ann. A Brief Discovery of that Which is called the Popish Religion. London, Printed for Giles Calvert, 1656. 20 pages. G 258. TT Reel 133:E.887(2).

Gargill, a Quaker, makes an unusually direct attack on Catholicism. She criticizes the clergy for their "vain titles" and says the pope is "carnall, and wicked and abominable before the Lord." She accuses the Church of deceit and murder.

317B Gargill, Ann. A Warning to all the World. London, Printed for Giles Calvert, 1656. 5 pages. G 259. EEB Reel 563:10 and TT Reel 131:E.865(2).

This Quaker call to repentance names the adulterous woman, the harlot and the merchant. Imagery is based primarily on the bitter root of the "Plant of the innocent." Gargill says the guileless shall reign, guided by the "Light of the Lamb." The author's name appears as "Gargel" on the title page.

318B Gethin, Grace Norton, Lady.   Misery's Virtues Whet-stone. Reliquiae Gethinianae. [London], Printed by D. Edwards for the author, 1699. 90 pages. G 625*. EEB Reel 982:37.

The prefatory poem to this posthumous collection was written by William Congreve. It includes essays about idleness, love, pleasure, flattery, boldness, revenge, prosperity, adversity, reading, custom and so on. Much was apparently adapted from Bacon and others. It was published by the Lady Gethin's nearest relatives to preserve her memory. Gethin's father was Sir George Norton of Somersetshire, who had helped Charles II escape from England. This publication was intended for private distribution.

319B Gilman, Anne. An Epistle to Friends; Being a Tender Salutation to the Faithful in God everywhere. London, 1662. 8 pages. G 768. EEB Reel 1384:61.

Gilman cheerfully assures fellow Quakers of their ultimate victory, despite persecution. She appeals to Charles II for toleration and compassion and warns: "...if Fire should be for us prepared, the ashes of our bones would rise as a witness against thee to plead the innocency of our cause before thee."

320B [Gould, Anne.] <u>An Epistle To all the Christian Magistrates and Powers in the whole Christendom, And Professors, and Teachers, and Christians that witness the end of the law</u>. London, Printed by Thomas Simmons, 1659. 16 pages. G 1414. EEB Reel 788:35.

Quaker Gould says persons should not be persecuted because of observance of the sabbath or religious holidays, for such things are inconsequential to Christ. She advises following one's conscience in these matters, and cites treatment of the Apostle by Jews and gentiles as an example. She asks, "And do ye ever persecute any till they come to that confession [as did Paul]?"

321B Greenway, Margaret. <u>A Lamentation against the Professing Priest and People of Oxford, and to all in the cages of unclean birds, called Colleges</u>. [London, 1657?] Broadside. G 1861. EEB Reel 1739:25.

Greenway chastises priests who claim only death can bring salvation and, therefore, cleanliness. She says "all that are born againe will witnesse against your Doctrine, for he that is born of God sins not, neither can he because the seed remaines in him." Greenway also maintains neither their preaching nor their lengthy prayers will save the priests.

322B H., M. <u>The Young Cooks Monitor: or, Directions for Cookery and Distilling</u>. Second Edition. London, Printed for the author at her House in Lime-street, 1690. 180 pages. H 96*.

The work is dedicated especially to "scholars." It includes recipes for dishes like "stewed carp, Batalia pye, pickled cowslip flowers," marrow pudding, almond florentine and quince water.

323B Halkett, Anne Murray, Lady. "Memoirs." In <u>The Memoirs of Anne, Lady Halkett and Ann, Lady Fanshawe</u>. John Loftis, ed. Oxford, The Clarendon Press, 1979. [78] pages. N.I.W.

Anne Murray (1623-1699) was the daughter of a tutor to Charles I and a governess to Princess Elizabeth. She was educated by tutors, particularly in the medical sciences. In this lively, suspenseful, personal account of her adult life, she effectively uses anecdote and dialogue. The salient events are her three courtships, including an incipient love affair with the duplicitous Colonel Joseph Bampfyld, and various royalist intrigues (including the Duke of York's escape in 1648 from St. James Palace). Lady Halkett was quite prolific, although most of her largely devotional writing remains in manuscript.

324B Hambly, Loveday Billing. <u>A Relation of the Last Words and Departure of that Antient and Honourable Woman Loveday Hambly</u>. London, Printed by John Gain, 1683. 11 pages. H 472.

A beloved Cornish Quaker woman is honored in this tribute which includes her final words. One of Hambly's servants describes her suffering during her final days. Testimonials from her congregation and friends discuss her faith and "Fame for Good Works, Charity and Hospitality."

325B Harcourt, Anne, Lady.   The Harcourt Papers.   Edward H. Harcourt, ed.
Oxford, Printed for private circulation by J. Parker, 1880-1905.   Vol. I, pages
169-196. N.I.W.

Extracts from this diary (1649-1661) describe Harcourt's religious life and
observances, her "transgressions" and family life. Excerpt: "The Lord was
pleased to visit my husband with many sad distempers, as with an ague...but
the Lord...did deliver him from his ague after 4 fits." Harcourt also recounts
her husband's imprisonment in Kent.

326B Harley, Brilliana Conway, Lady. Letters of the Lady Brilliana Harley. London,
The Camden Society, 1854. (Publications of the Camden Society, Series I, Number
58) N.I.W.

This volume contains letters in the Harley family papers by the Lady Brilliana,
third wife of Sir Robert, a Puritan member of the House of Commons. Early
letters are primarily to her husband, while later ones are to her son Edward at
Oxford. Often religious, the latter epistles offer advice about Edward's health,
studies and conduct. This period is notable for the siege of Brampton Castle,
the Harley estate, in 1643 by cavaliers. Excerpt: "The gentillmen of this cuntry
have affected theair desires in bringing an army against me...The Lord in mercy
presarve me, that I fall not unto theair hands."

327B Hatton, Lady Elizabeth. A True copy of a Letter from...left at the remove of
her household from Stoke, upon hearing of Prince Ruperts approach. London,
Printed by R. B. for William Ley, 1642.   Broadside.   H 1149.   TT Reel
245:669.f.6(84).

This interesting broadside is addressed to Charles I. The Lady Elizabeth says
she has enjoyed serving the queen mother and apologizes for fleeing when the
king is expected to visit. She says "Parliament is the only firme foundation of
the greatest establishment, the King...can attain." She warns if he tries to
"break" Parliament, "you shall concurre to destroy the best ground-work for his
Majesties prosperity."

328B Hayward, Amey. The Female's Legacy. Containing divine poems...On several
choice subjects. Commended to all Godly women. London, Printed by Benj. Harris
for the author, 1699. 104 pages. H 1227. EEB Reel 1636:1.

Hayward's twenty-six simple poems on religious themes and proper behavior
encourage women to pursue spiritual growth. She notes women have immortal
souls and stresses they are as responsible to God as are men.

329B Hendricks, Elizabeth. An Epistle to Friends in England. [London], 1672. 7
pages. H 1447. EEB Reel 815:24.

Hendricks' Quaker tract is meant to spread love to Friends who have seen and
heard the light and truth of God. Written from Amsterdam, this letter warns
them to keep faith and not arrogantly to claim the truth.

330B [Henrietta Maria, Queen Consort of Charles I.] The Best Newes from York,
That ever came to London and Westminster...with the Contents of a Letter lately
sent from the Queenes Majestie to the King, concerning her desire, that his Majestie

and the Parliament may concurre together. July 1, 1642. London, [1642].   6 pages. B 2058. EEB Reel 252:E.153(4) and TT Reel 27:E.153(4).

A letter from Henrietta Maria appears on page one of this document. The queen's brief note to Charles I reveals her affection: "No distance of place can divide our hearts, nor any length of time can lessen the reall and unfaigned love that is equal betweene us." She expresses her hope for "a happy Union betweene your Majestie and your Parliament."

331B Henrietta Maria, Queen Consort of Charles I. De Boodtschap Ende Briefvan de. n.p., Gedruckt by R. Barcker, 1642. H 1455.

This document is likely identical to 339B.

332B Henrietta Maria, Queen Consort of Charles I. A Copie of the Queen's Letter from the Hague to the King's Majesty residing at Yorke. London, Printed for John Price, 1642. Broadside. H 1456. TT Reel 245:669.f.3(62).

This letter expresses Henrietta Maria's continuing loyalty to Charles I and describes her displeasure at the deteriorating hospitality being shown to her and her entourage at the Dutch court. She links this situation to the growing hostility between the States of Holland and Prince Rupert. The queen also shows concern for the safety of the Prince of Orange and the intentions of the king of Denmark, who is sailing for England. She vows "either to live or dye at Your sacred feet, and in your owne Kingdome."

333B [Henrietta Maria, Queen Consort of Charles I.] A Coppy of 1. The Letter sent by the Queenes Majestie concerning the collection of the Recusants Mony for the Scottish Warre, Apr. 17, 1639. London, Printed in the Yeare of the discovery of plots, 1641. 2 pages. C 6196. EEB Reel 254:E.164(15) and TT Reel 29:E.164(15).

This "testification" concerns the raising of money for the king's impending war with the Scots. Henrietta Maria was able to obtain a pledge of 20,000 pounds from the Catholics for the cause. Her suggestion that the ladies of England should make a present to the king was rejected. Excerpt: "And as wee presume the summe they will raise will not be unworthy our presenting to the King; so shall we be very sensible of it...and will endeavor...to improve the merit of it."

334B [Henrietta Maria, Queen Consort of Charles I.] "Her Majesties Gracious answer to the Lord Digbies Letter." In Admirable and notable things of note. London, Printed for Francis Coules and Thomas Banks, 1642. Broadside. Item: N.I.W. Collection: A 586. EEB Reel 250:E.138(19) and TT Reel 25:E.138(19).

This item is the same as 336B.

335B Henrietta Maria, Queen Consort of Charles I. The Protestation of Her Royal Majesty Given at her departure from Scheveling, February 25, 1643. London, Printed for John Hancocke, 1643. Broadside. H 1466. TT Reel 245:669.f.5(142).

This letter protests the search and seizure of the queen's ship by the Lords of the States General of the Low Countries. The queen had been granted a passport by the Dutch to travel to England. Because her ship contained ammunition for the king, its mission violated a Dutch order prohibiting the shipment of arms to the British government. The queen maintains the present action violates a treaty between the two countries. This document reveals the queen's penchant for independent action and shows her strength in challenging Holland's neutrality.

336B Henrietta Maria, Queen Consort of Charles I. [The Queens] Majesties Gracious Answer to the Lord Digbies Letter. London, Printed for Tho. Powell, [1642]. [8] pages. H 1458. EEB Reel 250:E.138(8) and TT Reel 25:E.138(8).

In this one-page document, dated from Canterbury on February 3 [1642], the queen tells Sir Kenelm Digby, her chancellor, to stay in Middleborough until he receives further word and indicates the king has gone to a safe place. She answers Digby's letter of January 21 in which he asks for orders and reconfirms his allegiance. The remaining seven pages are a news summary.

337B Henrietta Maria, Queen Consort of Charles I. The Queens Letter from Holland: Directed to the Kings most Excellent Majesty. [London], Printed for I. Underhill, [1643]. 6 pages. H 1459. EEB Reel 243:E.90(2) and TT Reel 16:E.90(2).

This item is the same as 339B.

Henrietta Maria, Queen Consort of Charles I. The Queenes Letter to the Kings most Excellent Majesty. See 741A.

Henrietta Maria, Queen Consort of Charles I. The Queens Majesties Letter to the Parliament of England. See 743A.

338B Henrietta Maria, Queen Consort of Charles I. The Queens Majesties Message and Declaration. [London], Printed for L. White, [1649]. [6] pages. H 1462. TT Reel 83:E.538(7).

The declaration addresses those plotting to kill Charles I. It charges the king's enemies are congregating in large numbers in Yorkshire, while others are traveling there by freight. This document reports Holland denied a request to mediate between the king and Parliament because it was reluctant to interfere in the internal affairs of another country. Although the Prince of Wales was dispatched, he was prevented from landing in England by the navy.

339B Henrietta Maria, Queen Consort of Charles I. The Queens Majesties Message and Letter from the Hague in Holland. [October 14] [London], Printed for I. Underhill, [1642.] [6] pages. H 1463. EEB Reel 248:E.122(12) and TT Reel 21:E.122(12).

This short supportive letter to Charles was found in a ship loaded with munitions and grounded at Yarmouth. The queen says she can express her love only by acting as the king's "humble and faithfull Agent in accommodating and promoting your high affaires." She advises him to stand firm in his convictions and in the cause and offers assurances that Prince William of Orange is trying to gather support for him. See also 891A.

Henrietta Maria, Queen Consort of Charles I. The Queens Majesties Propositions to to [sic] the Kings Most Excellent Majesty. See 744A.

340B Henrietta Maria, Queene Consort of Charles I. The Queens Majesties Propositions to the States of Holland, Concerning the Differences betwixt His Majestie and His Parliament. London, Printed for T. H. and T. R., 1642. 6 pages. H 1465. EEB Reel 252:E.153(10).

The queen had asked the government of Holland to mediate between the king and Parliament, but Dutch officials were loath to do so. She beseeched them, whereupon they appointed the young Prince of Orange, Duke Robert and Gustavus Horn as representatives.

Henrietta Maria, Queen Consort of Charles I. The Protestation of. See 335B.

Henrietta Maria, Queen Consort of Charles I. The Queenes Speech. See 746A.

Henrietta Maria, Queen Consort of Charles I. A True Relation. See 891A.

341B Henshaw, Anne. To the Parliament of the Commonwealth of England, Scotland, and Ireland. The humble petition of Anne Henshaw, widow, late wife and executrix of Benjamin Henshaw, Esq. Deceased. [London], 1654. Broadside. H 1477. TT Reel 246:669.f.19(49).

This plea is addressed to Parliament by the widow of Benjamin Henshaw, Esq., owed money by the government. Henshaw is asking payment for herself (as executrix of his will) and her seven children.

342B Hewytt, Mary. To the Hon. the Knights, Citizens and Burgesses of the Commons House now assembled in Parliament. The humble Petition of Dame Mary Hewytt, widow, late wife of John Hewytt, Dr. in Divinity. [London, 1660?] Broadside. H 1640.

Hewytt's husband was accused of treason in Cromwell's High Court of Justice. He argued the Court was not established by statute and thus had no right to try him. Nevertheless, he was tried and executed at Tower-Hill "without Jury or Witness produced." Hewytt asks that head justice, John Lisle, be tried for murder, and other commissioners pay her family damages. Wing's STC spells the author's name "Hewitt."

343B Hildegard [A Nun]. A strange Prophecie, against Bishops, Prelates, and all other Priests, which have not kept the faithfull Order of Priesthood; And also against the Transgressors of Righteousnesse in these Times. London, Printed for John Thomas, 1641. 6 pages. H 1983.

Twelfth-century German mystic Hildegard predicted plagues, inveighed against the "Debauchery of Nunneries" and the hypocrisy of priests and monks. She said the Jesuits, accused of abuses, would lose their material possessions. After her death she was considered a prophet. Excerpt: "There will arise Men without a Chief, who shall feed and grow fat on the sins of the People." Hildegard's prophecies are also quoted in A Nunn's Prophesie (N 1472: EEB Reel 1640:20).

344B [Hincks, Elizabeth.]   The Poor Widow's Mite, cast into the Lords
Treasury...Justification of the Meetings of the People of God called Quakers.
[London], 1671. 47 pages. H 2050. EEB Reel 942:15.

In couplets Hincks defends and explains the distinctiveness of Quaker tenets.
She describes resistance, especially by the young, to the "truth."   Biblical
allegories demonstrate the difference between true and false professors of faith.
Questions and answers about the Quaker service follow. The primary issues
addressed are silence in meetings, the nature of darkness and the persecution
of Friends.

[Hobry, Marie.] A Hellish Murder Committed by a French Midwife. See 431A.

345B Holden, Mary. The Womans Almanack, Or, an Ephemerides For the Year of
our LORD, 1689. London, Printed by J. Millet, 1689. [no pagination] A 1827A*.
EEB Reel 1453:16.

Holden's almanac of weather conditions also describes the trajectories of
planets and movements of other heavenly bodies.

Holmes, Jane. False Prophets and their False Preachers Described. See 34B.

Hooten, Elizabeth. False Prophets and their False Preachers Described. See 34B.

346B Hooton, Elizabeth. To the King and both Houses of Parliament. [London,
1670.] 2 pages. H 2710A.

Hooton, probably the first female Quaker preacher, was an activist and
missionary persecuted during her ministry in New England.   This item,
comprised of two pages following Thomas Taylor's To the King, criticizes
Charles II for confiscating Quaker property, bankrupting families and
demolishing meetinghouses.

347B [Hopton, Susannah.]   Daily Devotions. Consisting of Thanksgivings,
Confessions and Prayers. [Two Parts.]   London, Printed by A. Maxwell for
Jonathan Edwin, 1673. 164 pages. H 2761. EEB Reel 384:8.

The basis for this volume is Reflections and Resentments of Holy David by a
"learned and pious Christian." Hopton's prayers are to be repeated on the way
to, during and after services. They are quotidian devotions, although some
occasional prayers are included for holidays. She does not address the
Christian or domestic duty of women.

348B Howgill, Mary. A Remarkable Letter of Mary Howgill to Oliver Cromwel, called
Protector. [London], 1657. 6 pages. H 3191. EEB Reel 791:18.

Quaker Howgill claims she gave her letter to Cromwell and conversed with him
at length about it. She accuses him of pride, denying God and acting cruelly
to "them who are in the fear of the Lord." Howgill says Cromwell seeks
personal glory and is "as a stinking dunghill in the sight of God." In a letter
to the inhabitants of Dover, Howgill assails the Anabaptists, water baptism and
transubstantiation rituals. This piece has a more distinctly Quaker tone than the

Cromwellian letter. Howgill was likely the wife of prominent Quaker Francis Howgill.

349B H[owgill], M[ary.] The Vision of the Lord of Hosts...Also, a few Words to Friends of Truth. [London], 1662. 7 pages. H 3192. EEB Reel 791:19.

Howgill had a vision of "the dark, horrible, and miserable estate that would fall on this Land of England." She describes an open pit filled with wild beasts somewhere in the south country. Although she was frightened, an angel said it was intended to "bow down a stiff-necked and a gain-saying People."

Hulton, Anne. Memoirs of the Life of...Mrs. Anne Hulton. See 515B.

The Humble Petition of many thousands of the poor enslaved...Men and Women. See 625B.

350B The Humble Petition of the Widdows and Fatherless Children of the West. [London? 1689.] Broadside. H 3585A. EEB Reel 498:14.

Over 1000 widows and children of Dorset, Somerset and Devon claim magistrate George Lord Jeffries has sold their estates or cut off their inheritances. A description of his tyranny is included. They ask that he be handed over to them to "give him another manner of Welcome than he had there three Years since."

351B Hutchinson, Lucy Apsley. "The Life of Mrs. Lucy Hutchinson written by herself." In Memoirs of the Life of Colonel Hutchinson with the Fragment of an Autobiography of Mrs. Hutchinson. London, Oxford University Press, 1973. 14 pages. N.I.W.

This volume was first published in 1806. Hutchinson (b. 1620) was an exceptionally bright, well-educated child who knew Greek and Latin and translated Lucretius into English. This short autobiography concerns her spiritual awakening and strong, independent personality, often unsuited to women's prescribed role. Excerpt: "When I was about seven yeares of age, I remember I had at one time eight tutors in severall qualities, languages, musick, dancing, writing, and needlework."

352B Hutchinson, Lucy. Memoirs of the Life of Colonel Hutchinson with the Fragment of an Autobiography of Mrs. Hutchinson. London, Oxford University Press, 1973. 292 pages. N.I.W.

Hutchinson wrote this memoir to clear her husband's name, for personal consolation and to present a noble example for her children. The Colonel was an acerbic Puritan who believed strongly in the subservience of women. His wife includes a detailed description of his contribution to the Civil War. She also recounts how she saved her husband's life by forging a letter. See also 351B.

J., R. A Letter of Advice to a friend. See 259B.

353B James, Elinor. Mrs. James' Advice to the Citizens of London. [London? 1688.] Broadside. J 415. EEB Reel 1741:7.

James was a printer and pamphleteer who defended the Church of England. Here she assures the citizenry she desires their well-being and advises them to seek God. James urges loyalty to the king and promises the "God that chang'd Nebuchadnezar's Heart, can convince my Sovereign Lord, and make him more zealous for the Protestant Religion than ever he was for Rome."

354B James, Elinor. The Case between a Father and his Children. London, Printed for Tho. James, 1682. Broadside. J 416. EEB Reel 498:42.

James presented this petition to the Lord Mayor of London and the Court of Aldermen. It concerns a friend, a "most Indulgent Father," whose children refused aid when he was in need and prevented the sale of his possessions when he attempted to raise money. James asks the Mayor and aldermen to heal the familial breach and try the case. She blames the children's disobedience on Satan's influence.

355B James, Elinor. Mrs. James's Defence of the Church of England. [London], Printed for me Elinor James, 1687. 8 pages. J 417. EEB Reel 816:17.

This pamphlet is an answer to Canting Address and The Quakers Good Advice. James criticizes the printer for publishing a work which "lampoons" her. She says although he claims to support religious toleration, he is really personally ambitious. She repeats that only the Church of England has a connection to royalty.

356B [James, Elinor.] An Injur'd Prince Vindicated, or, a Scurrilous, and Detracting Pamphlet Answered. [London? 1688?] Broadside. J 417A. EEB Reel 1595:105.

This broadside in verse is a defense of James II. It accuses the Whigs of treachery and fomenting disorder. While invoking the divine right of kings, James depicts King James as under assault by mobs.

357B James, Elinor. May it please your Majesty, to accept my thanks. [London, 1688.] Broadside. J 417AC. EEB Reel 1741:8.

In this letter to James II, James praises him for restoring the charter of London and encourages him to make peace with the Dutch. She says his subjects will gladly fight for him but not for Rome. James agrees there are some admirable Catholics, but decries the elevation of Mary and the pope over other mortals.

358B James, Elinor. May It Please Your Most Sacred Majesty, seriously to consider my Great Zeal. [London, 1685.] Broadside. J 417B. EEB Reel 1551:28.

James claims she has often fasted to demonstrate her loyalty to the king. Although she has nursed and raised many children herself, she made time to come to Whitehall to support the Crown. Her challenge: She will consent to sequestration with a faithful Catholic to see who can fast longer; the person with greater endurance will represent the true religion. She requests a witness if the Catholic is a male to "prevent scandal" (if the two are alone).

359B James, Elinor. Most Dear Soveraign, I cannot but love. [London, 1689.] Broadside. J 417C. EEB Reel 962:15.

In this fragment addressed to James II, the author characterizes him as humble. She says she values him above all his kingdoms, but fears for his corruption by priests and Jesuits, whom she calls "perverters" not "converters" and "implacable enemies to the Church of England." She charges the Roman Church has no faith, charity or self-denial. James says she would sacrifice 100 lives for the king if she but had them to give.

360B James, Elinor. My Lord, I thought it my bound duty. [London, 1687.] Broadside. J 418. EEB Reel 1617:13.

James thanks the Lord Mayor of London for preserving peace and prosperity and for supporting Charles II and James II. She praises him for resisting vengence against provocateurs and notes her twenty-year support of the Church and the crown.

361B James, Elinor. My Lords, I can assure your Lordships that you are infinitely admir'd. [London, 1689.] Broadside. J 419.

In a letter to the House of Lords, James praises their support of the Church of England, "the Best Church in the World." Alleging James II has been "sorely tempted," she advises them to keep Catholics away from him. Although she admires William of Orange, James does not support his ascension to the throne.

362B James, Elinor. My Lords, You can't but be sensible of the great Zeal. [London? 1688.] Broadside. J 419B.

James declares support for the king and kingdom, but especially for the Church of England. She asks Parliament to take nothing from James II beyond his kingdom and requests that they conform to God's laws. James also asks for assistance to William of Orange in proselytizing for Christianity and challenging the French king.

363B James, Elinor. Mrs. James her new answer to a Speech said to be lately made by a Noble Peer of this Realm. [London, 1681.] Broadside. J 420. EEB Reel 1741:9.

James criticizes the unnamed peer for responding to the king's speech with disrespect. She says he is mistaken to think of intimates of Charles as "popish mistresses, counsellors and favorites." James also takes offense at the peer's attack on the queen's religion. Signature: "I am your humble Servant and Souls Well-Wisher, E.J."

364B James, Elinor. Sir, my Lord Major [sic] and the Aldermen. [London, 1690?] Broadside. J 421.

In this letter James complains about the practice of discarding squibs in the streets of London.

365B James, Elinor. This being your Majesty's Birth-day. [London, 1690.] Broadside. J 421aA.

James thanks King William for saying "the Church of England is one of the greatest supports of the Protestant Religion" and offering his life in its defense. James calls the Church the only "Bulwark against Popery." She attacks dissenters who seize land and do not believe in a state church. James encourages William to support Anglicans and to give attention to England rather than Holland.

366B James, Elinor.   To the Honourable Convention, Gentlemen, you seem. [London? 1688.] Broadside. J 421A. EEB Reel 498:43.

James calls the gentlemen addressed, i.e., the Parliament, "honest and Religious" because they must subscribe to Church doctrine if they claim to be Christ's disciples. She speaks on behalf of the king and maintains they "ought to Act better by him, than by Unthroning him." She says the king cooperated in their attempts to "Free the Land from Popery" and blames them for the present governmental rift. She likens them to "some Women that love Changes which should be beneath such Noble Souls as Men of Wisdom."

367B James, Elinor. To the Honourable the House of Commons...I am very sorry. [London? 1696.] Broadside. J 422.

James speaks against a new bill which addresses "clipt money." She opposes changing the coin of the realm, citing the difficulty of identifying real silver and special problems the new system will present for the poor. She also suggests recalling silver tankards from pubs for replacement with pewter ones.

368B James, Elinor. To the Kings Most Excellent Majesty. The Humble Petition of Elinor James. [London, 1685.] Broadside. J 422aA. EEB Reel 1741:10.

James petitions James II to disavow Catholicism. In an anti-Marian, anti-transubstantiation document she describes his primary responsibilities: to honor God and pursue freedom. Excerpt: "to serve God is perfect Freedom, but to serve Popery is perfect Thralldom."

369B James, Elinor. To the right honourable Convention. Gentlemen, though you have a new name. [London? 1688.] Broadside. J 422bA.

James desires that the House of Commons be "Sons of that Blessed Church of England." She warns against succumbing to popery and urges them to turn to the House of Lords for guidance while they establish regulations for the reign of William and Mary.

370B James, Elinor.   To the Right Honourable the House of Lords. My Lords. [London? 1688.] Broadside. J 422A. EEB Reel 1551:29.

James opposes a tax on East Indian goods as unfair to English weavers and detrimental to trade, which is suffering in any case. She bases her argument on Christian ethics, maintaining punishment of the East India Tea Company would be counter to the will of God. This item is dated 1702 by the Houghton Library, Harvard University.

371B James, Elinor. To the right honourable, the Lord Mayor...and all the rest of the Loyal Citizens. [London, 1683.] Broadside. J 422B. EEB Reel 1617:14.

James says she appreciates the loyalty [to the king] of these officials during recent difficult times. She cites Sir John Moore in particular. James concludes with a caveat to resist the blandishments of popery and remain true to the king and the Church of England.

372B [James, Elinor.] Mrs. James's vindication of the Church of England, in an Answer to a Pamphlet entituled a New Test of the Church of England's Loyalty. [London?], Printed for Elinor James, 1687. 12 pages. J 423. EEB Reel 1150:34.

This document defends James II, The Book of Common Prayer and the Church of England. It argues against a pamphlet written by John Dryden that allegedly expressed disloyalty to the king. James calls Dryden's work "pernicious" and says she realizes the king will question why a woman is involved in such matters, but claims she is concerned about the country.

373B Jesserson, Susanna. A Bargain for Bachelors, or: The Best Wife in the World for a Penny. [London], Printed for E. A., 1675. 8 pages. J 686. EEB Reel 108:9.

Jesserson describes a good wife as temperate, chaste, companionate, modest, true and a "help-meet." Such a woman must copy "our mother Eve before she dialogu'd with the Serpent." Saying this wife "commands by obeying" and is "ashamed to show herself wiser than her husband," Jesserson is one of the few women to argue so directly for female submission. Men are entreated to consider wealth only after personal qualities.

374B Jevon, Rachael. Carmen [Triamveftikon] Regiae Majestati Caroli II. London, Typis Joannis Macock, 1660. 5 pages. J 729. TT Reel 161:E.1080(10).

The Greek word in the title derives from Plutarch and means an affiliation with triumphal families. This is a Latin version of 375B.

375B Jevon, Rachael. Exultationis Carmen. To the Kings most excellent Majesty upon his most Desired Return. London, Printed by John Macock, 1660. 7 pages. J 730. EEB Reel 459:23 and TT Reel 161:E.1080(11).

This typical royalist poem commending the restoration of Charles II was presented to him by Jevon. It is Jevon's first published work "though for my sexes sake I should deny." She criticizes the Revolution and expresses pleasure that England has regained its former glory. Excerpt: "Let shady Woods and Groves together dance/To see the Royal Oak to them advance."

376B Jinner, Sarah. The Woman's Almanack: Or, Prognostication For ever. Shewing the nature of the Planets, with the Events that shall befall Women and children born under them. With several Predictions very useful for the Female Sex. London, Printed for J. J., 1659. 16 pages. A 1848. TT Reel 243:E.2140(1).

Jinner consulted signs to predict the probability of marriage, types of marital matches, etc. She argues women should be familiar with astrology so they will be "patterns of civility to all the world." Jinner advocates women's education and, citing writers like Katherine Philips and the Duchess of Newcastle, warns her contemporaries "not to let their great worth with other learned authors of our sex ly in obscurity." She also claims women's judgment and memory are equal to those of men. Jinner supports female public speech, although she accepts the status quo in general.

377B Joceline, Elizabeth (Brooke). The Mothers Legacy, to her Unborne Child. Oxford, Printed and sold by Jo. Wilmot, 1684. 119 pages. J 756. EEB Reel 108:11.

Joceline died shortly after giving birth. Having a foreboding of her own death, she wrote this volume for her unborn child. She says a female child should learn writing and the Bible, how to perform housework and "good works." She suggests following examples of virtuous women and warns against pride and drunkenness.

378B Jones, Sarah. This is Lights appearance in the Truth to all the precious dear Lambs. [London? 1650.] 3 pages. J 989.

This Quaker tract is addressed to "babes" who are "little and weak in your own eyes." Jones encourages them to focus on the Lord and goodness within. She concludes with an exhortation to ignore worldly things.

379B J[ones], S[arah.] To Sions Lovers, being a Golden Egge, to avoid Infection: or, A short step into the Doctrine of laying on of hands. [London], 1644. [12] pages. J 990. EEB Reel 230:E.16(7) and TT Reel 3:E.16(7).

This argument based on scripture defends the laying on of hands as a healing device. It has the tone of a radical sectarian tract. Jones supports baptism and healing and criticizes Presbyterians and unenthusiastic congregations.

380B [Juliana of Norwich.] XVI Revelations of Divine Love, Shewed to a Devout Servant of our Lord, called Mother Juliana, an Anchorette of Norwich. [London?], 1670. 223 pages. C 6904. EEB Reel 1656:31.

The title page indicates this work was "published by R. F. S. Cressy," who states the author was "a Person of your own Sex" whose biography eluded him. Juliana was probably a Benedictine nun (c.1343) of the house at Carrow near Norwich. The text relates her mystical experiences in which Christ or other heavenly bodies revealed truths or foretold events.

381B K[emp], A[nne]. A Contemplation on Bassets down-Hill. [Oxford, Printed by H. Hall, 1658?] Broadside. K 257. EEB Reel 1151:12.

This poem describes a rural setting, perhaps in Gloucester. Excerpt: "Here are no smoaking streets, nor howling cryes,/Deafning the earcs [sic], nor blinding the eyes;/No noysome smells t' infect and choacke the aire,/Breeding diseases envious to the Faire."

382B Kent, Elizabeth Talbot Grey, Countess of. A Choice Manuall, or Rare and Select Secrets in Physick and Chyrurgery. London, Printed by G[ertrude] D[awson], 1653. 128 pages. K 310*. EEB Reels 152:3 and 1573:1.

Brief recipes and directions for making medicines are gathered in this duodecimo. Similar to many cookery/medical treatises, this was an early, popular one. The book went through nineteen editions.

383B Kent, Elizabeth Talbot Grey, Countess of. <u>A True Gentlewomans delight</u>
<u>wherein is contained all manner of Cookery</u>. [London], Printed by A. M. for
Margaret Shears, 1671. 140 pages. K 317C*.

Kent's cookbook was first published as part of 382B. It includes recipes for
food, directions for making candles and so on.

384B Killigrew, Anne. <u>Poems</u>. London, Printed for Samuel Lowndes, 1686. 100
pages. K 442.

These posthumously published poems include a prefatory ode by Dryden.
Killigrew's work is quite austere and often critical of greed and ambition. Much
of her poetry about the nature of women seems imitative of traditional male
views.

385B [Killin, Margaret.] <u>A Warning from the Lord to the Teachers and People of</u>
<u>Plymouth</u>. London, Printed for Giles Calvert, 1656. 6 pages. K 473. EEB Reel
539:18 and TT Reel 130:E.861(14).

Killin collaborated with Barbara Patison on this Quaker entreaty to repent
addressed to proud priests, rich men, corrupt magistrates, covetous lawyers,
drunkards, swearers, adulterers and whoremongers. One section is titled
"Queries to the Parish teachers of this Nation, who have great Sums of Money
for teaching the people." Here the festivities of Easter, Whitsuntide and
Christmas are called "pleasing to the flesh."

386B L., Elizabeth. <u>Short Remains of a Dead Gentlewoman and Wife</u>. n. p.,
[1690?] 3 pages. L 17A.

This fascinating document contains a letter the author wrote to her husband
during her final illness. She is frank in her criticism of him, saying he "has both
said and done several severe and hard things to me, which none stuck close
to me." She confesses she never answered him sharply because "I knew he
would not bear it." It is noteworthy that he published it after her death for "the
good Example of [others]."

387B <u>The Ladies Companion, or a Table furnished with sundry sorts of Pies and</u>
<u>Tarts, Gracefull at a Feast, with many receipts</u>. By Persons of Quality whose names
are mentioned. London, Printed by W. Bentley, and are to be sold by W. Shears,
1653[4]. 82 pages. L 152. TT Reel 194:E.1528(2).

This volume contains recipes for pies, tarts, preserves, and so on contributed
by individual women.

388B [La Fayette, Marie Madeline Pioche de la Vergne, Comtesse de.] <u>The</u>
<u>Princess of Cleves</u>. London, Printed for R. Bentley and M. Magnes, 1679. 259
pages. L 169*. EEB Reels 74:4 and 1703:18.

La Fayette's involved romance is set in France during the reign of Henry II. It
focuses on Madam de Chartres, a great beauty and heiress of the Prince of
Cleves. She was supposedly courted by the king.

389B [La Fayette, Marie Madeline Pioche de la Vergne, Comtesse de.]   The Princess of Monpensier. [London], 1666. 83 pages. L 171. EEB Reel 189:9.

This romance, set in France during the Civil War under Charles IX, involves the House of Bourbon, which favors marriage between the Prince of Monpensier and Mlle. Mezieres; and the House of Anjou, which tries to match her with the Duke of Maine. Although his brother, the Duke of Guise, is in love with Mlle. Mezieres, she marries Monpensier, who removes her from war-torn Paris. After thwarted romances with both the Duke of Guise and the Count de Charbanes, her husband's good friend, the Princess becomes ill and dies a depressed woman. The author concludes her fate might have been different had virtue and prudence dictated her actions.

390B [La Fayette, Marie Madeline Pioche de la Vergne, Comtesse de.] Zayde: A Spanish History. Two Parts. London, Printed by T. Milbourn for William Cademan, 1678. 175 pages. L 172*, L 173A. EEB Reel 74:5.

This novel was translated from the French by P. Porter. Set in Spain at the Court of Leon, it concerns the Castille family: Gonsalvo loves a mysterious beauty named Zayde, who is shipwrecked in Catalonia. Hermenesilde, his sister, is beloved by Don Garcia. Another plot revolves around the duplicity of Nugna Bella, Gonsalvo's former love, and his rival Don Ramires. A subplot recounts the saga of Zayde's triangular relationship with her female friend Felime and an Arab named Alamire, Prince of Tharsus. The romance uses a modern literary device: it relates one incident from several points of view. The British Library lists Jean Regnaud de Segrais as joint author.

391B [Lamb, Catharine.]   A Full Discovery of the False Evidence Produc'd by the Papists against the most Reverend and Learned Dr. Tho. Tenison. London, Printed for John and Thomas Lane, 1688. [6] pages. L 205C. EEB Reel 739:6.

This pamphlet concerns Tenison, a parish priest at St. Martin-in-the-Fields, later Archbishop of Canterbury, and his dispute with Andrew Pulton, head of the Jesuits in the Savoy. Tenison attacked the Roman Catholic system of indulgences and other matters of doctrine. The two men publicly debated at Long Acre on September 29, 1687. Catharine Lamb discusses a statement she signed indicating she was privy to the event. Because its caustic tone is atypical of writing by women, female authorship is questionable.

La Mothe, Marie Catherine, Countess d'Aulnoy. See Aulnoy, Catherine Jumelle de Berneville, Comtesse d'.

392B [La Vallierre, Louise Francoise, Duchesse de.]   The Penitent Lady: Or Reflections on the Mercy of God. London, Printed for Dorman Newman, 1684. 110 pages. L 623G*.

These twenty-three meditations were translated from the French by Lewis Atterbury. La Valliere encourages female novices to consecrate themselves to God and strengthen their resolve. She also provides comforting prayers for times of doubt. La Valliere's major purposes are to render Christ immediate, to discourage earthly bonds, and to express the difficulties she faced as a newly penitent soul.

393B Lead, Jane (Ward). The Ark of Faith: or a Supplement to the Tree of Faith. Together with a Discovery of the New World. London, Printed for J. Bradford, 1696. 23 [32] pages. N.I.W.

Lead was an important Protestant mystic, the founder of the Philadelphian sect, and a disciple of the visionary Jacob Boehme, originator of theosophy. Here Lead presents an allegory of the marriage of the ark of faith and the new Philadelphian Church under Christ's aegis. She says the union will lead to the founding of a utopian society in which manual skills and the practical arts form the basis of religious experience.

394B [Lead, Jane (Ward).] The Ascent to the Mount of Vision, where many Things were shewn. London, 1699. 39 pages. L 782.

Lead describes her vision of a mountain representing heaven and hell. Christ appears with male and female prophets; believers take their places in the structure. She it "The State of Separated Souls."

395B L[ead], J[ane] (Ward). The Christian Warfare. Being some Serious, Humble, and Practical Reflections on Psalm XV. London, Printed and sold by John Gain, 1680. 200 pages. L 27A.

This lengthy biblical commentary divides each verse   into fifteen or twenty responses, so the meaning of each section can be elucidated. Lead offers Hebrew word origins and Latin terminology. She focuses on the means of salvation and the rights of the innocent.

396B Lead, Jane (Ward).   The Enochian Walks with God, found out by a Spiritual-Traveller, whose Face towards Mount-Sion above was set.   [London], Printed for D. Edwards, 1694. 38 pages. L 783. EEB Reel 1743:10.

The title of this work derives from Genesis 5.22: "Enoch walked with God, and was not, for God took him." Lead argues for total communion with God based on the renunciation of earthly concerns and gifts accompanying communion: revelation, vision, the Kingdom of the Power. Lead also refers to the laying on of hands.

397B Lead, Jane (Ward). A Fountain of Gardens, Watered by the Rivers of Divine Pleasure, and springing up in all the variety of Spiritual Plants.   Three Vols. London, Printed for F. Bradford, 1696-1701. L 783aA*, L 783B, L 784. EEB Reel 1674:2.

In this spiritual diary Lead describes and interprets her visions and dreams. She presents discussions with the fictive Sophia, a mythical figure representing wisdom, complementing the male deity. Lead's magnum opus is stylistically imaginative: A predominant image of female power is the tree of life which supports an eagle's nest inhabited by Eve. The work is typical of spiritual autobiographies of the period.

398B Lead, J[ane] (Ward). The Heavenly Cloud now breaking. London, Printed for the Author, 1681. 40 pages. L 785. EEB Reel 1703:23.

Lead's spiritual guide identifies reason as the true enemy of faith. Lead describes a mystical ascent of the soul to the Mount of Glory and includes a scene of Christ prone on a table surrounded by followers. God's bound offspring ascend, as spirits leave behind the constraints of rationality. Lead calls herself God's messenger and "the oppressed and desolated Daughter of Sion."

399B [Lead, Jane (Ward).]   The Laws of Paradise given forth by wisdom to a translated Spirit. [London], Printed and sold by T. Sowle, 1695. 79 pages. L 786. EEB Reel 1785:2.

Lead claims divine laws are offered in ten "particulars," akin to the biblical Ten Commandments. The primary distinction seems to be their delivery by a divine female being representing virginal wisdom. Excerpt: "Thou shalt own, and bear witness to the True God, manifested through his Virgin Wisdom, as come to restore Nature to its own Eternal Originality which consisted in Light, Purity and Power."

400B [Lead, Jane Ward.]   A Message to the Philadelphian Society Whithersoever dispersed over the whole Earth. Two Parts. [London], Printed and sold by J. Bradford, 1696. L 787.

Lead addresses the sect she founded, dedicated to brotherly and sisterly love. She encourages them to "wait in the Unity of pure Love" for Christ's return. Lead employs wedding imagery, with Christ assuming the role of bridegroom and the sect members as virgin bride. She stresses that like the Virgin Mary, she (a virgin) can provide the leadership needed by the Society. Emphasis is on cleanliness and freedom. Three messages are actually included in this volume.

401B [Lead, Jane Ward.]   A Messenger of An Universal Peace. London, 1698. 72 pages. L 788.

Lead announces a New Jerusalem will be established on earth, and God's spirit will be offered to all "without distinction of Sex, Age or Person." She claims God's original message has been lost in the "decay of pure and primitive Christianity." Lead compares the coming emancipated generation to Adam in his innocence. She predicts progress towards the New Jerusalem between 1696 and 1700.

402B [Lead, Jane.]   The Revelation of Revelations Particularly as an essay towards the unsealing, Opening and discovering the Seven Seals. London, Printed for A. Sowle, 1683. 130 pages. L 789. EEB Reel 1507:11.

In this complex commentary on the Apocalypse, Lead says one must break the seven seals: success in the spirit of faith, peace taken from earthly life, the end of plenty among saints, etc. She claims salvation cannot be attained through earthly wisdom, and people are but living stones gathered to Christ, the cornerstone.

403B [Lead, Jane Ward.]   A Revelation of the Everlasting Gospel-message, which shall never cease to be Preached Till the Hour of Christ's Eternal Judgement.

London, Printed and are to be sold by the Booksellers, 1697. 39 pages. L 789A.
EEB Reel 1743:11.

Lead claims she has withheld her revelations, fearing an unfair reception: "...if
it be a Woman, who can therefore have no authority, and against whom many
not Unjust Prejudices do lie." Hoping to discourage opposition to her view of
God's love, she includes an elaborate dream/meditation sequence beginning
with a visit to the regions of the dead. Lead discusses the Second Coming,
punishments and rewards in the afterlife and a distinctively apocalyptic vision
of creation. She emphasizes childlike vulnerability in approaching a loving, not
a wrathful, deity.

404B [Lead, Jane Ward.]   The Signs of the Times: forerunning the Kingdom of
Christ and evidencing when it is come.   London, 1699.   48 pages.   L 790.   EEB
Reel 1743:12.

Lead addresses "Christ's flock," members of the Philadelphian sect. She presents
evidence that Christ's return is nigh, an event they eagerly await. She warns
divisiveness among His followers may delay Christ's coming. Among the signs
she describes are a golden head, three monarchs seated on their thrones, and
the decadence of the age, originally prophesied in the Bible.

405B Lead, Jane Ward (introduction).   Theologia Mystica, or, The Mystic Divinite of
the Aeternal Invisibles.   London, 1683.   162 pages.   P 2968.   EEB Reel 847:30.

This work was written by Behemenist John Pordage, although the nine-page
introduction is signed by J. L. (Jane Lead).   Lead was Pordage's "Second
Prophetess."

406B Lead, Jane Ward.   The Tree of Faith: or, The Tree of Life springing up in the
Paradise of God.   London, Printed and sold by J. Bradford, 1696.   222 [122] pages.
L 791.

Lead criticizes established religious institutions and asserts their uselessness in
attaining salvation.   She notes part of this work is an account of her own
spiritual travels.   The vision of the title is a tree of faith "which spread forth its
Branches for increase and fruitfulness," so the spirit of the Eagle could build
its nest.   There is much reproductive and feminine imagery in the volume.

407B Lead, J[ane] (Ward).   The Wars of David, and the Peaceable Reign of
Solomon...Set Forth in Two Treatises.   London, Printed by J. Bradford, 1700.   27
pages.   L 791A.

This work contains two treatises originally published in Holland and a
biographical introduction by Lead's publisher.   The treatises are "An Alarm to
the Holy Warriors" and "The Glory of Sharon."   Both center on religious
symbols that appeared to Lead during her final lengthy illness.   In "Alarm" she
describes a white horse and rider, symbols of faith, and a mill overflowing with
golden grain, symbolizing paradise.   It is a journal dated during her illness from
October of 1699 until January of 1700.   In "Glory" Lead says Christ spoke to
her, then a rose appeared, symbolizing good health.   She contrasts the purity
and beauty of future life with the pain and suffering of mortality.

408B [Lead, Jane Ward.] <u>The Wonders of God's Creation manifested in the variety</u> <u>of eight worlds</u>. [London], Printed and sold by T. Sowle, [1695?]. 89 pages. L 792.

Lead contends there are eight regions for human souls. She claims Christ revealed them to her, and she is sure of their existence, even though they are not described in scripture. Christ also warned Lead the earth is ready to give up the dead. She presents an elaborate description of the eight worlds, ranging from hell to earthly realms and, finally, to heavenly ones.

409B Leigh, Dorothy. <u>The Mothers Blessing. Or, The Godly counsell of a</u> <u>Gentlewoman, not long since deceased, left behind her for her children. Containing</u> <u>many good exhortations, and good Admonitions, profitable for all Parents to leave</u> <u>as a legacy to their children</u>. London, Printed by E. Cotes for Andrew Crooke, 1656. 244 pages. L 980*. EEB Reels 1704:4, 1743:22, 1744:1, 1744:2.

This religious homily is dedicated to Elizabeth, daughter of James I. Leigh encourages her children--all sons--to dedicate themselves to God and to shun earthly pursuits. This book was originally published c.1621 and went through fifteen editions during the seventeenth century. It was used as a catechism for children by many women during the period.

[Levingston, Anne.] <u>The State of the Case in Brief</u>. See 817A.

410B Lilburne, Elizabeth (Dewell). <u>To the Chosen and betrusted Knights, Citizens,</u> <u>and Burgesses, assembled in the High and Supream Court of Parliament. The</u> <u>Humble Petition of Eliz. Lilburne, Wife to Lieut. Col. John Lilburne</u>. [London, 1646.] Broadside. L 2077.

Lilburne was the devoted wife of John Lilburne, Republican leader of the extremist Levellers. This petition argues there are legal and constitutional precedents supporting Lilburne's contention her husband's abuse was illegal. It includes a discussion of the English concept of liberty.

[Lilburne, Elizabeth.] <u>Elizabeth Lilburne...against William Carr...The case</u>. See 326A.

411B Lisle, Alicia. "The Lady Lisle, at Winchester in September 1685." In <u>The Dying</u> <u>Speeches of Several Excellent Persons, who Suffered for their Zeal against Popery,</u> <u>and Arbitrary Government</u>. London, 1689. 2 pages. Item: N.I.W. Collection: D 2957. EEB Reel 491:4.

This document purportedly contains the final words of a woman beheaded for offering shelter to a Non-conformist minister. She denied her guilt and forgave Colonel Penruddock, who had arrested her and whose father had been sentenced to death by her husband, a member of Cromwell's House of Lords. Although she was originally sentenced to burn at the stake, she petitioned James who granted her wish to die by beheading. See also 312A.

<u>A Living Testimony from the power and spirit of our Lord Jesus Christ in our faithful</u> <u>Womens meeting</u>. See 374A.

412B Love, [Mary Stone.] <u>Love's Name Lives: Or, A Publication of divers Petitions presented by Mistris Love to the Parliament, in behalf of her Husband</u>. London, 1651. 15 pages. L 3141*. EEB Reel 389:4.

This publication includes copies of letters exchanged by Mary Love and her husband, an imprisoned minister. Mrs. Love tried to get his sentence either waived, reduced or postponed. She asked that his execution be delayed until their baby was born, but her requests were denied. The text includes letters from ministers jailed with him.

<u>Love Letters between Polydorus</u>. See 542A.

413B [Lynam, Margaret.] <u>The controversie of the Lord against the Priests of the Nations and Teachers of the People</u>. [London], 1676. 22 pages. L 3564. EEB Reel 719:36.

Quaker Lynam warns readers: "Howl and mourn, for your Desolation hasteneth." She addresses those who deny "the Power of God," even though they have professed religion. She criticizes ministers who pretend to know the Lord for self-serving reasons. Lynam calls herself God's messenger and cautions God's wrath will be visited upon those who "abide in the flesh."

414B L[ynam], M[argaret]. <u>For the Parliament sitting at Westminster</u>. [London? 1659.] Broadside. L 3564aA.

Lynam laments the treatment of Quaker missionaries in New England. She beseeches Parliament, "who hath hid your selves in osbscurity for a long time," to repent and "hearken to the cry of the oppressed within you."

415B Major, Elizabeth. <u>Honey on the Rod: or a Comfortable Contemplation for one in Affliction</u>. London, Printed by Tho. Maxey, 1656. 160 pages. M 305.

Major describes moral problems and situations, suggesting consoling passages from scripture. A similar, shorter document titled "Sin and Mercy Briefly Discovered" follows. It includes biographical material and "sundry poems" listed on the title page of <u>Honey in the Rod</u>. Major was raised by her father, worked as a servant, then returned home when she became lame. She comments on pride, drunkenness and other sins, emphasizing the "prison" of her own body.

416B [Makin, Bathshua Pell.] <u>An Essay to Revive the Antient Education of Gentlewomen, in Religion, Manners, Arts and Tongues</u>. London, Printed by J. D. to be sold by Tho. Parkhurst, 1673. 43 pages. M 309. EEB Reel 697:2.

In a prospectus for a secondary school at Tottenham High Cross, Makin bemoans the lack of advanced education available for women. She asks not for "female preeminence"; rather, she says men should dominate and women should "acquiesce." Makin recalls the golden age of Elizabeth when many women were educated. She says women excelled especially in languages, oratory, logic, philosophy, mathematics and poetry. Makin maintains gifted women should also learn domestic skills. In short, she argues for women's education on pragmatic grounds.

417B [Manley, Mary de la Riviere.]   Letters Written by Mrs. Manley. To which is Added a Letter from a supposed Nun in Portugal, to a Gentleman in France. [London], Printed for R. B., 1696. 88 pages. M 434. EEB Reel 36:5.

These fictionalized letters, published without Manley's permission, were supposedly written while she was traveling by public coach throughout England. The witty collection contains interesting descriptions of people and places. One letter by a nun is supposedly written in imitation of a similar work by Alcoforado.

418B Manley, Mary de la Riviere.   The Lost Lover; or, The Jealous Husband.   A Comedy.   London, Printed for R. Bently, F. Saunders, J. Knapton, and R. Wellington, 1696. 39 pages. M 435. EEB Reel 36:6.

Apparently responding to criticism, Manley claims to know her faults and promises to improve. She says writing is proper for females. The characters are Lady Young-Love (a vain, conceited old woman), Marina (her daughter), Sir Rustick Good-Heart (an ill-bred country gentleman), his son Wilmore, Belira (Wilmore's secret mistress), Sir Amorous Courtall and Wildman (Wilmore's son). Orinda, an "affected poetess," is an obvious reference to poet Katherine Philips.

419B Manley, Mary de la Riviere.   The Royal Mischief. A Tragedy. London, Printed for R. Bentley, F. Saunders, and J. Knapton, 1696. 48 pages. M 436. EEB Reel 36:7.

This play is dedicated to William, Duke of Devonshire. It also includes a tribute to Manley by Mary Pix. The setting is the Castle of Phofia in Libardian. Characters include Levan Adaian, Prince of Colchis; his uncle the Prince of Libardian; Osman, chief vizier; Ismael, cousin to Osman; Acmat, a eunuch; Bassima, Princess of Colchis; Homais, Princess of Libardian who is in love with Levan; and Selima, married to Osman.

420B [Marguerite de Valois.]   The Grand Cabinet-Counsels Unlocked.   London, Printed by R. M., 1656. M 593bA*. EEB Reel 607:5.

This item is the same as 423B.

421B Marguerite de Valois.   Heptameron, or the History of the Fortunate Lovers. London, Printed by F. L. for Nath: Elkins, 1654. 528 pages. M 593. TT Reel 188:E.1468(2).

This work contains eight journals, each comprised of several short tales. They are stories about a sick woman who, upon witnessing her husband kissing her chambermaid, became so enraged that she recovered; the continual repentance of a nun for losing her virginity before taking her vows; and the revenge in kind of a court lady whose husband made love to other women. Throughout the volume, the author addresses "Ladies."

422B Marguerite de Valois.   The History of Queen Margaret of Valoys.   London, Printed for R. H., 1649. M 593*. EEB Reel 466:2.

This item is a version of 423B.

423B Marguerite de Valois. The Memorialls of Margaret de Valoys, First Wife to Henry the Fourth, King of France and Navarre. London, Printed by R. H., 1641. 229 pages. M 595*. EEB Reels 466:3, 607:6, 1426:4, 1466:4, 1619:43 and 1620:1.

In this dramatic autobiography the author speaks of her youth, her devotion to her mother, and her marriage to Henry IV of France. She also discusses her Catholicism, fostered by a governess, and defends her actions during a controversy involving her brother, the Duke of Alenson. A good portion concerns the queen's role in French politics. This text was apparently published under several titles.

424B Maria to Henric, and Henric to Maria: or, The Queen to the King in Holland, and his Majesty's Answer; Two Heroic Couplets in Imitation of the Stile and Manner of Ovid. London, Printed for Joseph Knight, 1691. 12 pages. M 598. EEB Reel 466:5.

This long epistolary poem in two parts is attributed to a "lady." It was ostensibly written by the named figures (William Henry, or William III, and Mary II) to each other. This romanticized vision of their relationship includes references to William's role in the Dutch war with France. Written in baroque style, it includes many classical allusions.

425B. M[arsin], M. All the Chief Points Contained in the Christian Religion. London, Printed and are to be sold by J. Clark, E. Whitlock, and W. Reddish, 1697. 16 pages. Item: M 812*. EEB Reel 1574:36. Collection: M 813A EEB Reel 1406:6.

Marsin enumerates the basic tenets of Christianity, emphasizing salvation and grace, identifying God as the author of punishment but not sin. Excerpt: "...there is none that live in the perfection of good works, but shall be rewarded according to their works." This treatise is also titled A Short Collection of All the Heads of the Chief Points (433B). It is similar to 437B.

426B M[arsin], M. The Christian Belief, Showing What A Christian ought to Believe. London, Printed and sold by John Clarke, John Gwilliam, Mrs. Mitchel, and Mr. Gorin, 1697. [irregular pagination] Item: N.I.W. Collection: M 813A. EEB Reel 1406:6.

Marsin emphasizes the importance of inner spirituality, baptism and humankind's covenant with God. She notes the existence of "false faith"--confession without repentance. Marsin quotes at length from scripture to demonstrate the need for faith and total individual transformation.

427B Marsin, Mary. A Clear and Brief explanation upon the chief points in the New Testament, where by laying scripture to scripture, it is fully proved what it is to be a believer. London, Printed and sold by John Clarke, John Gwillim, Mrs. Mitchel and Mr. Gavin, 1697. 96 pages. Item: M 812A. EEB Reel 1639:6. Collection: M 813A. EEB Reel 1406:6.

Marsin argues against good works and for God's grace through faith as the means to salvation. She cites scriptural references and historical arguments for support. Marsin also notes Christ's rejection of many Jewish rituals.

428B Marsin, Mary. The Figurative Speeches: By Which God has Veiled his Secrets. London, Printed and sold by John Clarke, John Gwillim, Mrs. Mitchel, and Mr. Garin, 1697. 248 pages. Item: M 813. Collection: M 813A. EEB Reel 1406:6.

Marsin says her work will provide a key to the riddle of the scriptures and reveal what God wished to be veiled "until the end of the Time"--near to the Second Coming. Marsin notes the scripture omits mention of burning at Judgment Day but cites fire as one element of the body. This item is largely a linguistic analysis of projected events of the final days. The title page lists the author as "Mersen."

429B M[arsin], M[ary]. The First Book. [Seven Parts.] London, Printed and sold by Edward Pool, John Gwillim, Mrs. Mitchel, and Abel Roper, 1698. 627 pages. M 813A. EEB Reel 1406:6.

This volume contains seven of Marsin's works: The First Book: A Clear and Brief Explanation, Proving the near Approach of Christ's Kingdom, A Rehearsal of the Covenant of Moses, The Figurative Speeches, The Christian Belief, This Treatise Proving Three Worlds and Three Foundations, and A Short Collection of all the Heads of the Chief Points.

430B Marsin, Mary. A Full and Clear Account the Scripture gives of the deity. London, Printed, and sold by John Gouge at Mrs. Fabian, at John Clarks, and at John Gwillim's, 1700. 94 pages. M 813B. EEB Reel 1620:5.

This lengthy exegesis on the trinity emphasizes the three beings as the embodiment of the excellent characteristics of God. Marsin reiterates her conception of heaven as a state rather than a place. This book contains extensive biblical references.

431B M[arsin], Mary. The Near Aproach [sic] of Christ's Kingdom, Clearly proved by Scripture. London, Printed for M. M. and are to be sold by Tho. Fabian, 1696. 50 pages. Item: M 813C. EEB Reel 428:3. Collection: M 813A. EEB Reel 1406:6.

This tract, addressed to King William and Parliament, predicts Christ's impending return. Marsin calls herself a weak vessel to justify her presumption in writing. In her view, the immediate signal of Judgment Day is the restoration of Israel. Emphasis is on numerology and alleged biblical foreshadowing of the turbulent contemporary events in England, in the tradition of the writings of the Lady Eleanor Douglas. This item is called Proving the Near Approach of Christ's Kingdom in 429B.

432B Marsin, Mary. A Rehearsal of the Covenant by Moses made with the children of Israel, at Mount Horeb. [London, 1697.] [21] pages (incomplete). Item: M 813CA. Collection: M 813A. EEB Reel 1406:6.

Marsin says the covenant Moses made with God identified the Hebrews as a singular people. But the Christian elect are comprised of all who follow Christ, not just those descended from the tribes of Israel. Marsin uses the term "generation" for all children of Adam and claims their covenant with God concerns love for Him alone.

433B Marsin, M. A Short Collection of all the Heads of the Chief Points. London, Printed and are to be sold by J. Clark, E. Whitlock and W. Reddish, 1697. Item: N.I.W. Collection: M 813A. EEB Reel 1406:6.

This treatise is the same as 425B.

434B [Marsin, Mary.] Some of the Chief Heads of the most Miraculous Wonders, that have of late been in Christendom. [London, 1694?] [4] pages. M 813CB. EEB Reel 1763:9.

Dated from Jamaica in 1692, this document discusses a terrible earthquake which toppled masonry and stone buildings on the island. Marsin describes similar disasters in Sicily and Naples. Her conclusion: "These are the signs which the Lord gave us." Marsin warns all who seek the truth should acknowledge the significance of such natural phenomena.

435B M[arsin], M[ary]. This Treatise Proving Three Worlds. London, Printed for M. M. and are to be sold by Tho. Fabian and Henry Nelme, 1696. [159] pages. Item: N.I.W. Collection: M 813A. EEB Reel 1406:6.

Marsin discusses election, both absolute and conditional; God's mercy, eternal purpose, God's "foreknowledge" (particularly of Christ's martyrdom), etc. She says the Tree of Life represents Christ and the Tree of Knowledge, good and evil. Marsin maintains humans were originally immortal and perfectly righteous, and there was no election before creation.

436B Marsin, Mary. Truth vindicated against all Heresies, the Seed of the Woman, and the Seed of the Serpent Distinguished. Two Parts. Second Edition. London, Printed and sold by John Goudge at Mrs. Fabian, and at John Clarks, 1700. M 813D. EEB Reel 1128:3.

This religious treatise with many biblical allusions contains chapters about Adam's transgression, the light, election, rebirth, proof of Christ's divinity, agreement between the prophets and apostles, the trees of life and knowledge. There is very little about women.

437B Marsin, Mary. Two Sorts of Latter Days, Proved from Scripture. London, Printed and sold by J. Bradford, Mrs. Michael, and at John Guillum's, 1699. 46 pages. M 813E.

Marsin speaks of the inability of scholars to accept a single interpretation of the scriptures and maintains the simplicity of Christ's message. She encourages a return to the text and discourages dwelling on commentaries. Marsin speaks of afterlife as a state of salvation rather than a physical location. After Christ's coming, the earth is compared to a new garden, another Canaan. This is part two of 436B.

438B [Marsin, Mary.] The Womans Advocate. [London], Printed and sold by J. Clark, 1697. 16 pages. M 813F*. EEB Reel 1487:26.

This document is a prediction of the Second Coming and a call for renunciation of sinful behavior. Marsin argues although Eve's transgression led to women's greater affliction, men will rely on women in the final days preceding Judgment.

She says God "is no respecter of Persons, or Sex"; however, she wonders whether men may not choose to risk perdition rather than heed a woman's warning.

439B Martel, Margaret. A True Copy of the Paper Delivered by Margaret Martels own Hand, Before she went to the Place of Execution. July the 16th, 1697. London, Printed by Mary Edwards, [1697]. Broadside. M 817A.

Martel, a prisoner facing execution for murder, claims she committed crimes because she left the Catholic Church. She prays to Jesus, Mary and God for forgiveness of her sins. See also 374A.

440B Martel, Margaret. A true Translation of a Paper written in French, delivered by Margaret Martell to the Under-Sheriff at the Time...of her Execution...July 16, 1697. London, Printed for E. Mallet, 1697. Broadside. M 817B.

This document is essentially the same as 439B.

[Martindall, Anne.] A Relation of the Labour, Travail, and Suffering of that Faithful Servant of the Lord, Alice Curwen. See 253A.

441B [Masham, Damaris Cudworth, Lady.] A Discourse concerning the Love of God. London, Printed for Awnsham and John Churchill, 1696. 126 pages. M 905. EEB Reel 190:5.

Masham, a philosopher and author, was a friend of John Locke. This anti-papist tract, addressed to [John Norris] throughout, argues against the "Life of Contemplation" allegedly chosen by many Catholics. Masham discusses at length the role of reason and emotion in the love of God and humankind. The work is less religious and more cerebral than most by women. See also 654A, dedicated to Masham.

Mason, Margery, pseud. See 864A.

442B [Melvill, Elizabeth, Lady Culross.] Lady Culross Godlie Dreame, Complyit in Scotish Meter. Aberdene, Printed for E. Raban, 1644. 21 pages. M 1649.

This poem in Scottish dialect describes how a woman found relief from depression in religion.

443B [Montpensier, Anne Marie Louise d'Orleans.] The Characters or Pourtraicts of the Present Court of France. London, Printed by J. C. for Thomas Palmer, 1668. 135 pages. M 2507. EEB Reel 112:3.

This volume, ostensibly written for better understanding of the "affairs and interests" of France offers explanation, history, biography and anecdotes about court figures--from the king down. It is in turn sycophantic, chatty and factual.

444B [Moore, Mary.] Wonderfull News from the North. Or, a True Relation of the sad and Grievous Torments, Inflicted on the Bodies of three Children of Mr. George Muschamp...also the prosecution of said Witches. London, Printed by T. H. to be sold by Richard Harper, 1650. 28 pages. M 2581. TT Reel 95:E.618(10).

A child lost the use of its limbs, tongue, and jaw movement for sixteen weeks. Other children were also afflicted with symptoms typical of bewitching. Margaret White of Chatton confessed to having intercourse with the devil disguised as a man accompanied by a greyhound. She and Dorothy Swinow are accused of causing illnesses and death. Moore's own child is named as a victim of Swinow and her sister Jane.

445B Mordaunt, Elizabeth (Carey), Viscountess of County Down. The Private Diarie of Elizabeth Viscountess Mordaunt. R. Jocelyn, ed. Duncairn, [privately printed], 1856. N.I.W.

The author, the only daughter of Thomas Carey, was considered a great beauty. As wife to the royalist John Mordaunt, she bore eleven children. When her husband was condemned to death for conspiracy, she gained his release by appealing to Cromwell. The diary (1656-1678) is a record of events revealing Mordaunt as a self-effacing, religious woman of great fortitude.

446B More, Gertrude. The Holy Practices of a Divine Lover or the Saintly Ideots Devotions. Paris, Printed by Lewis de la Fosse, 1657. 330 pages. M 2631A. EEB Reel 445:20.

More was a nun in the order of our Ladies of Comfort and a grandchild of Sir Thomas More. She died in 1634 at twenty-seven. This compilation contains fifty-three occasional confessions and her other extant writings, mostly commentaries on patristic texts. (More cites Saints Catherine of Siena, Teresa, Gertrude and Bridget.)

447B More, Gertrude. The Spiritual Exercises of the most Vertuous and Religious...of the Holy Order...in Cambray. Augustine Baker, ed. Paris, Printed by Lewis de la Fosse, 1658. 112, 312 pages. M 2632. EEB Reel 1312:18.

This item is essentially the same as 446B.

448B Morton, Anne Douglas, Countess of. The Countess of Morton's Daily Exercise: Or, a book of Prayers and Rules. Seventeenth Edition. London, Printed by J. H. for Luke Meredith, 1696. [Various pagings.] M 2817*. EEB Reel 1364:7.

This book, originally published in 1692, is dedicated to two noble women who used it for religious observance. It includes the litany, rules, and daily and occasional prayers.

449B M[udd], A[nn.] A Cry, a Cry: A Sensible Cry for Many Months Together hath been in my Heart. London, 1678. 7 pages. M 3037. EEB Reel 1019:4.

This tract is addressed to Quakers, who are "backsliding," falsehearted," "fat and full" and "rich." Mudd entreats them to turn from "self-conceitedness"; she alleges their meetings are meant "to exalt your Selves and make You seem more holy than You are." This highly critical piece utilizes images of plague and famine. A postscript, "formerly writ by another," is included.

450B Newcastle, Margaret Cavendish, Duchess of.   De Vita et Rebus Gestis Nobilissimi Illustrissimque Principis Guilielmi Duci Novo-Castrensis, Commentarii. London, Execudebat T. M., 1668. 235 pages. N 848. EEB Reel 430:10.

Walter Charleton translated into Latin the duchess' life of her husband William, Duke of Newcastle. The appendix contains some of the author's observations.

451B Newcastle, Margaret Cavendish, Duchess of.   The Description of a New World. London, Printed by A. Maxwell, 1666. 122 pages. N 849*. EEB Reel 1509:10.

Cavendish's fantasy describes the adventures of a woman shipwrecked in the South Seas. After being rescued by the natives, she visits Paradise where she marries an emperor. She questions the natives about local customs and their views of nature. Cavendish uses this interchange as a vehicle to display her own knowledge of science.

452B Newcastle, Margaret Cavendish, Duchess of. Grounds of Natural Philosophy. Second Edition. London, Printed for A. Maxwell, 1668. 311 pages. N 851. EEB Reel 468:11.

This volume is the second edition of Philosophical and Physical Opinions.

453B Newcastle, Margaret Cavendish, Duchess of. "Letters of Margaret Lucas to William Cavendish." In William Cavendish. The Phanseys of William Cavendish, Marquis of Newcastle...and her Letters in Reply. Douglas Grant, ed. London, Printed for Nonesuch Press, 1956. [22] pages. N.I.W.

Margaret Lucas expresses wariness of William Cavendish's love and fears the queen might oppose their union. She is affectionate, but not subordinate. Shyness is revealed in her reluctance to be too forthright. Cavendish, in distinction, is passionate, writing daily poems to his beloved, stressing that his seasoned love is dependable.

Newcastle, Margaret Cavendish, Duchess of.   The Life of... William Cavendishe. See 464B.

454B Newcastle, Margaret Cavendish, Duchess of.   Natures Pictures drawn by Fancies Pencil. London, Printed for J. Martin and J. Allestrye, 1656. [404] pages. N 855*. EEB Reel 1575:38.

This work is a collection of verse commentaries about love, constancy, courage, the civil wars, and other topics. The ninth book is the same as the Female Oracle, published in 1766.

455B Newcastle, Margaret Cavendish, Duchess of. Observations upon Experimental Philosophy. To which is added, the Description of a New Blazing World. Four Parts. London, Printed for A. Maxwell, 1666. N 857*. EEB Reel 1532:17.

Cavendish says if her writing is a disease, she hopes it is a one of wit. She defends her opposition to the ideas of many "eminent and ingenious writers," claiming her motive is to discover the truth. She alludes to women's potential, but laments their lack of education. Among her topics are sense and perception, atoms, flying, the production of fire by flint, the eyes of flies, the nature of water, the seeds of vegetables and the Cartesian theory of motion. The second item is the same as 451B.

456B Newcastle, Margaret Cavendish, Duchess of. Orations of Divers Sorts, Accommodated to Divers Places. [London], Printed by A. Maxwell, 1662. 309 pages. N 859*. EEB Reel 1364:12.

This treatise on moral philosophy includes essays about friendship, truth, pride and the role of women. In "Female Orations," the Duchess offers several short dialogues which posit opposing views of women's status, while presenting some of the earliest examples of feminist writings. Cavendish comments on marriage, childbirth, and the nature and intellect of women. The text is somewhat ambiguous and fragmented.

457B Newcastle, Margaret Cavendish, Duchess of. The Philosophical and Physical Opinions. London, Printed by Thomas Roycroft for J. Martin and J. Allestrye, 1655. 174 pages. N 863*. EEB Reel 1489:37.

This early early work, dedicated to fame, is comprised of brief statements about topics in natural science: external matter, matter and motion, power, perfection, the unities, vacuum, pleasure, pain, the mind. The author questions an original motion and describes the characteristics of humans and animals.

458B Newcastle, Margaret Cavendish, Duchess of. Philosophical Fancies. London, Printed by Tho. Roycroft, for J. Martin and J. Allestrye, 1653. 94 pages. N 865. TT Reel 189:E.1474(1).

The duchess offers the usual apologies for her work, noting she wrote it in three weeks. Introductory dedications are to time, her brain, "troubled fancy." In brief essays, she comments on physical phenomena, emphasizing the underlying unity of nature. Topics include decay, death, motion, matter, sense and so on.

459B Newcastle, Margaret Cavendish, Duchess of. Philosophical Letters, or Modest Reflections Upon some Opinions in Natural Philosophy maintained by several Famous and Learned Authors of this Age, Expressed by way of Letters. London, 1664. 543 pages. N 866. EEB Reel 542:10.

In epistolary essays Cavendish discusses the writings of prominent philosophers--Descartes, Hobbes, More and van Helmont. She exchanges introductory notes with her husband. The text purports to explain 457B. Cavendish says she is "uncapable of Learning" and suggests "It is better to write wittily then [sic] learnedly." She claims her opinions are her own and requests fair criticism.

460B Newcastle, Margaret Cavendish, Duchess of. Plays, Never before Printed. Five Parts. London, Printed for A. Maxwell, 1668. N 867. EEB Reel 674:2.

Cavendish claims her books are intended for "future Ages," says she writes "for my own pleasure, and not to please others," and alludes to the alleged envy and malice of critics. This volume includes several comedies: The Sociable companions, or The Female Wits; The Presence, Scenes (an appendix to The

Presence), The Bridals, The Convent of Pleasure, and A Piece of a Play (the latter intended for Blazing-World). Their significance, especially The Convent of Pleasure, lies in Newcastle's positive portrayal of female scholars in a women's-college setting.

461B Newcastle, Margaret Cavendish, Duchess of. Playes Written by the Thrice Noble, Illustrious and Excellent Princess, the Lady Marchioness of Newcastle. London, Printed by A. Warren for John Martyn, James Allestry, and Thomas Dicas, 1662. 679 pages. N 868. EEB Reel 502:11.

Cavendish apologizes for her plays, calling them "dull dead statues." She admits she has not observed the unities, discusses the function of theatre and how to read plays (as if spoken), and claims her husband has illustrated the work, although no drawings accompany this edition. Plays: Loves Adventures, The Several Wits, Youth's Glory, and Death's Banquet, The Lady Contemplation, Wit's Cabal, Unnatural Tragedy, The Publick Wooing, Matrimonial Trouble, Natures Three Daughters, Beauty, Love, and Wit; The Religious, The Comical Hash, Bell in Campo, A Comedy of the Apocriphal [sic] Ladies and The Female Academy.

462B Newcastle, Margaret Cavendish, Duchess of. Poems and Fancies. London, Printed by T. R. for J. Martin and J. Allestrye, 1653. 214 pages. N 869*. EEB Reel 503:1.

Cavendish calls upon other women to support her attempts to excel in a traditionally male endeavor--creative writing. She says since poetry reflects the imaginative and fanciful aspects of human nature, the emotionality of women suits the enterprise. Further, the poet need not be wise or accurate.

463B Newcastle, Margaret Cavendish, Duchess of. CCXI Sociable Letters. London, Printed for William Wilson, 1664. 453 pages. N 872. EEB Reel 1553:10.

These epistles present Cavendish's views of many subjects, including the position of women. She expresses indignation at their exclusion from the duties and perquisites of citizenship: "If we be no Citizens in the Commonwealth, I know no reason we should be subjects to the Commonwealth. And the truth is, we are no Subjects, unless it be to our Husbands." She reiterates a conventional idea--with "beauty, and other good Graces," each woman can gain power.

464B Newcastle, Margaret Cavendish, Duchess of. "A True Relation of the Birth." In The Life of...William Cavendishe. London, Printed for A. Maxwell, 1667. [43] pages. N 853*. EEB Reel 1467:5.

Appended to her husband's biography is the story of Cavendish's life marked by a happy childhood, close family relationships, a competent mother, and a typically "feminine" education ("singing, dancing, playing of music, reading, writing"). She comments on the Civil War's effect on the family and includes courtship letters exchanged by herself and the duke.

465B Newcastle, Margaret Cavendish, Duchess of. The Worlds Olio. [London], Printed for J. Martin and J. Allestree, 1655. 216 pages. N 873*. EEB Reel 503:2.

This work was published five years after its completion. Following her standard apologetic introduction ("It cannot be expected I should write so wisely or wittily as men"), Cavendish offers a paean to men, then says they tyrannize women--"using us either like Children, Fools, or subjects." She claims women have become "stupid" through lack of education. This book curiously combines feminist anger and praise of male achievements. See also 308A.

[Norfolk, Mary (Mordaunt) Howard, Duchess of.] His Grace the Duke of Norfolk's Charge against the Dutchess, before the House of Lords, and the Duchesses Answer. See 649A.

466B [Northumberland, Elizabeth Percy.] Meditations and Prayers. To be used Before, At, and After the Receiving the Holy Sacrement [sic]. Second Edition. London, Printed for William Nott, 1687. 119 pages. N 1308A*. EEB Reels 1730:28, 1749:2 and 1749:3.

This well written, cogent work begins with "Meditations on the Sacrament." It contains prayers and meditations for daily use. The perspective is High Church, although the author was a Presbyterian. She rejects the notion of transubstantiation during the eucharist, but maintains Christ's blood is present in the ceremony.

467B An Ode, Occasion'd by the Death of Her Sacred Majesty. By a Young Lady. London, Printed for Richard Cumberland, 1695. 12 pages. O 132. EEB Reel 723:11.

This ode was written in the first person upon the death of Mary II. The author employs many classical allusions, typical of elegiac form, but this poem is more sophisticated and philosophical than most of the period. Attributes of the deceased queen include her majestic bearing, courage and industriousness.

468B [Oliver, Elizabeth.] Catalogue of Valuable Books. [London], 1689. 28 pages. O 274 and C 1416. EEB Reel 1419:2.

The books listed are to be sold at auction "for the Benefit, and Entertainment of the Clergy, Gentry, and Citizens" and for profit. They span the disciplines of divinity, history, the humanities and philology.

Orinda, The Matchless. See Katherine Philips.

Osborne, Dorothy. See Temple, Lady Dorothy Osborne.

469B Overton, Mary. To the Right Honourable, the Knights, Citizens, and Burgesses, the Parliament of England, assembled at Westminster. The Humble Appeale and Petition of Mary Overton prisoner in Bridewell. [London], 1647. 14 pages. O 617. TT Reel 61:E.381(10).

Overton discusses the right to petition and Parliament's duty to uphold the "common liberties of the people." She says her husband was illegally apprehended for breaking press laws, and she was dragged through the streets and vilified by soldiers while carrying her infant. Overton cites various documents to support her position, including the Magna Carta and the due process statute of Edward III.

[Oxford, Wendy.] A Prospective for King and Subjects. See 731A.

470B The Parallel: An Essay on Friendship, Love and Marriage. [London], Printed for Henry Playford, 1689. 35 pages. P 333. EEB Reel 645:2.

This short essay explores the roles of friendship and love in marriage. Although there is no explicit statement of authorship, the work is clearly by a woman. The publisher describes her as "modest." She speaks of her "Tim'rous Muse" and asks for aid from the classical muses in language revealing her gender.

471B Parr, Susanna. Susanna's Apologie Against the Elders. [Oxford], Printed [by Henry Hall for T. Robinson], 1659. 114 pages. P 551. TT Reel 223:E.1784(2).

Parr wishes to exonerate herself after excommunication by Mr. Lewis Stuc[k]ley's church. She says "Weaknesse is entailed upon my Sex in generall...I am a despised worme, a woman full of naturall and sinfull infirmities." A Congregationalist, Parr claims she was excluded for listening to another minister and refusing to return without "the liberty of communion with other of Gods people in this city." See also 22A and Addendum 157, about another ostracism by this minister.

472B Partridge, Dorothy. The Woman's Almanack for...1694. London, Printed for J. S., 1694. [No pagination.] A 2016.

This poorly organized, semi-intelligible almanac contains no personal material.

A Pattern or President for Princes to Rule By. See 261B.

Patison, Barbara. A Warning from the Lord to the Teachers and People of Plimouth. See 385B.

[Patrick, Lynn.] The Virgin Mary misrepresented by the Roman Church. See 689A.

473B Penington, Mary Proude. A Brief Account of my Exercises from my Childhood: Left with my Dear Daughter, Gulielma Maria Penn. Philadelphia, 1848. 39 pages. N.I.W.

Penington (1625-1682) was the daughter of Sir John Proude of Kent. She was twice married--first to Sir William Springett, a colonel in the Parliamentary army during the Civil War, and then to Isaac Penington, a Quaker. The first part of this autobiography concerns Penington's conversion to Quakerism, while the second is a letter to her grandson about her life with his grandfather (Springett). It tells of Penington's religious experiences, financial woes and family illness. Gulielma Maria was the wife of William Penn.

474B Penington, Mary Proude. Experiences in the Life of Mary Penington. Norman Penne, ed. Philadelphia, The Biddle Press; London, Headley Brothers, n.d. [modern edition] 116 pages. N.I.W.

This text similar to 473B except the editor modified Penington's style somewhat. "Abstract of the will of Mary Penington, dated 18th July, 1680," appended to this edition, is based on Some Account of Circumstances in the Life of Mary Penington (London, 1821).

475B [Pennyman, Mary (Heron).] The Ark is begun to be Opened. London, 1671. 14 pages. P 1403. EEB Reel 1039:4.

This item was written by John (listed as author in the Wing STC) and Mary Pennyman at the request of others. Mary says after eight years of widowhood, the Lord willed she marry Pennyman. She may have left her children, causing the disapproval of Quakers who interrupted the wedding celebration. The story is interspersed with religious passages.

476B Pennyman, Mary (Heron), ed. John Pennyman's Instructions to his Children. London, Printed and are to be given by the author, or to be had at Dorman Newman's shop, 1674. P 1407. EEB Reel 1039:7.

This volume is edited by Mary Pennyman.

477B Pennyman, Mary (Heron). Some of the Letters and Papers which were written by Mrs. Mary Pennyman, Relating to an Holy and Heavenly Conversation, in which she lived to her Dying-Day. London, 1700/01. 48 pages. N.I.W.

John Pennyman collected these writings after Mary's death. They contain her religious experiences, preservation from fire and plague in the mid-60s, hypocrisy among the Quakers, advice to her children and various letters.

478B P[ennyman], M[ary] (Heron). Something formerly writ foreseen and foretold. [London], 1676. 7 pages. P 1429. EEB Reel 1448:15.

This Quaker tract is a typical call to accept Christ. Pennyman says one should not rely on churches for salvation, but "to walk inwardly with God--is that State of a Spiritual Man."

479B Perrot, Lucy. An Account of Several Observable Speeches of Mrs. Lucy Perrot the late Wife of Mr. Robert Perrot of London, Minister. London, Printed for R. P., 1679. 35 pages. P 1643.

Perrot's words were recorded without her knowledge and published posthumously. The text is comprised primarily of religious ruminations about her life and reflects her attitudes towards children, death and pain. It is written primarily in the third person.

480B Pettus, Katherine. Katherine Pettus, plaintiffe, Margaret Bancroft, Defendant in Chancery. [London, 1654.] Broadside. P 1913. EEB Reel 1659:18 and TT Reel 246:669.f.19(30).

Pettus tried to sue Margaret Bancroft for twenty-three years for an "orphans portion" left by her father Thomas Bancroft. Bancroft was jailed for denying Pettus her portion. Pettus asks for relief from debts since she cannot procure her inheritance. She filed a bill for the Relief of Creditors and Poor Prisoners.

481B [Philips, Joan.] Advice to His Grace. [London, c1681.] Broadside. P 2029. EEB Reel 472:8.

This letter, addressed to the Duke of Monmouth (illegitimate son of Charles II), discourages him from trying to claim the throne. Philips suppports James II and warns of factions ("that busy piggling crew") who wish to exclude him from the throne.

482B [Philips, Joan.] Female Poems on Several Occasions. Written by Ephelia. London, Printed by William Downing for James Courtney, 1679. 112 pages. P 2030*. EEB Reel 645:16.

This collection consists primarily of love poetry to "Stephon." Philips mentions "Orinda" (Katherine Philips) and dramatist/novelist Aphra Behn. requesting a man's friendship, Philips states: "Think me all Man: my Soul is Masculine/And Capable of as great Things as Thine."

483B P[hilips], K[atherine.] Poems. London, Printed by J. G. for Rich. Marriot, 1664. 242 pages. P 2032*. EEB Reels 286:8 and 1211:6.

This wide-ranging volume is by "The Matchless Orinda," one of the most popular female poets of the century. Some poems are for members of her literary society, while others express friendship toward women and use phraseology similar to love poetry. Though modest, Philips was a talented poet who wrote about accepted topics.

Philomela. See Rowe, Elizabeth Singer.

484B [Pix, Mary (Griffith).] The Beau Defeated: Or, the Lucky Younger Brother. A Comedy. London, Printed for W. Turner and R. Basset [1700.] 47 pages. P 2326. EEB Reel 1192:3.

Pix was one of a few female playwrights to gain attention during the late seventeenth century. She says this farce is in part a translation of a French play based on Dancourt's Le Chevalier a la Mode. The characters include Sir John Rover, the elder Clerimont (a country squire), the younger Clerimont, Mrs. Bracegirdle, Mrs. Landsworth, Mrs. Rich (a widow), and her niece Lucinda. The theme is "quality," defined in polite society as possession of a title. The action revolves around Mrs. Rich's preoccupation with quality and Lady Landsworth's attempt, while disguised as a prostitute, to marry a virtuous and witty man. The British Library attributes this play to Henry Barker.

485B [Pix, Mary (Griffith).] The Deceiver Deceived. A Comedy. London, Printed for R. Basset, 1698. 48 pages. P 2327. EEB Reel 506:3.

This play concerns the feigned blindness of Venetian senator Melito Bondi, who believes his malady will exempt him from paying taxes. Bondi thinks his wife Olivia (courted by Count Andrea) is unfaithful, and his daughter Ariana is unwilling to marry his designated suitor, Count Insulls. Olivia deduces her husband's ploy, and he is eventually hoist on his own petard. Ariana marries her lover, Fidelio, and Olivia proves her faithfulness.

486B Pix, Mary (Griffith). The False Friend, or, the Fate of Disobedience. London, Printed for Richard Basset, 1699. 60 pages. P 2328. EEB Reel 506:4.

This drama, dedicated to the Countess of Burlington, finds the hero Emilius in Sardinia with his new fiancee, Louisa. They decide that until his father, the Viceroy, is apprised of their plans, he will assume a disguise, and she will remain sequestered. The plot is complicated when Appamia, who secretly loves Emilius, tricks him into administering a poison to Louisa. In the end, the Viceroy vows to punish Appamia for her treachery.

487B Pix, Mary (Griffith). Ibrahim, the Thirteenth [Twelfth] Emperor of the Turks. A Tragedy. London, Printed for John Harding and Richard Wilkin, 1696. 41 pages. P 2329. EEB Reel 506:5.

This play is set in the Middle East. Sheker, favored mistress of the Sultan Ibrahim, loves the dashing General Amurat who, in turn, loves Morena. Their fathers agree to the betrothal. The wicked Ibrahim rapes Morena, notwithstanding a holy law against the act. Eventually he is murdered by an ally of Amurat, Morena poisons herself, and Amurat kills himself.

488B Pix, Mary (Griffith). The Innocent Mistress. London, Printed by J. Orme for R. Basset and F. Cogan, 1697. 52 pages. P 2330. EEB Reel 506:6.

In this comedy about forced marriage, the Lady Beauvlar and her brother Cheatall are guardians of Arabella. Their father had left a will requiring Arabella and Cheatall to marry to inherit his money. After a series of tricks and mistakes, Arabella and Beaumont (who truly loves her) are coupled.

489B Pix, Mary (Griffith). Queen Catharine: or, the Ruines of Love London, Printed for William Turner and Richard Basset, 1698. 52 pages. P 2331. EEB Reel 1099:3.

This drama revolves around Catherine of Valois, widowed in 1422 when Henry V died. Forbidden to remarry without her small son's permission, she apparently secretly married Owen Tudor, a Welsh squire. Pix offers a version of the story in which Edward IV, vowing revenge for Catherine's rejection of him, plots to thwart the lovers' plans and of the Queen's servant Isabella and her betrothed, the Duke of Clarence, a Plantagenet. The play, dedicated to Mrs. Cook of Norfolk, includes an epilogue by Catherine Trotter.

490B Pix, Mary (Griffith). The Spanish Wives. London, Printed for R. Wellington, 1696. 48 pages. P 2332. EEB Reel 396:7.

Pix claims this play is a burlesque of Ovid's epistles. The characters include the governor of Barcelona, a trusting husband; his wife, who is being courted by an English officer; his guest, the suspicious elderly Marquess of Moncada; his wife, Elenora; and Camillus, a Roman count who is pursuing her. In the end, the governor's wife remains true, while Camillus wins Eleanor. A satire on controlling, jealous husbands, the play is apparently borrowed from The Pilgrim, a Spanish novel.

491B [Pix, Mary (Griffith).] When I Languish'd...Song in the Innocent Mrs. [London], Printed for T. Cross, [1697?] Broadside. P 2333.

This song was written for Pix's play 488B. The heroine longs for a sign of interest from a prospective lover while inadvertently revealing her own coquettish nature.

492B A Poem on the Death of the Queen. By a Gentlewoman of Quality. London, Printed for R. Cumberland and to be sold by J. Whitlock, 1694/5. 4 pages. P 2692. EEB Reel 1408:20.

This elegy for Mary II is similar to those written by men. It deplores Albion's [England's] great loss and recounts the poet's vision of Mary in heaven riding in a chariot surrounded by angels. Female authorship is questionable because the poet does not comment on her or Mary's womanhood and attends primarily to William.

493B Poole, E[lizabeth.] An Alarum of War, Given to the Army, and to their High Court of Justice. [Two Parts.] [London], 1649. 14 pages. P 2808*. TT Reel 24:E.555(23) and (24).

Radical sectarian Poole speaks directly to the army whose authority she questions. Poole uses her faith as a shield against the power of Parliament and the army, which has threatened her bodily harm. She says "To the pretended Church, and Fellowship of Saints, in London who pursued me with their weapons of Warre, to shoot me to death at the General Councell of the Army, not regarding the Babe Jesus in mee, Greeting." Poole also speaks against execution of Charles I.

494B Poole, Elizabeth. A Vision wherein is manifested the disease and cure of the Kingdome. London, 1648 [1649]. 6 pages. P 2810. TT Reel 83:E.537(24).

This fascinating broadside reproduces a speech delivered before the Council of War on December 29, 1648. Poole asks this body to address the condition of the country, which she likens to "a woman crooked, sick, weak and imperfect in body." Poole reminds them of their obligation to keep the public trust. She refers to the king's loss of authority and concedes Charles I should be tried, although she opposes his physical punishment.

495B P[ope], M[ary]. Behold Here is a Word, Or an Answer to the late Remonstrance of the Army...Answer to a Book, cal'd the Foundation of the Peoples Freedomes. [Two Parts.] [London], Printed and to be sold by Mrs. Edwards, 1649. 18 pages. P 2903. TT Reel 84:E.539(8) and (10).

Pope, a young woman from Nottinghamshire, holds the king responsible for the Civil War and calls him a traitor. She predicts the end of the war. Excerpt: "And that mens backs or rather estates have been broken in pieces, and their hearts too almost at the sad events."

496B P[ope], M[ary]. A Treatise of Magistracy. [London], 1647. 131 pages. P 2904. TT Reel 66:E.417(13).

Pope challenges the Presbyterian and Independent view that the magistrate is not the chief officer of the church. She discusses the trinity, bishops, deacons, the sabbath, John the Baptist, the ark and various sacraments. She also addresses Parliament, decrying the length of the war and its effect on taxation and trade. She requests her document, which took three years to write, be examined by three or four "godly" men and volunteers to answer questions about it.

497B [Elizabeth Powys.] A Ballad upon the Popish Plot. [London, 1679-80.] Broadside. P 3118/G 75. EEB Reel 1449:8.

This royalist poem in three parts was to be sung to the tune of "Packington's Pound." Excerpt: "They scorn to submit to Scepter and Crown;/And into confusion, or Common-wealth turn,/A People that Hastens to be undone." Although originally attributed to Powys, the song may have been penned by John Gadbury.

498B [Pretty, Miss.] An Elegy upon the Death of that Worthy Gentleman Mr. Peter Pretty. The Son of a Divine. From his sister. London, [1679]. Broadside. P 3320A.

The author praises her brother's noble character, regretting he died a virgin and left no children who might reflect his image. She describes their sibling affection and praises the children of the minister. The Houghton Library, Harvard University, attributes this work to "Miss Pretty."

499B Quarles, Ursula. "A Short Relation of the Life and Death of Mr. Francis Quarles, by Ursula Quarles, his Sorrowful Widow." In Francis Quarles. Solomon's Recantation. London, Printed by M. F. for Richard Royston, 1645. 6 pages. Item: N.I.W. Collection: Q 116*. EEB Reel 773:22.

Quarles discusses her husband's ancestry and education (Christ's College, Cambridge). He was an author and Chronologer to London--religious, courteous, discreet, patient, charitable, studious and forgiving. His dying words were "God will be a husband to the Widow." She declines to judge his published work for two reasons: incompetence because of her sex and bias because of their close relationship. They had eighteen children. Quarles also edited her husband's Judgement and Mercie for Afflicted Souls (1646).

The Queens Majesties declaration and desires. See 742A.

500B R., S. A Tender Visitation of Love to Professors and Profane, But especially to the Inhabitants of the Town of Waymouth. Being written from the breathings of life by a handmaid of the Lord, S. R. London, Printed for Thomas Simmons, 1661. 14 pages. R 77.

The author warns the inhabitants of Weymouth of their possible damnation if they ignore their consciences and continue to mock the Lord. She notes they have not heeded many ominous signs; she claims "Babylon" must be destroyed if its sinners are to be saved. She also speaks of Christ as the husband of women. Finally, she notes the Lord cares not for sabbath or feast days.

Radford, Eleanor. Memoirs of the Life and Character of...Mrs. Eleanor Radford. See 512B.

501B Redford, Elizabeth. A Warning, a Warning from the Lord in mercy to the people, to see if they will yet seek him. [London, 1696.] 8 pages. R 661.

In this Quaker call for repentance, Redford says the cries of the poor and distressed are growing and must be heard.

502B Redford, Elizabeth. A Warning from the Lord to the City and Nation, in mercy to the people, to see if they will yet seek him. [London?, 1695.] Broadside. R 661A.

This item is essentially the same as 501B.

503B Redford, Elizabeth. The Widow's Mite, Humbly Offer'd, not impos'd. [London, 1690?] 36 pages. R 662.

This involved argument contends the seventh day of the week should be the sabbath for Christians and Jews.

504B Richardson, Elizabeth. A Ladies Legacie to her Daughters. In Three Books. London, Printed for Tho. Harper, 1645. 168 pages. R 1382. TT Reel 251:E.1165(4).

The author was the widow of Sir Thomas Richardson, Lord Chief Justice of the King's Bench. This volume is dedicated to her six daughters and four daughters-in-law. She apologizes for publishing these forty-eight brief prayers or petitions to God because she worries some will find such an act "contemptible" for a woman. Yet she argues: "the matter is but devotions, or prayers, which surely concerns and belongs to women, as well as to the best learned men."

505B Rolph, Alice. To the chosen and betrusted Knights, Citizens and Burgesses, assembled in Parliament...The humble petition of Alice Rolph, wife to Major E. Rolph, close prisoner at the Gate House. Broadside. [London, 1648.] R 1889. TT Reel 246: 669.f.12(73).

Rolph says two conspirators lied, claiming the army wanted to poison the king and that her husband was involved in the plot.

506B [Rone, Elizabeth.] A Reproof to those Church Men or Ministers that Rejected the Kings most Gracious Declaration. [London?], Printed for Elizabeth Rone, 1688. Broadside. R 1914A. EEB Reel 1293:7.

This poem attacks Tory ministers who refused to read the king's 1688 declaration in their pulpits (presumably the Declaration of Indulgence of James II, which suspended the penal laws against Roman Catholics and dissenters). Rone maintains they should obey the king's laws and expect strong criticism for failing to do so.

507B [Rowe, Elizabeth Singer.] Poems on Several Occasions. Written by Philomela. London, Printed for John Dunton, 1696. [Divided pagination: 1-72, 11-69.] R 2062.

Rowe's collection of poetry has some feminist content, but it is generally about individuals. Rowe comments on the Athenian Society pastorals and paraphrases classics like Ovid's Metamorphosis. Earlier poems reveal an attraction to men and an interest in romantic themes, while her later work emphasizes liberty and independence. From Elizabeth Johnson's preface: "We complain, and we think with reason, that our <u>Fundamental Constitutions</u> are destroyed [when men refuse education to women]; that here's a plain and an open design to render us meer Slaves, perfect <u>Turkish Wives</u>, without Properties, or Sense or Souls."

508B Rowlandson, Mary White. <u>The Sovereignty and Goodness of God...Being a Narrative of the Captivity and Restauration of Mrs. Mary Rowlandson</u>. Cambridge [Massachusetts], Printed by Samuel Green, 1682. 73 pages. R 2093. EEB Reel 399:10.

A Connecticut minister's wife was captured by a group of Indians. She describes the act and the conditions of her captivity. The unrelated last sermon of her deceased husband is appended.

509B Rowlandson, Mary White. <u>A True History of the Captivity and Restoration of</u>. London, 1682. R 2094.

This item is the same as 508B.

<u>The Royal Wanton</u>. See 31A.

510B Russell, Rachel, Lady. <u>Some Account of the Life of Rachel Wriothesley Lady Russell...followed by A Series of Letters from Lady Russell to her Husband William Lord Russell from 1672 to 1682</u>. London; Longman, Hurst, Rees, Orme and Brown, 1819. 110 pages. N.I.W.

Rachel Wriothesley was the daughter of Lord Southampton and his first wife, Rachel de Ruvigny. She was married first to Francis, Lord Vaughan, who died in 1667, and then to Russell in 1669. Their warm and tender relationship is reflected in their correspondence. Russell was eventually arrested for his alleged complicity in the Rye House Plot. He was committed to the Tower and executed in 1683.

511B Sandilands, Mary. <u>A Tender Salutation of Endeared Love</u>. London, Printed for J. Bradford, 1696. 12 pages. S 654.

In this Quaker tract, Sandilands glorifies Christ, describing his suffering and "unspeakable" love for humankind. She encourages Friends to be an "Inward Retired People" to reflect God's spirit. She recalls Christ prepared the way for his followers and says they should follow his path.

512B Savage, Sarah. <u>Memoirs of the Life and Character of Mrs. Sarah Savage...to which are added, Memoirs of the Life and Character of Mrs. Anne Hulton and Mrs. Eleanor Radford</u>. John Bickerton Williams, ed. Philadelphia, Presbyterian Board of Publication, 1845. 360 pages. N.I.W.

This volume contains numerous excerpts from the journals of Savage, Hulton and Radford. Savage's private multi-volume diary begins in 1686 and covers most of her remaining years. (She died in 1752.) Much of it concerns her religious studies. Hulton (1668-1697) studied Latin, English and the Bible and wrote sermons. Her sister Eleanor Radford (1667-1697) also wrote sermons despite her frail constitution.

513B Schurman, Anna Maria van (of Utrecht). <u>The Learned Maid: or, Whether a Maid may be a Scholar?</u> London, Printed by John Redmayne, 1659. 55 pages. S 902. TT Reel 237:E.1910(3).

Dutch scholar Schurman argues for the education of bright upper-class Christian women. She suggests learning to gain integrity and experience greater love of God. The treatise utilizes logic, posing contradictory statements that refute her original premises. In addition to religious piety and household maintenance, Schurman encourages study of the "liberal arts," especially theology, rhetoric, grammar, physics, metaphysics, history, language, politics and scripture. She disapproves of law, military science or oratory for women. Schurman laments the lack of female educational institutions and women's absence from public office. She notes famous educated women along with the writings of male advocates of female education.

514B Scudery, [Madeline] de. <u>Almahide; or the Captive Queen</u>. [Three Parts.] London, Printed by J. M. for Thomas Dring, 1677. S 2142. EEB Reel 1732:7.

Scudery was a noted French novelist who encouraged women to pursue serious endeavors. Almahide, daughter of Don Pedro de Leon, Duke of Medina Sidonia is captured by pirates as a child. Most of the action focuses on a conflict between the Moors and the Spanish. The title page attribution is "Monsieur de Scudery, Governour of Notre Dame." The Library of Congress considers Scudery the "supposed author," although it may have been written by Georges and Marie de Scudery, her brother and sister-in-law. Or "Georges" may have been her pseudonym.

515B Scudery, Madeline de. <u>Amaryllis to Tityrus, Being the First Heroick Harangue of the Excellent Pen of Monsieur Scudery</u>. London, Printed for W. Cademan, 1681. 86 pages. S 2143. EEB Reel 511:14.

In this fiction the poet Vergil assumes the persona of the shepherd Thyrus, dissatisfied with his bucolic surroundings. His mistress Amarilus reproaches him for devaluing the country, reminds him of its appeal and attempts to persuade him of its superiority to the city. Two other pieces are included --"An Essay on Dramatic Poetry" (in praise of Dryden) and "Artemisia to Isocrates," the first of several heroic harangues.

516B [Scudery, Madeline de.] <u>Artamenes; or, The Grand Cyrus ...Romance</u>. Five Vols. London, Printed for J. Darby, R. Roberts, B. Griffin, and R. Everingham, 1691. S 2145*, S 2162. EEB Reels 292:2, 579:2 (Vol. 3) and 1157:1.

This lengthy romance contains song lyrics as well as descriptions of many battles and romantic intrigues. The translator claims Persian glory is now exceeded by the accomplishments of England. He also says de Scudery can relate history through her fiction more effectively than historians. Moreover, she avoids the exaggerations and jingoism of most romances. He says the novel is about the "Height of Prowess, intermix'd with Virtues and Heroick Love." It is attributed to "Monsieur de Scuderi," a pen name of Scudery.

517B [Scudery, Madeline de.] <u>Clelia, An Excellent New Romance</u>. [Five Parts.] London, Printed and are to be sold by H. Herringman, D. Newman, et al., 1678.

736 pages. S 2151-S 2156. EEB Reels 646:9, 10, 11; 578:7, and 1557:25 (Part Five).

In this lengthy romance two young lovers are separated after an earthquake. The heroine, Clelia, with many womanly virtues, travels through several countries and has many adventures, while her lover seeks her. The Roman Horatius is her primary suitor. The convoluted action involves political intrigue in Greece, Crete, Rome and Africa. The novel is attributed to "Monsieur George de Scudery."

518B Scudery, [Madeline] de. Conversations upon several subjects. [Two Vols.] London, Printed for H. Rhodes, 1683. 235 pages. S 2157. EEB Reel 646:12.

This work is dedicated to the Countess of Ossory. The essays are about various subjects: conversation, speech, pleasures, complaisance, idleness, raillery.

[Scudery, Madeline de and Camus, Jean Pierre.] Elise, or Innocencie Guilty. See 147A.

519B [Scudery, Madeline de.] Les Femmes Illustres or the Heroick Harrangues of the illustrious women. Edinburgh, Printed by Thomas Brown, James Glen and John Weir, 1681. 235 pages. S 2158*. EEB Reel 1130:6.

This compilation of speeches by classical and mythical heroines is addressed to the men in their lives, e.g., Cleopatra to Mark Antony, Octavia to Augustus. Some are directed to children, and all either teach virtue or explain why women must abide by their personal moral codes. The comments of Sappho to Ermina contain the most clearly feminist material; they urge women to eschew "false shame" and claim the "portion of women" comprises more than mere beauty. The text is attributed to "Monsieur de Scuddery," a pen name of Mlle. de Scudery.

520B [Scudery, Madeline de.] Ibrahim, or the Illustrious Bassa. Four Parts. London, Printed by J. R. and Sold by Peter Parker and Thomas Guy, 1674. 390 pages. S 2161*. EEB Reels 579:1 and 647:1.

This romance is about the exploits of Ibrahim Bassa, Grand Visior and governor of Constantinople. Except for the exotic setting, it is quite similar to other elaborate novels popular in seventeenth-century France. The preface notes it was written by Monsieur de Scudery, a pen name.

521B [Scudery, Madeline de.] A Triumphant Arch erected and consecrated to the Glory of the Feminine Sexe. London, Printed for William Hope and Henry Herringman, 1656. 229 pages. S 2163. EEB Reel 1130:6 and TT Reel 203:E.1604(4).

This text, by "Monsieur de Scuderi," is essentially the same as 519B.

[Scudery, Madeline de.] Zelinda: an Excellent new Romance. See 925A.

The Second Part of the Amours of Messalina. See 31A.

522B Sharp, Jane. The Midwives' Book, Or the whole Art of Midwifery discovered. London, Printed for Simon Miller, 1671. 418 pages. S 2969B.

Sharp's manual is based on extensive experience and her reading of similar continental handbooks. She presents standard descriptions of female anatomy and delivery procedures. Sharp defends the position of female midwives against the advance of men, who claimed to have a systematic, and thus a superior knowledge. Sharp believed women are naturally suited to midwifery, and it is their skill, "not hard words that perform the work." This guide went through four editions by 1725.

Shaw, Dorothy. [Writings.] See 801A.

523B Shaw, Hester. Mrs. Shaw's Innocency Restored, and Mr. Clendon's Calumny Retorted. London, Printed by T. M. for G. A. and may be had at Ralph Smith's, 1653. 30 pages. S 3018. EEB Reel 1770:19 and TT Reel 112:E.730(7).

Shaw answers Clendon's reply to 524B, repeating that he has refused to return her money. She includes accounts of witnesses, reproduces the minister's charges against her and, (apologizing for writing "in the plain style of a weak woman") defends her reputation.

524B Shaw, Hester. A plaine relation of my sufferings by that miserable combustion which happened in Tower Street. London, 1653. S 3019.

During an accidental gunpowder explosion, some valuables of midwife Hester Shaw were blown out of her home and taken to her neighbor's house for safekeeping. Clendon, a minister, returned most of them, but Shaw accused him of keeping some money. He and his wife maintained their innocence, while Shaw insisted upon their guilt. After Clendon condemned her as a slanderer, she published her view of the incident. The outspoken Shaw was supported by a number of her female friends.

She Ventures, and He Wins. See 11B.

Shinkin ap Shone. Shinkin ap Shone Her Prognostication for the Ensuing Year 1654. See 803A.

Shipton, Ursula [Mother]. See 730A.

Sicurus, Dorotheus, pseud. The Origine of Atheism. See 671A.

525B Simmonds, Martha (Calvert). A Lamentation for the lost Sheep of the house of Israel. London, Printed for Giles Calvert, 1655. 16 pages. S 3791. TT Reel 129:E.855(2).

This typical Quaker tract warns against turning against God. The most interesting sections contain Simmonds' criticisms of government. She demands the authorities cease their persecution of the Friends.

526B Simmonds, Martha (Calvert). O England; thy time is come. [London, 1656-65.] 16 pages. S 3793.

Short pieces by Simmonds appear along with those by other Quakers like Hannah Stranger and James Nayler. Simmonds attacks foolish virgins, who waste time in frivolous activities rather than seeking salvation. She strongly berates this "Generation of Unbelievers," who are unmindful of God's generosity in sending Christ to earth for their salvation. Simmonds advocates meekness and asks, "Why hath thy Rod been so light upon me, seeing my sins have been multiplied?"

527B Simmonds, Martha (Calvert).   When the Lord Jesus came to Jerusalem. London, 1655. Broadside. S 3794. TT Reel 246:669.f.19(73).

Simmonds claims the Lord built the city of Jerusalem, then wept because of the sin rampant within it. She says salvation must be considered during life on earth.

Simpson, Mary. Faith and Experience. See 219A.

528B Six Familiar Essays Upon Marriage, Crosses in Love, Sickness, Death, Loyalty, and Friendship. Written by a Lady. London, Printed for Tho. Bennet, 1696. 110 pages. A 4066/S 3912. EEB Reels 163:13 and 1579:15.

This work has been attributed to Mary Astell, and in places it resembles her writings; however, the author is less clearly feminist than Astell. Although she raises questions about women's status, she asks women to conform to social norms for their own happiness. She asks them to appreciate her work for "all woman-kinds" sake, but tells men: "I am one that never promotes Rebellion against your Arbitrary Sway." The style seems more terse and less philosophical than Astell's.

529B Skelton, Anne.   Comforts Against the Fear of Death: Being some short meditations composed by that precious Gentlewoman, late of Norwich...A. Skelton. London, Printed by J. M. for Nathaniel Brooks, 1649. 95 pages. S 3932A.

This publication includes portions of Skelton's funeral sermon by John Collinges, Anglican minister of Norwich, that contains little about her. He notes she wrote several works besides her meditations ("Infallible Signes of Saving Grace") in which she advocates direct communication with both God and one's fellows; she says a sign of His grace is our ability to deal with adversity. She further discusses virtuous living modelled after Christ's example.

530B [Smith, Mary.]   These few lines are to all such as have...[been] persecuting the Innocent People of God called Quakers. [London?], 1667. [No pagination.] S 4130.

Smith, a Quaker, asks enemies of the Friends to desist from persecuting them. She calls herself "one who is a Lover of the souls of all people, and travels for the Redemption of the embondaged Seed, which lies in spiritual Sodome and Egyptian this day."

531B S[mith], R[ebecca.]   The foundation of True Preaching Asserted. London, Printed by Andrew Sowle, 1687. 12 pages. S 4150.

Smith attacks a sermon preached before the Society of Friends which allegedly contained references to earthly learning. According to Smith, it was not inspirational--i.e, it came "by Humane Learning, School Divinity, or the Notions of Plato and Aristotle," rather than from contact with Christ.

532B [Smyth, Anne.]   The Case of Anne Smyth, the Wife of Daniell Smyth. [London], 1650. Broadside. S 4358.

Smythe claims she is about to be defrauded of her estate. She alleges the executors (all men) have mismanaged and misused it. She asks for interest and damages and requests her husband, an executor himself, be exempt from suits brought by the others.

533B [Sophia, Amelia, Queen of Denmark.] The Queen of Denmark's letter to the King of Scots, now resident in the city of Paris, Nov. 16, 1651, together with the removal of Major General Massey, and the sending of him prisoner to the tower. London, Printed for George Horton, 1651. 6 pages. S 4689. TT Reel 99:E.649(1).

This letter from the queen of Denmark to the future Charles II is dated from Hamburg. She expresses regret over his loss of a Scottish battle (presumably Edinburgh) and congratulates him on his escape from England and sanctuary in Paris. She says she believes fate will eventually see the end of unrest in England.

534B Stirredge, Elizabeth (Tayler). A Salutation of my Endeared love in God's holy Fear and Dread, and for the Clearing of my Conscience. [n.p., 1683.] 12 pages. S 5685A.

Stirredge recalls her trial in Bristol and credits the Lord with saving and transforming her. She advises fellow Quakers: "The People that live most Chaste, keep nearest to the Lord, and they that are nearest, hear most of his Counsel." Dorcas Dole's six-page epistolary entreaty to repent follows ("To you that have been Professors of the Truth of God, in the City of Bristol"). It is dated from Bridewell Prison on March 30, 1683.

535B Stone, Katharine. To the High Court of Parliament...The Humble Petition of Katherine Stone, Widdow.   [London, 1654.]   Broadside.   S 5731.   TT Reel 246:669.f.19(38).

The widow claims Sir Henry Ferrers mortgaged a manor to her deceased husband, then registered him as delinquent without her knowledge. Ferrers then put the property up for sale to two men, Foxley and Snape. She is petitioning to have the manor returned to her. The document includes counter arguments from the current owners as well. No judgment is rendered herein.

Stout, Mary. The Case of. See 168A.

536B [Stout, Mary.] "Letter to W. Haworth." In John Crook. Rebellion Rebuked: In an answer to a scandalous pamphlet...by one William Haworth. London, 1673. Broadside. C 7212.

Stout's commentary responding to Haworth's anti-Quaker tract follows a lengthy one by James Crook and William Bayly. Stout refutes Haworth's notion that scripture, not the light, should provide individual guidance.

537B [Stout, Mary.] "Reply by M. Stout to what concerns her in W. Haworth's former book, entituled, The Quaker converted to Christianity re-established." In Richard Thomas. The Testimony of the Hertford Quakers. London, 1676. [15] pages. T 819. EEB Reel 1537:39.

Stout continues the dialogue about Quaker dogma in response to Haworth's rejoinder to Rebellion Rebuked.

538B [Strong, Damaris.] Having seen a paper Printed, reflecting on the person and labours of my Dear Husband Mr. William Strong. [London, 1655.] Broadside. S 5988. EEB Reel 266:E.245(9) and TT Reel 130:E.861(2).

This notice was written by the wife of a recently deceased minister. She denies his notes were written in a "character of his own divining," claims eventually all his work will be published, and maintains only "a careful review" (not substantial editing) will be done. Strong says publication without permission offends her and the Church and costs the family royalties.

539B Sunderland, Dorothy Sidney, Countess of. "Letters from Dorothy Sidney, Countess Dowager of Sunderland, to George Saville, Earl of Halifax, in 1680." In Some Account of the Life of Rachel Wriothesley, Lady Russell. London; Longman, Hurst, Rees, Orme and Brown, 1819. [39] pages. Item: N.I.W.

The Countess was the niece of Sir Philip Sidney and the eldest daughter of Dorothy Percy and Robert Sidney, Earl of Leicester. She first married Henry Lord Spencer, later Earl of Sunderland, and then Sir Robert Smythe of Kent. Beautiful and talented, she was celebrated by the poet Edmund Waller as "Sacharissa." These letters were written by her at sixty to her son-in-law. They concern an English expedition sent to Tangier, the involvement of the Dutch in it, various family matters, events at court, and commentary on reaction to the Exclusion Bill.

540B Temple, Dorothy Osborne, Lady. Love Letters of Dorothy Osborne to Sir William Temple, 1652-54. G. C. M. Smith, ed. Oxford, The Clarendon Press, 1928. N.I.W.

Dorothy Osborne was the youngest child of a wealthy royalist family which disapproved of her betrothal to Temple. Their long relationship, initiated when she was twenty-one, ended in union after a protracted courtship, during which she was disfigured by smallpox. These letters represent only her correspondence. Her wit and charm are evident in discussions of familial and social events and political figures.

The Ten Pleasures of Marriage. See 858A.

Terry, Ann. [Writings.] See 567A.

541B A Testimony for the Lord, and his Truth. [York? 1688.] 9 pages. T 810A* (formerly W 2051). EEB Reel 950:22.

Subtitled "Epistle from the Womens Yearly Meeting at York, 1688," this document encourages local Quaker women to live peaceably, righteously and modestly. It is signed by Whitton, Judith Boulby, Elizabeth Sedman, Frances Taylor, Mary Waite, Deborah Winn, Elizabeth Beckwith and Mary Lindley.

The Third Part of the Amours of Messalina. See 31A.

542B Thornton, Alice. The Autobiography of Mrs. Alice Thornton, of East Newton, County York. Durham, Published for the Surtees Society by Andrews and Company, 1875. 360 pages. N.I.W.

Thornton (1626-1707) was married to Robert Thornton in 1651 and widowed in 1668. She eventually survived all of her relatives. This account was written to vindicate her name, allegedly tarnished by slander. It is dedicated to her "careless," bankrupt husband and the memory of her parents. Thornton describes various calamities, including fires, difficult pregnancies, falls, seizures, chokings, convulsions, infant deaths, and monetary problems. She also comments on contemporary political events.

543B Tillinghast, Mary. Rare and Excellent Receipts. Experienc'd, and Taught by Mrs. Mary Tillinghast. [London], 1690. 30 pages. T 1183*.

This cookbook, lacking introductory material and an index, offers recipes with directions. It is intended for use by the author's students and other cooks in training.

544B Tipper, Elizabeth. The Pilgrim's Viaticum: or, The Destitute, but not Forlorn. London, Printed for Thomas Ballard, 1699. 83 pages. T 1305*. EEB Reel 1662:10.

This book of religious poetry is dedicated to the Lady Coventry. Tipper's work is preceded by laudatory poems by men, one of whom compares her to Aphra Behn and Katherine Philips. Tipper's topics include her struggles with temptation and her resolve finally to imitate Christ. Excerpt: "Baptismal Vows engage Heroick Minds,/Women are valiant, tho' of different Kinds,/And tho' my Sex is weak, my Heart's not so."

545B To the Parliament of the Commonwealth of England. The Humble Petition of divers afflicted Women, in behalf of M: John Lilburn, prisoner in Newgate. [July 25, 1653.] Broadside. T 1585. TT Reel 246:669.f.17(26).

Leveller women ask Parliament to avoid haughtiness and needless violence. They accuse the body of excessive taxation and request suspension of John Lilburne's trial and an inquiry into his sentence of banishment. See also 548B, 550B and 575B.

546B To the Queens most Excellent Majestie. The Humble Petition of divers Gentle-women. [London, 1642.] Broadside. T 1599. EEB Reel 1242:15.

In an obsequious petition Royalist women (tradesmen's and citizens' wives) assure Henrietta Maria her presence has been an impetus to trade and a comfort to the people. They request that she remain in England.

547B To the Right Honourable, the High Court of Parliament; The Humble Petition of many hundreds of distressed Women, Trades-mens Wives, and Widdowes.

[February 4, 1642.] London, Printed for John Hammond, 1642. Broadside. T 1621. TT Reel 245: 669.f.4(57).

Women lament the lack of trade, the power of bishops, and the state of the country ("put into a present posture of Warre, for the safety and defense thereof"). They say the bishops and lords in Peeres ignored prior grievances, suggest placing teachers in the ministry, and request aid for "distressed Protestants" in Ireland. They claim trials for incendiaries and delinquents contribute to the decay of business. See also 570B.

To the Right Honourable the House of Peeres Now Assembled in Parliament. The Humble Petition of Courtiers, Citizens, Gentlemen and Tradesmens Wives inhabiting London, concerning the staying of the Queenes Intended Voyage into Holland. See 25B.

548B To the Supreme Authority of England the Commons Assembled in Parliament. [May 5, 1649.] [London, 1649.] T 1724. TT Reel 246:669.f.14(27).

This Leveller petition, signed by 10,000 women, was presented by 1,000 to Parliament. They remind the House that like men, they are made in the image of God and deserve a proportionate share of freedoms. They complain about lack of response to their earlier petition and request a review of it. They compare their right to petition to the rights of due process and trial by jury. They claim Leveller prisoners (Lilburne, Walwyn, Prince, Overton, Sawyer and Bray) are victims of "extrajudicial imprisonment and force" and should be given due process and reparations for their treatment. See also 545B, 550B and 575B.

549B To the Supreme Authority of this Commonwealth, the Parliament of England. The humble Petition of severall of the Wives and Children of...Delinquents. [London, 1650.] Broadside. T 1734. TT Reel 246:669.f.15(46).

Wives of delinquent royalist landowners protest the sale of their appropriated estates. Using submissive language, they request continuance of the practice of granting one fifth of such property to dependents in the projected Act for the Sale of Delinquent Estates. "August 1650" has been written on the copy examined.

550B To the Supream Authority of this Nation, the Commons assembled in Parliament: The humble Petition of divers wel-affected Women Inhabiting the Cities of London, Westminster...In behalf of Lt. Col. John Lilburn, Mr. William Walwyn, Mr. Thomas Prince, and Mr. Richard Overton, (Now Prisoners in the Tower of London) And Captain William Bray...and Mr. William Saywer. [April 24, 1649.] [London], 1649. 6 pages. T 1736. TT Reel 85:E.551(14).

Leveller women allege Parliament is acting unfairly toward the named prisoners, whose release they demand, along with reparations. They also claim trade is being driven away, food is expensive, and unemployment and taxes are high. They express fear for the lives of their husbands, servants and children, given the environment of "hostile violence" which presently obtains. Finally, the women request that soldiers be prevented from exercising civil authority. See also 545B, 548B and 575B.

551B [Townsend, Theophila.] <u>An epistle of love to Friends in the womens Meetings in London, To be read among them in the fear of God</u>. [London, 1686.] 8 pages. T 1987A. EEB Reel 1662:11.

Townsend was a Quaker minister imprisoned in 1681 for preaching. Here she expresses love and sisterhood to the women's meeting and offers condolences on the death of Anne Whitehead. She emphasizes the commitment needed to retain religious zeal and control the vanity of youth. Townsend ends with a strong appeal to follow Christ: "Bear with my plainness and homely expressions, Charity make way for it, for the truths sake."

552B Townsend, Theophila. <u>An Epistle of tender Love to all Friends that are tender hearted, who are tender of the Honour of God</u>. [London, Printed for Thomas Northcott, 1690.] Broadside. T 1988.

This appeal to Quakers, dated from Cirencester, warns against those who issue "Orders for Friends, and how they shall keep their Men and Womens Meetings." Townsend charges they want to bar the young and foreigners from meetings. She maintains Friends' inner sensibility cannot be structured by orders.

553B [Townsend, Theophila.] <u>A Testimony, Concerning the Life and Death of Jane Whitehead</u>. London, 1676. 28 pages. T 1989. EEB Reel 583:6.

This testimonial honors Quaker Jane Whitehead, formerly Jane Waugh, of South Cadbury in Somerset. Whitehead traveled with other Quaker women and was often arrested for speaking in public in the early 1660s. During one imprisonment for interrupting an Anglican service, her child was nursing. Her life is described as a series of "cruel mockings, scoffings and scornings, beating and reviling, and cruel Imprisonments in nasty places in the cold of Winter, and heat of Summer." Her husband's statement attests to her strength in the face of these persecutions.

554B Townsend, Theophila. <u>A Word of Counsel, in the Love of God, To the Persecuting Magistrates and Clergy</u>. [London, 1687.] 12 pages. T 1990.

Townsend addresses residents of Gloucester who "carry that unchristian work of Persecution, against their honest Neighbours." She supports freedom of conscience and rails against authorities who regarded "neither age nor sex" in pursuing Quakers to collect tithes.

555B Trapnel, Anna. <u>The Cry of a Stone: Or a Relation of Something spoken in Whitehall</u>. [London], 1654. 76 pages. T 2031. TT Reel 112:E.730(3).

Trapnel, a Fifth Monarchist daughter of a shipwright in Stepney, describes prophecies resulting from a religious trance she experienced at Whitehall. Known as the "singing prophetess," she relates her visions for "Governors, Army, churches, ministries, universities, and the whole nation," but first for virgins. Criticizing Cromwell's arrogant title (The Lord Protector), she reminds army officers of their bond to the people and rejects the notion of tithing.

556B Trapnel, Anna. <u>A Legacy for Saints, Being several Experiences of the dealings of God with Anna Trapnel</u>. [London], Printed for T. Brewster, 1654. 64 pages. T 2032. TT Reel 123:E.806(1).

Writing from prison at Bridewell, Trapnel speaks of her spirituality and humility. She includes a message of support from her London congregation of All-Hallows.

557B Trapnel, Anna. Anna Trapnel's report and plea. Or, a Narrative of her Journey from London into Cornwal [sic]. London, Printed for Thomas Brewster, 1654. 59 pages. T 2033. EEB Reel 1537:53.

Trapnel criticizes the people of Cornwall for treating her in a "rough, boisterous, rugged, inhumane, and uncivil" manner during her visit. She claims abusive reports about her (including accusations of witchcraft) have been circulated by "professors and clergie...who have a form of godliness, but deny the power." This work is written in a lyrical style with some sexual imagery: "The next day the Lord greatly ravished my soul with his smiling looks on me."

558B Trapnel, Anna. Strange and Wonderful Newes from White-Hall: or, The Mighty Visions Proceeding from Mistris Anna Trapnel, to divers Collonels Ladies and Gentlewomen, concerning the Government of the Commonwealth of England, Scotland, and Ireland. London, Printed for Robert Sele, 1654. 8 pages. T 2034. EEB Reel 263:E.224(3) and TT Reel 39:E.224(3).

This pamphlet contains descriptions of Trapnel's visions, especially those about Cromwell, whom she opposed. She was imprisoned for two months at Whitehall for "aspersing the government," a charge levelled by local clergy and magistrates.

559B Trapnel, Anna. [A] Voice for the King of Saints and Nations; Or A testimony...poured forth by the Spirit through Anna Trapnell. London, 1658. 91 pages. T 2035.

Trapnel's poems describes visions she had over several months, the "testimony of Jesus, the Spirit of prophesy." She utilizes marital imagery extensively to illustrate Christ's selection of her as a vessel: "O spouse my love saith he still sing,/Thou art the married wife."

560B T[ravers], R[ebeckah] [Booth.] For those that meet to worship at the Steeplehouse called John Evangelist, in London. London, 1659. 61 pages. T 2059.

Converted from Baptism to Quakerism by James Nayler, Travers was the most prolific woman Quaker writer after Margaret Fell and Dorothy White. She oversaw the conducting of Quaker marriages in London and was a frequent prison visitor. Here she chastises a group for interfering with Friends and resisting God. She offers a history of her enlightenment and says God sent her and others to witness the living gospel.

561B Travers, Rebeckah Booth (postscript). The Good old way and truth. By Ambrose Rigge. n.p., 1669. 39 pages. R 1483. EEB Reel 675:3.

Travers wrote the postscript to this tract by Ambrose Rigge.

562B Travers, [Rebeckah Booth.]   The Harlots Vail rent, and her impudency rebuked. In a short answer to one E. Atkinson her Babylons Brat against the people called Quakers. [With Elizabeth Coleman] n.p., 1669. 8 pages. N.I.W.

This pamphlet, co-authored by a leading Quaker minister, is a vituperative attack against an apostate Quaker in response to her charge of rampant immorality among the Friends.   The authors accuse Atkinson of betrayal, deceit, backsliding and acting "like a silly ignorant woman." They claim she inverts the language and values of Quakerism to criticize her former colleagues unfairly. See also 16B and Addendum 8.

563B Travers, Rebeckah Booth (preface).   A Message from the spirit of Truth.   By James Nayler. London, Printed for T. Simmons, 1658. 16 pages. N 298. EEB Reel 769:32.

Travers wrote the address to the reader for this piece written by James Nayler, a Quaker leader who was tongue-bored and pilloried.

564B [Travers, Rebeckah Booth.] Of that Eternal Breath begotten and brought forth not of flesh and blood. [London, 1659.] 8 pages. T 2060.

Travers warns the parishioners of Ashted not to heed "Hireling Teachers" who interpret the gospel but ignore the living spirit of Christ. She entreats them to follow their consciences. Accused by a local minister of sitting in darkness during his sermon, she responds the light showed her the truth.

565B [Travers, Rebeckah Booth.]   A Testimony Concerning the Light and Life of Jesus. London, 1663. 24 pages. T 2061. EEB Reel 1623:23.

This tract echoes the Quaker emphasis on spiritual rather than earthly things. Travers advocates renunciation of power and urges nations to avoid arrogance. She utilizes feminine imagery throughout: "All drawing from the one breast the milk of the Word." Travers dedicates this document to Quakers "who in the one Spirit warre against the many spirits gone out into the World."

566B [Travers, Rebeckah Booth.]   A Testimony for God's everlasting truth. [London], 1669. 47 pages. T 2062. EEB Reel 1515:25.

Travers answers Robert Cobbit's God's Truth attested according to Scripture, claiming he renders God into human form and ignores the truth of the light. She addresses each passage of Cobbit's work, an attack on the Quaker concept of the light. Her major concerns are the nature of Christ, the facts of the ascension, the relation of God to Christ and the accuracy of Cobbit's interpretation of Genesis and Revelations.

567B T[ravers], R[ebeckah Booth.]   This is for all or any of those...that resist the Spirit, and despise the grace. London, 1664. 12 pages. T 2063. EEB Reel 1537:54.

Travers' warns enforcers of the Conformity Act "made against such as meet to worship contrary to the Lyturgy of the Church of England." She says Quakers follow Paul's religion--that of a "consuming fire," and they choose martyrdom rather than giving up their services.

568B [Travers, Rebecca Booth.] This is for any of that generation. London, Printed for Mary Westwood, 1659. Broadside. T 2064*.

Travers addresses millenarians who think they can control destiny. She describes the Second Coming as a mighty force sweeping away false believers. She says "...your offerings stink before him, and your prayers are an abomination unto him, whose flight shall come on you in Winter, and on the Sabbath day."

569B Triumphs of Female Wit, In Some Pindarick Odes, or The Emulation...an Answer to an Objector against Female Ingenuity and capacity of learning. London, Printed for T. Malthus and J. Waltho, [1683]. 20 pages. T 2295. EEB Reel 519:15.

In the preface the author, supposedly a young lady, says she expects to be ridiculed for her views. She claims women could "out-do" men with the advantage of a "suitable education" and calls men "unjust Invaders of our native Rights." Charging men allow women only enough education to restrain their passions, she says men are fearful of women's political ambitions. In reply, a Mr. H. calls the author bold, but subscribes to the traditional view of women. In another rejoinder, a Mr. F. advances female superiority.

Trotter, Catherine. See Cockburn, Catherine (Trotter).

570B A True Copie of the Petition of Gentlewomen, and Tradesmens- Wives, in and about the City of London. London, Printed by R. O. and G. D. for John Bull, 1641[2]. [7] pages. T 2656*. EEB Reel 1296:57 and TT Reel 24:E.134(17).

This political petition was delivered to the House of Commons on February 4, 1642 by Anne Stagg, a brewer's wife, and her peers. It defends the right of women to petition, denounces the horrors of war in Germany and Ireland, and excoriates the abuse of women in Ireland. Other concerns are "Popery and Idolatry," the mass and women's right to "the free enjoying of Christ in his own Laws." They also ask that Archbishop Laud, in the Tower, be punished. M. P. John Pym advises them to go home and pray. See also 547B.

571B Trye, M[ary.] Medicatrix; or The woman-physician, vindicating Thomas O'Dowde a chymical physican...against the calumnies...of Henry Stubbe. London, Printed by T. R. and N. T. and sold by Henry Broome and John Leete, 1675. 126 pages. T 3174. EEB Reel 1296:67.

Trye defends the chemically-based cures of her father and his colleague T. O'Dowde against followers of Galen. Arguing women should learn medicine to treat other females, she says she continued her father's practice after his death. Trye's wide-ranging, cogent defense addresses academic pedantry, professional issues and political disputes with verve. As her controversial father's only daughter, Trye vows to carry on in his tradition.

572B Turner, J[ane.] Choice Experiences of the Kind Dealings of God before, in, and after Conversion. London, Printed by H. Hils, 1653. 208 pages. T 3294.

Sectarian Turner was reluctant to publish this spiritual autobiography, but her husband encouraged her when he saw her manuscripts. His preface testifies

to her solo effort.   She discusses doctrinal matters, including religious
conversion and the Quaker concept of "inner light," under six headings.

573B Twysden, Isabella. "The Diary of Isabella, Wife of Sir Roger Twysden, 36
Baronet, of Royden Hall, East Peckham, 1645-1651." In Rev. F. W. Bennet, ed.
Archaeologia Cantiana, Transactions of the Kent Archeological Society, LI (1939),
116-136. N.I.W.

Twysden was the youngest daughter of Sir Nicholas Saunders of Nonsuch in
Surrey.   She was born in 1605, married in 1635 and died in 1657.   Her
husband was arrested in 1642 and imprisoned for his support of the Petition of
Kent. This diary of abbreviated entries was written largely during the seizure
of the family estate. Excerpt: "at 4 a clock in the morning came tropers to our
liamhous at peck: to serch as they sed for armes, and letters, for letters there
was none they cared for, yet carried a waye 4 or 5 of my husbands and armes
what was, and they carried a waye my husband, and my bro: cho: to leeds
castell prisoners, for no cause, I thank Christ."

574B The Unnatural Mother. A Tragedy. Written by a Young Lady. London, Printed
by J. O. for R. Basset, 1698. 52 pages. U 87. EEB Reel 1076:21.

The setting for this tragedy is Siam.   The primary characters are Bebemeah,
betrothed to Munzaffer under her father Pechai's order; Pechai's second wife,
the evil Callapia; her equally malicious son, Cemat, who attempts to rape his
own sister, Choufer; and Sennorat, father to Munzuffer. By chance Bebemeah
and Munzuffer meet in an orange grove and fall in love.   Ignorant of each
other's identity, they nearly break their marriage contract because of their
clandestine romantic involvement. Cemat and Callapia try to foil their match
through violence and attempted murder. Meanwhile, Choufer is pursued by her
brother while she loves her half-sister's lover (Munzuffer). The primary themes
of the tragedy are incest, rape, jealousy, greed and arranged marriage.

575B Unto Every Individual Member of Parliament: The humble Representation of
divers afflicted Women-Petitioners to the Parliament on the behalf of Mr. John
Lilburn. (July 29, 1653.) [n.p., 1653.] U 99. TT Reel 246:669.f.17(36).

Leveller women submitted this petition on behalf of John Lilburne. They protest
withholding of their right to petition, citing the biblical story of Queen Esther,
who successfully petitioned against the actions of the wicked Hamen.   The
women express fear that any citizen might be treated like Lilburne. This petition
was probably written by Katherine Chidley. See also 545B, 548B and 550B.

576B Veitch, Marion Fairly. "Memoirs of the Life of Mrs. Veitch." In Memoirs of Mrs.
William Veitch, Mr. Thomas Hog of Kiltearn, Mr. Henry Erskine, and Mr. John
Carstairs. Edinburgh, Committee of the General Assembly of the Free Church of
Scotland, 1846. 60 pages. N.I.W.

These previously unpublished memoirs were written by the wife of a minister in
the Church at Dumfries. The couple was married in 1664, then fled to England
after banishment from Scotland. The document relates their "domestic affliction"
and "vexatious persecution."   Pious and humble in tone, it was meant as
instruction for Veitch's children. Excerpt: "When the news of [her son's wounds]

came to me, I was put to admire his free love and faithfulness to such a worm as I am."

577B Venn, Anne. A Wise Virgins Lamp Burning; or, Gods sweet incomes of Love to a gracious soul waiting for him. London, Printed for E. Cole, 1658. 152, 201-331 pages. V 190.

The first sixty-one pages of this book comprise a history of Venn's religious conversion. The remainder, following it, concerns questions of scripture.

578B Vokins, Joan. God's Mighty Power Magnified: As Manifested and Revealed in his Faithful Handmaid. Sansom O[liver], ed. [London], Printed for Thomas Northcott, 1691. 130 pages. V 685. EEB Reel 902:45.

This compilation of Vokins' religious and personal writings was published posthumously and edited by Sansom O[liver]. Vokins, a Quaker, speaks of her "Work of the Ministry." The text includes testimonies by fellow Quakers and her seven children, her letters to various women's meetings and to congregations she visited, including American ones. Her husband and eldest son were jailed in Reading for refusal to pay tithes. Several of her sermons are also included.

579B [Vokins, Joan.] "A Loving Advertisement unto all those who joyn together to persecute the Innocent." In God's Mighty Power Magnified. Sansom O[liver], ed. [London] Printed for Thomas Northcott, 1670. 8 pages. Item: V 686. Collection: V 685.

This item is included in Vokins' collected writings (578B). It describes the willingness of Herod and Pilot to prosecute Christ without sufficient evidence. Vokins compares them to contemporary persecutors of the Quakers whom she advises to turn to Christ. Pagination is irregular.

580B [Vokins, Joan.] "A Tender Invitation unto all those that want peace with God." In God's Mighty Power Magnified. Sansom O[liver], ed. [London], Printed for Thomas Northcott, 1670. 7 pages. Item: V 687. Collection: V 685.

This item is included in Vokins' collected writings (578B). The author reminds her audience that although Christ atoned for the sins of humankind, they must continue the effort toward reconciliation with God. Vokins fears God's mercy will cease if non-Quakers do not join in the quest for salvation.

581B [Waite, Mary.] A Warning to all friends who professeth the everlasting truth of God. [London, 1679.] 10 pages. W 224. EEB Reel 402:22.

The household duties of masters and mistresses are described in this Quaker guide. Roles are more egalitarian than those in most documents of the period. Emphasis is on humility ("humble self denying Life"). The author requests that her work be read at all Friends' meetings.

Walker, Elizabeth. [Writings.] See 930A.

582B Warren, Elizabeth. The Old and Good Way Vindicated. London, Printed for Henry Shepheard and William Ley, 1646. 38 pages. W 958*. TT Reel 51:E.311(33).

Christians are encouraged to develop a personal relationship with Christ in this Quaker guide. Warren says this is a troubled time because people are becoming alienated from ministers.

583B Warren, Elizabeth. <u>Spiritual Thrift. Or, Meditations Wherein humble Christians (as in a Mirrour) may view the verity of their saving Graces</u>. London, Printed by R. L. for Henry Shepherd, 1647. 83 pages. W 960. TT Reel 59:E.373(7).

This lengthy didactic compendium of biblical and Christian stories is about persons who used their time on earth in commitment to Christ. Warren is particularly concerned about "the pious improvement of precious time."

584B Warren, Elizabeth. <u>A warning-peece from heaven, against the sins of the Times, inciting us to fly from the Vengeance to come</u>. London, Printed by Richard Constable for Henry Shepheard, 1649. 54 pages. W 961. TT Reel 89:E.581(5).

This tract contains a Quaker discussion of God's wrath as manifested in earthly phenomena as well as a defense of the power of faith to illuminate divine truth.

585B Warwick, Mary Boyle Rich, Countess of. <u>Autobiography of Mary Countess of Warwick</u>. T. Crofton Croker, ed. London, Printed for the Percy Society by Richards, 1848. 50 pages. N.I.W.

Lady Warwick's autobiography was abridged by the Reverend Thomas Woodrooffe. The original manuscript records her domestic activities and public life for twelve years after the Restoration. This version is a brief account of her origins, her courtship by and marriage to Charles Rich (against her father's wishes), her religious awakening, her husband's intemperance, their social life in London and at court, and various bouts with illness and death. See also 381A and 929A.

586B Warwick, Mary Boyle Rich, Countess of. "Occasional Meditations Upon Sundry Subjects: With Pious Reflections upon Several Scriptures." In Anthony Walker. <u>[Eureka, Eureka,] The Virtuous Woman</u>. London, Printed for Nathanael Ranew, 1678. [7] pages. Item: N.I.W. Collection: W 301.

Each meditation refers to a fact or a scene, an elaboration of the lesson it teaches, and a prayer. Examples are the setting sun, a peaceful river, a silkworm spinning, the simultaneous lighting of many candles, a person dozing and a hog eating acorns. Rich's purpose is to "bring all my passions into subjection to my reason, and my reason to my religion."

587B [Warwick, Mary Boyle Rich, Countess of.] "Rules of Holy Living." In George Berkeley, Earl of Berkeley. <u>Historical Applications and Occasional Meditations</u>. London, Printed by J. Flesher for R. Royston, 1666. 28 pages. Item: N.I.W. Collection: B 1963*. EEB Reels 13:5, 857:45 and 858:1.

This unsigned essay was apparently written in 1659 at Berkeley's request. The Countess advises not to rise or retire late, to read the scriptures regularly, worship twice daily with one's family, choose friends wisely, meditate, indulge infrequently in recreation and to avoid dice and cards.

588B W[eamys], A[nna.] A continuation of Sir Philip Sydney's Arcadia: Wherein is handled the Loves of Amphialus and Helena Queen of Corinth, Prince Plangus and Erona. London, Printed by William Bentley, and are to be sold by Thomas Heath, 1651. 199 pages. W 1189. TT Reel 173:E.1288(2).

In a lengthy romantic tale, Weamys continues Sydney's work in the relationship of Amphialus and Helena. Introductory poems lend credibility to her work by supporting sexual equality of writers: "The only difference 'twixt you and men/Tis Tyrannie to keep your sex in aw,/And make wit suffer by a Salick Law./Good wine does need no Bush, pure wit no Beard,/Since all souls equal are, let all be heard."

589B [Webb, Mary.] I being moved of the Lord, doth call unto you that are gathered together in Parliament. London, Printed for Thomas Simmons, 1659. 4 pages. W 1205.

Warning the powerful and arrogant to seek God, Webb also attacks organized religion: "Who ordained those houses to be called Churches?" She says all may spread Christ's word, not only the educated or credentialed. Webb criticizes hollow honoring of the sabbath as blasphemy and claims the Lord hates fasting.

590B Wells, Mary. A Divine Poem written by Mary Wells, who Recommends it as a fit Token for all Young Men and Maids, instead of profane Songs and Ballads. [London], Printed by James Astwood, 1684. Broadside. W 1296.

Wells asks forgiveness for her sins: "Make me think vilely of my self;/Shew me the want of Grace;/Let not the love of any sin/Within my heart have place."

591B Wentworth, Anne. The Revelation of Jesus Christ. [London], 1679. 23 pages. W 1355. EEB Reel 1162:7.

Baptist Wentworth recorded these numbered revelations after they came to her while she slept. Her message is the usual caveat against sinfulness with an anti-papist twist. An unsigned section describes her forcible eviction from her house by Mr. Wentworth. She defends herself against charges of being "an impudent Hussy," a "disobedient wife," and living a scandalous life in an almshouse. She claims her husband has not supported her for two years and blames relatives and his pastor for setting him against her.

592B [Wentworth, Anne.] A Vindication of Anne Wentworth... preparing...all people for Her Larger Testimony. [London], 1677. 22 pages. W 1356.

Wentworth says she has suffered for eighteen years because of her abusive husband and persecution from the Baptists. She says her enemies have accused her of being "proud, passionate, revengeful, discontented, and mad" and of publishing "things to the prejudice and scandal of my Husband." Wentworth maintains her husband threatened her life and tried to seize her writings. She expresses willingness to return to him if he allows her to work.

Wharton, Anne. [Letters.] See 399A.

593B [White, Dorothy.] <u>An alarmum sounded to Englands inhabitants, But most Especially to Englands Rulers</u>. London, Printed for Robert Wilson, 1661. 8 pages. W 1745. EEB Reel 929:40.

Dorothy White of Weymouth, a prolific female Quaker writer, warns of judgment day and cautions against sinful behavior.

594B White, Dorothy. <u>A call from God out of Egypt, by His Son Christ the Light of Life</u>. London, 1662. [10] pages. W 1746. EEB Reel 930:1.

This pamphlet is a call to recognize the "Spirit of Truth" within (the light). It also suggests a gathering of nations to communicate Quaker dogma.

595B White, Dorothy. <u>The Day Dawned Both to Jews and Gentiles...The Bright and Morning Star appearing</u>. [London], 1684. 16 pages. W 1747.

White announces the arrival of the day of "Light and Righteousness." She lyrically discusses the creation and the development of nations, languages and so on. Likening the "ark of faith" to that of Noah, she refers to herself as a wise virgin and to Christ as a bridegroom.

596B White, Dorothy. <u>A Diligent Search amongst Rulers, Priests, Professors and People</u>. [London, 1659.] 8 pages. W 1747A.

White claims she was divinely inspired to write this Quaker tract. She speaks against the "blood-thirsty Rulers of England," comparing them to those of Sodom and Egypt in their declines. She refers to Christ's encounter with the Samarian woman at the well. Finally White discusses biblical episodes in which crafty men "[lead] silly women captive."

597B W[hite], D[orothy.] <u>An Epistle of Love, and of consolation unto Israel</u>. London, Printed for Robert Wilson, 1661. 13 pages. W 1748. EEB Reel 1297:29.

This typical Quaker tract is more optimistic and less aggressively critical than many. White reiterates the cheerful promise that God's love is being dispersed among the faithful. Images of nature predominate: "the Winter is passing away" and "the Lilly begins to appear in the field of pleasure." The tone becomes progressively more rapturous and the style more lyrical.

598B White, Dorothy. <u>Friends. You that are of the Parliament, hear the Word of the Lord</u>. 8 pages. [London,] 1662. W 1749.

White reminds fellow Friends their authority derives from God. She elaborates His destructive powers and warns "the oppressor that oppresseth the just" (Parliament) will be judged harshly on judgment day. White also criticizes collectors of tithes.

599B [White, Dorothy.] <u>Greetings of pure Peace and perfect Love, sent unto all the Poor, Scattered, Little Holy Flock of Jesus Christ</u>. [London, 1662.] 23 pages. W 1750.

In verse and prose, White offers God's love and joy to those who accept the truth of the light. The reward of total devotion to Christ is purification and union with Him. Excerpt: "We must be subject into Light within,/Wherein is known the Cleansing from all Sin;/Subject unto Christ, the Light alone."

600B [White, Dorothy.] <u>A Lamentation Unto this Nation: And also, A Warning To all People of this present Age</u>. London, Printed for Robert Wilson, [1661]. 8 pages. W 1751. EEB Reel 1581:14.

White maintains the spirit of the Lord impels her to offer this warning to the faithless. She says, "The Lord is stretching forth the Arms of his Everlasting Love, and he is drawing you with the cords of his Love." Glories of judgment day, great changes to be wrought by God and the "Everlasting Habitation" for true believers are meant to appeal to the uninitiated.

601B White, Dorothy. <u>A Salutation of Love to All the Tender Hearted, who follow the Lamb wheresoever He Leadeth them</u>. [London, 1684.] 8 pages. W 1752.

Addressing Friends ("Abraham's seed") White says God is good "to that Israel who are of a clean Heart." Citing Mary and Martha, White notes those called to Christ lose their identities in Him: "And then it is no more two, but Christ Liveth in [His followers]." The postscript emphasizes Christ's permanent prophecy.

602B White, Dorothy. <u>This to be delivered to the Counsellors that are sitting in counsel</u>. London, Printed for Thomas Simmons, 1659. 8 pages. W 1753. EEB Reel 1452:11.

Urging repentance, White claims in a vision God asked her to remind the rulers and judges of God's power. She charges corruption among authorities and predicts God's vengeance against the guilty.

603B White, Dorothy. <u>To all those that worship in Temples made with Hands</u>. [London, 1663.] Broadside. W 1754.

White cites the historical worship of false idols among nations, entreating "the people who meet at Pauls" to leave doomed Babylon and "walk in the Light of the Lord." She claims God is now communicating through handmaidens like herself. White signs this document from the "Counter Prison in Wood-Street."

604B W[hite], D[orothy.] <u>A Trumpet of the Lord of Hosts, Blown unto the city of London</u>. [London], Published by me D. W., 1662. 16 pages. W 1755. EEB Reel 930:2.

White warns Londoners the day of judgment is nigh. She likens the city to Sodom and writes of God's vengeance, to be visited upon those "who live in Lust, Pride, and Envy." The second section, in verse, refers to God's trumpet--herself--as communicator of His word. She claims the elect will find true happiness.

605B White, Dorothy. <u>Universal Love to the Lost: With the Voice of the Chief-Shepherd, to gather the scattered Number together</u>. 16 pages. [London, 1684.] W 1756.

White warns of judgment day, when all will return to "the Ark of God's Covenant" or "the strong Tower, a safe Defence and hiding Place." She compares the sorrow of sinners to that of a "Woman in Travel" and calls the saved "not Children of the Flesh, nor of the Bond-Woman, but of the Free-Woman, which is Married, and in covenant with Christ her Husband."

606B [White, Dorothy.] Unto all Gods Host, in England. [London, 1660.] 8 pages. W 1757. EEB Reel 1109:10.

White directs two four-page letters to groups of Friends, calling the first a "Heavenly Visitation." She maintains the Lord has called her "to declare the day of free Love, and of everlasting consolation" unto Israel. The second epistle concerns the coming of Zion (Judgment Day) and its rewards for the faithful. White concludes: "So from the Spirit of Truth I this publish, as the Counsel of God unto all Israel."

607B White, Dorothy. Upon the 22nd day of the 8th month, 1659. The word of the Lord came to me. London, Printed for Thomas Simmons, 1659. 8 pages. W 1758. EEB Reel 1136:9.

White says she is relaying a message from God calling for redemption of sins. She chastises iniquitous rulers, directing her unstructured words to "you that are ruling and governing this nation."

608B W[hite], D[orothy.] A Visitation of Heavenly Love Unto the Seed of Jacob. London, Printed for Robert Wilson, 1660. 11 pages. W 1759. EEB Reel 907:5.

White says a prophet who speaks as thunder is proclaiming the imminence of judgment day. She claims God's wrath is turned against the current generation: "And the Lord God is not come to bring Peace, but a Sword, and the Sword of the Lord Jehovah is drawn, to cut down and destroy the Man of Sin."

609B White, Dorothy. A Visitation of Love, sent unto all: That those that do not see, may see. London, Printed for the Author, 1684. 10 pages. W 1760.

White addresses those blind to God's truth who do not realize all persons are His prophets. She brings good tidings from God, who is now communicating His message directly, rather than through prophets.

610B White, Elizabeth. The Experiences of Gods gracious dealing with Mrs. Elizabeth White, late wife of Mr. Thomas White of Coldecot in the county of Bucks. As they were written under her own hand, and found in her closet after her decease, she dying in childbed, Decemb. 5, 1669. Glasgow, Printed for Robert Sanders, 1696. 22 pages. W 1762*.

White's personal account portrays conflict between fear and doubt and a growing love of God. Her notes reveal her initially weak faith and early temptations, e.g., reading "Histories, and other foolish Books." After reading Shepards Sincere Convert, she says she gained a fear of God and glimpsed ultimate salvation.

611B Whitehead, Anne (Downer). An Epistle For true love, Unity and order in the Church of Christ. London, Printed by Andrew Sowle, 1680. 15 pages. W 1882*. EEB Reel 1244:6.

Whitehead's work appears on the first ten pages; 266B follows. She answers a charge against the Quaker women's meeting that the "tender Consciences of the Weak" have been forced in unnatural directions. She portrays women not as seekers of influence, but as companions to men who willingly accept male authority. This is one of the most thorough descriptions of the women's meetings available. See also 266B.

612B [Whitehead, Anne (Downer).] For the King and both Houses of Parliament. [London, 1670.] Broadside. W 1884.

This document was signed by thirty-six Quaker women, the first of whom was Whitehead. They contend Christ's truest followers have shed their blood in the streets. They recall Christ was killed by magistrates and abandoned by the people. They plea for freedom to worship God and remind authorities that some Quakers have been imprisoned for nearly seven years.

613B Whitrow, Joan. Faithful warnings. London, Printed and are to be sold by E. Whitlock, 1697. [192] pages. W 2032A.

Whitrow, a Quaker originally from Covent Garden, then Surrey, directs this tract to the king and Parliament, acknowledging her presumption. She argues strongly against heavy taxation of the poor and proposes a new system wherein taxes would be levied for sins. The second and larger section is entitled Some Remarks on a Sermon, Preached on the Death of the Late Queen. It supports the queen and criticizes judgments of her in the sermon. Only the latter is paginated.

614B Whitrow, Joan. The humble Address of the Widow Whitrow to King William. With a faithful warning to the inhabitants of England. [London], 1689. 13 pages. W 2033. EEB Reel 338:13.

Whitrow criticizes the king for wasting his time in hunting. She suggests if he is to rule well and with compassion, he must accept Christ.

615B Whitrow, Joan. A Humble Salutation and faithful Greeting of the Widow Whitrow to King William. [London, 1690.] 20 pages. W 2034.

This piece is both a greeting and a warning to William: Although God has rewarded him with the English throne, he is still doing His work. She encourages him to develop inner faith and trust God's power. Whitrowe invokes the tale of Daniel in the lion's den to assure William of God's protection.

616B Whitrow, Joan. The Widow Whitrow's humble Thanksgiving for the King's safe return. London, Printed for D. Edwards for J. B., 1694. 40 pages. W 2035.

Whitrowe blames rabbis, physicians and scholars for Christ's crucifixion and warns the proud and arrogant to repent. She criticizes wealth and extravagance, employing biblical passages to emphasize humility before God.

In her own defense, Whitrowe asks: "And why should it be thought incredible for a woman to write truth, any more than a man?"

617B [Whitrowe, Joan.] To King William and Queen Mary, grace and peace. The Widow Whitrow's humble Thanksgiving for the King's safe return to England. London, 1692. W 2036.

This item is the same as 616B.

618B [Whitrow, Joan.] To Queen Mary: The Humble Salutation, and Faithful Greeting of the Widow Whitrowe. [London], 1690. 20 pages. W 2037.

Whitrow's warning about God's wrath is directed to all rulers. She prays for the queen's longevity and advises her to "take the holy Women in former ages for your Example," especially with regard to their simple dress and avoidance of earthly pleasures.

619B Whitrow, Joan. The Word of God in a Dying Maid...Susannah Whitrow. [London], 1671. 48 pages. W 2039*. EEB Reel 1559:36.

Whitrow writes about her daughter, Susannah, who died when she was fifteen. She believes the girl became closer to God and her mother during her illness. The work attempts in part to apologize for the young Susannah's critical comments about the women's meeting. It includes testimonies by Rebeckah Travers and others.

620B Whitton, Katharine. An Epistle to Friends everywhere: To be Distinctly read in their Meetings. London, Printed for Benjamin Clark, 1681. [10] pages. W 2050. EEB Reel 403:3.

Whitton testifies to the Lord's lovingkindness and mercy. She entreats Quakers to do His work--to care for the sick and needy. Whitton claims that in obedience (to God) she has found peace.

The Whole Duty of a Woman: Or a Guide to the Female Sex from the age of Sixteen to Sixty. See 492A.

621B Wight, Sarah. A Wonderful Pleasant and Profitable Letter written by Mrs. S. W., to a friend. Edited by R. B. London, Printed by James Cottrel for Ri. Moone, 1656. 81 pages. W 2106. TT Reel 210:E.1681(1).

Occasioned by the death of Wight's brother, this text was published by a friend without her permission. Wight expresses her view of the comforting aspects of religion during illness. She describes God's strength during difficult times. See also 485A.

622B [Wiginton, Leticia.] The Confession and Execution of. [London, Printed for Langley Curtis, 1681.] 4 pages. W 2110. EEB Reel 950:32.

This confession was supposedly written shortly before Wiginton's execution in 1681. Her alleged crime was the whipping death of Rebecca Clifford, an apprentice of eleven. Wiginton said her lodger killed the girl. Apparently he moved in when Wiginton's husband, a seaman, failed to provide for her and their three children and two apprentices. Wiginton's defense is reasoned, detailed and plausible. It includes detailed information about her economic circumstances.

[Wilks, Judith.] The Confession of Mrs. Judith Wilks, The Queens Midwife. See 231A.

623B [Wolley, Hannah.] The Accomplish'd Lady's Delight in Preserving, Physick, Beautifying and Cookery. Second Edition. London, Printed for B. Harris, 1677. 380 pages. W 3268*. EEB Reel 371:16.

Wolley was a school mistress, governess and personal secretary of middle-class origins and considerable ambition. Although some of her writing concerns social behavior and decorum, this is primarily a cookbook with no political or ideological content. The author's name is also spelled "Woolley."

624B Wolley, Hannah. The Compleat Servant-Maid; or the Young Maidens Tutor. London, Printed for Thomas Passinger, 1677. 167 pages. W 3273A*.

Wolley dedicates her guide to female servants, saying if they learn skills, they will enhance their chances of marriage. The author stresses modesty and courtesy, legible handwriting, neat dress, proper grammar, mathematical proficiency, and expertise in domestic arts like carving and preserving. Recipes are interspersed with discussions of culinary techniques.

625B Wolley, Hannah. The Cooks Guide: or, Rare Receipts for Cookery. London, Printed for Peter Dring, 1664. 100 pages. W 3276*.

Wolley dedicates this cookbook to Anne Wroth in repayment of her "love and bounty." It is organized alphabetically by recipe, rather than by type of food. It includes instructions for preparing almond custard, artichoke pie, Dutch sausages, ginger bread and so on.

626B Wolley, Hannah. The Gentlewoman's Companion: or, A Guide to the Female Sex. London, Printed by A. Maxwell for Edward Thomas, 1675. 262 pages. W 3277*. EEB Reel 1602:55.

Acknowledging a debt to guides in French and Italian, Wolley offers practical advice for women in all classes and situations. Her emphasis is on skill rather than education. She blames men for restraining women and encourages girls to think seriously and critically. Wolley presents recipes and medical advice as well as material about social behavior. Topics include bad breath, sore breasts, courtship, jellies, and duties of governesses. An introductory section includes biographical material.

627B Wolley, Hannah. The Ladies Delight: or a Rich closet of Choice...Preserving and candying both fruits and flowers. London, Printed by E. Milbourn for A. Crouch, 1672. 137 pages. W 3279.

This book includes sections titled "The Exact Cook" and "The Ladies Physical Closet." It is comprised of many recipes for items like damson marmalade, licorice juice, anti-plague syrup and artificial walnuts.

628B Wolley, Hannah. <u>The Ladies Directory</u>. London, Printed by Thomas Milbourn for the authress [sic], 1661. 111 pages. W 3280*.

This book includes recipes for preserving and candying fruits and flowers, making cakes, perfumes, various potions, "consumption drinks" and so on.

629B Wolley, Hannah. <u>The Queen-like Closet, or, rich cabinet: stored with all manner of rare receipts for preserving, candying and cookery</u>. London, Printed for R. Lowndes, 1670. 383 pages. W 3282*.

This work covers primarily cookery and popular medicine.

630B Wolley, Hannah. <u>A Supplement to the Queen-Like Closet</u>. London, Printed by T. R. for Richard Lownds, 1674. 194 pages. W 3287*. EEB Reel 1138:7.

This is the second part of 629B. Like 626B the introduction includes some biographical information.

<u>Woman Turned Bully</u>. See 963A.

631B <u>The Womens Petition to the Right Honourable...Lord General Cromwell. The Humble Petition of many thousands of the poor enslaved, oppressed and distressed Men and Women in this land, who by these their subscribed representators, most humbly complaining</u>. [October 27, 1651.] [London, 1651.] Broadside. W 3332. TT Reel 246:669.f.16(30).

The women request an alternative to imprisonment for debtors. They ask Cromwell to devise a way "that the poor may by some easie and speedy way reap the fruit of Justice." They claim two acts which were to have provided for the release of those indebted for fewer than five pounds have not proven beneficial. The petition is signed by E. Balsfield, E. Cole, K. Frefe and D. Trinhale.

632B Woodforde, Mary Norton. "Mary Woodforde's Booke, 1684-1690." In <u>Woodforde Papers and Diaries</u>. Dorothy Heighes Woodforde, ed. London, Peter Davies, 1932. [28] pages. N.I.W.

Although a Protestant, Woodforde supported James II. This is a candid and brief account of familial and social affairs at Binstead, her home. Excerpt: "Bless our Late King James (wheresoever he is), with all the grace of thy holy Spirit open his eyes to the ways of truth, and embrace them before it is too late."

Woolley, Hannah. See Wolley, Hannah.

633B Worcester, Margaret Somerset, Countess of. <u>To the Parliament of the Commonwealth...The humble Petition of</u>. [London, 1654.] Broadside. W 3537. TT Reel 246:669.f.19(27).

The Countess was married to Edward, Earl of Worcester in 1639, when her portion amounted to 20,000 pounds. Here she claims in nine years she has received only four hundred pounds from his estate. Having discovered the house remains unsold, she asks for it along with other things "as may be discovered."

634B [Wyndham, Anne Gerard.] <u>Claustrum Regale Reservatum or the Kings Concealment at Trent</u>. [London], Printed by A. W. for Will: Nott, 1667. 48 pages. W 3772. EEB Reel 1055:11.

This story concerns the smuggling of Charles II out of England by Jane Lane following the battle of Worcester during the Civil War. The author notes "persons of both sexes" provided assistance during his flight. Publication was apparently at first delayed by the king. Strong royalist views are presented in opposition to legal and religious arguments for rebellion against the crown.

635B Yeamans, Isabel. <u>An Invitation of Love to all who hunger and thirst after Righteousness</u>. [London], 1679. 51 pages. Y 20. EEB Reel 403:13.

Writing from Swarthmore Hall, the home of Margaret Fell Fox, Yeamans advises about the correct path to righteousness, while warning of the perils of sin. The Quaker principle of the light underlies her views. Yeamans notes the importance of the discovery by a woman that Christ's body was missing after the Resurrection, and mentions both "Sons and Daughters" witnessed Christ's visit to earth.

Yeats, Susannah. <u>An Account of Some of the Dying Sayings of</u>. See 971A.

636B York, Anne Hyde, Duchess of. <u>A Copy of a paper written by the late Dutchess of York</u>. [London, 1686.] Broadside. Y 46. EEB Reel 1055:21.

Anne Hyde explains her conversion to Catholicism, saying she realizes leaving the Church of England renders her "lyable to many censures," particularly because she had been a vocal critic of Catholicism. Hyde claims England shunned the religion for the worst of reasons: Henry VIII wanted to divorce, Edward VI's uncle exploited Church lands, and Queen Elizabeth denied the Church out of political expediency. Hyde concludes: "I would never have done, if I had thought it possible to save my soul otherwise." See also 609A.

637B Zins-Penninck (Sewel), Judith. <u>Some Worthy Proverbs left behind by...to be read in the congregation of the Saints</u>. London, Printed for William Warwick, 1663. 10 pages. Z 13. EEB Reel 1272:22.

This translated Dutch Quaker tract encourages wisdom and love as the way to salvation. It also argues for the importance of friendship. Zins-Penninck was known as Judith Zinnspinning or Zinnspenning.

Part II

Works For and About Women

1A A., I. <u>The Good Womans Champion Or, A defence of the Weaker Vessell</u>. London, Printed for Francis Grove, [1650?]. [14] pages. A 9A.

The author defends women against the "envious revilings, slanderous raylings, and malignant writings of some inveterate ill-bred spirits." Like Agrippa, he thinks women are purer than men, but their closest companions. He cites virtuous biblical and classical women as examples. A humorous poem is appended by another author entitled "A Carefull Wives [sic] Good Counsell to a Carelesse bad Husband, in a Dialogue."

2A Abbadie, Jacques. <u>A Panegyric On our late sovereign lady Mary Queen of England, Scotland, France and Ireland, of Glorious and Immortal Memory</u>. London, Printed for Hugh Newman, [1695]. 32 pages. A 56. EEB Reel 1:11.

Abbadie, a doctor of divinity and minister of the French Church in the Savoy, lauds the recently deceased Mary II. He calls her "the ornament of her nation, and glory of her sex," dwelling on her modest heroism.

3A Abbot, Robert. <u>Milk for Babes; or, A Mother's Catechism for Her Children</u>. London, Printed by John Legatt for Philemon Stephens, 1646. 326 pages. A 69. EEB Reel 46:2.

In this children's catechism written by an Anglican minister, Abbot speaks of their original sin, the power of God and the mercy of Christ. The maternal conceit-- "I have brought thee forth into this world in great sorrow"--assuages the harshness of the message. Despite the title, the book only obliquely addresses the duties of women. Three other sermons are appended.

4A <u>Abstersae Lacrymae. The Poet Buffoon'd...a vindication of the Unfortunate Ladies</u>. London, Printed for Randal Taylor, 1694. 110 pages. A 113. EEB Reel 46:13.

This lewd misogynistic piece attacks an unidentified poet, a woman-hater. It portrays lusty women discussing their sexual needs and bemoaning their husbands' impotence and incompetence. It contains many double entendres, including allusions to women's "broad" natures and to drooping penes.

5A An Abstract of the Unfortunate and unpallarel [sic] case of Elizabeth Wandesford Widdow and Relict of Garret Foulkes, Esq.   [Dublin?, 1693.] Broadside. A 145A.

This case involves Wandesford, a loyal Irish Protestant, her elderly mother and her children. Her husband and brothers died in Irish-English battles, and their castle was placed under seige. Wandesford wants William III to continue her annual stipend of 200 pounds, originally designated by Mary to be drawn from Irish forfeitures. After a three-year hiatus in the payment schedule, the widow's misfortune was compounded by the deaths of five family members.

6A The Account Audited, or the Date of the Resurrection of the Witnessess. London, Printed by T. R. and E. M., 1649.   16 pages.   A 169.   TT Reel 85:E.550(21).

The author criticizes Mary Cary's writings, giving special attention to her projections for the Second Coming of Christ. Cary had said it would occur on April 5, 1645, and to lend credence to her prediction, she identified herself as "M. Cary a Minister." See also works by Mary Cary in Part B.

7A The Account Of several of the most Remarkable Tryals that were Tryed at the Sessions-house in the Old-Bailey...And The Tryal and Sentence of Mrs. Eliz. Cellier the Popish Midwife. [London, Printed for T. Davies, 1680.] 4 pages. A 222. EEB Reel 2:29.

This document relates trial details of both men and women. It includes the sentencing of Elizabeth and Mary Johnson for theft, Mary Bucknal for murdering her illegitimate male child, Elizabeth Browne for robbery and Elizabeth Cellier for publishing her allegedly libelous work Malice Defeated. The women were sentenced either to death or lashing.

8A An Account of the Manner, Behaviour and Execution of Mary Aubry, who was Burnt...in Leicester Fields. London, Printed for E. Mallet, 1687. Broadside. A 319D.

A French midwife was accused of strangling and dismembering her husband. Notwithstanding a show of remorse during her imprisonment, she was hanged and then burned. Aubry was also known as Mary Hobry. See also 431A, 793A and 940A.

9A An Account of the Proceedings of the New Parliament of Women.   [London], Printed for J. Coniers, [1683].   [6] pages.   A 370.   EEB Reel 339:10.

In this bawdy satire "languishing maidens" submit a petition decrying widows who have had several husbands, and bachelors who promise more than they can deliver. Among the participants: Lyddy Long-Tongue, Ann Ape-like, Alice Allcock. They ask bachelors to be kind to maids or be "gelded"; women with old husbands to take younger lusty ones; and widows of forty to be content with husbands and one "friend." They claim bachelors should be available to young women over seventeen.

10A An Account of the seducing of Ann...Ketelbey...to the Popish Religion. [London, Printed for J. Nutt, 1700.] 7 pages. A 382. EEB Reel 3:21.

This anti-Catholic piece is about the secret conversion to Catholicism of a young Protestant woman. After her parents learned about it, Catholics hid her because she feared her father would do her harm. She reluctantly returned to her parents. The story is told from the parents' perspective.

11A An Account of the Tryal and Examination of Joan Buts, for being a Common Witch and Inchantress. [London, Printed for S. Gardener, 1682.] Broadside. A 413. EEB Reel 47:18.

Buts was accused of lacking a fear of God, following the devil and causing two females to languish and, in one case, to die. The parents of Mary Farmer, a sick child, claimed Buts acted strangely near the site where they buried Mary's urine and burned her clothing--remedies prescribed by a physician. Joan Burrige, a servant who survived enchantment, leveled a similar charge. Buts was acquitted. See also 836A.

12A Acrostick on Mary, Queen to...James II. London, Printed by J. S. for William Cox, [1689-94]. Broadside. A 445.

This encomium for the queen, "Great Britains Boast, and Glory of her Sex," is fashioned from the acrostick "Mary Queen of Great Britain."

13A Adams, Richard. "How Child-bearing Women ought to be encouraged and supported against, in, and under the Hazard of their Travail?" In The Morning Exercises at Cripplegate. Samuel Annesley, ed. Vol. Three. London, 1682. Item: N.I.W. Collection: A 3231*. EEB Reel 1085:1.

This sermon, based on biblical texts, is meant to cheer women during childbirth. Adams says their pain atones for Eve's sin, their salvation lies in bearing children and the "sorrows of child-bed should not dishearten Christian women from entering into a marriage-state."

14A An address of Thanks, On Behalf of The Church of England to Mris. James, For Her Worthy Vindication of that Church. London, Printed by George Larkin, 1687. Broadside. A 546. EEB Reel 3:43.

This satire mocks Elinor James for beseeching the king while seeking the passage of laws to benefit herself. It describes her work as an effort "to upbraid and affront the King, whilst we seem to complement Him." The author claims only James would come to the defense of the Church, even though others are living on ecclesiastical pensions. See also works by James in Part B.

Advertisement be [sic] Agnes Campbel, relict. See 129B.

15A Ady, Thomas. A Candle in the Dark: or, a Treatise concerning the nature of Witches. London, Printed for R. I. to be sold by Tho. Newberry, 1656. 172 pages. A 674. TT Reel 131:E.869(5).

This thoughtful scholarly work advises judges, justices of the peace and jurors about "what to do before pass[ing] sentence on...witches." Ady does not deny the existence of witchcraft, but suggests most persons prosecuted are not witches. He rejects many myths about witches, e.g., copulating with satan, consorting with familiars like black dogs, and strange body marks.

16A Ady, Thomas. A Perfect Discovery of Witches. London, Printed for R. I. and to bee [sic] sold by H. Brome, 1661. A 676.

This item is essentially the same as 15A.

17A Agrippa von Nettesheim, Henrich Cornelius. Female Pre-eminence: or The dignity and excellency of that sex, above the male. London, Printed by T. R. and M. D. and are to be sold by Henry Million, 1670. 83 pages. A 784. EEB Reel 444:4 and TT Reel 173:E.1289(3).

This 1509 treatise was not published until 1532 (Cologne) as De Nobilitate et Praecellentia Foeminei Sexus. Agrippa, historian to Emperor Charles V, studied Cabalistic and Neoplatonic thought, reflected here in preoccupation with etymology and hierarchy. For example, he says women are superior because they were created last. Other arguments are based on achievements of biblical and ancient figures and the physiology and behavior of both sexes. Agrippa blames female status on male tyranny and poor education, claming females have the "same Rationall Power and Speech" as do males.

18A Agrippa von Nettesheim, Henrich Cornelius. The Glory of Women; or, A Looking-glasse. London, Printed by T. H. for F. Coles, 1652. A 787*.

This item is essentially the same as 17A.

19A Albion's Tears on the Death of Her Sacred Majesty Queen Mary. A Pindarick Poem. London, Printed for J. Place and sold by J. Whitlock, 1695. 11 pages. A 880. EEB Reel 444:9.

This eulogy for Mary II follows traditional form, emphasizing her generosity and tenderness. It is most interesting for its entreaty to the "fairest sex," to emulate the queen and strive to be "free from Cloisterous Austerity." Mary is called both women's friend and "Great Protectress."

20A The Ale-Wives Complaint, against the Coffee-Houses, In a Dialogue between a Victuallers Wife and A Coffee-Man Being at difference about spoiling each others Trade. London, Printed for John Tomson, 1675. 6 pages. A 905. EEB Reel 1298:9.

In a satirical dialogue an ale-wife complains of losing business to coffee-houses, mocks their menus, and accuses a coffee-man of regaling clientele with unimportant news. He says she fills glasses half full with froth and "droppings." She likens the coffee he serves to soot. Since women worked in ale houses, and men in the coffee-houses, this work may be a whimsical view of competition between sex-typed occupations.

21A All the Proceedings at the Sessions of the Peace holden at Westminster...against Elizabeth Sorrell the Elder, Margaret Dunlape, Anne Burley,

Frances Bedwell, Elizabeth Sorrell the Younger. London, Printed for Thomas Harper, 1651. 14 pages. A 946. TT Reel 98:E.637(18).

Four female and six male defendants were accused of believing that John Robins, alias Roberts, was the father of Christ and his wife would bring forth the Savior. All were imprisoned. Their petition requests pardons and claims they were seduced.

22A Allein, Toby. Truths Manifest: or A Full and Faithfull Narrative, of all Passages relating to the excommunication of Mrs. Marie Allein. London, Printed for F. E., 1658. [42] pages. A 958. EEB Reel 830:22.

The husband of a woman excommunicated from a church in Exon attempts to counter lies and vindicate his wife. Marie (Mary) Allein left her church when the minister (Lewis Stucley) petitioned on behalf of the congregation (without its approval) to dissolve Parliament. When her request for an impartial hearing was denied, the minister defamed her in a sermon. See also 471B and Addendum 152.

23A [Allestree, Richard.] The Ladies Calling. Two Parts. Oxford, Printed at the Theatre, 1673. 245 pages. A 1141*. EEB Reels 705:6, 7; 781:6,7; and 831:8,9; 1413:11 and 1582:3.

This popular guide for female behavior went through seven impressions before 1701. A politically active Anglican divine, Allestree prescribes proper familial, domestic and personal behavior for gentlewomen. The book is divided thematically according to the virtues expected of women--"Of Modesty, of Meekness, of Compassion, etc." and according to marital status--"Of Virgins, of Wives and of Widows."

24A Ambrose, Isaac. Redeeming the Time...A Sermon preached At Preston in Lancashire...at the Funeral of...the Lady Margaret Houghton. London, Printed by T. C. for Nath. Webb and William Grantham, 1658. 32 pages. A 2968. TT Reel 141:E.945(3).

In this sermon Houghton is discussed for only about five pages. She is noted for her prayer, needlework, humility, patience, charity and her respect for ministers. Ambrose claims she desired death so she could join Christ.

25A [Ames, Richard.] The Female Fire-ships. A Satyr against Whoring. London, Printed for E. Richardson, 1691. 19 pages. A 2979. EEB Reel 198:10.

Ames was one of several men who wrote misogynistic pieces with anti-male replies. This one, written after the death of a fellow student who consorted with prostitutes, is a warning in verse for innocent young men about the evil of streetwalkers. The author says London strumpets are "true canibals [sic] who can with ease devour/A dozen Men while Time shapes out an Hour."

26A [Ames, Richard.] The Folly of Love. A new Satyr against Woman. The Second Edition, Corrected and Enlarged. London, Printed for E. Hawkins, 1693. 22 pages. A 2981. EEB Reel 1194:24.

This satyrical verse argues the world's problems began with Eve. Ames says women's single positive quality--their beauty--is used to tempt men to sin. He claims little good can be said of women who make of marriage "slavery for men." On women's creation: "And of that Crooked shapeless thing did frame The Worlds Great Plague and did give it Woman's name."

27A [Ames, Richard.] The Pleasures of Love and Marriage. A Poem in Praise of the Fair Sex. London, Printed by H. N. and R. Baldwin, 1691. 26 pages. A 2987. EEB Reel 340:12.

Ames answers recent satires of women, especially his own The Folly of Love. Typical of sycophantic defenses of women, it argues for female purity and male envy.

28A [Ames, Richard.] Sylvia's Complaint, of her Sexes Unhappiness. A Poem. The Second Part of Sylvia's Revenge. London, Printed and sold by Richard Baldwin, 1692. 24 pages. A 2992A. EEB Reels 298:25 and 1734:15.

Ames assumes a female persona to continue the poetic satire begun in 29A. He calls men women's "deadly foes": women are warned to beware of male duplicity. Ames says women will ultimately seek revenge against men by shunning cosmetics: "Our Minds, and not our Faces we'll adorn/That's the Imployment for which we were born."

29A [Ames, Richard.] Sylvia's Revenge, or a Satyr against Man; in answer to the Satyr against Woman. London, Printed by Joseph Streater and are to be sold by John Southby, 1688. 22 pages. A 2992D*. EEB Reels 298:26, 948:23, 1663:4 and 1754:5.

This extended poetic attack on men is ostensibly by a woman angry about the proliferation of misogynistic literature. In reply to 400A, Ames satirizes men, calling them villains, monsters and traitors. Robert Gould answered with A Satyrical Epistle (1691). See also 251B, a woman's reply to Gould's satire.

30A The Amours of Bonne Sforza, Queen of Polonia. London, Printed by T. M. for R. Bentley, 1684. 155 pages. A 3021B. EEB Reel 1772:11.

This novel is supposedly based on true exploits of a Polish princess. Sigismundus, King of Poland, took Bonna, the daughter of John Galeas, Duke of Milan, as his second wife. Her intrigues and romances in the duchy of Barr in Naples provide material for an obviously embellished tale.

31A The Amours of Messalina, late queen of Albion. By a Woman of Quality. Four Parts in One Vol. London, Printed for John Lyford, 1689. A 3023. EEB Reels 1114:24 and 1661:3.

This four-part roman a clef is characterized by the British Library as a libel of Mary of Modena. Although the novels are attributed to a woman, the Library of Congress suggests Gregorio Leti as the possible author. Other volumes in the series are The Second Part of the Amours of Messalina and Love Letters between Polydorus (also published as The Royal Wanton). Here part four is titled The Amours of the French King. See also 542A.

32A [Anderton, Lawrence.]   The English Nunne. Being a Treatise Wherein the Author Endeavoreth to Draw Yong [sic] and Unmarried Catholic Gentlewomen to imbrace a votary and religious life.   London, St. Omers, English College Press, 1642.   175 pages.   A 3109.   EEB Reel 1375:2.

Anderton encourages young English women to enter the convents of Western Europe. He praises monastic life and enumerates the hardships of marriage for women: irresponsible husbands, pain in childbirth and unruly children. He implies those who refuse a religious vocation because it precludes marriage should view celibacy as appealing.

33A An Answer to a Book, Intituled, the Doctrine and Discipline of Divorce, or, A Plea for Ladies and Gentlewomen, and all other Married Women against Divorce. London, Printed by G. M. for William Lee, 1644. 44 pages. A 3304. EEB Reels 7:4 and 231:E.17(12); TT Reel 3:E.17(12).

In a carefully reasoned refutation of Milton's famous treatise on divorce (594A), the author criticizes his view that "a man may divorce or put away his wife for indisposition, unfitnesse, or contrariety of mind." He says adultery is the only true ground for divorce.

34A An Answer to a Pamphlet, entituled, the Parliament of Ladies. London, 1647. 2 pages. N.I.W.

This satirical response to Neville's Parliament of Ladies criticizes his slander of several lords and ladies. The author suggests Neville should be left to the mercy of the women's parliament.

35A An Answer to a Printed Paper, Entituled, The Case of Mary Dutchess of Norfolk. [London, 1700]. Broadside. A 3339A.

The author defends the Duke of Norfolk against charges he's depleted his estranged wife's estate. He claims the duchess became indebted "tho' she had a 1,000 pound a year pin-money all the while." The document also describes the duchess' flight to France and her change of religion. See also 164A, 649A, 886A and 920A.

36A An Answer to the Poor Whore's Complaint. London, Printed for F. Bissel, [1685-1692]. Broadside. A 3431. EEB Reel 1414:42.

"A bully spark" addresses this broadside to Mistress Nell (possibly Nell Gwynne, who died in 1687), "the common Crack of Fleet-street." He sympathizes with her complaint that a surfeit of strumpets is lowering the going rate. He proposes that only those whose mothers were prostitutes should practice the profession.

37A An Answer to a Scoffing and Lying Lybell, Put forth and privately dispersed under the Title of A Wonderfull account of the Cureing the Kings-evil, by Madam Fanshaw the Duke of Monmouth's Sister.   London, Printed by T. B., 1681. Broadside. A 3347. EEB Reel 1245:31.

The author blames the Jesuits for a pamphlet ridiculing the Duke of Monmouth and his half-sister, Mary Fanshawe. He claims it discredits Monmouth, viewed as an obstacle to the succession of James, Duke of York. (Monmouth was an illegitimate son of Charles II.) Fanshawe's supposed authorship (she was apparently converted to Protestantism by her husband) questions Monmouth's legitimacy and religious commitment. The "Kings-evil" both alludes humorously to Monmouth and refers to a popular notion that only royalty could cure scrofula, a disease characterized by running sores. See also 887A.

38A An answer to the Character of an Exchange-wench. London, Printed for Thomas Croskill, 1675. 6 pages. A 3397. EEB Reel 1394:2.

This item replies to an earlier attack on the morality of women working in the London Exchange. It exaggerates the integrity and skill of a typical female worker beyond credulity: Her shop is like a nunnery, and her financial acumen makes her a desirable wife. See also 40A.

39A Answers for James Anderson and Agnes Campbell his Mother, To the Complaint Exhibited Against them. [London? 1688]. Broadside. A 3463A.

The printers are charged with publishing proclamations of the Council and other items belonging to the office of their Majesties Printers "without taking the Oath of Allegiance and Certificate of Appointment to be taken by persons in Public Trust." The accused are to be deprived of said office. The broadside argues the oath is for military personnel and others in the public trust, not printers, but claims the pair are "most willing to swear the Oath of Allegiance."

40A The Ape-Gentlewoman, or the Character of an Exchange-Wench. London, Printed for Francis Pye, 1675. 6 pages. A 3527. EEB Reel 1029:3.

This misogynistic publication attacks female apprentices or traders at the London Exchange. It is replete with double entendre and invective. See also 38A.

The [Ap]prentices Answer to the Whores Petition. See 724A.

41A [Argences, D'.] The Countess of Salisbury; or, The most Noble Order of the Garter. Two Vols. London, Printed for R. Bentley and S. Magnes, 1683. A 3630*. EEB Reel 1434:26.

This translated French romance, set in medieval England, concerns the origins of the Order of the Garter. Based on the affair between Joan, Countess of Salisbury and Edward III, the story shifts between romantic intrigues of the nobility to developments in the French and English wars.

42A Aristotle's Masterpiece: or, The Secrets of Generation...very necessary for all midwives, nurses and young-married women. London, Printed for W. B., 1695. 182 pages. A 3689BA*. EEB Reel 7:22.

This popular midwifery volume is based largely on work by Nicholas Culpeper, Albertus Magnus and common folklore. The first part concerns propitious timing of sexual intercourse, conditions for conception, female infertility, monstrous births, genitalia, copulation. It propounds the "semence theory"--both parties must experience pleasure during intercourse for conception to occur. The second part covers maladies of the womb, a prolapsed uterus, false conception, miscarriage, treatment during and after labor, etc.

43A The Arminian Nunnery: or, a Briefe Description and Relation of the late erected Monastical Place...at little Gidding in Huntingdonshire. London, Printed for Thomas Underhill, [1641].   10 pages.   A 3699.   EEB Reel 255:E.171(10) and TT Reel 30:E.171(10).

This publication requests that Parliament close the famous girls' school at Little Gidding because of its alleged Catholic affiliation.   The author claims the director's son is a "priest-like man," his nieces are old-maid virgins, and the school's regulations represent Arminianism, "a bridge to popery."

44A The Arraignment and Acquittal of Sir Edward Mosely, Baronet; Indited at the King's-Bench Bar for a Rape, upon the Body of Mrs. Anne Swinnerton. London, Printed by E. G. for W. L., 1647. 12 pages. A 3740.

The Swinnerton family claims no lawyer will take their case, presumably because of Mosely's title.   The charge of premeditated rape is supported by Swinnerton's maid.   Mosely's witnesses claim the victim was his mistress and had a history of staging rapes for profit.   Mosely is told to "heed what company you keep hereafter."

45A The Arraignement, tryal and examination of Mary Moders, Otherwise Stedman, now Carleton, (Stiled the German Princess). London, Printed for N. Brook, 1663. 16 pages. A 3764. EEB Reel 730:22.

The "German Princess" was accused of deceiving her husband (who had also falsely claimed to be a gentleman) by feigning royal origins and concealing her first marriage to a shoemaker.   Moders claims her husband's father-in-law stole her jewelry; he claims she deceived his son, the victim of her bigamous deceit. This is one of many publications about her.

The Articles and Charge of Impeachment against the German lady.   See 151A.

46A Articles of High Treason and Other High Crimes and Misdemeanors Against the Dutchess of Portsmouth. [London, 1680.] Broadside. A 3845*. EEB Reels 1414:47 and 1434:28.

The Duchess of Portsmouth, Louise Renee de Keroualle, mistress of Charles II, is accused of crimes against the English people--having relations with the king while harboring "contagious distempers," subverting the government by attempting to introduce popery, gossiping about her alleged marriage to the king, etc. It is a poitical attack on one of the king's most extravagant and least popular lovers.

47A Arwaker, Edmund. An Elegy on her Grace Elizabeth Duchess of Ormond, who died July the 21st 1684. London, Printed for Thomas Newcomb, 1684. 5 pages. A 3905. EEB Reel 8:18.

This typical elegy expresses sympathy for the widower James Butler, first Duke and twelfth Earl of Ormond and Ossory, who had lost his son, wife and sister in succession.   The duchess had been a ward of the Crown.

48A Arwaker, Edmund. A Pindaric Ode upon our late Sovereign Lady of Blessed Memory, Queen Mary. London, Printed for Rich. Parker, 1695. 12 pages. A 3910. EEB Reel 805:46.

This formal eulogy, written for Mary II who died of smallpox, is largely about the grief of England and William, her husband. It includes a dramatization of the death scene and encourages eschewing grief in exchange for thought about "the haughty Insolence of France."

49A Arwaker, Edmund. A Poem Humbly Dedicated to the Queen on the Occasion of her Majesty's Happy Conception. London, Randal Taylor, 1688. 7 pages. A 3911. EEB Reel 198:14.

This poem for Mary of Modena honors her conception after her lengthy infertility. Such poems were written by supporters of James II who favored his dominion, rather than his replacement by his adult Protestant daughters, Anne or Mary.

50A Atherton, Henry.   The Resurrection Proved: or, The Life to come Demonstrated...Relation of what Hapned to Mrs. Anna Atherton. London, Printed by T. Dawks, 1680. Broadside. A 4114. EEB Reel 1245:44.

This broadside records the deathbed vision of a girl, aged fourteen, who had lain in a trance for seven days and then told of having seen heaven. Her brother, a physician, recorded her story. She also claimed to have seen some people who died during her trance.

51A Atterbury, Francis.   A Discourse Occasioned by the Death of the Right Honourable the Lady Cutts. Second Edition. London, Printed for Tho. Bennet, 1698. 40 pages. A 4148*. EEB Reel 341:14.

This publication is dedicated to John Cutts, Commander in Chief of the King's Forces in Ireland and Colonel in the Coldstream Guards. The author notes the gravity of death and considers the deceased, a biblical scholar, diligent in her devotions. The essay concludes with a brief biography, stressing her role as a model for her sex. Lady Elizabeth, Cutts' second wife, died at eighteen in childbirth. See also 457A, 733a, 851A and 955A.

52A Atterbury, Lewis. A Sermon Preached at the Funeral of the Lady Compton. London, Printed by R. E. and are to be sold by Randal Taylor, 1687. 24 pages. A 4156A.

Aterbury, rector of Sywell in Northampton, dedicated this sermon to William Willmer, Esq. The text is based on Psalms 90.12 and concerns the uncertainty and brevity of life, and its enhancement through virtue and piety. Aterbury offers little about Lady Compton other than her description as a devoted Anglican.

53A An Auction of Whores, or, The Bawds Bill of Sale, for Bartholomew-Fair, held in the Cloysters, near Smithfield. London, Printed for N. H., [1691]. Broadside. N.I.W.

This satire announces an auction of disreputable women along with pick-pockets, pimps and the like. The list includes brief descriptions of those for sale:

"...Country Whores, Ubiquitarian Whores, Journey women Whores...about 65,000." Single men and bachelors are advised to "bring Money with you, and I'll secure you shall carry none home."

54A Austin, William. A Joyous Welcome to...Catherine. [London, 1662.] [6] pages. A 4261. EEB Reel 1323:21.

This poem welcomes Catharine of Braganza to London on her initial visit with Charles II. It was apparently presented to her on the Thames. Many classical allusions are explained in footnotes.

55A A[ylett, Robert.] "Susanna: or the Arraignment of The two unjust Elders." In Divine and Moral Speculations. London, Abel Roper, 1654. 44 pages. Item: N.I.W. Collection: A 4285. TT Reel 184:E.1439(3).

This poetic parable in four books is about the unsuccessful attempt of two judges to corrupt a virtuous maiden. Excerpt: "Old letchers that in beastly lust delight,/See here your deeds of darkness brought to light."

56A A[ylett], R[obert.] A Wife, Not Ready Made, But Bespoken. Second Edition. London, Printed for A. R., 1653. 26 pages. A 4286. TT Reel 184:E.1439(2).

These amusing debates, about the pros and cons of marriage, take place between a poor young shepherd and a friend who tells him how to succeed in love without marrying. The tone is fairly light in comparison to more caustic satires. The final pages contain brief elegies for Mary Alleyn, who died in childbirth, and her husband Edmund.

57A B. An elegy on the most accomplished virgin Madam Elizabeth Hurne, who departed this life on the 27th of July, 1683. London, Printed by N. T., 1983 [1683]. Broadside. B 2. EEB Reel 1583:25.

This typical eulogy alludes to Hurne's religion ("that which the Pope and Presbyter oppose"). She was certainly a dissenter and possibly a Quaker. The author also alludes to her political activity; apparently Hurne was harassed by the Whigs but withstood their persecution.

58A B., A. A Letter of Advice Concerning Marriage. London, Printed for William Miller, [1676]. 29 pages. B 15. EEB Reel 374:7.

A gentleman advises his younger male cousin who is contemplating marriage. He claims wives can do chores unseemly for men and can preserve one's estate. He cautions against marrying a lazy woman and recommends one who can administer an estate and will bring an adequate dowry.

59A B., A. An Ode Occasion'd by the Death of the Queen. London, Printed by Tho. Warren for Francis Saunders, 1695. 2 pages. B 25. EEB Reel 1394:30.

The author includes a rather sarcastic prefatory letter to John Dryden. Written on Queen Mary's death from smallpox, the ode is grim and cynical. Excerpt:"The Queen is dead and Lewis lives/O Justice, tho' from Earth long since you flew,/Will you forsake the heavens too?" (Lewis is presumably Louis XIV of France.)

60A B., E. <u>Strange and Wonderful News Of the Birth</u>. London, 1685. Broadside. B 55. EEB Reel 1604:16.

In a letter the author writes of a stillborn monstrous child born with two heads and three arms in the county of Meath in Ireland. He marvels that the mother is yet alive and reports a similar birth and autopsy elsewhere.

61A B., F. <u>The Office of the good House-wife, With Necessary Directions for the Ordering of her Family and Dairy</u>. London, Printed by T. Ratcliffe and N. Thompson for Richard Mills, 1672. 143 pages. B 63. EEB Reel 49:31.

This guide provides directions for keeping a dairy and maintaining a country family. A woman is reminded she is a helpmate and warned to avoid "meddling above her place." A full description of the typical farm woman's duties is included along with flora and fauna she cares for--swine, cattle, poultry, ducks, peacocks, geese, honeybees, silk worms and so on.

62A B., F. <u>Vercingetorixa: or, The Germane Princess Reduced to an English Habit</u>. London, 1663. 42 pages. B 65. EEB Reel 445:8.

Mary Carleton, an alleged imposter who claimed to have been a German princess, is the butt of this satire and subject of several other pieces.

63A B., J. <u>Mrs. Wardens observations upon her husbands reverend speech</u>. [London, 1642.] 8 pages. B 114. EEB Reel 247:E.115(20) and TT Reel 20:E.115(20).

This piece apparently satirizes women's insistence on expressing their political views. Mrs. Warden is a schoolmistress, midwife and minister's wife. Her humorous language may imply inebriation. She discusses the militia, Ireland, Scotland, religion and learning. Excerpt: "We can...prove it as lawfull for women as men to be BISHOPS. We have just cause to vent our HOLY malice against the lawes for putting a PROPHANE bridle on us." This item is also included in 863A.

64A B., M. <u>The Ladies Cabinet. Enlarged and Opened: Containing Many Rare Secrets</u>. London, Printed by T. M. for M. M., G. Bedell and T. Collins, 1654. 227 pages. B 135*. EEB Reels 50:1 and 1394:37; TT Reel 194:E.1528(1).

The preface notes an earlier edition was well received. The book is divided into three parts: preserving and candying, physick and surgery, and cookery and housewifery. It is similar to, but somewhat more lengthy than, other guides for homemakers.

65A B., R. <u>The Coppie of a Letter sent to a Gentlewoman</u>. London, 1642. 8 pages. B 163. EEB Reel 1626:36.

This letter responds to an earlier one by the gentlewoman to her Anabaptist sister. Arguing from scripture, the author claims there is no necessity for infant baptism. He notes sprinkling with water is not a substitute for total immersion and encourages independent thinking.

66A B., T. Extraordinary Newes. From the Court of Spain: declaring The late Solemnities that were perform'd in the highest way of magnificence at the Reception of the Young Queen, the Emperors Daughter. London, Printed for Richard Lowndes, 1650. 13 pages. B 183. TT Reel 93:E.603(11).

This publication describes the marriage of Philip IV of Spain, forty-six, and Maria Anna of Austria, age sixteen. The festivities took place in both Italy and Spain.

67A B., W. Sacred To the Precious Memory of Mrs. Mary Boyleston, Daughter of Mr. Thomas Boyleston, of Fan-Church Street, London. London, Printed for John Macock, 1657. 35 pages. B 225.

Boyleston apparently boarded with the author's family and died in their Staffordshire home. This funeral sermon is dedicated to her family in London. She is lauded for her strength, revealed through voracious scriptural reading. Aside from a description of her final days, there is little biographical material.

68A Baber, John. To the King, upon the Queens being deliver'd of a son. June the 10th. A Poem. London, Printed by Mary Thompson, [1688]. 10 pages. B 246. EEB Reel 445:17.

This congratulatory poem celebrates the birth of the long-awaited heir, James Francis Edward Stuart, son of James II and Mary of Modena. There is praise for the glory of Britain and the monarchy, but little about the queen.

69A The Batchellors Answer to the Maids Complaint or the Young Men's Vindication...setting forth the subtle Tricks and Vices of the Female Party. London, Printed for J. Coniers, 1675. 8 pages. B 257. EEB Reel 1085:8.

The bachelors' lament is they have loved better than earlier generations and could continue to be passionate if not forced to wed. This typical anti-marriage satire contains pungent language: "...to be tyed for term of life like a monkey by the loyns to a bedpost, with the same woman...[is unthinkable]."

70A The Batchelor's Directory: Being a Treatise of the Excellence of Marriage...an Apology for the Women against the Calumnies of the Men. London, Printed for Richard Cumberland and Benjamin Bragg, 1694. 253 pages. B 260*.

This text says although both sexes are commanded to marry, women, do so more readily than men. Women are also influenced more by their parents with regard to marriage. Even when a woman denies it, "there is nothing she desires with greater passion than to marry." The author claims "marriage puts men under engagements, which come very near to servitude."

71A Bacon, Francis. The Felicity of Queen Elizabeth: and her Times. London, Printed by T. Newcomb, for George Latham, 1651. 42 pages. B 298. EEB Reel 806:27.

In a summary of Elizabeth's life and reign, Bacon calls her a "wonder of her Sex" and focuses on her statesmanship. Bacon notes "her single status gave her no partner in [her] glory." He gives virtually no attention to her scholarship.

72A Baker, Daniel. <u>A True Account of the Great Tryals and Cruel Sufferings undergone by those two faithfull Servants of God, Katherine Evans and Sarah Cheevers</u>. London, Printed for R. Wilson, 1663. 277 pages. N.I.W.

Baker defends the right of Quaker missionaries to speak regardless of sex. He notes those who are under "the grace and truth that is in the one seed, Christ...are not under the law, which saith, the woman is not to usurp authority over the man." Baker describes the experience of Cheevers and Evans, who were incarcerated for three years in Malta. See also 143B and 268B.

73A Banks, John. <u>The Innocent Usurper, Or, the Death of the Lady Jane Gray</u>. A Tragedy. London, Printed for R. Bentley, 1694. 60 pages. B 658. EEB Reel 51:15.

The remarkable, bright and honorable Lady Jane Grey is the subject of this play. The cousin of Edward VI, she was matched by her powerful relatives with Guildford Dudley (Northumberland) in the hope she would succeed the king. The ploy failed, and she and her husband were finally beheaded for treason. The drama is sympathetic to the Lady Jane and critical of her political exploitation and forced marriage.

74A Banks, John. <u>The Island Queens: Or, the Death of Mary Queen of Scotland</u>. London, Printed for R. Bentley, 1684. 70 pages. B 659.

This dramatization of Queen Elizabeth's tortured deliberation over whether to execute her cousin Mary is quite similar to later plays and contains a lengthy discussion which allegedly took place between Mary and Elizabeth. Mary is treated favorably notwithstanding her seemingly heavy dependence upon men in the play.

75A Banks, John. <u>Vertue Betrayed: or, Anna Bullen</u>. A Tragedy. London, Printed for R. Bentley and M. Magnes, [1682]. 79 pages. B 667*. EEB Reel 51:19.

Dedicated to Elizabeth, Countess of Somerset, this play presents a thoroughly sympathetic picture of Anne Boleyn as a woman used and cast aside by Henry VIII, a tragic figure seemingly victimized by fate.

76A Barbaro, Francesco. <u>Directions for Love and Marriage</u>. In Two Books. London, Printed for John Leigh and Tho. Burrell, 1677. 128 pages. B 683A.

Divided into two parts, "the endowments of a wife" and "the duty of a wife," this work argues for a highly circumscribed role for women. It advises young men to marry a competent, wealthy woman, restrict her to the home and require her silence in public.

77A [Barecroft, Charles.] <u>A Letter to a Lady, Furnishing her with Scripture, Testimonies against the Principal Points and Doctrines of Popery</u>. London, Printed for John Taylor, [1688]. 83 pages. B 757. EEB Reel 621:21.

This anti-Catholic tract is intended to be "obvious to a female capacity." Because poorly educated women supposedly "understand nothing of logical reasoning," the author provides them with scriptural arguments against the priestly function and transubstantiation.

78A Barker, Edmund. <u>A Sermon Preached At the Funerall of the Right Honourable and most Excellent Lady, the Lady Elizabeth Capell Dowager</u>. London, Printed by I. R. for John Williams, 1661. 55 pages. B 766. EEB Reel 1626:51.

Dedicated to Capell's son, the essay stresses her total Christian devotion. The sermon includes biographical material interspersed with praise of Capell's piety and modesty.

79A Barnett, Andrew. <u>A Just Lamentation for the Irrevocable Loss of the nation, by the doleful death of the late Queen Mary</u>. London, Printed for Thomas Parkhurst, 1695. 30 pages. B 875B.

This sermon was preached on the occasion of the death of Mary II. It emphasizes her strengths of character: cordiality of affection, constancy of resolution and compassion. Barnett employs the metaphor of a building (Britain) which remains upright even if its foundation has been weakened.

80A Barret, Robert. <u>A Companion for Midwives, Child-Bearing Women, and Nurses</u>. London, Printed for Tho. Ax, 1699. 111 pages. B 913. EEB Reel 120:6.

This volume addresses the "indispositions of women with child," illustrated with examples from this physician's own practice. Its three sections: the character of midwives and instructions for their practice; the physiology of women, causes of infertility and prevention of miscarriage; and the care of neonates. Barret characterizes the ideal midwife as neither too young nor too old, cheerful, strong, inured to fatigue, courteous, sober and chaste.

81A Baston, Edmund. <u>A Funeral Sermon on the Death of Mrs. Paice, Late Wife of Mr. Joseph Plaice Merchant of Clapham</u>. London, Printed by Samuel Bridge, 1700. 61 pages. B 1141. EEB Reel 407:13.

This sermon, dedicated to Mr. Plaice, was published at his request. There is little about the deceased, described as patient, strong, prudent, discreet, cheerful and resigned to the will of God.

82A Batchiler, John. <u>The Virgins Pattern: in the exemplary life and lamented death of Mrs. Susanna Perwick</u>. London, Printed for Simon Dover, 1661. [228] pages. B 1077. EEB Reel 53:1.

This biography tells of a talented musician who died at twenty-four. Taught by several eminent musicians, Perwick played the lute and harpsicord. She had also mastered harmony, calligraphy, cookery and accountancy. She was a lovely, religious woman and a good conversationalist. She bequeathed her belongings to those who attended her in her last days.

83A Bates, William. <u>A Sermon Preached upon the...Death of...Queen Mary</u>. London, Printed for Brabazon Aylmer, 1695. 23 pages. B 1120*. EEB Reels 200:1; 834:2, 3 and 4.

The theme of this sermon is the enduring memory of the righteous. Bates links immortality with the "unchangeable Everlasting Perfection of God," the true foundation of the Church. A second theme is the contrast between the perfection and permanence of God and the imperfection and impermanence of humanity.   Bates stresses even those of high station cannot escape the inevitability of death.

84A Baudier, Michel. The Bawds Tryal and Execution. London, Printed for L. C., 1679. 6 pages. B 1166. EEB Reel 1087:11.

This semi-pornographic fictional account describes the life and travels of a "wicked woman" as she becomes more embroiled in a life of sin. Ultimately she dies, rotting of a "contagious disease."

85A Baxter, Richard. A Breviate of the Life of Margaret, The Daughter of Francis Charlton...and Wife of Richard Baxter. London, Printed for B. Simmons, 1681. 107 pages. B 1194. EEB Reel 200:9.

Puritan Baxter enumerates the sacrifices his recently deceased wife made so he could follow his own principles. He details the many relocations and financial losses she endured. Among her qualities were her cheerfulness, thoughtful counsel and judgment, housekeeping skills, piety and generosity. Baxter hoped his book would encourage more accurate assessments of women's abilities. He also includes a tribute to Margaret Baxter's mother along with her letters.

86A Beaumont, Francis. Bonduca: or, The British Heroine. A Tragedy. London, Printed for Richard Bentley, 1696. 53 [45] pages. B 1584. EEB Reel 166:13.

This play is based on the story of the legendary Boadicea, Queen of the Iceni, who led the Britons against the Roman invaders led by Suetonius in East Anglia. The Beaumont and Fletcher tragedy was originally published in 1647. See also 456A.

87A Beckwith, Marmaduke [and Elizabeth Beckwith]. A True Relation of the Life and Death of Sarah Beckwith, Daughter. London, 1692. 19 pages. B 1655B. EEB Reel 167:3.

The Beckwiths offer testimony and commentary by friends and relatives about Sarah Beckwith, who died at twenty in 1691. She was obedient, pious and serious.

88A Bekker, Balthasar. The World Bewitch'd: or, An Examination of the Common opinions concerning Spirits. Vol. I. [London], Printed for R. Baldwin, 1695. 264 pages. B 1781. EEB Reel 203:10.

This four-part work by a Flemish pastor, translated from the French, presents proofs against the existence of witchcraft. Bekker resolves to follow reason and the Holy Scripture in his analysis. He cites evidence of concepts of demons, apparitions, magic and the devil from pagan, ancient, African and modern cultures. He blames the clergy more than government officials for widespread popular belief in witchcraft.

89A [Betterton, Thomas.] The Revenge. London, Printed for Nathaniel Thompson, 1682. Broadside. B 2084.

This play is attributed to Aphra Behn by Langbaine, Genest and Hargreaves, but to Betterton by Montague Summers, the Wing STC and the Library of Congress; thus authorship is in question. It is based on John Marston's The Dutch Courtesan.

90A [Bilain, Antoine.] A Dialogue Concerning the Rights of Her most Christian Majesty. London, Printed by Thomas Newcomb, 1667. 78 pages. D 1362. EEB Reel 1548:25.

The Folger Shakespeare Library, Washington, D.C., attributes this work to Bilain, although the Wing STC lists it under title. It presents a discussion among French, Flemish and German advocates about the French king's rights to property in the Low Countries inherited by his wife upon the demise of her parents and only brother, Prince Don Baltazar.

91A Birch, Peter. A Funeral Sermon Preached on the Decease of Grace Gethin, Wife of Sir Richard Gethin. London, Printed by D. Edwards, 1700. 28 pages. B 2937. EEB Reel 375:6.

This typical funeral oration was to be preached at Westminster Abbey every Ash Wednesday to perpetuate the subject's memory. Grace Gethin was the only child of Lady Norton, to whom the preface is directed. The sermon praises her general religious and moral qualities and laments her tragic death at twenty-one. There is a commemorative monument of her in the Abbey.

92A [Bishop, John] The fruitful Vi[ne] growing in the good man's gar[den]. [Boston], [1680]. 34 pages. N.I.W.

This wedding sermon emphasizes the wife's role as described in Psalms 128.3: "Thy wife shall be like a fruitful vine." It is an excellent example of the contemporary male view of marriage's advantages. The final two pages discuss how a man can help his wife be a good companion. The remainder of the text is about the glory and usefulness of a good wife. The Houghton Library, Harvard University, attributes it to Bishop.

[Blackley, James.] A Lying Wonder Discovered. See 828A.

93A Blake, William. The Ladies Charity School-House Roll of Highgate: or, A Subscription of many Noble, well-disposed Ladies for the easie carrying of it on. [London?, 1670?] 292 pages. B 3152. EEB Reel 84:2.

The author was Housekeeper to the Ladies Charity School-House. He encourages wealthy women to support the school, although they are not specifically named in the letters included.

94A Blake, William. A New trial of the ladies. Hide-park, May-day. London, Printed by T. Butler and T. Brewster, 1658. B 3153.

This work is the same as 96A.

95A Blake, William. A Serious Letter sent by a private Christian. London, Printed, and are to be sold by Mr. Butler, 1655. B 3153A.

This piece is essentially the same as 97A.

96A Blake, William. The Triall of the Ladies. Hide Park. May Day. Or, The Yellow Books Partner. London, Printed and are to be sold by Mr. Butler, 1656. 46 pages. B 3153B*. EEB Reels 122:8 and 1543:15; TT Reels 132:E.878(2) and 141:E.945(2).

Blake's Puritan diatribe addresses sexual immorality allegedly rampant in Hyde Park. A fictitious trial of indiscreet London lords and ladies takes place before the apostles in hell. The defendants are given symbolic or humorous names, e.g., Mris. Never-repent, Mris. Silver-stuff, Mris. Jewel, and are condemned for their behavior. Punishments specified in scripture are prescribed for the errant socialites. See also 97A.

97A [Blake, William.] The Yellow Book, or A Serious Letter sent by a private Christian to the Lady Consideration, the first day of May, 1658. London, Printed and are to be sold by Tho. Butler and Tho. Brewster, 1658. 23 pages. B 3153E*. EEB Reel 122:9 and TT Reel 127:E.835(2).

Blake's religious tract warns of the evil that befalls drunkards, prostitutes and nonbelievers. It is a tale about Hyde Park, the allegedly sinful women who congregate there, and men who pursue them. He advises young women to read scripture rather than novels. See also 96A.

98A Blegny, Nicholas de. A True History of a Child Anatomized: Which remained Twenty five years in his Mothers Belly. London, Printed by Thomas James for Samuel Lee, 1680. 47 pages. B 3187. EEB Reel 55:4.

Margaret Mathews went into labor for the eleventh time in 1652. She supposedly remained in that state for eighteen or nineteen years. After her death at sixty-two, the autopsy revealed a deteriorated male fetus. Thirteen pages are devoted to this tale; the remainder considers the details of the story. The author was surgeon to the king of France. Illustrations of the fetus are included.

99A The Bloody Husband, and Cruell Neighbour; or, A True historie of Two Murthers lately committed in the Isle of Thanet by the hands of Adam Sprackling, 12 Dec. London, Printed for Tho. Warren, 1653. 14 pages. B 3254. TT Reel 107:E.697(10).

The author presents a grizzly account of Sprackling's murder and mutilation of his wife before two witnesses. He was allegedly a drunken reprobate.

Blow, John. Three Elegies upon the Much Lamented Loss of our Late Most Gracious Queen Mary. See 433A.

100A [Boate, Arnold.] The character of a trulie vertuous and pious woman...Mistres Margaret Dungan. Paris, By Ste. Maucroy for the author, 1651. [187] pages. B 3369. EEB Reel 55:13.

Boate's touching eulogy for his wife, who died of a hemorrhage during pregnancy, recounts her demise in some detail. He describes her piety, compassion, forgiving nature, expansive and charitable personality, and even her eating habits. In spite of her many virtues, Boate apparently valued her obedience the most.

101A Bohun, Edmund. <u>The Character of Queen Elizabeth. Or, a Full and Clear Account of Her policies</u>. London, Printed for Ric. Chitwell, 1693. 376 pages. B 3448. EEB Reel 15:1.

This history is based on Elizabeth's exploits throughout her reign. Drawn from the work of a Dr. Johnston, a "learned Scotch physician," the book also includes materials from contemporary histories. Bohun notes Elizabeth's faults and discusses her coterie. The text is primarily a political assessment rather than a personal account of her reign; it is not a panegyric to Elizabeth.

102A [Boileau, Jacques.] <u>A Just and Reasonable Reprehension of Naked Breasts and Shoulders</u>. London, Printed for Jonathan Edwin, 1678. [152] pages. B 3463A. EEB Reel 127:7.

Boileau is described by the translator as "a great and learned papist." The book, which includes a preface by Richard Baxter, contends exposed breasts are offensive and, even if they are attractive to sensual men, they should not be to Christian men.

103A Bold, Henry. <u>Elegy on the death of her Highness Mary Princess Dowager of Aurange</u>. London, Printed for Edward Husbands, 1660. Broadside. B 3470. TT Reel 247:669.f.26(55).

This eulogy was written at the death of Mary, daughter of Charles I. She is said to have been summoned to heaven to join her great namesake, Queen Mary. The emphasis is on qualities desirable in both sexes: "The mothers Virtues and the Fathers Spirit."

104A Bolton, John. <u>A Justification of the righteous judgement of Godon Nathaniel Smith...As also a witness against E[lizabeth] Atkinson</u>. [London], 1669. 28 pages. B 3508. EEB Reel 1276:10.

The first part of this volume attacks Smith, who had criticized the Quakers. The second section concerns Atkinson, guilty of a similar transgression. Bolton focuses on Quaker dogma rather than on Atkinson's personal attributes or actions. See also 16B and 17B.

105A <u>A Book of Cookery, and the order of Meates to be served to the Table...Medicines for grievous Diseases</u>. London, Printed for Jeane Bell, 1650. 102 pages. B 3705. EEB Reel 56:4 and TT Reel 178:E.1350(1).

This book contains information about ordering meats, cooking foods and making medicines for migrain, stomach disorders, shingles, scabs and the like.

106A <u>A Book of Fruits and Flowers, shewing the Nature and Use of them, either for Meat or Medicine</u>. London, Printed by M. S. for Tho. Jenner, 1653. 49 pages. B 3708. TT Reel 106:E.690(13).

Recipes and instructions for preserving candy and concocting medicines for cold, consumption, nosebleed, weak back, etc. are contained in this volume.

107A [Boreman, Robert.] A Mirrour of Christianity... Or ...the Life and Death of...Lady Alice Dutchess Duddeley. London, Printed by E. C. for R. Royston and J. Collins, 1669. 48 pages. B 3758. EEB Reel 836:17.

This eulogy is dedicated to Katherine Levison, widow of Sir Richard and sole surviving daughter of the duchess. The deceased was the mother of five daughters. Content to live within her means, she was prudent, affable, humble, patient and had a winning disposition. An apppendix catalogs charitable deeds, including gifts to churches, the poor and widows.

108A Bossuet, Jacques Benigne. Quakerism A-la-mode: or, a History of Quietism, Particularly...Madame Guyone. London, Printed for J. Harris and J. Bell, 1698. 128 pages. B 3789. EEB Reel 1479:11.

Bossuet was the Bishop of Meux, a noted French cleric. This tract is typical of his attacks on Protestantism in general and Quietism in particular. He criticizes the deceased Madame Guyone for religious arrogance. He infers a peculiar arrogance in her manuscripts, comparing her self-described spirituality with the Quakers' continual talk of divine inner light.

109A Bossuet, Jacques Benigne. A Sermon preached at the funeral of Mary Terese of Austria, Infanta of Spain, Queen of France and Navarre, at St. Denis, September 1, 1683. [Paris] London, Reprinted by J. C. and F. C. for H. H. and sold by Samuel Crouch, 1684. 31 pages. B 3791. EEB Reel 128:3.

Bossuet describes the descent of the House of Burgundy and French naval activity; however, most of the sermon is quite personal and immediate. He explores Marie Terese's role as mother and wife, her generosity to her servants, her personal attributes and the tragic deaths of her children.

110A Bower, Edmund. Doctor Lamb Revived, or, Witchcraft Condemn'd in Anne Bodenham. London, Printed by T. W. for Richard Best and John Place, 1653. 44 pages. B 3869. TT Reel 109:E.705(24).

Anne Bodenham was arraigned and executed for witchcraft at the Salisbury Assizes. Judge Baron Wild wanted this lengthy trial transcript published as a warning for others. It is an unparagraphed account of the strange foreknowledge she had of future deaths and locations of stolen property. An elderly wife of a clothier, a "cunning woman," Bodenham supposedly had unusual interactions with other servants. See also 292A.

111A [Boyle, Robert.] The Martyrdom of Theodora, and of Didymus. London, Printed by H. Clark for John Taylor and Christopher Skegnes, 1687. [232] pages. B 3986*. EEB Reel 446:27.

This novel embellishes a legend about the early Christian martyr, Theodora, who was brought before the ruler of Antioch and forced to burn incense to the Roman Gods or risk either sacrifice or forced prostitution. She tried to convince her first ravager to kill her. The second section is a fictionalized account of her death.

112A Braithwaite, Richard. The English Gentleman and the English Gentlewoman
...with A ladies love-lecture and supplement lately annexed. Third Edition. London,
Printed for John Dawson, 1641. [454] pages. B 4262*. EEB Reel 680:24.

Braithwaite's popular work about English gentlemen was first published in 1630;
his text about women followed in 1631. It describes the admirable qualities of
women--modesty, constancy and other traditional feminine virtues. Witty
aphorisms accompany the volume, divided into nine sections, each of which
addresses a different female duty or characteristic.

113A [Bremond, Gabriel de.] The Apology: Or, the Genuine Memoires of Madame
Maria Manchini, Constabless of Colonna. London, Printed for J. Magnes and R.
Bentley, 1679. 160 pages. B 4344. EEB Reel 525:12.

Defending the niece of Cardinal Mazarin, Bremond speaks of her rivalry with her
more beautiful younger sister, who came to England as the Duchess of Mazarin.
Bremond argues against the allegedly false popular image of her improper
behavior and presents a lengthy account of her childhood and days at the
French court.

114A Bridgewater, Benjamin. A Poem Upon the Death of Her Late Majesty Queen
Mary, of Blessed Memory. London, Printed for Richard Baldwin, 1695. [9] pages.
B 4485. EEB Reel 16:13.

In a poetic tribute to Mary II which employs several metaphors (including a ship
at sea and a wounded stag), Bridgewater laments the passing of Mary's serene
rule. He says her tenure saw neither civil strife nor foreign aggression. He
describes her as a powerful, mild and courageous ruler and an able diplomat,
although William is considered responsible for foreign affairs.

115A Bridgman, Robert. Some reasons why Robert Bridgman, and his wife...Have
left the...Quakers. London, Printed for Brab. Aylmer and Char. Brome, 1700. 21
pages. B 4494. EEB Reel 731:31.

This anti-Quaker tract by a former Friend argues specifically against their form
of Christianity. Bridgman claims they speak about the "Light and Truth," but
ignore the special grace of the Holy Spirit. He includes a letter from George
Whitehead bemoaning the baptism of his family within the Anglican Church.

116A A Brief Anatomie of Women: Being an Invective Against, and an Apologie for
the Bad and Good of that Sexe. London, Printed by E. Alsop, 1653. 6 pages. B
4524. TT Reel 111:E.722(2).

The author advises women to eschew vice by admitting their own "deformities."
He alludes to both good and "evil" biblical women, then cites female physical
characteristics, imputing a lascivious purpose for each (hair, lips, eyes, etc.).
He concludes although good women are commendable, and bad women are
"extreamly evil," most gravitate toward the mean. A caveat notes women often
deceive men through their beauty.

117A A Brief Narrative of a Strange and Wonderful Old Woman that Hath a Pair of
Horns. n.p., Printed by T. J., 1676. 7 pages. B 4610. EEB Reel 1417:1.

An old midwife from Shotwick, Cheshire wore a straight hat for several years. It first caused a soreness, then she grew horns, which she shed every three or four years. Many could testify to her condition, including a minister and his wife. Although the tone is serious, the story ends with the guarantee that if it is proven false, the woman would "pull in her Horns."

[Brilhac, Jean Baptiste de.] Agnes de Castro: or, The force of generous love. See 40B.

118A [Brinley, John.] A Discourse proving by Scripture and Reason...That there Are Witches. London, Printed for J. M. and sold by John Weld, 1686. 127 pages. B 4697. EEB Reel 16:26.

Brinley discusses the exaggerated common belief in witches and claims it derives from lack of faith. He suggests maladies supposedly caused by witches actually stem from natural causes; however, he admits witchcraft does exist and says weak, emotional people are most vulnerable to it. Brinley discusses traits of witches, how the devil enters their bodies, their body markings and so on. The second section explores astrology.

119A [Brinley, John.] A Discovery of the Impostures of Witches and Astrologers. London, Printed for John Wright, and sold by Edward Milward, in Leitchfield, 1680. B 4698.

This item is essentially the same as 118A.

120A Brinsley, John. A Looking-glasse for Good Women. London, Printed by John Field for Ralph Smith, 1645. 48 pages. B 4717. TT Reel 50:E.305(23).

Brinsley writes about the inherent physical and moral weaknesses of women. He speaks to Anglican women who have deserted the Church for separatist congregations. As a minister, he assures women he wishes to help them reform, but he seems most interested in exposing their failings. Brinsley advises women to follow the Church and its catechism unquestioningly to avoid temptation.

121A Britains Sorrowful Lamentation For the Loss of Their Gracious Queen Mary. London, Reprinted at Edinburough by John Reid, 1695. Broadside. B 4812.

In this poetic tribute to Mary II, a recent victim of smallpox, the author describes the nation's sorrow and Mary's courage.

[Brome, Richard.] The Debauchee: Or, The Credulous Cuckhold. See 47B.

122A [Brown, David.] The Naked Woman; or, a rare Epistle. London, Printed for E. Blackmore, 1652. 19 pages. B 5014. TT Reel 105:E.681(20).

A young woman stripped before an Anglican congregation in Whitehall to protest a sermon. Brown criticizes the minister because he did not question the woman closely or expel her. The minister said he thought she was simply deranged. See also 213A.

123A Bruce, Lord. The Lord Bruce and the Lady Elizabeth Bruce his wife, desire a bill may be passed in Parliament, relating no manner of way to the cutting off entails. [London?, 1680.] Broadside. B 5219.

Those named in the title are requesting settlement of a dispute over an estate. Other parties include the Duchess of Beaufort, mother of Elizabeth Bruce. Lord Bruce was Thomas K. Bruce, Third Earl of Elgin and Second Earl of Ailesbury.

124A Buchanan, George. A Detection of the Actions of Mary Queen of Scots, concerning the Murther of her Husband, and her Conspiracy, Adultery and pretended Marriage with the Earl Bothwel. [London], Printed and are to be sold by Richard Janeway, 1689. 80 pages. B 5282*. EEB Reels 1417:10 and 838:8.

This anti-Stuart, anti-papist tract written originally in Latin attacks Mary as "headstrong and rash." It includes letters and materials from the trials and confessions of the principals. Buchanan reiterates popular tales about Mary's infidelity and alleged participation in her husband's murder.

125A Bugg, Francis. Jezebel Withstood, and Her Daughter Ann Docwra Publickly Reprov'd. [London, 1699.] 16 pages. B 5372.

Quaker leader Anne Docwra, who had charged Bugg with fraud, claimed he had lied about a letter she allegedly wrote and the authorship of one of his books. He retorts when Quakers are attacked, they "Lie, Dissemble and Prevaricate." This argument is a detailed rebuttal of 175B. See also 179B and 127A.

126A Bugg, Francis. The Painted-Harlot Both Stript and Whipt. London, Printed by J. Gain for the author and are to be sold by F. Smith, 1683. 92 pages. B 5380. EEB Reel 1351:7.

In this anti-Quaker tract Bugg claims the Quakers are attempting to "exercise Dominion over the consciences of their Brethren." He argues against the Quaker practice of requiring prospective spouses to appear twice before the men's and women's meetings. Although this is primarily an attack on the Quaker leadership, Bugg also questions the legitimacy of the women's meeting and asks for a precedent for it--"unless in the Pope's Nunnery."

127A Bugg, Francis. "A Winding-Sheet for Ann[e] Docwra." In William Penn, the Pretended Quaker. [London, 1700.] 13 pages. Item: N.I.W. Collection: B 5399. EEB Reel 1146:5.

Bugg reples to a charge by Quaker Anne Docwra that his criminal past undermines his credibility as a critic of the Friends. Docwra had claimed he and his son concocted an illegal scheme to transfer funds from their estate to establish a jointure for Bugg's wife. Bugg angrily denies the charge and says Docwra is attempting to set his daughter-in-law and her family against him. He also justifies a jail-term and fines he paid while a Quaker. See also 175B, 179B and 125A.

128A [Bunworth, Richard.] The Doctresse: A plain and easie method, of curing those diseases which are peculiar to Women. [London, Printed by J. F. for Nicholas Bourne, 1656.] 149 pages. B 5474. TT Reel 213:E.1714(2).

The primary foci of this gynecological text are women's diseases and childbirth. Menstrual irregularities are linked to small pox, measles, spotted fever, and other contagious diseases. Distinct male and female physiologies are emphasized throughout. The format is common for such texts.

129A [Burdet, W.] A Wonder of Wonders. Being A faithful Narrative and true Relation, of one Anne Green. [London], Printed for John Clowes, 1651. 6 pages. B 5620. TT Reel 95:E.621(11).

A pregnant servant in Oxfordshire delivered her own stillborn child. Embarrassed and terrified, she buried the child in a rubbish heap. Although she maintained her innocence, she was hanged for one half hour. At her request the executioner beat her breasts with a musket to ensure a quick death. She survived, and witnesses agreed this miracle confirmed her innocence. See also 943A.

130A Burgess, Daniel. A Funeral-Sermon Preach'd upon the Death of Mrs. Sarah Bull. London, Printed and sold by A[ndre] Bell and J Lansley, 1694. 80 pages. B 5706B.

The themes of this sermon are the brevity of life, the importance of good health and patience in waiting for the Lord's will. Six pages describe the deceased: She was a good student of religion, valued the hereafter above worldly things, kept house well, and was a loving mother who "reverenced [her husband] as her head."

131A B[urnell], H[enry]. Landgartha. A Tragie-Comedy. Dublin, 1641. [74] pages. B 5751. EEB Reel 1456:27.

The prologue to this play is delivered by an Amazon with a battle-ax, in apparent imitation of Jonson's prologue to The Poetaster. The setting is Sweden, and the plot involves the conquest of Fro (Frollo), King of Suethland, by Regner (Reyner), King of Denmark, and the repudiation of his queen, Landgartha. It is apparently based on a true historical episode (from D. E. Baker, Biographia Dramatica, 1966).

132A [Burnet, Gilbert.] The Conversion and Persecutions of Eve Cohan, now called Eliz. Verloon. London, Printed by J. D. for Richard Chiswell, 1680. 27 pages. B 5772. EEB Reel 484:30.

The author, an important Anglican divine, was the Bishop of Sarum. He says Verloon has been threatened by her family since her conversion from Judaism to Christianity. The story involves her family's efforts to withhold her estate in Holland, annul her marriage and kidnap her.

133A Burnet, Gilbert. An Essay on the Memory of the Late Queen. London, Printed for Richard Chiswell, 1695. 197 pages. B 5783*. EEB Reels 85:4 and 1610:38.

Burnet calls the late Mary II "the best part of us," lauds her extraordinary virtue, compares her to earlier female monarchs and comments on her joint sovereignty with William. He also discusses her approach to religious and state matters.

134A Burnet, Gilbert. A Sermon Preached at St. Dunstans in the West at the Funeral of Mrs. Anne Seile, the 18th of July 1678. London, Printed for Mary Clark, 1678. 29 pages. B 5871. EEB Reel 272:3.

The author did not know the deceased, and there is nothing about her in the text. The sermon concerns righteous living.

135A Burnet, Gilbert. A Sermon preached at the Funeral of...Anne, Lady-Dowager Brook. London, Printed for Ric. Chiswell, 1691. 34 pages. B 5895. EEB Reel 682:10.

Burnet praises the Lady Anne's modesty, industry, faith and discretion, notwithstanding her wealth. He speaks about her visits to poor houses, care of the sick, and lack of concern about contracting contagious disease (except for smallpox). Apparently six sons and her husband predeceased her.

136A Burroughs, Thomas. Christ the Sts. Advantage both in Life and death. A Sermon...Funerall of Ms. Elisabeth Coke, wife to Colonel Thomas Coke of Pebmersh. London, Printed by T. R. and E. M. for John Bellamy, 1646. 49 pages. B 6130. TT Reel 168:E.1200(3).

This sermon is based on Philippians 1.21. A few pages at the end describe the deceased: She was religious, lively, virtuous, public spirited and tended the souls of her children and servants in her husband's absence.

137A [Butler, Samuel.] A New Ballad of King Edward and Jane Shore. London, 1671. Broadside. B 6326.

The story of Edward IV and Jane Shore is told through a battle metaphor. Butler refers to various mythical and classical female rulers and soldiers, depicting Shore as a warrior fighting for England.

138A C., Mr. Upon the Death of that Incomparable Princess, Queen Mary. With an address to His Majesty. Edinburgh, Printed by the Heirs and Successors of Andrew Anderson, 1695. Broadside. C 3.

The exemplary qualities of Mary II and the grief of William are subjects for this typical eulogy. The queen had succumbed suddenly to smallpox.

139A C., B. A Letter Touching a Colledge of maids; or, A virgin-society. [London,] 1675. [7] pages. C 14. EEB Reel 409:19.

The author describes the curriculum of a hypothetical boarding school for wealthy girls where they would be taught history, poetry, practical divinity, languages, music, and philosophy, including experimentation. Daughters would go home periodically or they could withdraw to marry. This item was supposedly included in a letter from one man to another.

140A C., I. The Gyant whipt by his Godmother; A Loving Epistle. [London, 1682?] Broadside. C 49. EEB Reel 861:37.

This vitriolic attack on journalist/pamphleteer Roger L'Estrange is by a self-described "anti-papist" who uses "godmother" as a double-entendre. Here she is an enraged Amazon, while L'Estrange is a pigmy. She claims his wicked tongue properly belongs to "our Sex," whose teeth [to bite] and tongues [to scold] he should fear. Apologizing for her impertinence, she claims to speak the truth naturally, "after the womans manner, that is, laying it on according to her Female ability."

141A C., J. An Elegie upon the death of the most incomparable, Mrs. Katharine Philips, The Glory of her Sex. London, [1664]. Broadside. C 53. EEB Reel 1566:9.

The author asks the heavenly bodies to postpone the departure of poet Philips' soul because she died prematurely. The focus is Philips' affectional poetry and loving nature. Excerpt: "She, who in Tragique buskins drest the Stage,/Taught Honour, Love, and Friendship to this Age."

142A C., T. A brief relation of the life and death of Elizabeth Braythwjaite [sic]. [London, 1684.] 8 pages. C 128. EEB Reel 1326:22.

A teenaged girl was arrested after a month's absence from church while she was attending Quaker services. After refusing bail-money from neighbors, she was imprisoned for two months where she became ill and died. Her family describe her virtuous life, suffering and death. She is called innocent, meek and accepting.

143A Calamy, Edmund [younger.] A Funeral Sermon, Preached Upon Occasion of the Decease of...Mrs. Elizabeth Williams. London, Printed for J. Lawrence, 1698. 92 pages. C 272. EEB Reel 1418:23.

This typical funeral sermon praises a devoted minister's wife, called "a Domestick Instance of Exemplary Patience." She disagreed with those who felt her husband mistreated her. Calamy includes a brief account of her life and religious writings.

144A Cambridge University. Threni Cantabrigienses in Funere Duorum Principum...Marie Arausionesis. Cantabrigiae, Exudebrat Joannes Field, 1661. [97] pages. C 354. TT Reel 161:E.1082(6).

Dons of Cambridge Uiversity wrote these Latin eulogies for Mary, Princess of Orange, sister to Charles II.

145A Camden, William. The History of the Most Renowned and Victorious Princess Elizabeth, late Queen of England. Fourth Edition. London, Printed by M. Flesher for R. Bentley, 1688. 661 pages. C 363A*. EEB Reel 558:6.

This treatment of the early years of Elizabeth's reign was written by an important Jacobean historian. Camden wrote it at the request of Lord Burleigh, who gave him the queen's rolls, memorials and records. A massive index enhances the history. Camden discusses the queen's womanhood only as it relates to her decisions about state matters.

146A [Camfield, Benjamin.] A Consolatory Discourse for the support of Distressed Widows and Orphans. London, Printed for John Newton, 1690. 31 pages. C 378. EEB Reel 1588:11.

This volume helps the religious and virtuous bereaved gain hope through scriptural readings. Stories of biblical widows like Naomi, Ruth and the widow of Naim are included. A "Distressed Widows Prayer" is added.

147A [Camus, Jean Pierre and Madeline de Scudery.] Elise, or Innocencie Guilty. London, Printed by T. Newcomb for Humphrey Moseley, 1655. 150 pages. C 413.

The authorship of this novel is in dispute. It concerns Elise, who is the bride of Timoleon, forced to leave his country in disgrace. This novel describes their journey home. It contains an account of the couple's encounter with Amazonian characters.

148A Captain Charles Newey's wonderful Discovery, of several Remarkable and strange things...Case and Vindication, About his having 18 Wives. [London, Printed for Jer. Wilkins, 1700.] Broadside. N 918. EEB Reel 503:3.

This story is about a polygamist. The copy examined is a fragment.

149A C[are], H[enry.] The Female Secretary. Or Choice New Letters. Wherein each degree of Women may be accommodated with Variety of Presidents for the expressing themselves aptly and handsomly on any Occasion proper to their Sex. With some replies. London, Printed by Thomas Ratcliffe and Mary Daniel for Henry Million, 1671. 115 pages. C 519.

Amusing letters with some replies exemplify proper forms for correspondence. Examples: "A Gentlewoman to her Father, being marryed against his will," "On the inconstancy of her Servant," "To her too familiar Servant." From the preface:"If He have [sic] not here copied every womans mind, since there are so many of them that scarce know their own."

150A [Carisbrick, Edward.] The life of the Lady Warner of Parham In Religion Call'd Sister Clare of Jesus. London, Printed for Tho. Hales, 1691. 289 pages. C 574*.

This lengthy, involved biography of a nun includes many of her letters. They reveal her early interest in monasticism while she was poor. It is superior to many biographies because it includes much primary material.

151A [Carleton, John.] The Articles and Charge of Impeachment against the German lady...according to the records of the City of Canterbury. London, Printed for G. Winnam, 1663. 8 pages. [A 3804+.]

Carleton, credited with this pamphlet by the Houghton Library, Harvard, includes materials from the trial of his infamous bigamous wife, Mary (the "German Princess"). He tells of her "strange pranks and unheard of designs" and calls her a "rare inchantress." This item is nearly identical to his The Replication, or Certain Vindicatory Depositions...concerning the late acted cheat (1663) in the Harvard Law School library.

152A Case, Thomas. The Excellent Woman: A Sermon Preached at the Funeral of Mrs. Elizabeth Scott, Relict to Humphrey Scott of Conghurst in Kent...and Daughter unto Sir Mathew Howland Knight. London, Printed for Robert Gibs, 1659. [222] pages. C 829. EEB Reel 1183:9.

Halfway through this eulogy, based on Proverbs 31.29, Case describes Scott as godly, wise, prudent, humble and merciful. Her incredible generosity, including gifts to poor scholars, is estimated at one fifth of her annual income. A separate section includes testimonials of other clergy about Scott's character and her own interesting writings. Excerpt: "I was born a child of wrath, and an heir of hell...Yet I did duties in a formal way, and was very confident."

153A The Case Betwixt Thornton Cage, Esq. and his Wife. [London, 1684?] 4 pages. C 860.

A wealthy young man was tricked into marriage by his mother-in-law, who claimed her daughter was an heiress. Their marriage was a comedy of errors: The mother-in-law lived with them, drank their liquor and spent money on the gardens; his wife caroused with friends who robbed him; and a cousin sowed dissension.

154A The Case is Altered. Or, Dreadful news from Hell...discourse between...Oliver Croomwell [sic], and Sir reverence my lady Joan his wife. London, Printed for John Andrews, [1660]. 16 pages. C 871. TT Reel 233:E.1869(2).

Cromwell's ghost stalks the country observing evidence of his own evil. He speaks of occasional disagreements with the devil. His wife Joan has not yet died, and she talks of permanent residence in the Tower or Bridewell. A goc portion of the satire concerns Cromwell's son Richard's alleged reluctance to continue his father's tyranny.

155A The Case of Ann, Wife to the late Baron Slane. n.p., [1698]. Broadside. C 881.

The widow Slane describes her marital agreement, stipulating an annual 800-pound jointure plus a 200-pound independent allowance. After the Baron's exclusion because of his support of James II, the Earl of Athlone assumed control of his estate and allowed Ann Slane only the smaller payment. She requests that her original agreement be honored before Parliament passes the Act on Irish Forfeitures.

156A The Case of Anne Smyth, the wife of Daniell Smyth...Northampton...truly stated. [London, 1650.] Broadside. S 4358. TT Reel 246:669.f.15(61).

This petition is addressed to the House of Commons. Smyth was willed one thousand pounds by her father with the Danvers brothers named as executors. Her husband, who was collecting money for them, was imprisoned and became ill. Now destitute, she alleges Danvers will not answer her entreaties. Fearful of being defrauded of her estate, Smyth asks for the original bequest plus damages. Her husband is to be spared unnecessary suits, like the one threatened by Danvers.

157A The Case of Angela Margarita Cottington, the lawful Wife of Charles
Cottington Esq. [London, 1680.] Broadside. C 882.

An Englishman married an Italian woman in Torino.   When she became
pregnant, he left her. She followed him but he denied they were married.
English courts awarded her alimony of 300 pounds, of which he paid only one
third. Here she is suing for the remaining 200 pounds.

158A The Case of Arabella Lady Howard, on the Behalf of Her Protestant Relations.
[London, 1690?] Broadside. C 885. EEB Reel 1756:10.

Lady Howard was the only child of Sir Edmund and Frances Alleyn, both
Protestants. When Arabella was two, they died and left her 1400 pounds.
William Thompson removed her from her custodian, Sir William Dalston. He
wished her to marry his son, and kept her away from her Protestant relations
by sending her to a nunnery. Eventually he cut timber from her estate, thus
reducing her income from it to 1000 pounds. This case concerns an attempt
to block the sale of her land and consequent control by her son. See also
Addendum 69.

159A The Case of Elisabeth and Margaret Cholmley, Sarah Smith, and Sir Kings-Mill
Lucy Bart. [London, 1673.] Broadside. C 911.

This appeal to the House of Lords is by three women and a man for repayment
of money they advanced to a company which had lent Parliament 9000 pounds
in 1642.   The plaintiffs contend although they received payments for both
principal and interest until 1666, they were denied reimbursement thereafter.
When they originally asked for settlement of the loan through sale of the
company's assets, investors in Parliament denied it.

160A The Case of Elizabeth Dutchess of Albemarle, and Christopher Monke, Esq.
against John, Earl of Bath. [London? 1695]. 4 pages. C 911A.

In a dispute over property of the Duke of Albemarle [George Monck], the
plaintiffs request a settlement based on stipulations in his will. The argument
includes a history of the Chancery appeal and trial and maintains trustees and
friends of the Duke were unaware of a secret transfer of deeds. See also 172A.

161A The Case of Elizabeth, the Wife of Charles Stuteville Esq., and of their Five
Children. [n.p., 1699-1700.] Broadside. C 912.

This confused and complicated case involves several Stutevilles. Upon Charles'
death, his estate was encumbered by his creditor, Lady Glenham, who took the
case to Chancery and forced foreclosure. Stuteville's mother Judith had sued
him for being twenty-nine years late in payment of her jointure and had
obtained a decree of 5800 pounds against him. A dispute involving custody
of the children further confounds the issues.

162A The Case of Her Grace the Dutchess of Cleveland, the Dukes of Grafton and
Northumberland, touching an Annuity of 4700 [pounds] per annum. [London,
1690?] Broadside. C 919.

This account concerns money put in trust for the Duchess of Cleveland, Barbara Villiers, former mistress to Charles II. It was to have been paid by the Post Office. A Parliamentary act had earlier settled the Post Office "upon the Duke of York and the Heirs Male of his Body." This document is meant to ensure Post Office profits to the stipulated heirs.

163A The Case of Margaret Mortimer, Widow and Seventeen more Sufferers by a dreadful Fire...in Derby Court, Westminster. [London, 1697.] Broadside. N.I.W.

Although this legal document describes events following a fire of April 16, 1697, dates mentioned in the document cover a period ending in 1701. The case involves insurance fraud.

164A The Case of Mary, Dutchess of Norfolk. [London, 1700.] 4 pages. C 949.

This item concerns the bill for divorce between the duchess and Henry Howard, the Duke of Norfolk, begun in 1692. See also 35A, 649A, 886A and 920A.

165A The Case of Mary Howard, Relict of Henry Howard Esq. [London, 1680?] N.I.W.

This document responds to the appeal of Sir John Edwards. The dispute concerns jointure lands settled on Mary Howard by her deceased husband. Edwards had procured a mortgage but now claims it was a purchase. The court ruled the land was not purchased: If she had paid principal and interest on it, then she owned it.

166A The Case of Mary Walwyn, Widow of John Walwyn Esq; petitioner against the Right Honourable Earl of Monmouth. [n.p., 1691.] Broadside. C 950.

The widow Walwyn is suing for damages and money to pay her husband's debts and support her family. She claims the family's land fell to her two male children, "both lunaticks or Ideots." Trustees were to be appointed to protect their interest and enable payment of debts. Before the patent could be granted, the Earl of Monmouth won it. When the tenants fell in arrears, he captured Walwyn's remaining living son and forced payment of the rent.

167A The Case of Mary Watkinson, Mother of Hannah Gooding (later Hannah Knight), an Infant and Thomas Gooding Son of Serjant Gooding. Broadside. [London, 1697?] N.I.W.

Hannah Knight Gooding, the minor daughter of Mary Knight Watkinson and John Knight, was to receive a dowry of 5000 pounds from Knight, if she had no surviving brothers. The trustees claim her mother wanted Hannah's jointure and tried to marry her to Thomas Gooding, a student of twenty-three. They wish to have the marriage annulled. Gooding charges the trustees with attempting to seize the jointure. See also 169A.

168A The Case of Mrs. Mary Stout, Widow [in the appeal against Spencer Cowper and others for the alleged murder of Sarah Stout]. [London, 1700?]. 4 pages. C 962*/S 5771A. EEB Reel 1629:12.

Stout brought suit against men charged with slaying her daughter Sarah. After the sheriff delayed serving her writ, it was burned. The men named wanted it dismissed because the term of the King's Bench had ended. Stout contended she was simply trying to find the murderers and, if the men were innocent, they should have welcomed a trial. See also 258A, 280A and 882A.

169A The Case of Richard Taylor...and John Clerkson...Trustees of Hannah Knight, an Infant. [n.p., 1656]. Broadside. N.I.W.

A girl of ten was allegedly offered in marriage to a student by her mother and step-father. The man's family was apparently told she was twelve, above the age of consent. The girl's trustees, both uncles, brought suit and, after one court appearance, the girl disappeared. The men fear she will be sequestered until she reaches twelve. Hannah Knight is a pawn in this drama because she has a settlement of sixty pounds. See also 167A.

170A The Case of Susanna Smith...Widow and Executrix of William Smith, Esq. [n.p., 1689]. Broadside. C 1007.

This petition was filed by Susanna Smith, widow of the Comptroller of His Majesty's revenue in Ireland. She is asking for leniency; the case concerns foreclosure on houses against a debt owed her late husband. The tenants apparently failed to pay rent, and she could not maintain the properties herself. Because the debt is longstanding, and the rent is her only income, she wishes to be made an exception under a law requiring forfeiture of the properties.

171A The Case of the Daughters of the Late Earl of Rochester...and Heirs to John Mallet. n.p., 1692. Broadside. C 1060.

This case involves a petition for "settling the Navigation of the New Cut River, leading from Bridgwater to Taunton." The women say their grandfather, Jolen Mallet, received a royal commission to cut a path for the river, build a sluice and erect a bridge--all at his own expense. They request that ships plying the river pay a fee for maintenance of the bridge and to "cleanse the said Cut."

172A The Case of the Dutchess of Albemarle and Christopher Monke, Esquire, Appellants Against the Earl of Bath. London, [1694.] 31 pages. C 1064. EEB Reel 1481:19.

This document presents a widow's claims at the highest level of English society, the peerage. The dispute concerns a 1665 bequest of the Duke of Albemarle [George Monck] for support of his sons and wife and two later wills of his son. The involved case, told from the perspective of the duchess [Elizabeth Monck] and her cousin (Christopher Monck), states the Earl of Bath lacks witnesses to prove his claim. See also 160A.

173A The Case of the Dutchess of Richmond, and others concerned in the Duties of Subsidy and Aulnage. [London? 1682.] Broadside. C 1064A.

The plaintiffs oppose passage of a bill in the House of Commons to abolish the tax traditionally levied by the king on the exportation of certain goods. Tax monies had contributed to the duchess' jointure. She (Frances Teresa Stuart) was a favorite of Charles II.

174A The Case of the Executors, Creditors, and Legatees of the late Countess Frances of Portland...Exportation of White Clothes. [London, 1700?] Broadside. C 1070.

This case concerns the status of a license granted to Sir James Hayes and Sir Peter Apsley by Charles II in trust to the Countess of Portland. It had been granted originally to her father, the Duke of Lenox, by James I. The license levied a duty on the exportation of non-dyed woollen goods; the proceeds were to support the dependents of the recently deceased countess. Relatives and servants maintain income from her estate is insufficient because it is committed to debt service.

175A The Case of the Ladies Margaret, Catherine and Elizabeth McCarty, Daughters of Calaghan late Earl of Glencarty. [London, 1700?] Broadside. C 1101.

The daughters of the late Earl are requesting their just portions from their parents' estate. Although their father had instructed his solicitor to allow each woman a 4000-pound share, he died before settlement was made. When the estate devolved upon a minor brother, both the daughters' and the wife's claims were stayed. After the government seized the land during the Irish Rebellion, the House of Lords passed a bill restoring their rights; however, Parliament was prorogued before the king could sign it.

176A The Case of the Lady Anne Poole in the behalf of her self, her sister, her Daughter the C. of Newburgh...concerning a debt of 6000 [Pounds] due from the late Earl of Cleaveland. [London, 1677.] Broadside. N.I.W.

The plaintiffs maintain the Earl of Cleaveland, trustee for heirs of the Countess of Newburgh, appropriated money from the estate for his sister's portion. Funds were released from his estate for his heirs (including the Lady Wentworth), but the money he used from the estate of the countess was not repaid. See also 177A and 656A.

177A The Case of the Lady Henrietta Maria Wentworth...Grandchild...of the Right Honourable...Earl of Cleaveland. [London, 1677.] Broadside. C 1102.

This case involves a dispute over claims to the estate of the Earl of Cleaveland. It had been seized during the Interregnum, when no income accrued; however, an act restoring property rights was not invoked by the Lady Poole, a creditor, in time to receive payment. Poole requested the Lady Wentworth's claim be pursued through the courts. Wentworth's guardian defends her right to the inheritance, maintaining debts have been incurred against the sum due Poole. Henrietta Maria Wentworth was the mistress of James, Duke of Monmouth. See also 176A and 656A.

178A The Case of the Lady Wandesford. [London? 1660.] Broadside. C 1102A.

In this case Parliament is asked to honor a patent of Charles I for a land-grant to Mary and William Wandesford and their heirs. Mary allegedly spent much money to clear it of water and would lose the estate without title to it. She requests "all the land in Hampshire between the High and Low-Water-marke."

179A The Case of the Poor Widdows and Orphans of the City of London. n.p., [1685]. Broadside. C 1143.

Fourteen hundred orphans and widows, whose inheritances were forced into the Chamber of London, ask the king and Parliament to look into their case. They also ask for an investigation into a charge that the Chamber has "made some to bring in the Moneys." ("Not one in Twenty could procure such large and unreasonable Security as they insisted on...")

180A The Case of the Widow and Children of John Sayer, Esq. [London? 1690?] Broadside. C 1178A.

This document is a defense of the rights of the Widow Sayer and William Lightfoot to the manor of Bidstone. They wish to restrain an imminent act of Parliament which will restore the manor to the Earl of Derby. In 1662 the Earl had tried to claim other manors, but never Bidstone. Now that several persons have purchased the manor at full price, he wishes to regain the property, transferred by his grandmother to William Steel and his heirs in 1653.

181A The case of Ursula Cartwright, Widow. [London], 1680? Broadside. C 1191.

This involved case concerns the rights of heirs of William Cartwright's second wife Ursula. The petition accuses Mary, daughter of Cartwright's first wife, of attempting to usurp their portion of the estate. Ursula Cartwright claims the case should not be heard on appeal before the House of Lords.

182A A Catalogue of Ladies to be set up by Auction. [London, 1695.] Broadside. N.I.W.

This satirical piece announces an auction of women between fifteen and twenty-five with fortunes of 1000 to 10,000 pounds. Men "who have clear Limbs and members entire" are invited to bid at Lincolns-Inn-Gardens.

A Catalogue of valuable books. See 468B.

183A A Caution to Married Couples: Being a true Relation How a Man in Nightingale-Lane Having Beat and abused his Wife. London, Printed for D. M., 1677. 4 pages. C 1561. EEB Reel 1522:12.

A lighterman argued with his wife and began to beat her. She fled, and he followed with a half-pike. A tubman witnessed the chase and tried to prevent further abuse of the wife, but became a victim himself. The killer acknowledged the attack, but claimed the tubman was "hindering him to correct his wife." The lesson: Men should not abuse their wives, but rather love and cherish them after God's will.

184A A Caveat for Wives to love their Husbands, or Pleasant News from Hell. By Niccolo Machiavelli, pseud. London, 1660. 12 pages. M 132A.

The author contends that when men reached hell they blamed their wives for sending them. Princes of the Underworld decided to come to earth to test this allegation and sent one devil to report back. He married a prideful woman who spent his money, and he eventually decided life was better in hell.

[Cellier, Elizabeth.] An Abstract of the Tryal of Elizabeth Cellier. See 136B.

185A A Certain and True Relation of the Heavenly Enjoyments and Living Testimonies of God's Love...declared upon the Dying-Bed of Sarah [Beck]. [London], 1680. 12 pages. C 1686A. EEB Reel 12:7.

Sarah Beck died after giving birth to a daughter. In this touching testimonial, family members describe her sweet and loving character. Paraphrases of her words are included. Example: "My Soul is near ready to be offered up unto the Lord as a Living Sacrifice."

186A Certain Letters evidencing the Kings steadfastness in the Protestant Religion: sent from the Princess of Turenne and the Ministers of Charenton, to some Persons of Quality in London. London, Printed by Thomas Newcomb for Gabriel Bedell and Thomas Collins, 1660. 46 pages [irregular pagination]. C 1702.

Only the first letter was written by Anne de la Tour d'Auvergne, wife of the Marshall-General of France and grandchild of the Duke and Marshall of the Force. It is addressed to her English cousin in London, Mme. de Castelnaut. She speaks mostly of her affection for her and expresses hope the exiled Charles II will return. Claiming his power is divine, she notes his demonstrations of piety, including participation in spiritual exercises held twice daily.

187A The Challenge, sent by a Young Lady to Sir Thomas--etc. Or, The Female War. Wherein the Present Dresses and Humours, etc. of the FAIR SEX are Vigorously Attackt by Men. By Philaret, pseud. Two Parts. London, Printed for E. Whitlock, 1697. C 1796. EEB Reel 1279:12.

This elaborate debate over the characteristics of women seems to be a satire of feminist ideas. In "the female war" men attack, and women defend their sex. Women are said to take pity on men in love, letting them "now and then make love to them, or at least to their Fan or Picture." The author claims if women did not indulge them, men would love only themselves. "Philaret" was used by John Dunton, although this book may be by another author.

Chamberlain, Hugh.] The Compleat Midwifes Practice Enlarged. See 226A.

[Chamberlain, Hugh.] Dr. Chamberlayne's Midwives Practice. See 189A.

188A [Chamberlayne, Edward.] An Academy or College: wherein Young Ladies...may be...instructed in the true Protestant Religion. [London], Printed by Tho. Newcomb, 1671. 10 pages. C 1818. EEB Reel 20:5.

Students of the proposed college were to be educated there through puberty. The school was to be "under the tuition of a Lady Governess, and grave society of Widdows and Virgins." Chamberlayne believed women should return to pre-Civil-War piety. The school was based on the German Protestant academies; its curriculum, typical of a finishing school, includes French, cookery, and dancing.

189A C[hamberlen], P[eter]. <u>Dr. Chamberlayne's Midwives Practice</u>. London, Printed for T. Rooks, 1665. C 1817H. EEB Reel 327:10.

This text draws on work of prominent gynecologists Mauriceau and Culpeper, as well as Rodericus e Castro. It is typical of treatises about women's diseases that focus on sexual malfunctions. The preface is notable for its discussion of the emotional, social and psychological aspects of women's diseases as they were perceived by seventeenth-century physicians. Although the dedication is signed by "P. C.," the work has been attributed to both Hugh and Peter Chamberlen.

190A Chamberlen, Peter. <u>A Voice in Rhama: or, the Crie of Women and Children</u>. London, Printed by William Bentley for John Marshall, 1647. C 1910. TT Reel 167:E.1181(8).

Most of this document, addressed to the College of Physicians, contains iconoclast Chamberlen's defense of his own conduct. He speaks of his birth and education, his charitable works and service. He defends state regulation of midwives, advocating their incorporation into the College which, with the midwives, opposed his plan to license them himself. Excerpt: "The Objection infers thus much, Because there was never any Order for instructing, and governing Mid-wives, therefore there never must be. Because multitudes have perished, therefore they still must perish."

191A <u>The Character of a Town-Misse</u>. London, Printed for W. L., 1675. 8 pages. C 1994.

This pamphlet describes the socially aspiring, sexually promiscuous woman of the Restoration. A semi-pornographic work, ostensibly supportive of moral precepts, it is filled with sexual innuendo. The author laments contemporary usage of the term "miss" for someone "our unmannerly ancestors call'd whore and strumpet." The reply, which defends prostitution, is entitled <u>The Town-Misses Declaration and Apology</u>.

192A <u>Characters of Several Ingenious designing Gentlewomen, who have lately put in to the Ladies Invention</u>. [London, 1699.] Broadside. N.I.W.

This bawdy satire is about a lottery meant for gambling women, including a widow and a rich Quaker's daughter. The prizes include husbands and sexual favors. The broadside attacks several groups, including physicians, elderly women, widows and Quakers. It is apparently meant to mock <u>The Ladies Invention</u>.

193A [Charles I.] <u>A Briefe Abstract of the Kings Letters to the Queene</u>. London, Printed for Hannah Allen, 1648. 12 pages. C 2152.

These letters describe an alleged agreement between Charles and Henrietta Maria and the Catholic party. He expresses trust in her as his intermediary with Parliament. The king says he will nullify all laws biased against Catholics, requests that she bring the Duke of Loraine's army into England, and vows he will use Irish troops against the Scots and English. The document is of questionable authenticity.

194A Charles I.   The Kings Majesties Letter to the Queen; concerning the differences betwixt the English and the Scots, and the Great distraction within the city of London. London, Printed for G. Oreton, 1648. 6 pages. C 2418.

This letter was written to Henrietta Maria, queen consort of Charles I. It concerns the differences between the English and the Scots, distractions within London, the French army, etc. It is affectionate and loyal.

195A Charles I. Munday [sic] 29th January 1648. [London, 1649.] Broadside. C 2840. TT Reel 246:669.f.14(9).

This broadside reproduces the king's speech to his young children, the Lady Elizabeth and Henry, the Duke of Gloucester, on the day before his execution. It reports Elizabeth's version of his words--don't grieve for me, and forgive my enemies but don't trust them. Assuming his son Charles would succeed him, he told Henry to regard his elder as his sovereign. The king also requested the children's obedience to his wife.

196A Charles II. Prince Charles His letter to the lady Marie His most loyall sister. London, Printed for William Reynor, 1642. [8] pages.   C 3115. EEB Reel 240:E.140(16) and TT Reel 25: E.140(16).

Charles writes to his young sister, recently married to the Prince of Orange, telling her how much he misses her and their mother, who was with her in Holland. He says he received a letter from her new husband revealing his fondness for his bride and laments domestic troubles that are distracting his father the king. He asks Mary to write to their father at York.

197A Cheesman, Thomas.   Death Compared to a Sleep...Funeral of Mrs. Mary Allen. London, Printed for Thomas Parkhurst, 1695. 18 pages. C 3774.

This sermon was preached in East Ilsly, Berkshire. Cheesman suggests it is inadvisable to grieve too much for pious persons like Mary Allen. His primary metaphor is the comparison of death to sleep. Little attention is given to Allen, except insofar as she was "a fruitful Mother in Israel" who raised many children "in the fear of God."

198A [Chevreau, Urbain.] A Relation of the Life of Christina Queen of Sweden. London, Printed by J. C. for Henry Fletcher and Nath. Heathcoate, 1656. 42 pages. C 3803. TT Reel 131: E.870(9).

This biography was supposedly written by a domestic who accompanied Christina to Germany. Chevreau discusses her reasons for renunciation of the crown and her voyage to Brussels and Rome. The queen was allegedly corrupted by a Frenchman named Bourdelot and the Spaniard, Pigmentelli. There is much about Christina's early development and personal qualities, including her wit and intellectual curiosity. Chevreau maintains she raised herself above the limitations of her sex.
See also 365A and 415A.

199A The Christian life and death, of Mistris Katherin Brettargh, late wife of Master William Brettargh, of Bretterghoult in the county of Lancaster. London, Printed by

Felix Kingston for John Wright, the Elder, 1641. 20 pages. C 3946. EEB Reel 1327:18.

This document is primarily an anti-papist diatribe, although its ostensible purpose is to vindicate the reputation of the deceased. The author says papists contend she died in despair; by implication, her religion was of no comfort. He maintains she was pious and charitable. Married at twenty, she had only one child who died at two. The author offers a detailed account her illness, as well as alleged intimidation of the Brettarghs by "Seminary Priests" and "Recusants."

200A Chute, Chaloner. Mr. Chutes Case upon the Lady Dacres Appeal. n.p., [1685]. Broadside. C 4277. EEB Reel 1629:116.

This complex case centers around a dispute between Chute, son of the former Speaker of the House of Commons (d. 1659) and the Lady Dacre, his stepmother (the elder Chute's second wife). She says his estate owes her 5000 pounds against a debt apparently incurred while the younger Chute's parents were living. He argues he should pay no interest for the period when he was a minor, as she should have been paying it off with monies accruing from his parents' estate. (He was ten years old when his parents died.) See also 504A.

201A Chute, Chaloner. Mr. Chute's Case Upon the Decree obtained against his father (by the Lady Dacres). [n.p., 1685.] 2 pages. C 4278. EEB Reel 1683:62.

This broadside summarizes the case described in 200A.

202A Chute, Chaloner. Mr. Chute's Petition of appeal consists of these Nine Points. n.p., [1685]. Broadside. C 4279. EEB Reel 1629:117.

In the case described in 200A, Chute agrees to abide by the decision of two impartial lords.

203A Cibber, Colley. A Poem on the Death of Our Late Soveraign Lady, Queen Mary. London, Printed for John Whitlock, [1695]. 15 pages. C 4282. EEB Reel 486:21.

This formal heroic poem was the first published by Cibber, an actor and dramatist. He extols Mary's religious toleration, piety and charity, noting that the court mourns her as a friend, mother and queen. (Cibber incidentally forgives her for producing no heir.) William is consoled in his grief: "While to his Sorrows this Relief is Giv'n,/Has lost a Queen on Earth and gain'd a Friend in Heav'n."

204A The Citizens Reply to the Whores Petition, and Prentices Answer. London, 1668. Broadside. C 4344. EEB Reel 1547:23.

This broadside continues a humorous series. The "citizens" attack both whores and apprentices, claiming the whores' behavior is worse than the apprentices', who allegedly ransacked their lodgings. The prostitutes are called impudent and are advised to seek legitimate work. See also 716A, 724A and 952A.

205A The City-dames petition in the behalfe of the long afflicted, but well-affected cavaliers. Presented to the supreme powers of the kingdome. [London], 1647. 6 pages. C 4350. TT Reel 65:E.409(12).

This bawdy satire is a request by the "wives" of shopkeepers, signed by fourteen women with humorous names like Mrs. Stradling, Han. Snatchall, Mrs. Overdooe, A. Troublesome, and P. Horne. They lament their loss of business since the king's flight and claim they must staff the shops while their husbands are at war (or the men have fled because of royalist views).

206A The Citie Matrons, or The Three Monumentall Mobbs. [London], Printed in the Yeer of Womens honesty, 1654. 8 pages. C 4356. EEB Reel 135:10.

In this satire three matronly "polecats" meet as the Committee for the election of a governess of Bridewell. The three--Mistris Holland, Sarah Salisbury, and Bess Broughton--offer their qualifications for the job. Excerpt: "All Partyes heard, with most mature discretion,/She carried it, that did the most transgression."

207A The City-wifes petition, against Coffee. London, Printed for A. W., 1700. 4 pages. C 4362A. EEB Reel 135:11.

This humorous, lewd petition is addressed to the public. The "women" complain about inconveniences caused by excessive coffee drinking by "Frenchified" men. They say it renders men lethargic and unable to perform sexually. They also note that men seem to gravitate between ale houses, where they become drunk, and coffee shops, where they hope to become sober.

208A [Clagett, William.] An Abridgment of the Prerogatives of St. Ann, Mother of the Mother of God. London, Printed for Ric. Chiswell, [1688]. 20 pages. A 108.

Clagett provides information about the lives of Anne and the Virgin Mary, even though scriptural verification is insubstantial. The remainder of the work is a translation of the Prerogatives, a catechism for St. Anne's Christian followers.

209A [Clagett, William.] A Discourse concerning the Worship of the Blessed Virgin and the Saints. London, Printed for Tho. Bassett and Tho. Newborough, 1686. 114 pages. C 4384.

Directing his comments to recent Catholic writings encouraging adoration of deceased persons, Clagett argues against worship of Mary and the saints. He says Mary did not wish to compete with Christ; although she was suprahuman, she was not a deity. Clagett denies a patristic rationale for the worship of Mary and the saints.

210A Clarke, Samuel. The History of the Glorious Life, Reign, and Death, of the Illustrious Queen Elizabeth. Second Edition. London, Printed for Henry Rodes, 1683. 208 pages. C 4524*. EEB Reel 1683:64.

This book is a narrative of the events of Elizabeth's reign. Like most such histories, it is laudatory. Clarke notes the queen was revered by all the princes of her time. The second edition contains a section about the difficulties she encountered before ascending the throne.

211A Claude, Isaac. A Sermon Upon the Death of the Queen of England Preach'd In the Walloon Church at the Hague. London, Printed for John Dunton and sold by Edm. Richardson, 1695. 20 pages. C 4587.

The textual reference for the funeral sermon is Acts 9.36-37. It describes Tabitha, a noble and generous woman, who died while performing charitable acts. Claude offers her exemplary life as an analogue to that of Mary II.

212A A Closet for Ladies and Gentlewomen. Or, The Art of Preserving, Conserving, and Candying. London, Printed by R. H. for Charles Greene, 1647. [no pagination] C 4728*. EEB Reel 1523:22.

In this typical household guide, approximately one third is devoted to cookery; the remainder discusses home remedies. It includes a large section about fruit-based syrups and medicines for many ailments.

213A Cloathing for the Naked woman, or The second part of The Dissembling Scot, set forth in his Colours...errors in...The Naked Woman. London, Printed for Giles Calvert, 1652. [9] pages. C 4736. TT Reel 105:E.683(25).

This pamphlet responds to 122A. It concerns the Ranters, John Lilburne and original sin, but does not address the woman mentioned in the earlier piece.

214A Cobb, Samuel. A pindarique ode: Humbly Offer'd to the Ever- Blessed Memory of our Late Gracious Sovereign Lady Queen Mary. London, Printed for John Witlock, 1694[5]. 12 pages. C 4772*. EEB Reel 412:4.

In this formal eulogy for Mary II, Cobb dwells on England's grief and the queen's virtues--piety, patience, humility, charity and strength. Excerpt: "Tho' a Woman, like some Rock she stood [frightening away birds of prey]." Cobb also alludes to "Insulting Paris" which he claims "laughs" at England's grief.

215A Cockburn, John. Bourignonism Detected. Or the Delusions and Errors of Antonia Bourignon. Narrative I. London, Printed for W. Keblewhite and H. Hindmarsh, 1698. 76 pages. C 4804*. EEB Reel 734:7.

This attack on an eccentric religious leader was published after her death in 1680. Cockburn accuses her of vanity and self-importance, alleging most of her disciples deserted her, while her present followers reside in Scotland. Cockburn wishes to demonstrate Bourignon was not inspired, and her doctrine is contrary to scripture. By implication he hopes to discredit Quakerism and Quietism as well. In this first volume of a series, Cockburn includes biographical material and examines Bourignon's character. See also works by Bourignon in Part B.

216A Codrington, Robert. The Second Part of Youth's Behaviour; Or, Decency in Conversation Amongst Women. London, Printed for W. Lee, 1664. 230 [32] pages. C 4878*. EEB Reel 1438:10.

Codrington maintains woman's office is to "please in all companies." He recommends discretion, silence and modest language, while addressing deportment, general behavior and administration of the family. Chapters discuss ornaments and apparel, recreation, learned ladies, marriage, diet, preserving, etc.   Codrington also includes proverbs and sample correspondence.

217A A Collection of the Funeral Orations...upon the death of...Mary II. London, Printed for John Dunton and sold by Edmund Richardson, 1695. [219] pages. C 5203. EEB Reel 660:4.

These five funeral orations were written by admirers in the Low Countries: Peter Francius of Amsterdam, John Ortwinius of Delph, J. G. Grevius of Utrecht and Francis Spanheimius of Leyden. The first is unsigned.

218A Collier, Giles. The Taking Away of Righteous and Merciful Persons...Funeralls of Mrs. Anne-Mary Child, wife of Thomas Child, Esq. of North-wick...Worcester Oxford, Printed for W. Hall, 1661. 15 pages. C 5238. EEB Reel 1328:7.

This sermon is devoted largely to Isaiah 57.1, which addresses saving the righteous from evil. Only the preface and final three pages concern Child, referred to as Thomas Child's eldest daughter rather than his wife (see title). She is characterized as pious, meek, helpful, tenderhearted, charitable, humble and sweet.

Collinges, John. The Excellent Woman Discoursed. See 220A.

219A Collinges, John. Faith and Experience: or, A Short Narration of the holy Life and Death of Mary Simpson...to which is added a sermon preached at her funeral upon Romans 14, 6 and 7. Two Parts. London, Printed for Richard Tomlins, 1649. C 5316A.

This publication includes Faith and Experience, a transcript of Simpson's religious views, revealing her strong but simple faith. It also contains a sermon written by John Collinges for her funeral: The Life and Death of a True Christian. He focuses on scripture rather than Simpson's personal qualities.

Collinges, John. The Life and Death of a True Christian. See 219A.

Collinges, John. Light in Darkness. See 220A (Courten funeral sermon, enlarged).

220A [Collinges, John.] Par Nobile. Two Treatises. The one, concerning The Excellent Woman. [Frances Hobart of Norfolk] The Other ...at the Funeralls of...the Lady Katharine Courten. London, 1669. 303 pages. C 5329. EEB Reels 683:11 and 1306:3.

A Presbyterian divine pays tribute to daughters of the Earl of Bridgewater. Hobart, the eldest of eight daughters, was tutored in the arts, married a widower, became a widow and managed the property, reducing her husband's debt by 6000 pounds. She survived most of her nine children. Courten's poignant life was marked by the deaths of many children, the ruin of her husband's estate and his escape to Italy, and a final confining illness. In a postscript the author denies the Courtens were papists.

Collinges, John. A Sermon composed for the Funeral of that precious Woman Mrs. Anne Skelton. See 529B.

221A Collinges, John. <u>Strength in Weakness: A Sermon Preached at the Funeral of Mrs. Martha Brooks, late wife to Mr. Tho. Brooks minister of gospel in London</u>. London, Printed for John Hancock, 1676. 39 pages. C 5342.

Brooks, who died after a lengthy illness, was a clergyman's wife. Her funeral sermon contains little about her life or personality, but dwells on her piety.

222A Comber, Thomas. <u>The Occasional Offices of Matrimony, Visitation of the Sick, Burial of the Dead, Churching of Women</u>. London, Printed by M. C. for Henry Brome, and Robert Clavel, [1679]. 580 pages. C 5480.

Dedicated to the Archbishop of Canterbury, this guide tells ministers and church officials how to conduct ceremonies relating to marriage, death, childbirth and sickness. The section devoted to churching, or "The Thanksgiving of Women after Childbirth," is most relevant for the Church's view of women.

223A <u>A Compendious Narration of the Most Exemplar Life of the Right Honourable and most Virtuous Lady Mary, late Countess of Shrewsbury</u>. [London], 1677. 59 pages. C 5608A.

The author was the countess' spiritual leader of long acquaintance. He describes her noble birth in Westminster in 1599 and her early proclivity toward religion. She prayed daily before attending to her household tasks, listened to hymns during childbirth, and engaged in austere demonstrations of piety.

224A <u>The Complaint of Mrs. Celliers, and the Jesuits in Newgate, To the E. of D.[anby] and The Lords in the Tower</u>. London, Printed for T. Benskin, [1680?]. Broadside. C 5613.

Although credited to Elizabeth Cellier in the Wing <u>STC</u>, this broadside was not written by her (a midwife implicated in the Meal-tub Plot). The author, purportedly a Catholic seeking the Romanization of England, calls her anti-English and claims the Plot (like Eve's sin) is a case of complicity between the devil and a woman. Cellier supposedly called England "one poor silly Heretical island" and argued the Catholics could make the public believe a Protestant was responsible for the plot.

225A <u>The Complaint of Mrs. Page, for causing her Husband to be Murthered, for the love of Strangewidge, who were executed together</u>. [London], Printed for F. Coles, T. Vere and I. Wright, [1680?]. Broadside. C 5613A.

This allegedly true sixteenth-century story concerns a woman forced by her father to marry. She was executed for killing her husband, even though she repented. Maids are warned to be faithful wives. Excerpt: "Me thought his sight was loathsom to my eye/My heart did grudge against him inwardly." See also 271A.

226A <u>A Compleat History of the pretended Prince of Wales...to the Fatal Exit of his True Mother Mrs. Mary Grey</u>. London, 1696. 40 pages. C 5640.

This piece concerns the alleged "false prince" born to James II. It substantiates rumors that he was actually the son of an Irish gentlewoman brought to

England in the Monmouth yacht to give birth to a child supposedly born of Mary of Modena.

227A The Compleat Midwifes Practice Enlarged. John Pechey, ed. Fifth Edition. London, Printed for H. Rhodes, I. Philips, J. Taylor and R. Bentley, 1698. 352 pages. C 1817G*/P 1022*. EEB Reels 1546:7 and 1611:1.

This guide for midwives, nurses and mothers is based on teachings of Hugh Chamberlain, Theodore Mayern, Nicholas Culpeper and Louise Bourgeois, midwife to the queen of France. It discusses the structure and functions of genital organs, fetal development, delivery, infant and child care, barrenness, desired attributes of midwives, etc.

228A A Compleat Narrative of the Tryal of Elizabeth Lillyman, Found Guilty of Petty Treason...For the Barbarous and Bloody Murthur of William Lillyman her late Husband. London, Printed for Phillip Brooksby, 1675. 6 pages. C 5647. EEB Reel 1630:14.

Lillyman was condemned at Old Bailey and burned at the stake for treasonous acts against her sixth husband, a cooper. She was jealous of him, "a lusty comely man," and after accusing him of drinking ale with a servant, stabbed him in the heart. Her confession appears in the document. The charge of treason, not murder, highlights a political view of marriage.

229A Concubinage and Poligamy [sic] Disprov'd: or, the Divine Institution of Marriage Betwixt the Man, and One Woman Only, Asserted. London, Printed for R. Baldwin, 1698. 95 pages. C 5714.

This text answers a work by the Reverend John Butler. The author says toleration of any marital state except monogamy will turn mothers into prostitutes and lead to a loss of respect for fathers by children. He maintains that although the Bible does not limit men to one wife, it does not authorize more.

230A A Conference between Lady Jane Grey and F. Feckman a Romish Priest... with her Behaviour and last Speech and Prayers at her Suffering. n.p., 1688. Broadside. C 5726.

This broadside tells of the arranged marriage of the Lady Jane to the son of the Duke of Northumberland. The duke persuaded Edward VI to name Grey his successor in lieu of his two sisters, although she had requested that the crown be offered to them. Grey is described as superior to the King "in Learning and Knowledge." The "conference" relates the supposed interchange between Lady Jane and a priest sent by Mary to convert her. Grey's final speech and details of her execution at sixteen are included.

231A The Confession of Mrs. Judith Wilks, the Queen's Midwife. London, Printed for E. R., 1689. Broadside. W 2257. EEB Reel 950:41.

Mrs. Wilks was midwife to Mary of Modena, queen consort of James II. The ostensible purpose of this satirical antipapist letter (supposedly written by Wilks to her cousin Wilifred) is to relate her role in the birth of the Prince of Wales. The author begins with effusive praise of the queen, then accuses Mary of complicity with the papacy in dominating James to further the Church's mission.

232A <u>A Continuation of the "Dialogue" Between Two Young Ladies Lately Married.</u>
<u>Concerning the Management of Husbands</u>. Part the Second. London, 1696. 44
pages. C 5963. EEB Reel 1400:21.

This piece continues a satire in which a happy and a sad wife exchange notes
about their marital problems. They discuss the advantages of obedience to win
over a husband. Seemingly obsessed with sex, one claims since Abelard was
castrated, he was hardly worth Eloise's efforts. Finally the notions of
compromise and consideration are raised as means to a happy marriage. See
also 284A.

233A <u>The Cony-Catching Bride. Who after she was privately married...sav'd her</u>
<u>selfe...from being Coney-caught</u>. London, Printed for T. F., 1643. 6 pages. C
5992. EEB Reel 177:11.

This story tells of a young bride who outwits both her father and husband on
her wedding night, making off with her own portion. Excerpt: "...never was the
like trick shewed by the wit of a Woman on her Wedding Day."

234A Cooper, Edmund. <u>On the Recovery of our Most Gracious Queen Katherine</u>
<u>from her Late Grevious and Deplorable Fit of Sicknesse</u>. London, 1664. 13 pages.
C 6054. EEB Reel 1684:23.

Dedicated to Henrietta Maria, this poem was written during the near fatal illness
of Catherine of Braganza, queen to Charles II. It contains standard praise of
her character and thanks to God that she was spared. This copy includes
another poem, in Cooper's own hand, to Ann Hyde, Dutchess of York, on her
recent illness.

235A [Cotton, Charles.] <u>Erotopolis: The Present State of Betty-land</u>. London,
Printed by Thomas Fox, 1684. 31 pages. E 3242.

This parody of contemporary regional studies meant to encourage travel is firstly
a burlesque that analogizes land to a woman's body. The extended metaphor
describes the climate, topography, inhabitants, and history of an area which
supposedly adjoins the Isle of Man. Part of the text lampoons papists, but the
primary intent is pornographic, with emphasis on woman as nature.

236A <u>The Court and Kitchin of Elizabeth, commonly called Joan Cromwel, the Wife</u>
<u>of the late usurper, truly described and represented</u>. London, Printed by Tho.
Milbourn for Randal Taylor, 1664. 133 pages. C 7036. EEB Reel 137:10.

The first forty-five pages of this book comprise a vicious criticism of Elizabeth
Cromwell's domestic management skills. Her table is called ordinary and
vulgar, while Cromwell herself is said to be "100 times fitter for a barn than a
palace." The remainder of the text contains recipes, supposedly used by her.

237A <u>The Crafty Whore: Or, The Misery and Iniquity of Bawdy Houseslaid open, in</u>
<u>a dialogue between two Subtle Bawds, wherein, asin a Mirrour, Our City-Curtesans</u>
<u>may see their Soul-Destroying Art, and Crafty Devices, whereby they Ensnare and</u>

Beguile Youth. London, Printed for Henry Marsh, 1658. 112 pages. C 6780. TT
Reel 239:E.1927(1).

> This anecdotal dialogue between two fictional Roman characters is apparently
> meant to demonstrate the cunning of prostitutes. One claims to sell her sexual
> favors for both money and enjoyment: "For what Woman is so affectionate, as
> to be satisfied with one man?" The author attacks the English for adopting the
> French preoccupation with courtesans, bawds and prostitutes. This work may
> be modelled on Pietro Aretino's Ragionamenti.

[Cressy, Hugh Paulin, ed.] XVI Revelations of divine love. See 380B.

238A Crooke, Banks. A Sermon Preach'd in the Parish Church of St. Michael
Woodstreet at the Funeral of Mrs. Hannah Bullivant. Who was Barbarously
Murdered. London, Printed for Joseph Wild, 1698. 23 pages. C 7229.

> This sermon was printed at the request of Bullivant's relatives. Crooke warns
> about the evils of malicious gossip: Even though the murderer knew Bullivant,
> she was apparently mistakenly attacked. As a result, her character was
> impuged. Bullivant seemed near death at one point and declared herself ready
> for her end. Her courage is cited as exemplary. See also 879A.

239A C[ross], J[ohn]. Contemplations on the Life and Glory of holy Mary, The
Mother of Jesus. With a Daily Office, agreeing to each Mystery thereof. Paris, 1685.
103 pages. C 7250. EEB Reel 46:11.

> Dedicated to Catherine of England, Scotland, France and Ireland, this defense
> of Catholic doctrine responds to a Protestant attack on transubstantiation. It also
> supports Mary's role as intercessor between humans and Christ. The work
> contains eight occasional "contemplations" directed to Mary.

240A Cross, Walter. Caleb's Spirit Parallell'd in a Sermon Preach'd at the Funeral
of the Late Mrs. Constancy Ward of East-Smith-field, London. London, Printed by
J. D. for Andrew Bell, 1697. 48 pages. C 7257. EEB Reel 913:12.

> Most of this sermon discusses Numbers 14.24. Only the final memorial poem
> concerns the deceased. She gave sound advice, valued reason and
> thoughtfulness, and was charitable and humble. Her husband, apparently
> harrassed by papists, fled from their persecution. Excerpt: "She labour'd much
> for Knowledge, and attain'd/Degrees therein beyond her Sex, yet still/A deep
> Humility in her remain'd."

241A [Crouch, John.] An Elegie, Upon the Death of the Right Honourable Anne,
Countess of Shrewsbury. London, 1657. 7 pages. C 7295. EEB Reel 178:1.

> This poem, dedicated to the countess' husband and mother, considers the
> earl's grief, the couple's contentment and the mystery of death. The countess,
> who died in childbirth, was apparently the last in her familial line. Excerpt: "She
> was her Fathers heir, and must disclaim/Not only his Estate, but House, and
> Name: /That Dower must vast and comprehensive be,/Whose Total is the whole
> posterity."

242A [Crouch, John.] The Muses Joy for the Recovery of that weeping Vine, Henrietta Maria. London, Printed for Tho. Batterton, 1661. [4] pages. C 7302. TT Reel 155:E.1050(3).

Dedicated to the Countess of Shrewsbury, this royalist poem celebrates the queen's return to England. Crouch refers to Charles I's execution, the reign of Charles II and the continuing rule of the Stuarts. He concludes: "Let proud Rebellion, sunk as low as Hell,/ Forever There, in its own Region, dwell."

243A [Crouch, Nathaniel.] Female Excellency, or the Ladies Glory. By R[ichard] B[urton], pseud. London, Printed for Nath. Crouch, 1688. 177 pages. C 7326. EEB Reel 178:7.

Crouch's book praises great women of the past, usually biblical, classical or mythical figures. It discusses the lives of nine, including Esther, Deborah and Judith from the Old Testament, and rulers such as Boadicea of Britain and Clothilda, Queen of France. It includes biographies, biblical and classical quotations and portions of the women's allegedly real conversations.

244A Crowne, John. Juliana, or The Princess of Poland. A Tragi-comedy. London, Printed for Will. Cademan and Will. Birch, 1671. 46 pages. C 7393. EEB Reel 812:14.

This tragi-comedy is set in Warsaw at the meeting of the Ban and the Areer Ban, armed in the field for the election of a king. Juliana, supposedly an historical figure, is the daughter of the deceased king of Poland. She is in love with and betrothed to Ladislaus, Duke of Curland. During an expedition to Moscow, he is taken prisoner. Paulina, daughter of the Czar of Muscovy, also loves him, helps him to escape, then pursues him to Poland dressed as a man.

245A The Cruel French Lady...Relation of the...Murthers committed by a French Lady...of her own Father, two Brothers and Sister. London, Printed for Roger Vaughan, 1673. 8 pages. C 7418. EEB Reel 1631:8.

This supposedly true account concerns a French woman who, after fourteen years of marriage, discovered her husband's fortune was being squandered. She poisoned her family in order to inherit her father's estate, collaborating with a French apothecary to concoct potions that would take effect at varying times. The author claims she may have murdered as many as fifty people. The tale seems exaggerated if not fabricated.

246A The Cruel Midwife. Being a True Account of...many children that have been murdered. London, Printed for R. Wier, 1693. 8 pages. C 7419A.

Madame Compton, alias Norman, was a midwife of eighty living in Stepney. A number of infant corpses were discovered in her cellar, and her garden was possibly a burial ground for others. She attended wealthy clients, some of whose bastard children were left in her care. Compton was committed to Newgate Prison.

247A The Cruel Murtherer, or The Treacheous Neighbor; being A True and full Relation of the horrid Murther of Alice Stephens, and Martha her Daughter. London, Printed for Edward Robinson, 1673. 8 pages. C 7421. EEB Reel 24:3.

Thomas Reignolds, a nearly illerate idler, slit the throats of two women, then set their house afire. His story warns against male drunkenness, carding, swearing, lying and stealing. See also 824A.

248A The Cukoo's Nest at Westminster, or the Parliament between two Lady-birds. By Mercurius Melancholicus, pseud. [London], 1648. 8 pages. C 7459. TT Reel 71:E.447(19).

This royalist satire depicts Anne, Baroness Fairfax and Joan Cromwell as ravenous, treasonous birds of prey--harpies or vultures. The Baroness, wife of General Thomas Fairfax, was noted for her ambition. The women are said to have roosted for eight years at Westminster. The author refers to their jewels and gowns and portrays Anne as an aspirant to the throne.

249A Cullen, Francis Grant. Sadducismus debellatus: or, a True Narrative of the Sorceries and Witchcraft exercis'd by the Devil and his instruments upon Mrs. Christian Shaw. London, Printed for H. Newman and A. Bell, 1698. 60 pages. C 7475A*.

Christian Shaw, a Scottish child of eleven, accused a young woman of stealing milk. She took revenge by placing thirteen curses on her. The child underwent a violent seizure while asleep and sustained bruises. Seven persons were tried as a result of the incident.

250A Culpeper, Nicholas. A Directory for Midwives: Or a Guide for Women. London, Printed by John Streater and are to be sold by George Sawbridge, 1671. 161 pages. C 7492*.   EEB Reels 1631:10 and 1757:12; TT Reel 177:E.1340(1).

This influential gynecological text was written by a pharmacist/pronatalist physician who defended the rights of midwives over physicians. Alice Culpeper, his widow, vouches
for the authenticity of this edited version. It describes genitalia, labor problems, medicines and proper care for mothers and babies. See also 251A.

251A Culpeper, Nicholas. Culpeper's Directory for Midwives, or A Guide for Women. The Second Part. London, Printed by J. Streater...sold by Geo. Sawbridge, 1671. 270 pages. C 7498.

This work focuses on women's diseases, especially those affecting the sexual organs. It is divided into fourteen sections about maladies to which women are susceptible during and after birth.   Culpeper includes descriptions and treatment of female illnesses.

252A Curtain-conference...Discourse betwixt (the late Lord Lambert, now) John Lambert, Esq; and his Lady, As they lay a Bed together.   London, 1659. Broadside. C 7688. EEB Reel 1254:19 and TT Reel 247:669.f.23(10).

This satirical broadside is a political attack on John Lambert, an officer who served under Fairfax. It relates a conversation supposedly overheard by a servant of Lady Lambert. Lambert claims his wife's pride and haughtiness have inspired his "ambitious attempts."

253A [Curwen, Thomas, ed.] A Relation of the Labour, Travail, and Suffering of that Faithful Servant of the Lord, Alice Curwen. [London], 1680. 55 pages. M 857.

This collection of testimonials was written by Friends about the character of Curwen's deceased wife. Prominent Quaker Rebecca Travers includes an account of Curwen's pilgrimage to Boston to free her husband, imprisoned for refusing to pay tithes. Curwen's own account of her ministry in America and Barbados is included (called good "both among Whites and Blacks") along with letters exchanged by the spouses. This item is attributed in the Wing STC to Anne Martindall.

254A [Cutts, John.] On the Death of the Queen. London, Printed for R. Bentley, 1695. 4 pages. C 7708A. EEB Reel 1328:37.

This turgid elegy by the Commander in Chief of the King's Forces in Ireland expresses England's grief at the passing of Mary II, who died from small pox. She is idealized: "Her Form proclaim'd Her Mind, as well as Birth;/So graceful and so lovely; ne're was seen/A finer Woman, or more awful Queen."

255A D., J. The Coronation of Queen Elizabeth, with the Restauration of the Protestant Religion: or, The Downfall of the Pope. London, Printed for Ben. Harris, 1680. [23] pages. D 31.

This play stresses the triumph of Protestantism under Elizabeth against Rome. It begins with the banishment of papists from the court. Simple folk--including a tinker, cooper and cook--witness Elizabeth's coronation as "King of England." There is also a scene where satan, the pope and cardinals plan the queen's murder.

256A D., J. A Sermon Preached at the Funeral of that incomparable Lady, the Honourable, the Lady Mary Armyne. London, Printed for Nevil Simmons, 1676. 48 pages. D 43. EEB Reel 1381:9.

This sermon is dedicated to Armyne's nephew, the Hon. William Pierreponte. Prominent Puritan Richard Baxter wrote the introductory section. It stresses the existence of a heavenly abode awaiting the faithful after death. The latter part discusses Armyne's life and education, her genealogy and religious devotion.

257A D., M. A Brief History of the life of Mary Queen of Scots, And the Occasions that brought Her, and Thomas Duke of Norfolk, to their Tragical Ends. London, Printed for Tho. Cockerill, 1681. 67 pages. D 57. EEB 687:7.

Based on materials taken from the Walsingham papers, this treatise focuses little on Mary and discusses her Catholicism only insofar as it posed a threat to the throne. The author warns his contemporaries that popish intrigue during Elizabeth's reign provides a basis for suspicion of current Catholic activity.

258A D., P. The Hertford Letter...Murder of Mrs. Sarah Stout. London, 1699. 16 pages. D 75. EEB Reel 1758:1.

This publication concerns the drowning of Sarah Stout, an alleged murder victim. It dwells on details of the flotation of a drowning person--the author wishes to establish the amount of water necessary for drowning. There is also testimony from a trial held to determine if Stout was killed. See also 168A, 280A and 882A.

259A Dalton, James. A Strange and True Relation of a Young Woman Possest with the Devill. London, Printed by E. P. for Tho. Vere, 1647. 6 pages. D 142. TT Reel 59:E.367(4).

Four years prior to this account, Joyce Dovey of Worcester heard a sermon, then went into a "passion" and experienced convulsions. The seizures occurred particularly during private prayer. At these times she spoke of a pharaoh and threw a Bible into the fire that did not burn. She claimed soldiers came to visit her, speaking of papists and crucifixes.

260A Dangerfield, Thomas. Thomas Dangerfield's answer to a certain scandalous lying pamphlet entituled Malice Defeated, or the Deliverance of Elizabeth Cellier. London, Printed for the Author, 1680. 20 pages. D 183*. EEB Reel 413:10.

Dangerfield, a notorious rogue, attempts to discredit Cellier, his alleged co-conspirator in the Meal-tub Plot. He refutes her accusations against him, calls her a "lying Jezebel" and labels her associates "caterpillers." Dangerfield includes two incriminating letters that he claims were written by Cellier to her lover. See also 137B, 138B, 512A, 603A, 787A and 880A.

261A Dangerfield, Thomas. Mr. Tho. Dangerfeild's [sic] Second Narrative...charge against the Lady Powis...and Mrs. Cellier. London, Printed for Thomas Cockerill, 1680. 28 pages. D 193. EEB Reel 913:16.

This document records Dangerfield's version of his involvement in the Meal-tub Plot. It contains a chronology of events, the testimony of witnesses, and describes Elizabeth Cellier's alleged role in the murder of Sir Edmund Bury-Godfrey. Dangerfield levels charges against the Lady Powis and Cellier's nurse; he also describes methods he claims were used to invalidate testimony at his and Cellier's trial. He lists crimes of imprisoned papists and their bail charges.

262A Dankerman, Cornelius. Batavia maerens in obitum illustrissimae principis Mariae. London, Printed for A. Roper and E. Wilkinson, 1695. Broadside. D 210. EEB Reel 1255:1.

English title: An Elegy from Holland, Upon the Death of that most Incomparable Princess, Mary, Queen of England. Composed by a don at the University of Utrecht in both Latin and English, this elegy emphasizes the combined grief of England and Holland at the death of Mary II: "Those Nations whom before one League did join,/Must now Confederates in Grief combine."

263A Darby, Charles. An Elegy on the Death of the Queen. London, Printed for John Chamberlain and are to be sold by Peter Parker and John Whitlock, 1695. 10 pages. D 245A. EEB Reel 1001:22.

This poem honoring Mary II is addressed to King William. Darby emphasizes continuity and utilizes the metaphor of an eclipsed sun: The Thames freezes,

264A Darrell, William. A letter to a lady from W. D. of the Society of Jesus. Wherein, he desires a conference with the gentleman who writ her a letter, furnishing her with scripture testimonies against the principal points and doctrine of popery. [London, 1688]. Broadside. D 267. EEB Reel 451:18.

Darrell challenged a Mr. Pulton to discuss religious doctrine, e.g., purgatory, papal authority, divine forgiveness. The woman of the title, although "endow'd with more than a Female Judgement," provides a vehicle for the expression of his views.

265A [Dauncey, John.] The History of the Thrice Illustrious Princess Henrietta Maria de Bourbon, Queen of England. London, Printed by E. C. for Philip Chetwind, 1660. 132 pages. D 293. EEB Reel 139:6.

This publication attempts to redress the allegedly false negative picture painted of Henrietta Maria during the Civil War period. It is a royalist defense, noting the queen's heroic virtues-- despite her sex. The author emphasizes her support of her husband during his last years.

266A [Davenport, John.] The Witches of Huntingdon, Their Examinations and Confessions; exactly taken by his Majesties Justices of Peace for that County. London, Printed by W. Wilson for Richard Clutterbuck, 1646. 15 pages. D 368. TT Reel 56:E.343(10).

The accuracy of this report, dedicated to the justices of the peace of Huntingdon, is defended in the preface. It includes the confessions of several accused witches from Catworth, who admitted making agreements with the devil for personal gain, as well as testimony against them. The female victims were allegedly sexually molested either by rodents (instruments of the witches) or by a man dressed in black clothing.

267A Davis, Isaiah. A Sermon at the Funeral of the Vertuous and truly Religious Lady, Mrs. Margaret Andrewes. London, 1680. 19 pages. D 418A.

This funeral sermon was preached upon the death of the only daughter of Sir Henry Andrewes who died at thirteen. Details of her life are mentioned only insofar as they provide moral and religious examples for other young ladies. See also 523A.

268A A Declaration, of a Strange and Wonderfull Monster born in Kirkham Parish in Lancashire (the Childe of Mrs. Houghton, a Popish Gentlewoman). London, Printed for Jane Coe, 1646. 8 pages. D 603. TT Reel 53:E.325(20).

A child was born who allegedly lacked a head, but had a face upon its chest. Its mother had stated she would rather bear a child with no head than a Roundhead. (The child was said to have been stillborn.) The text includes a certificate verifying the incident signed by a minister and the attending midwife.

269A A Declaration of the most High and Mighty Princesse, The Queen of Sweden, concerning Prince Charles. London, Printed for R. W., 1649. 6 pages. C 3963*.

This document concerns a possible match between the Queen of Sweden and Prince Charles. It includes a letter about military matters involving Cromwell and Prince Rupert. It is likely that the Earl of Brainford wrote most of the part comparing her to Elizabeth.

270A A Declaration Of the Queen of Bohemia concerning her coming. December 14, 1642. London, Printed for H. Blundell, 1642. 2 pages [incomplete]. E 526A. EEB Reel 1685:33.

This document, signed by John Warner, discusses the reasons for a visit to Parliament by Elizabeth, Queen of Bohemia. She and her son, the Prince Elector, report their dismay at her son Rupert's alleged tyranny and cruelty. They also wish for peace and unity in England. An unrelated resolution of Parliament follows this incomplete item, which also mentions Prince William's promise of support for Charles I and mobilization of troops in Spain and France.

271A D[eloney], T[homas]. The Lamentation of Mr. Page's Wife. [London], Printed for Alex Milbourn, [1670-80]. Broadside. D 956*.

This ballad is based on the supposedly true story of a woman who married a Mr. Page of Plymouth under duress. She and her lover, George Strangwidge, were executed after murdering Page. Her final words condemn arranged marriages and wifely rebellion. See also 225A.

272A The Deportment and Carriage of the German Princess. Immediately before her Execution. London, Printed for Nath. Brooke, 1672. 5 pages. D 1078. EEB Reel 1439:42.

Mary Carleton, accused of bigamy and deception, was the infamous "German Princess," subject of many publications. Here she appears penitent, but disclaims current rumors: She "...did dye well satisfied and unconcern'd, with a Resolution and courage beyond the weakness of her frail sex." Carleton was supposedly executed on her baptism day.

273A A Description of the Sect called the Familie of Love. London, 1641. 6 pages. D 1168. TT Reel 29:E.168(2).

A beautiful and devout young woman rode six miles from Surrey to observe members of this religious sect, founded in Germany in the sixteenth century. Seduced by the leader, she remained with the group for a week, after which she became unruly, incontinent and then mad. She eventually recanted and, under the guidance of a male sect member recovered from her mental anguish. This account is interesting because of the reputed influence of male figures on a naive maid.

274A The Divell a Married Man. By Niccolo Machiavelli, pseud. [London, 1647.] M 133.

This item is the same as 184A.

275A The Devil and the Strumpet. London, Printed for E. B., 1700? 8 pages. D 1217. EEB Reel 959:34.

Jenny Freeman, a prostitute by reputation, is alleged to have seen the devil at various times. He beat her, threatened her with a knife, and, in a warning to lewd women, suspended a flaming sword above her head for three hours. She is charged with contributing to the delinquency of twenty young "virgins."

276A The Devil pursued: or, The right Saddle laid upon the right mare; A Satyr upon Madam Celliers standing in the Pillory. London, Printed for T. Davies, 1680. Broadside. D 1220. EEB Reel 1714:20.

This satire attacks Catholicism through midwife Elizabeth Cellier, a protagonist in the Meal-tub Plot. Excerpt: "But who would think it from the Woman fine/A thing whom Nature itself has made Divine,/That she should act such horrid barbarous thing,/As to design to stab Statesmen, and to murder KINGS?"

277A The Divels Delusions or A faithful relation of John Palmer and Elizabeth Knott two notorious Witches lately condemned at the Sessions of Oyer and Terminer in St. Albans. London, Printed for Richard Williams, 1649. 6 pages. D 1227. TT Reel 87: E.565(15).

Palmer supposedly seduced Knott to "consort with him in his villany." They made a clay frame for a picture of Goodwife Pearls of Norton and set it afire. She then expired. The deed avenged her locking Palmer out of his house for nonpayment of rent. Knott is also accused of bewitching a cow. This epistolary account supposedly contains the accusations and confessions of witches in Hartford County; however, they are omitted from the copy under examination.

278A Dialogue [between M(ary) and J(ames)]. [London?, 1688.] Broadside. D 1288B. EEB Reel 1775:22.

This satirical broadside presents a dispute between the monarchs about blame for their unexciting sexual relations and barrenness. James claims Mary brought him enemies, concluding: "Consult your Oracle of Rome,/For next fair Wind before they come."

279A A Dialogue between a Gentleman and a Lady Relating Chiefly to the Nursing and Bringing up of Children. London, Printed for I. Nutt, 1694. 44 pages. D 1293A.

The title page links this item to 232A. Euthrapelus and Fabulla debate the merits of male versus female children, then discuss issues of language, human behavior and other topics. The document is unusual in its presentation of the sexes discussing a wide range of ideas. The Folger Shakespeare Library notes the date has been altered by hand to read 25 October 1698.

280A A Dialogue Between a Quaker and his Neighbour in Hertford, about the Murder of Mrs. Sarah Stout. London, Printed for the author, 1699. [No pagination.] D 1299.

This fictitious dialogue questions the acquittal of two men for the murder of Sarah Stout. The defense argued successfully that Stout, an innkeeper, became enamoured of a guest. When he spurned her, she supposedly committed suicide. The Quaker doubted this story, believing the defendants guilty. See also 168A, 258A and 882A.

281A A Dialogue between Mistris Macquerella, a Superb Bawd, Mistris Scolopendra, a Noted Curtezan, and Mr. Pimpinello, an Usher...Bemoaning the Act against Adultery and Fornication. London, Printed for Edward Crouch, 1650. 6 pages. D 1318. TT Reel 93:E.607(13).

Two bawds lament a decrease in their trade and an increase in security necessary to protect against detection and consequent "hanging, burning, carting, whipping or so."

282A A Dialogue between the D[uchess] of C[leveland] and the D[uchess] of P[ortsmouth] at their meeting in Paris. [London], Printed for J. Smith, [1682]. 4 pages. D 1328. EEB Reel 488:18.

This dialogue is actually an imaginary squabble between two mistresses of Charles II, each claiming his affections and maintaining her superior beauty, intelligence, etc. Their argument is interrupted by the ghost of Jane Shore, mistress of Edward IV, who reminds them she too was a "Royal whore," and that her office led not to fame, but to a tainted reputation.

283A A Dialogue between the Dutchess of Portsmouth and Madame Gwin, at parting. London, Printed for J. S., 1682. Broadside. D 1329. EEB Reel 180:21.

This conversation in verse allegedly took place between two mistresses of Charles II, Nell Gwynne and Louise Renee de Keroualle, upon the departure of the latter.

284A A Dialogue between two Young Ladies Lately Married, concerning Management of husbands. London, 1696. 37 pages. D 1345. EEB Reel 1525:24.

Two young women compare their husbands--the one a cheap wastrel who patronizes prostitutes, the other a generous and thoughtful mate. The wife of the first is a scold, while the other woman is pleasant, empathizes with her husband, and offers constructive criticism. The piece is satirical and somewhat salacious. See also 232A.

A Dialogue concerning the rights of Her most Christian Majesty. See 90A.

285A Dialogue M. Why am I daily thus perplext?/Why beyond womans patience vext? [London, 1688.] Broadside. N.I.W.

This poetic broadside satirizes Mary of Modena and her husband, James II.

286A Diggs, Dudley. The Compleat Ambassador: or two Treatises of the Intended Marriage of [Queen] Elizabeth. London, Printed by Tho. Newcomb for Gabriel Bedell and Thomas Collins, 1655. 441 pages. D 1453. EEB Reel 92:5.

These letters, exchanged by Ambassador Francis Walsingham in France and Secretary Burleigh in London, concern negotiations to marry Queen Elizabeth to a member of the Valois family. Both attempts, of course, failed. Diggs contends efforts were initiated by the French and the queen's ministers, and says the queen thought each match "a thing doubly inscrutable, both as she was a Woman and a Queen."

287A Dillingham, William. A Sermon at the funeral of the Lady Elizabeth Alston. London, Printed for Johnathan Robinson, 1678. 44 pages. D 1487. EEB Reel 625:10.

This funeral sermon praises the religious, charitable nature of the deceased, "a most loving, faithful and dutiful wife, an Help meet for [her husband]." Alston is lauded for being a good mother, a helpful neighbor, and for caring for the poor, especially with "Physick for their bodies."

288A A Directory for the Female Sex: Being a father's advice to a daughter: Wherein all young ones (especially those of that sex) are directed how they may obtain the greatest beauty, and adorn themselves with a holy conversation. London, Printed for George Larkin, 1684. Broadside. D 1543.

The author's general advice to the young: remember your own mortality, live a pious and virtuous life, shun evil companions, be sincere and temperate, concentrate on building your character, keep secrets and beware of sycophants.

289A A Discourse of Women, Shewing Their Imperfections Alphabetically. London, Printed for Henry Brome, 1662. 204 pages. D 1611. EEB Reel 92:6.

Written originally in French, this book is for use by English ladies and serves to warn against "feminine" failings such as avarice, concupiscence, envious rage, garrulity of tone, etc. It is a typical diatribe against alleged female vanity, lust and deceit.

290A A Discourse upon prodigious Abstinence, occasioned by the Twelve Months Fasting of Martha Taylor, the famed Derbyshire damsel. London, Printed by R. W. for Nevil Simmons and Dorman Newman, 1669. 37 pages. N.I.W.

The author wrote this treatise for physician Walter Needham. It describes the effects of extended fasting on body processes. The account of Taylor's fast comprises a small portion of the text. Only one observation is directly related to the sex of a given subject: "seminal humours" in virgins are held to gain in acidity over time and thus increase the blood's "ferment."

291A Discoverie of six women preachers...in Middlesex, Kent. [London], 1641. D 1645. EEB Reels 92:7 and 254:E.166(1); TT Reel 29:E.166(1).

In this risque satire of women preachers, the author claims they are tolerated only because there are not enough good male speakers. He describes six types--including one who pontificates about hair and the wife of a mason who offers bricks for congregational seating. The author closes by suggesting, "where their University is I cannot tell, but I suppose that Bedlam or Bridewell would be two convenient places for them."

292A Dr. Lamb's Darling: or, Strange and terrible News from Salisbury... Engagement made between the Devil, and Mistris Anne Bodenham. London, Printed for G. Horton, 1653. 8 pages. D 1763. TT Reel 109:E.707(2).

Anne Bodenham, accused of witchcraft, could transmogrify into a mastiff, a lion, a white bear, a wolf, a bull and a cat. She could send her victims soaring into the air at forty miles per hour. She received a death sentence for bewitching Anne Stiles and forcing her to inscribe her name in blood in the devils's book. See also 110A.

293A Dreadful news from Southwark: or, A most true relation how one Margaret Simpson, widow, together with Elizabeth Griffin an infant...were wonderfully struck dead with a thunderbolt. [London, 1679?] D 2153. EEB Reel 1401:19.

A woman and a child were killed by a bolt of lightening immediately after Simpson had spoken a number of oaths about having to pay a farthing. The moral: Do not offend the Lord as one never knows when death is near.

294A Dryden, John. Eleanora: A Panegyrical Poem: dedicated to the Memory of the Late Countess of Abingdon. London, Printed for Jacob Tonson, 1692. 24 pages. D 2270. EEB Reels 181:20 and 208:42.

This panegyric honors Eleanora Bertie, Countess of Abingdon. She is called pious, benevolent, charitable, modest, active and a good wife and mother. Excerpt: "Not aw'd to Duty by superior sway;/But taught by his indulgence to obey." See also 401A.

295A Dryden, John. A Prologue to the Dutchess, on her return from Scotland. [London], Printed for Jacob Tonson, 1682. Broadside. D 2337. EEB Reel 489:18.

This poem is about Mary of Modena, driven into exile in Scotland with her husband, James II. Dryden says that distempered zeal, sedition and hatred will no longer vex the Church or tear the fabric of the state.

296A [Du Bosc, Jacques.] The Accomplish'd Woman. Written originally in French. London, Printed for Gabriel Bedell and Tho. Collins, 1656. 135 pages. D 2407*. EEB Reel 141:7.

Du Bosc's widely read, lengthy treatise about women was translated from the French by "T. D." and dedicated to Lady Mary Walcot. He describes desirable and undesirable female qualities and advocates serious learning for women, along with the traditional cultivation of humility and morality.

297A [Du Bosc, Jacques.] The Excellent Woman Described by her true Characters and their opposites. Two Parts. London, Printed for Joseph Watts, 1692. 304 pages. D 2407B*. EEB Reel 276:7.

This volume is an abbreviated version of 296A, including part one and three sections of part two of Du Bosc's L'Honnete Femme. It minimizes his emphasis on scholarship for women and dwells on the cultivation of modesty and chastity. This edition focuses on women's allegedly negative qualities such as cruelty, pity and jealousy. It includes only twelve of the twenty-one chapters contained in a complete English edition of Du Bosc's work (296A).

298A The Dutchess of Mazarines farewel. [London], Printed for Langley Curtiss, 1680. Broadside. D 2424.

This poem supposedly describes Mazarin's regret at leaving Windsor and her lover Charles II. The duchess bemoans her situation and admits beauty and social station are not sufficient to insure happiness.

299A The Dutchess of Monmouth's Lamentation for the Loss of her Duke. London, Printed for J. Millet, 1683. 4 pages. D 2425*. EEB Reel 489:25.

This humorous poem is directed to the supposed abandonment by the Duke of Monmouth of his wife in pursuit of the crown. Monmouth was an illegitimate son of Charles II.

300A The Dutchess of Portsmouths and Count Connigmarks Farwel to England. [London, Printed for J. Bayly, 1682.] Broadside. D 2426. EEB Reel 1282:9.

This anti-papist satirical broadside attacks the French mistress of Charles II, Louise Renee de Keroualle. She is indicted for greed, promiscuity and her religion. England is said to be well rid of these cutthroat Tories (including "Connigmark"). The author avers that the two will now become the French pestilence.

301A Dugard, Thomas. Death and the Grave; or, a Sermon Preached at the Funeral of...Ladie Alice Lucie. London, Printed by W. Dugard, 1649. 54 pages. D 2463. EEB Reel 761:2.

This sermon is dedicated to the children of the deceased. There are profuse marginalia in Hebrew as well as Latin. Dugard stresses the need to be prepared for death. He also elaborates on the Lady Alice's piety and familial responsibilities. Material about her is contained in the final quarter of the sermon.

302A [Duke, Richard.] Floriana. A Pastoral, Upon the Death of Her Grace The Duchess of Southampton. [London, Printed for Samuel Cooke, 1681.] 4 pages. D 2505. EEB Reel 453:2.

Duke's pastoral is recited by a shepherd for his deceased love, whom he calls "the Goddess of the Plain." It expresses great sadness and contains effusive praise for the dead lover. The duchess is largely ignored in the poem.

303A Duncon, John. The Holy Life and Death of the Lady Letice Viscountess Falkland...Represented in Letters to that Honourable Lady, and exemplified in Her. Third Edition, Enlarged. London, Printed for Rich. Royston, 1653. 192 pages. D 2604*. EEB Reel 689:1.

This compilation of various works praises Letice Morison Cary, the daughter of Sir Richard Morison of Leicester and wife of Lucius Cary, second Viscount Falkland. It includes elegies, a description of her life in a letter to her mother and epistolary testimonials by individuals who offer thanks for her aid and inspiration. The Lady Letice died in 1646.

304A [Duncon, John.] The Returnes of Spiritual comfort and grief [sic] in a Devout Soul. London, Printed for Rich: Royston, 1648. D 2605*.

This item is the same as 303A.

305A [Dunton, John.] An Essay Proving that we shall know our friends in Heaven. Writ by a disconsolate widower, on the death of his wife. By Philaret, pseud. London, Printed and are to be sold by E. Whitlock, 1698. [95] pages. D 2624.

Dunton was the publisher of The Athenian Mercury; his wife was Elizabeth. The first half of this book describes the widower's own grief. There is also some discussion of the couple's marriage and the proper role of a wife. See also 773A.

306A [Dunton, John.] The Parable of the Top-Knots. London, Printed for R. Newcome, 1691. 3 pages. D 2631. EEB Reel 867:5.

In this "parable" Nature is astonished to see a lady bedecked fashionably in "Ribbons, Laces, Silks and Jewels." Nature assumes she must have left her work unfinished if women try to improve upon it. She says a woman needs only "unstained Vertue" to complement her natural endowments. Dunton mocks the influence of France: "We Eat, Drink, and Sleep in plain English, but we manage the rest of our actions in French." See also the rejoinders 686A and 912A.

307A [Dury, John.] Madam, although my former freedom and Madam ever since I had a resolution. [London, 1645.] 8 pages. D 2870 and 2871. TT Reel 47:E.288(14).

In Dury's letters to Lady Konalot he explains his avoidance of women in the past because of "the silly weaknesse and want of capacite which doth appeare in most of the Female kind"; however, he claims because the Lady Konalot is different, he wishes to propose marriage. The letters concern his decision to marry and explain the importance and purpose of a Christian marriage.

308A Du Verger of Douai. Du Vergers Humble Reflections upon some passages of the...Lady Marchioness of Newcastle's Olio. Or, An Appeale From her mesinformed [sic], to her owne better informed judgement. London, 1657. 168 pages. D 2921. EEB Reel 182:9.

In Du Verger's dedicatory epistle to the Duchess of Newcastle, he claims he enjoyed The World's Olio until he read about monastic life. He reponds to her assertions that monks serve as nurses "to quiet the people." He also questions her criticism of their practices of mortification. See also 465B.

309A The Earl Marshal's Order Touching the Habits of the Peeresses at the Coronation of...William and...Mary. [London] In the Savoy, Printed by Edward Jones, 1688. Broadside. E 70. EEB Reel 1650:14.

This edict specifies the types and colors of garments to be worn by peeresses at the coronation of the king and queen. The greatest detail is afforded dress of the highest ranking ladies.

310A An Elegie and Epitaph for Mistris Abigail Sherard, Daughter to the Right Honourable Philip Baron of Lentrimm. [London, 1648.] Broadside. E 342. TT Reel 246:669.f.12(92).

This neo-Platonic poem is about a recently deceased young woman. The author notes that she was "fair, chaste, noble, young/And fit for marriage," and that she was "courted by many all deny'd."

311A An Elegy in Commemoration of Madam Ellenor Gwinn. London, Printed for D. Mallet, 1687. Broadside. E 348. EEB Reel 1590:45.

Nell Gwynne, an actress and mistress of Charles II, who died of a stroke, is the subject of this moving tribute. She is characterized as courteous to the poor, charitable, modest and free with praise. Excerpt: "Tis but her shadow that we now have lost;/She left but this for a more enduring Coast."

312A An elegy on Mrs. Alicia Lisle...Which for High-Treason was Beheaded at Winchester. London, Printed for J.M. and are to be sold by Randal Taylor, [1685]. Broadside. E 358. EEB Reel 1590:53.

Lisle's case is presented as an example to her sex. The author portrays her as a criminal deserving of punishment, even though she had claimed her innocence. She had been accused of harboring a Non-confirmist minister. Excerpt: "She Patroniz'd the Cause, the Cause./Against the Church and stablish'd Laws." See also 411B.

313A An Elegie On that great Example...the Countess Dowager of Thanet. London, Printed for D. M., 1676. Broadside. E 363A. EEB Reel 1590:57.

In this elegy, the author says the subject is a grand example of "Charity and Vertue" as well as a generous hostess, a loving wife and a tender mother.

314A Elegy on the Death of her Highness Mary Princess Dowager of Aurange, Daughter to Charles I, King of England, Scotland, France and Ireland. [London], Printed for Edward Husband, 1660. Broadside. E 371.

This broadside is more accurately a tribute to Charles I and other royalty than an elegy for Mary.

315A An Elegie on the Death of Mrs. Rebecca Palmer. [n.p., 1667.] Broadside. E 377. EEB Reel 1591:5.

The deceased expired at the early age of fifteen. She is praised for her cheerfulness and purity.

316A An Elegie On the Death of the Most Serene Majesty of Henrietta-Maria, The Queen Mother of Great Britain. London, Printed by and for Thomas Ratcliffe and Thomas Daniel, 1669. Broadside. E 398B. EEB Reel 1569:6.

The poet compares the queen's loss to a general slain on a battle-field and lauds her bravery in supplying arms to Charles. Her loyalty to the king and the author's contempt for her detractors are emphasized: "Proclaim'd her Traytor, How did they proclaim/In that Her Loyal and Her matchless Name!"

317A An Elegie on the Famous and Renowned Lady, for eloquence and wit, Madame Mary Carlton, otherwise styled, The German Princess. London, Printed for Samuel Speed, 1673. Broadside. E 417.

This slightly humorous epitaph was written for a notorious woman accused of bigamy and deception. It is one of many publications about her.

318A An Elegy on the lamented death of Miss Edwards, who departed this life. London, Printed for T. Davis, [1700?]. Broadside. E 417B.

This epitaph was written for a young woman jilted by a man with whom she had relations; she supposedly died of grief. It is addressed to virgins who are cautioned to guard their chastity lest they be exploited.

319A An Elegie On the Lamented Death of the most Illustrious Princess, Anne, Dutchess of York. [n. p., 1671.] Broadside. E 418. EEB Reel 1591:23.

Privately married to James II in 1660, Anne Hyde was the mother of queens Mary II and Anne. She died from breast cancer. This monodony is primarily about the grief of the court, especially the women. Excerpt: "Each Lady drowns with tears her sparkling Eyes,/Becoming Martyrs to Griefs cruelties."

320A An Elegy on the Truly Honourable, and most Virtuous, Charitable, and Pious Lady, Countesse of Devonshire. [London, 1675.] Broadside. E 442. EEB Reel 1591:36.

At the writing of this elegy, Christina Cavendish, Countess of Devonshire ("a Hundred and odd Years of Age") was lying in state in Holborn. The author says she was informed, religious, "Handsome, Brisk...Complaisant and Gay" and kind. Royalist Cavendish was a friend of many wits and humanists, including the poet Edmund Waller.

321A An Elogy [sic] upon that never to be forgotten matron, Old Madam Gwinn, who was unfortunately drowned in her own fishpond, on the 29th of July 1679. [n.p., 1679.] Broadside. E 459. EEB Reel 1591:47.

This slightly humorous poem is about the mother of Nell Gwynne who supposedly drowned, inebriated, in a pond. See also 885A.

322A An Elegy Upon the Death of Mrs. A. Behn; The Incomparable Astrea. By A Young Lady of Quality. London, Printed for E. J., 1689. Broadside. E 467A. EEB Reel 1569:13.

The self-described neophyte author praises Behn's skill and says "our sex for ever shall neglected Lye" because of Behn's passing; however, female authorship is questionable because of the poet's emphasis on young female vocalists, Behn's beauty and her promiscuity. The poet also remains surprisingly distant from Behn.

323A An Elegie Upon the Death of my pretty Infant-Cousin, Mris. Jane Gabry. London, 1672. Broadside. E 468.

Jane Gabry lived only one day after her baptism. The author discourages mourning and advises "Rather convert our Sorrows into Joy/To build new hopes for a more lasting Boy." The subtitle suggests that nurses may have been negligent, as three infant girls had already died at their hands.

324A An Elegy upon the Death of the Most Illustrious Princess Heneretta [sic] Dutchess of Orleans. [London], Printed for John Clark, [1670]. Broadside. E 474*. EEB Reel 1698:53.

In a hyperbolic poem, the author describes the despair of English citizens, with nature in sympathy, at the passing of Princess Henriette-Anne, sister of Charles II. Excerpt: "Hence let us seek some doleful Gloomy Shade,/By Nature only for our Sorrows made."

325A An Elegy upon the decease of the most incomparable pious lady, the Princess Elizabeth, who dyed in Carisbrook Castle in the Isle of Wight, Septemb. 8, 1650. [London], 1650 [1]. 5 pages. E 479. TT Reel 96:E.625(2).

Elizabeth, the second daughter of Charles I, studied under Bathsua Makin. She supposedly knew Hebrew, Greek, Latin, French and Italian before she was eight. She died of a fever. The elegy describes the sadness of her final days when the royal family was exiled. Excerpt: "Sit down and cry, thy guide, Thy Guide is gone/Cry, Cry aloud, till God attend thy moan."

326A Elizabeth Lilburne Widow, and Elinor Lilburne, her Eldest Daughter, Petitioners, against William Carr, Esq, Nephew of the said Elizabeth. [n.p., 1696.] Broadside. L 2077aA.

Both Lilburne women petitioned from Newcastle jail where they had been held for eighteen months as a result of a suit instigated by Mrs. Carr, Elizabeth's own sister. The dispute concerns William Lilburne's estate, of which Elizabeth was sole executrix. William Carr had neglected to pay her rent for use of a colliery and lands and withheld its profits, thus precluding payment of the debt owed his mother by the women.

327A Ellis, Humphrey. Pseudochristis: Or, A True and Faithful Relation of the Grand Impostures, Abominable Practices, Horrid Blasphemies...lately spread abroad...by William Franklin and Mary Gadbury. London, Printed by John Macock for Luke Fawn, 1650. 62 pages. E 579. TT Reel 92:E.602(12).

Written by a minister, this piece tells of Franklin and Gadbury, who claimed to be Christ and his wife, "the lady Mary, the Queen and bride, the Lamb's wife." It describes their visions, confessions, trials and imprisonment in 1649. In Gadbury's "recantation," she claims to have been seduced by the devil.

328A England. Laws, Statutes. The Lawes Against Witches and Conjuration...Confession of Mother Lakeland...condemned for a Witch, at Ipswich in Suffolke. London, Printed for R. W., 1645. 8 pages. E 918. TT Reel 50:E.307(11).

This statement concerns the repeal of an act against conjuration passed under Elizabeth. The new, more severe, rules are adumbrated with a description of the attributes of witches. Lakeland, allegedly a witch for twenty years, confessed to bewitching her husband, who died after great suffering. She was accused of other murders accomplished through animals provided by Satan. Two victims recovered on the day she was executed.

329A England. Parliament. An Act of Parliament of the Twenty-seventh of Queen Elizabeth, to preserve the Queen's Person, the Protestant Religion, and Government, from the Attempts of the Papists. [London], 1679. 6 pages. E 1146. EEB Reel 1569:29.

This act responds to papist political conspiracies conceived to kill or overthrow the monarch. It excludes forever participants in such plots from claims of power. (The crime was punishable by death.) The act calls for revenge against papists if the king should be assassinated. It includes the text of the Bill of Exclusion. A parallel is drawn with the plot to murder Queen Elizabeth by Mary's supporters.

330A England. Parliament. Two Petitions of the Lords and Commons to his Majestie. With his Majestie's answer. Also his Majestie's consent for the Princesse Marie's going to Holland and her Majestie to accompany her. London, Printed by Robert Barker and the Assignes of John Bill, 1641 [2]. 18 pages. E 2429. EEB Reel 249:E.134(20); TT Reel 24:E.134(20).

Two items about women are appended to these petitions. The first is the king's consent for the Princess Mary to go with her mother, Henrietta Maria, to Holland. The second is the queen's answer to a message from both houses. She claims she was advised of the Commons' intent to accuse her of treason, but she never saw the article in writing. She has now been assured by the House that "never any such thing came into their thoughts."

331A The English Midwife Enlarged. London, Printed for Rowland Reynolds, 1682. [320] pages E 3104. EEB Reel 1007:16.

Primarily for midwives, this guide covers conception, labor and nursing. It includes sections about female pre- and post-birth maladies and those of children. The author says he sees no reason to keep secrets from midwives. Dialogues containing a physician's questions and a midwife's responses communicate information.

Erotopolis. See 235A.

332A [Estienne, Henri.] The History of the Life of Katharine de Medicis. London, Printed for John Wyat, 1693. 96 pages. E 3353. EEB Reel 93:7.

This translated biography is based on an English edition of 1575. Estienne implies that Catherine's cunning derived from her Italian origins, and her family was only publicly religious. He claims she and Louis XIV enlisted the aid of Protestants only to forsake them after gaining power. In general the biography tries to portray the perfidy of political power.

333A Every Woman Her own Midwife: Or a Compleat Cabinet Opened for Child-Bearing Women. London, Printed for Simon Neale, 1675. 207 pages. E 3553. EEB Reel 1700:40.

Pregnant women are advised about proper behavior and medical care here. They are to eat and drink moderately, avoid medications, lie dorsally, apply herbal essences and discourage induction of labor. Advice for midwives is included. The work is most interesting for its emphasis on comfort and good sense. An addition to this volume lists various diseases and their cures.

334A Eves, George. The Churches patience and faith in Afflictions. Delivered in a Sermon at the Funeral of the Right Worshipfull, and Vertuous Cecelia Lady Peyton. London, Printed for G. Bedell and T. Collins, 1661. 31 pages. E 3554. TT Reel 156:E.1057(8).

This sermon is dedicated to Baronet Thomas Peyton, husband of the deceased. Material about her begins on page twenty-one. The author says next to his own mother, he owes "the greatest part of that which I am" to her. She is described as patient during her long illness, humble, pious and charitable.

335A An Exact and Faithful Relation of the Process Pursued by Dame Margaret Areskine. Edinburgh, Printed at the Society of Stationers, [1690]. [50] pages. E 3598. EEB Reel 1283:19.

Dame Margaret was a widow petitioning Parliament to oppose a decision of the Lords of Session that allegedly violated a law which "ought to protect widows." The lengthy convoluted presentation includes her marriage contract, setting forth her rights to various properties. It maintains her son (or step-son) was illegally assuming portions of her estate. See also Addendum 67.

336A An Exact and true Relation of a most cruell and horrid Murther committed by one of the Cavaliers on A Woman in Leicester, billetted in her House. London, Printed for E. Husbands and I. Franck, 1642. [5] pages. E 3612. EEB Reel 247:E.117(20) and TT 21:E.117(20).

A pregnant woman was allegedly shot in the back five weeks before the date when her child was due. She was apparently killed when a cavalier argued with her husband.

337A An Exact and True Relation of the behaviour of Edward Kirk [and others] During their Imprisonment, and at the place of Execution. London, Printed by Elizabeth Mallet, [1684]. 4 pages. E 3615. EEB Reel 738:8.

A man murdered his fiancee and left her in a field near Paddington. Her throat was slit "and her Head and Face miserably beat and bruised." He says at first he resisted her relentless pursuit. When he finally proposed, she refused, thus inciting him to anger. He appears repentant and says she had "given me perpetual occasions to be passionate, but not to that degree."

338A An Exact and True Relation of the Examination, Tryal, and Condemnation of The German Princesse...Mary Carlton. London, Printed for R. O., 1672. 8 pages. E 3619. EEB Reel 210:33.

A woman supposedly tricked a jeweler's son into marriage, then absconded with silver and pewter items. Here she returns from her banishment to Jamaica to tell the truth of her treachery. The introduction speaks to the evil of temptation. Carl[e]ton's case was notorious.

339A <u>An Exact and True Relation of the Landing of her Majestie at Portsmouth</u>.
London, Printed for C. Wildebergh and John Ruddiard, 1662. Broadside. E 3620.

The occasion for this poem was the arrival of Catharine of Braganza at
Portsmouth. It includes a description of her marriage to Charles II. The author
mentions the anticipation of English men, stimulated by her beauty.

340A <u>An Exact Narrative of the Bloody Murder and robbery committed by Stephen
Eatan, Sarah Swift, George Rhodes, and Henry Pritchard</u>. [London], Printed for R.
Taylor, 1669. 9 pages. E 3665. EEB Reel 914:21.

A minister in London was attacked by several persons who slit his throat and
left him for dead. Swift, a notorious thief, was heard by the victim to exclaim,
"Kill the rogue." She was found guilty of robbery and, along with the others,
sentenced to be executed.

341A <u>An Exact Relation of the Bloody and Barbarous Murder, committed by Miles
Lewis and his Wife, a Pinmaker upon their Prentice in Barnsby-Street in Southwarke.
Also the examination of this bloody woman</u>. London, Printed for J. C., 1646. 6
pages. E 3684. TT Reel 58:E.364(2).

This tale relates the abuse of a young orphan by his masters. Forced to work
long hours with little food, he was beaten severely and branded with irons.
Neighbors and a female apprentice were witnesses against the woman, but her
husband fled. Nothing about his apprehension is included. Only the wife was
imprisoned.

342A <u>The Examination and Tryall of Margaret Fell and George Fox</u>. [London],
1664. 17 pages. E 3710. EEB Reel 66:17.

According to Fell, she and Fox were tried for their obedience to Christ's
commandment to "Swear not at all." This document includes a transcript of
their trial wherein she was accused of holding religious services privately in her
home. She was told she would be set free if she gave a security and promised
to refrain from this practice in the future.

343A <u>The Examination, Confession, Triall, and Execution, of Joane Williford, Joan
Cariden, and Jane Holt: Who were Executed at Feversham...for being Witches</u>.
London, Printed for J. G., 1645. 6 pages. E 3712. TT Reel 50:E.303(33).

These women were executed one week after confessing to practicing witchcraft:
They supposedly suckled dogs, cats and the like, and sold their souls to or
consorted with the devil--often many years earlier. The confessions were
witnessed by the mayor of Feversham.

344A F., E. <u>The Emblem of a Virtuous Woman</u>. [London?, 1650.] [48] pages. F
12. EEB Reel 867:19.

Didactic poems about biblical figures, including Eve, Sarah, Hagar, Rebeccah,
and Potipher's and Lot's wives comprise this volume. It includes verses about
good women in general, i.e., those who are modest, truthful, religious, and
content with their lot. Excerpt: "A vertuous woman thinks it no disgrace/To have

the lowest roome in any place;/And though she hath a noble pedigree/She loves to sit hard by humility."

345A Fair Warning to murderers of Infants: Being an Account of the Tryal...Mary Goodenough. London, Printed for Jonathan Robinson, 1692. 14 pages. F 105. EEB Reel 1009:33.

This warning is directed to sinners like Goodenough, a destitute widow seduced by a notorious cad. She gave birth to a child who "perish'd for want of suitable Help and due Attendance [and] she was justly convicted of Murder." The pamphlet says she admitted her guilt and asked her neighbors to care for her two remaining children. In a letter by the widow to her children she notes no men comforted her before her execution.

346A The Famous Tragedie of the Life and Death of Mris. Rump. London, Printed for Theodorus Microcosmus, 1660. 8 pages. F 385A*. EEB Reel 981:11.

This satirical political tract attacks the Rump Parliament, using the image of a prostitute in labor. Her profession is acceptable because of "the weakness of her sex." The author accuses her of taking gold from captured lands and of shedding the innocent blood of Charles I. Members of Parliament are characterized as "gossips." The pseudonymous "Mercurius Melancholicus" is likely the author. See also 602A, another version of this item.

347A F[arnworth], R[ichard]. A Woman forbidden to speak in the Church. The grounds examined, the Mystery Opened, the Truth cleared, and the Ignorance both of Priests and People discovered. [London], Printed for Giles Calvert, 1654. 8 pages. F 514*. EEB Reel 1592:26 and TT Reel 112:E.726(16).

Farnworth, possibly a Quaker, expresses support for women's right to speak in church. He claims although a woman is the "weaker Vessell" she may be "full of His wisdom." He says the spirit of truth can speak anywhere and is manifested in both men and women.

348A A Farther Essay relating to the Female Sex. Containing six characters, and Six Perfections. With the description of Self-love. To which is added, a character of a Compleat Beau. London, Printed for A. Roper and E. Wilkinson, 1696. 115 pages. A 4061. EEB Reel 445:1.

This adapted work has been attributed to both Judith Drake and Mary Astell; however, internal evidence indicates male authorship. Six prototypical characters are presented to help women correct their moral defects. They are the coquette, the conceited female, the domestic woman, the gamester, the litigious person and the hypocrite. The author claims women should be excluded from hard labor because of their delicate physiques; however, female education is called the foundation of reason and the cornerstone of faith. The author stresses the subordination of learning to faith. The text may be based on Madame de Prigny's Les Differens Caracteres des Femme du Siecle (1694).

349A Featley, Daniel. A Fountaine of teares emptying it selfe into Three Rivelets. Amsterdam, Printed for I. Crosse, 1646. 725 pages. F 598*. EEB Reel 94:1.

Featley's comprehensive collection of meditations is addressed particularly to women--thus it is in "noe language but English" for easy comprehension. It includes prayers for mothers at the illness and death of children, for recent widows and dying women.

350A The Female Hector, or the Germane Lady Turn'd Mounsieur [sic]. London, Printed for N. Dorrington, 1663. 8 pages. F 667.

Mary Moders Carl[e]ton, popularly known as The German Princess, is the subject of these tales. She supposedly deceived a young lawyer's clerk by hiding her first marriage and claiming wealth and royal descent. This account is unique among many because it describes her transvestism, alluded to in The German Princess Revived.

351A Fenelon, Francois de. The Education of Young Gentlewomen. London, Printed for N. R. and sold by T. Leigh and D. Midwinter, 1699. 149 pages. F 674C.

This translation of an important French treatise is about women's education by the mystic Archbishop of Cambrai. The translator notes Fenelon's Catholicism is of secondary importance. Fenelon believed women should be educated so they would be serious and good Christians, trained for family roles.

352A [Ferguson, Robert.] A letter to a Person of Honour concerning the King's disavowing the having been married to the D.[uke] of M.[onmouth]'s mother. [London, 1680]. 23 pages. F 750. EEB Reel 211:2.

Ferguson's interesting lengthy letter analyzes the characters of Charles II and James I. He discusses why Charles denied Lucy Walter a marriage contract legitimizing their son, the Duke of Monmouth. Ferguson argues James persuaded Charles to disavow his marriage to Walter to avoid questions about his succession. He says James encouraged Charles since he had denied his own marriage to Anne Hyde and had tried to impugn her character. Ferguson reviews the history of political royal deception at the expense of women.

353A [Fergusson, David.] The Lady Bark. [Aberdeen, Printed for Forbes, 1680?] 7 pages. L 163. EEB Reel 1062:17.

This light Scottish pastoral presents a dialogue between a young lass and the skipper of a ship. The dominant image is the ship as woman: "Now Nakedness seems no great punishment,/For many Women are right well content/To have their breasts, and their Raw- Spaulds behind like Galley Slaves exposed to sun and wind."

354A The XV Comforts of Rash and Inconsiderate Marriage, or Select Animadversions upon the Miscarriage of a Wedded State. London, Printed for Walter Davis, 1682. 104 pages. F 885AB*. EEB Reel 1686:5.

This French publication is a parody of the fifteenth-century The Fifteen Joys of the Virgin. The "comforts" are wives, all protagonists of bawdy tales. They intimidate, use or cuckold their husbands. Family life is depicted as dangerous and onerous for men.

The Fifth and last Part of the Wandering Whore. See 935A.

355A A Fight between the Scots women, and the Presbyterian Kirkmen. Edinburgh, 1652. 5 pages. N.I.W.

This satirical attack on the Presbyterians commemorates the removal by women of some ministers during a reading from the Book of Common Prayer. Here women assault men of the Synod with "clubs and bagge-pipes." The author calls them Amazons and describes their attack in the local marketplace. He says they are pregnant with children of an unwanted reformation.

356A [Filmer, Robert.] An Advertisement to the Jury-Men of England, Touching Witches. Together with a difference between an English and Hebrew Witch. London, Printed by I. G. for Richard Royston, 1653. 24 pages. F 909. TT Reel 106:E.690(6).

Written after executions following the Maidstone trials, this work rebuts the views of William Perkins, who cited eighteen proofs of witchcraft. Filmer says understanding witchcraft is important because sentencing in England is closely guided by law. He discusses covenants with the devil, means for extracting confessions, and biblical accounts of witchcraft. Filmer does not discuss the sex of witches.

357A Fisher, James. The Wise Virgin: or, a Wonderfull Narration of the Various dispensations of God towards a Childe of eleven. Fourth Edition. [London], Printed for John Rothwell, 1658. 170 pages. F 1007*. EEB Reels 1187:24 and 25; TT Reel 193:E.1510(2).

A child who was deaf, dumb and blind was nevertheless heard to praise Christ. Several of her speeches are included.

358A [Fleetwood, William.] An Account of the Life and death of the Blessed Virgin. According to Romish Writers. With the Grounds of the Worship paid to Her. London, Printed by H. Clarke for Th. Newborough, 1687. 39 pages. F 1243*. EEB Reels 353:26 and 1441:47.

Fleetwood addresses veneration of the saints as well as superstitions about Mary, citing scriptural and liturgical sources and patristic writings. His concern is the authority of original sources: "For by this we Protestants may see, how far we are to trust those Catholic Doctors."

359A Fonteyne, Nicholas. The Womans Doctour, or an Exact and distinct Explanation of all such Diseases as are peculiar to that Sex. London, Printed for John Blague and Samuel Howes, 1652. 250 pages. F 1418A. TT Reel 173:E.1284(2).

In this important gynecological text, Fonteyne cites the womb as a source for many female illnesses. Like other medical writings about women, it mentions hysteria, prolapsed uteruses, and the difficulties of conception. It is more a discussion of the physical problems of women than a guide for midwives.

360A Ford, Simon. <u>Heuchia Christianou, or a Christian's acquiescence...Preached at...the Internment of...Lady Elizabeth Langham</u>. London, Printed by R. D. for John Baker, 1665. 226 pages. F 1485. EEB Reel 692:1.

This lengthy funeral sermon honors the wife of Sir James Langham, Knight of Northampton. The epistolary dedication addresses her husband and mother, Lucy, Countess of Huntingdon, daughter of mystic Eleanor Douglas. The countess is lauded as a mother and compared to Roman heroines. There are also elegies by Sir James and friends, some in Latin or French, but there is little biographical information.

361A <u>The Form of the proceeding to the Funeral of...Queen Mary II</u>. [London], Printed by Edward Jones, 1694/5. 4 pages. F 1582. EEB Reel 1092:12.

This document specifies the order of participants in the funeral march for Queen Mary, consort of William III, which crossed from Whitehall to Westminster Abbey. It began with "three hundred poor Women, four and four" and ended with the body, the "chief mourner" and so on.

362A Fox, George. <u>The Cause Why Adam and Eve Were driven out of Paradise</u>. London, Printed for Benjamin Clark, 1683. 14 pages. F 1758. EEB Reel 1460:49.

Fox, the founder of Quakerism and later the husband of Margaret Fell Fox, argues Adam and Eve were forced to leave Eden because of their disobedience to God. Both men and women are alleged to be evil. Fox does not blame Eve alone for the expulsion from Eden.

363A Fox, George. <u>This is an Encouragement to All the Womens-Meetings, In the World</u>. [London], 1676. 96 pages. F 1934. EEB Reel 1188:29.

Fox speaks about proselytizing efforts of women in the New World, emphasizing their successes in Rhode Island and New York. He cites biblical precedents for female participation in religious service and direct communication with God. He calls men who oppose women's meetings "ignorant of the universal spirit" and notes widows, virgins and wives of nonbelievers cannot heed the Paulist admonition to learn from their husbands. Fox also encourages women to hold meetings.

364A Fox, George. <u>The Woman Learning in Silence: or, the Mysterie of the Woman's Subjection to her Husband</u>. London, Printed for Thomas Simonds, 1656. 6 pages. F 1991. TT Reel 131:E.870(8).

Fox questions the ubiquitous proscription against female speaking in places of worship. He invokes biblical examples of prophesying females and warns, "You that will not have Him to reign in the Female, as well as in the Male, you are against Scripture." Maintaining Christ speaks through all but reprobates, Fox still calls the husband the "head" of the family, as Christ is head of the church.

365A [Frankenstein, Christian Gottfried.] <u>The History of the Intrigues and Gallantries of Christina, Queen of Sweden...whilst she was at Rome</u>. London, Printed for Richard Baldwin, 1697. 328 pages. F 2076A.

This book is dedicated to Charles, Earl of Dorset and Middlesex. The manuscript was supposedly acquired by a French abbot in Italy who claimed it was written by one of the queen's officers. Christina is described as extraordinarily witty, self-confident, strong and passionate. The author discusses her early abdication in favor of the Prince Palatine of the Rhine, ostensibly because of her conversion to Catholicism. He confides the real reason--her love of Count Magni of Gardin. There are anecdotes about the absentee court, Christina's relations with ecclesiastics and the aristocracy and her financial affairs. See also 198A and 415A.

366A The Freedom of the Fair Sex Asserted: Or, Woman The Crown of the Creation. London, Printed and are to be sold by J. Nutt, 1700. 28 pages. F 2125B.

Defending women against their detractors, the author says criticisms are of two sorts: either the "railling" type or those "more Serious and Settl'd Invectives." Women are advised to follow their natural inclinations and help men; however, they are warned against becoming servants to them. The author lauds women's conversational ability and beauty, but notes women have inherited from Eve the pain of childbirth.

367A The French Convert: Being a true Relation of the happy Conversion of a noble French lady, from the errors and superstitions of popery. [By A. d'Auborn, pseud.] London, Printed for John Gwillim, 1696. 144 pages. F 2183B*.

A French aristocrat was converted by Protestant clergymen, including d'Auborn. She survived an assassination attempt by hiding in the forest for two years until she was found by her husband, a military officer. Although this supposedly true account reads like fiction, it is primarily an anti-Catholic tract.

368A A Full and True Account Both of the Life: And also the...Delusions...of Susan Fowls. London, Printed for J. Read, 1698. 8 pages. F 2292A.

Susan Fowls, the wife of a Hammersmith laborer, was apparently made to seem possessed (perhaps under hypnosis) so the techniques of Catholic and Protestant exorcism could be compared. Anglican clergy claimed she was not legitimately possessed, and she was fined and imprisoned for blasphemy. See also 790A.

369A A Full and True Account of a most Barbarous Murther and Robbery committed by John Davis, on the Body of Esq. Bowles' Lady. London, Printed for A. H., 1699. Broadside. F 2293F.

John Davis, servant to the Lady Bowles, was charged with beating her to death, slitting her throat, and stealing three hundred pounds. He claimed valuables found in his trunk were inherited. After he fled, Esq. Bowles offered a reward for aid in his capture.

370A A Full and True Narrative of one Elizabeth Middleton, a Roman-Catholick, Living...Westminster. [London], Printed for F. T., 1679. 7 pages. F 2312A. EEB Reel 1593:15.

Middleton was overheard saying she hoped she might never see the "light" if there were such a thing as the Popish Plot. According to this anti-papist piece, she became both blind and ill thereafter.

371A A Full and True Relation of a Maid living in Newgate-Street. [London, 1680.] Broadside. F 2315B. EEB Reel 1593:16.

Grace Ashborne, apprentice to an abusive tailor's wife, supposedly died from a large head wound. Three days after her funeral, she was disinterred--apparently yet alive. She stopped breathing shortly after her body was recovered, and the corpse was displayed. The curious were charged to view it.

372A A Full and True Relation of a most Barbarous and Dreadful Murder; Committed on the Body of Mrs. Kirk. London, Printed for Elizabeth Mallet, 1684. 2 pages. F 2315C.

When the bruised body of a woman was found near a field, her husband was charged. Although he denied guilt, the author speculates he killed his pregnant wife because he was forced to marry her. Apparently his recent viewing of an execution had not deterred him.

373A A Full and True Relation of the Tryal, Condemnation, and Execution of Ann Foster, (Who was Arrained [sic] for a Witch)...at Northampton. London, Printed for D. M., 1674. 8 pages. F 2335. EEB Reel 1670:17.

An old woman was blamed when thirty sheep were found with their legs broken, and fires blazed in barns and cornfields. While incarcerated, she was said to fornicate with the devil (who appeared as a rat). Foster first pleaded not guilty but later confessed to sorcery. Although she requested burning at the stake, she was hanged.

374A A Full Relation of the Birth, Parentage, Education, Life...of Mrs. Margaret Martel...who was executed for a...murther committed by her on the body of Madam Pullen...Account of the Paper delivered at the Place of Execution. London, Printed and sold by J. Bradford, 1697. 8 pages. F 2360A.

Martel was born of middle-class Parisian parents and showed an early interest in the academies. When her father denied her request to attend, she went to England, where she turned to prostitution. After a gay life at court, her reputation waned, and she resorted to theft and eventually murder, for which she was executed. Martel's final statement is included here. See also 439B.

375A The Full Tryals, Examination, and condemnation of Four Notorious Witches, At the Assizes held at Worcester. London, Printed by I. W., [1690?]. 8 pages. F 2378. EEB Reel 1653:26.

Four women condemned as witches were charged with consorting with the devil, bringing illness upon one child and murdering two others. All were sentenced to burn at the stake. Two were identified as repentant and urged young women to learn from their example. The midwives charged to inspect their bodies said they found strange teats in their "privy parts."

376A Fuller, Ignatius. <u>A Sermon at the Funeral of Mrs. Anne Norton, Widow and Relict of W. Norton</u>. London, Printed by E. T. and R. H. for R. Royston, 1672. 37 pages. F 2391. EEB Reel 1616:20.

Norton was from Berkshire where, the minister notes, the people follow a practical Christianity. Much of the sermon describes Norton's exemplary religiosity. Fuller notes she was naturally pious and always performed good works but had little interest in dogma.

377A F[uller], T[homas.] <u>A Comment on Ruth</u>. London, Printed for G. and H. Eversden, 1654. 223 pages. F 2476. EEB Reel 890:19.

This elaborate biblical commentary concerns the proper role of the father, the nature of marriage, the general structure of the family and women's special spheres. It is dedicated to Lady Anne Archer, Countess of Warwick.

378A Fuller, William. <u>A Brief Discovery of the True Mother of the Pretended Prince of Wales</u>. Printed at London and Re-printed at Edinburgh, 1696. 42 pages. F 2480*.

Fuller reiterates the widely circulated story that the son born to James II and Mary of Modena was an impostor. He claims the real mother, Mary Grey, was housed in St. James Palace, and the queen falsely claimed it was her child. See also 379A.

379A Fuller, William <u>A Plain Proof of the True Father of the Pretended Prince of Wales</u>. London, Printed for the author, 1700. 16 pages. F 2485. EEB Reel 144:14.

Fuller contends a pregnant woman from Ireland was lodged at Lady Strickland's quarters in the royal palace until she delivered a child by midwife Judith Wilks. Fuller claims he witnessed the removal of the child in a warming pan to the rooms of Queen Mary of Modena. The child was declared to be hers, and the mother was sent to Paris and murdered. Fuller includes several letters supposedly written by the queen and the Lady Powis which buttress his account. See also 378A.

380A <u>A Funeral Eclogue sacred to...Queen Mary</u>. London, Printed for John Whitlock, 1695. 8 pages. F 2531. EEB Reel 69:8.

This bucolic poem depicts two shepherds, Celadon and Thyris, mourning Mary, who died suddenly of smallpox. The pathetic fallacy is used as a device: "The Trees with hang'd down Heads do seem to grieve,/As if they too her Absence did perceive."

381A <u>A Funeral Elegy Upon the much lamented Death of...Mary, Lady Dowager, Countess of Warwick</u>. London, Printed for Tho. Parkhurst, 1678. Broadside. F 2536A. EEB Reel 1593:23.

This formal elegy describes the deceased Countess: pious, faithful, humble, charitable, affable and so on. See also 585B and 930A.

382A G., E. A Prodigious and Tragicall History of the Arraignment, Trial, Confession and Condemnation of Six Witches, at Maidstone, in the County of Kent. London, Printer for Richard Harper, 1652. [6] pages. G 13. TT Reel 103:E.673(19).

Of six women arraigned, two confessed to relations with the devil, while three claimed he impregnated them. Two supposedly gave a "piece of flesh" to satisfy themselves. During the hearing, a pin was thrust into one's arms, drawing no blood and eliciting no pain. Another swelled up in a fit of ecstasy. These events allegedly confirmed their identity as witches. A tale about Mrs. Atkins, a victim of witchcraft who disappeared, is also included.

383A [G., J.] The Memoires of Mary Carlton: Commonly Stiled, the German Princess. London, Printed for Nath. Brooke...and Dorman Newman, 1673. 120 pages. G 35A.5*. EEB Reel 1593:24.

Mary Carleton was accused of falsely assuming the identity of a German princess. The author argues Englishmen are susceptible to deception by sophisticated continental women, and Carleton took advantage of their gullibility. This chatty, titillating account of her life, treats satirically her collusion with her husband to defraud others. This is one of many publications about Carleton.

384A [Garden, George.] An apology for M. Antonia Bourignon. London, Printed for D. Brown, S. Manship, R. Parker, and H. Newman, 1699. 444 pages. G 218. EEB Reel 380:16.

This defense was apparently written by a friend or supporter of Flemish visionary Antoinette Bourignon, who believed her writings "revive the Life and Spirit of Christianity." Garden claims prejudice against Bourignon results in part from the fact she was untrained. Materials quoted or summarized include a biography, documents about predestination, free will, grace and the spiritual state of infants.

385A [Gauden, John.] A Discourse of Artificial Beauty, in point of Conscience, between Two Ladies. London, Printed for R. Royston, 1662. 262 pages. G 353*. EEB Reel 277:18.

This dialogue presents traditional arguments for and against cosmetics. Adornment is characterized as unlawful, vain and evil--a mark of pride, arrogance and hypocrisy frowned on by Church fathers. The more lengthy rejoinder argues in favor of cosmetics, maintaining abuse should not preclude discreet use. This book has also been attributed to Jeremy Taylor and Obadiah Walker.

386A [Gauden, John.] Discourse of Auxiliary Beauty. Or Artificiall Hansomenesse, in point of Conscience between Two Ladies. [London], Printed for R. Royston, 1656. 200 pages. G 355. TT Reel 201:E.1594(1).

This item is essentially the same as 385A.

387A Gaule, John. Select Cases of Conscience Touching Witches and Witchcrafts. London, Printed by W. Wilson for Richard Clutterbuck, 1646. 208 pages. G 379. TT Reel 168:E.1192(1).

Originally preached as several sermons at Great Staughton, Huntington, this work argues strongly for the existence of witches. Gaule claims it would be as valid to contend there is no devil as no witches. He says witches are frequently seen with strange companions and unusual animals. To find a witch the devil supposedly looks for "a faithlesse heart, a forward nature, a feeble sex, an impotent age, an illiterate Education, a melancholy Constitution, and a discontented condition."

388A The Generous usurer Mr. Nevell in Thames-street, who alloweth his maid usually a black pudding to dinner. London, Printed for Salomon Johnson, 1641. 6 pages. G 513. EEB Reel 456:9.

A stingy master mistreated his wife's nurse and their maid. These women catalog his abuses, including their poor wages, board and quarters.

389A The Genteel Housekeepers Pastime: Or, the Mode of Carving at the Table Represented in a Pack of Playing Cards. London, Printed for J. Moxon, 1693. 46 pages. G 521. EEB Reel 1285:5.

This book, supposedly written by the Faculty of Carving, claims the art is worthy for both sexes and lists outstanding carvers. The text includes recipes and instructions for carving.

390A [Gerbier, Charles.] Elogium Heroinum: or, The Praise of Worthy Women. London, Printed by T. M. and A. C. and sold by William Nott, 1651. 164 pages. G 583. EEB Reel 145:8.

Dedicated to Elizabeth, Princess of Bohemia, this work compares her to Minerva, the vestal virgins and great women from the past. The author calls women "the miracle of the world, and the marvel of marvels." He notes their goodness, beauty and intelligence and refers to Lady Jane Grey, Christine de Pisan and Anna van Schurman as particularly learned women. Most examples cited are from antiquity.

391A The German Princess Revived: or the London Jilt. [London], Printed by George Croom, 1684. 8 pages. G 613. EEB Reel 145:9.

Jenny Voss was executed at Tyburn on December 19, 1684. Although her parents were not destitute, she began stealing as a teenager, often from them, and later joined a band of gypsies. Finally she took a male companion and together they performed eighteen robberies while she was dressed as a man. The "German Princess" of the title is the infamous impostor, Mary Carleton.

392A Glanvill, John. A Poem. Dedicated to the Memory, and Lamenting the Death of her late Sacred Majesty of the Small-Pox. London, Printed for John Newton, 1695. 7 pages. G 796. EEB Reel 494:9.

This is an effusive poem, typical of the period, offered in memory of Mary II, who died suddenly of small pox. Excerpt: "What Charms, what Vertues must be Hers, to move/That Heart to such a Grief, and such a Love."

393A [Glanvill, Joseph.] Some Philosophical Considerations touching the Being of Witches and Witchcraft. Written in a Letter to the much Honour'd Robert Hunt, Esq.

London, Printed by E. C. for James Collins, 1667. 62 pages. G 832. EEB Reel 31:6.

> Glanvill, a fellow of the Royal Society, supports the existence of witches and claims rationality has become too powerful if it no longer allows the idea of witchcraft.

394A Glascock, John.   Mary's Choice, or, The Choice of the truly Godly Person...Sermon Preached at the Funeral of Mrs. Anne Petter. London, Printed by J. H. for Samuel Gellibrand, 1659. 84 pages. G 842. EEB Reel 628:10.

> Although Glascock, a Fellow of Magdalen College, Oxford, was Petter's son, he minimizes her life's work in this sermon. More of a scholastic exercise than a funeral eulogy, it includes only one section about her life. There is little discussion of her character.

395A The Good-wives Lamentation: Or, The Womens Complaint On the Account of their being [sic] to be Buried in Woollen. London, Printed for L. C., 1678. 8 pages. G 1085. EEB Reel 1331:41.

> This satirical piece depicts drunken women returning from a speech opposing a law requiring burial in wool rather than linen, which is for "making of paper at home." The women (Tattleswell, Prate-a-Pace, etc.) say their delicate skin won't tolerate wool. See also 396A.

396A The Good-wives Vindication: or, An answer to a late saucy pamphlet intituled The womens complaint on the account of their being to be buried in woollen. London, Printed for L. C., 1678. [6] pages. G 1086. EEB Reel 983:6.

> The author of 395A is charged with eavesdropping on women's conversations. Here public matters are called "a scandal to [women's] disposition." The author claims women don't care if, after their deaths, their clothing is used as paper for young gallants' books or as dressings for surgeons. In either case, men will have the use of it.

397A The Good Womens Cryes against the excise of all their Commodities ...[they] have convened together in a Feminine Convention in Doe-little-lane. Written by Mary Stiff, Chari-woman, in Vinegar Verse. [London], Printed at the Signe of the Hornes in Queen Street...and are to be sold at the Dildoe in Distaffe-Lane, 1650. 6 pages. S 5551. TT Reel 90:E.589(1).

> A women's parliament, whose members have attained their positions through sexual favors, convenes to protest the excise tax. They claim women cannot maintain their households because of the tax on commodities. Although the satire lampoons female sexuality, it is primarily an anti-Parliamentary piece, noting, for example, that although the government has sold the bishops' houses, it is still in arrears.

398A Gouge, William.   A Funeral Sermon Preached...at the Funeralls of Mrs. Margaret Ducke Wife of Dr. Ducke, one of the Masters of Requests to his Majesty. With a short Relation of her Life and Death. London, Printed by A. M. for Joshua Kirton, 1646. 42 pages. G 1390. TT Reel 58:E.365(3).

Margaret Ducke, who died of a stroke, is described as retiring, meek, mild, patient and forgiving. Material about her final illness is included. She appears to have been reclusive, if not agoraphobic, in her reluctance to leave her home.

399A [Gould, Robert.] A Funeral Eclogue to the Pious Memory of the Incomparable Mrs. Wharton. [London], Printed for Joseph Knight and Francis Saunders, 1685. 6 pages. G 1419. EEB Reel 31:11.

Two nymphs, Damon and Alexis, lament the loss of poet Anne Wharton. Her virtues--sweetness, piety, charity--are idealized. Their most interesting comment praises Wharton's talent. Excerpt: "So sweet, so fraught with Heav'nly Innocence,/I dare believe, She cou'd not give Offence."

400A Gould, Robert. Love given o're: or, a Satyr against the Pride, lust and Inconstancy, etc. of Woman. London, Printed for Andrew Green, 1682. 12 pages. G 1422*. EEB Reel 598:6.

Gould says women, the "Original of Mischief," are more fit for satire than scholarly treatises. He declares war against women, whom he calls lewd, deceitful and lustful. See also 29A and 251B. The British Library names Thomas Brown as a possible author.

401A [Gould, Robert.] Mirana. A Funeral Eclogue: sacred to the memory of that Excellent Lady, Eleonora, late Countess of Abingdon. London, Printed for Francis Saunders, 1691. 6 pages. G 1427. EEB Reel 1403:13.

In this eclogue Damon and Alexis discuss their grief for Eleanora Bertie. Their depression is accute--particularly because she was "so Young, so Good, so Fair." They note her sister had died after terrible convulsions. This romantic poem offers little about Bertie's life. See also 294A.

402A Gould, R[obert. A Poem most humbly Offered to the memory of Her Late Sacred Majesty, Queen Mary. Second Edition. [London], Printed for Jacob Tonson and Francis Saunders, 1695. 15 pages. G 1430*. EEB Reel 788:37.

In this typical laudatory poem, Gould discusses events involving England during the reign of Mary and William. He mentions Mary's care of the poor, her humility and other virtues. The poet also suggests princes should "Not perish meanly with the Vulgar Herd."

403A [Gould, Robert.] A Satyr against Wooing: with a view of the ill Consequences that attend it. London, 1698. 23 pages. G 1435. EEB Reel 1385:6.

In a poetic satire, Gould mocks courtship roles. Women's coyness and artificial beauty are especially disdained. The poet closes noting the vanity of women and male stupidity for being beguiled by it. Excerpt: "O Sot that knows not Wedlock is a more Incessant Toyl than tugging at the Ore."

404A [Gould, Robert.] A Satyrical epistle to the Female Author of a poem, call'd Silvia's Revenge, etc. London, Printed for R. Bentley, 1691. 24 pages. G 1436. EEB Reel 983:15.

Gould chides the "female" author of Sylvia's Revenge (Richard Ames) as unwisely and unfairly scornful of men, while foolishly indulgent of women. He says [Ames] spitefully and unfairly rails against female writers, their immodesty and coarseness. Excerpt: "Ephelia, poor Ephelia, Ragged Jilt/And Sapho, Famous for her Gout and Guilt/Either of these, tho' both Debaucht and Vile/Had answer'd me in a more Decent Style."

405A The Gracious Answer of the most illustrious Lady of Pleasure the Countess of Castlem---to the Poor-Whores Petition. [London], [1668]. Broadside. G 1472.

This anti-papist broadside, ostensibly by Charles II's mistress Barbara Villiers, replies to London prostitutes. The "countess" attacks the Catholic view of prostitution and promises to help the "Sisterhood." See also 717A.

406A Graham, Richard. Poems upon the Death of the most honourable, the Lady Marchioness of Winchester. York, Printed by Alice Broad and John White, 1680. 4 pages. G 1476. EEB Reel 1633:21.

These poems are dedicated to the widower and daughters of the deceased, the Ladies Mary and Elizabeth Paulet. They are more laudatory than many elegies and include many references to the the stages of life.

407A Grantham, Thomas. A Marriage Sermon. A Sermon called A Wife mistaken, or a Wife and no Wife. London, 1641. 12 pages. G 1554*. EEB Reel 255:E.172(19) and TT Reel 30:E.172(19).

Grantham says men are generally deceived by women and, to support his argument, he refers to the biblical exchange of Leah for Rachel. He claims women are able to indulge in adultery easily; marital deception appears to be a solely female province. As Grantham describes it, "The married man is intangled like a fish in a net."

408A Great-Britain's Lamentation for her deceased Princess. London, Printed for John Whitlock, 1695. Broadside. G 1667a. EEB Reel 31:15.

This eulogy for Mary is typical of others. She is said to have shared equally in the governing of the kingdom with William, who "managed Martial Work" while she "kept Peace at home." She is called a pious, obedient wife, a protector of the innocent, a terror to her foes, and a sage, modest and courageous leader. An acrostic spells "Mary Queen of Britain is Deceased."

409A A Great Discovery of the Queen's Preparation in Holland...as it was sent in a letter from Rotterdam...to M. [J]ohn Blackston a member of the House of Commons. London, Printed for J. Wright, 1642. [6] pages. G 1686. EEB Reel 146:4.

This document, supposedly relaying information sent in a letter of December 1642, reports Newcastle merchants have sent ships, men, stores and money to Henrietta Maria in Rotterdam. It alleges her men are spending much time and money preparing for war in Newcastle, and Catholics are raising money for a 16,000-pound loan to her guaranteed by the Prince of Orange.

410A The Great Eclipse of the Sun; or Charles eclipsed by the destructive perswasions of his Queen. London, Printed by G. B., 1644. 8 pages. G 1688. TT Reel 247:E.7(30).

This document reiterates the oft repeated accusation that Henrietta Maria was dominating Charles I and inciting the "Popish faction." The Commonwealth is likened to the heavens, while the king is called the sun; the Parliament, the stars; the king's advisors, the planets, and so on. The queen is compared to the moon in eclipse of the sun. Most of the work concerns the king's alleged abuse of his Protestant subjects and his alliance with Catholics. He is also criticized for his false claim to conscience.

411A Great News from a Parliament of Women, Now Sitting in Rosemary-Lane. London, Printed for A. Chamberlain, 1684. Broadside. G 1714.

This satire utilizes the popular format of a governing body of women identified by comical names like Mrs. Tattel and Mrs. Rattle-pate. They complain about their husbands' poor sexual service and vote to allow three husbands for every female. They celebrate the law by dancing, singing and drinking.

412A Great News from Middle-Row in Holbourn: or a True Relation of a Ghost which appeared...to a Maid-Servant. [London, 1679/80.] 4 pages. G 1727. EEB Reel 1403:18.

An apparition of a Mrs. Adkins appeared to her servant and told of the murder and gravesite of two children. Their bones were found near a fireplace and disinterred. They were later identified as two illegitimate children whose mother had killed and hidden them to conceal their births.

413A Great News from the West of England...Account of Two Persons lately Bewitched. London, Printed for T. M., 1689. Broadside. G 1738A. EEB Reel 1332:19.

A young man and woman were allegedly bewitched in Beckenton in Somersetshire. The two expelled pins, needles, pewter, and other metal objects. An old woman was charged with the crime after women discovered marks on her body. When she was thrown into the water with her legs tied, she supposedly "swam like a cork." Six men confirmed the story. The woman was detained until the next Assize.

414A The Great Tryall and Arraignment Of the late Distressed Lady...Germain Princess. London, Printed for W. Gilberton, 1663. 7 pages. G 1758.

Mary Carleton was tried for impersonating a German princess and committing bigamy. This document presents supporting evidence, including testimony of witnesses who claim they knew her as a child in Germany. Carleton says she came to England not to cheat her husband but to make her fortune. The jury reportedly acquitted her of bigamy and deception. Other items also describe her exploits.

415A Gualdo Priorato, Galeazzo. The History of the Sacred and Royall Majesty of Christina Alessandra, Queen of Swedeland. London, Printed for A. W., 1660. 478 pages. G 2172.

This history describes the queen's life and conversion to Catholicism, her resignation from the throne and travels to Rome. The author identifies noble families who entertained her along the way. The biography is also a defense of Catholicism that maintains the Church is permanent, while other institutions are ephemeral. See also 198A and 365A.

416A H., E. A Plain and True Relation of a Very Extraordinary Cure of Mariane Maillard. London, Printed for Randal Taylor, 1693. 16 pages. H 20. EEB Reel 1424:15.

A French girl was cured of lameness while reading about Christ's healing and pardoning of the paralytic. She was the daughter of a Protestant who caused her deformity by tossing her into the air during her infancy. The tale provides some detail about the social and economic situation of the lame girl. See also 898A.

417A H., I. A Strange wonder or a wonder in a woman, wherein is plainely expressed the true nature of most women. London, Printed for I. T., 1642. 5 pages. H 50. EEB Reel 251:E.144(5) and TT Reel 26:E.144(5).

Women are accused of coyness, laziness, pride, drunkenness, sullenness, hypocrisy, mendacity, and so on. Wives are called scolding, pouting, proud or sluttish. The piece closes with a poem dedicated to [the few existing] good women.

418A H., J. The Family-Dictionary; or Houshold Companion. London, Printed for H. Rhodes, 1695. [33] pages. H 66. EEB Reel 1462:24.

This general household guide contains remedies for diseases; recipes for beautifying waters, perfumes and cookery, and directions for wine-making.

419A H., M. The Young Cooks Monitor: Or, Directions for Cookery...Excellent Receipts. London, Printed for William Downing, 1683. 149 pages. H 95*. EEB Reel 1778:22.

The author, an instructor of cookery, dedicates this work to "all ladies and gentlewomen, especially those that are my scholars." A variety of recipes is included, although formulae for medical potions and general household advice are omitted.

420A H., N. The Ladies Dictionary: Being a General Entertainment for the Fair-Sex. London, Printed for John Dunton, 1694. 528 pages. H 99. EEB Reel 667:1.

The author discusses the accomplishments of women in "a Compleat Directory to the Female-Sex in all Relations, Companies, Conditions and States of Life." Directed to "the Lady at Court, to the Cookmaid in the country," it includes the etymology of female names, brief biographies of famous women and commentary on the positive aspects of marriage. Emphasis is on women's role as helpmate.

421A H., T. A Looking-Glasse for Women, or, A Spie for Pride. London, Printed for R. W., 1644. 10 pages. H 139. TT Reel 1:E.2(18).

In this diatribe against certain current hairstyles, the author says women should not braid or "crisp" their hair. Biblical allusions support the argument.

422A [Hale, Matthew.] A Collection of Modern Relations of Matter of Fact, Concerning Witches and Witchcraft...Upon Occasion of a Tryal of several Witches. London, Printed for John Harris, 1693. 64 pages. H 224. EEB Reel 72:8.

One of the period's leading jurists, Hale discusses the characteristics of witchcraft. He argues Christianity makes clear the power of the devil to set his servants against mankind and presents tales about witches, some translated from the French, and some from English trials and confessions.

423A [Halifax, George Saville, First Marquis of.] Advice to a Daughter, as to Religion, Husband, House, Family and Children. Sixth Edition. [London], Printed for M. Gillyflower and B. Tooke, 1699. 164 pages. H 290*. EEB Reel 133:29 and 146:11.

This popular advice book saw seventeen editions by the late eighteenth century. Addressing his daughter directly, Halifax sympathizes with her powerlessness within marriage, but says she must conform to matrimonial and familial demands. He allows little room for disagreement with her husband and cautions against resistance to his mistreatment.

424A [Halifax, George Saville, First Marquis of.] The Lady's New-Years Gift: or, Advice to a Daughter. London, Printed and are to be sold by Randal Taylor, 1688. H 304*. EEB Reels 564:10, 1463:6; 1655:26 and 1672::9.

This volume is essentially the same as 423A.

425A Hardy, Nathaniel. Death's Alarum; or Security's Warning-Piece. A sermon preached...at the Funerall of Mrs. Mary Smith. London, Printed by J. G. for Nath. Web and William Grantham, 1654. 32 pages. H 714. TT Reel 112:E.725(4).

The first and largest part of this sermon addresses preparation for the coming of Christ. Only the last two pages concern Smith. She was the young, pious, modest daughter of a minister who lived like a "lamb"--meekly and quietly. An oblique reference is made to the "danger of child-bearing"; perhaps it caused her death.

426A Harst, de. A Panegyrick of the Most Renowned and Serene Princess Christina, By the Grace of God, Queene of Swedland, Goths and Vandals. London, Printed for Thomas. Dring, 1656. 75 pages. H 923. TT Reel 212:E.1704(2).

This lengthy romantic poem praises Christina's masculine qualities and notes the success of her reign.

427A [Hart, John.] Trodden Down Strength. By the God of Strength. Or, Mrs. Drake revived...how the Lord revealed himselfe unto her a few days before her death. London, Printed by R. Bishop for Stephen Pilkington, 1647. 193 pages. H 960. TT Reel 251:E.1156(1).

This book is a detailed description of a decade-long depression. Drake seemed lively until her forced marriage and subsequent birth of her daughter, the "cause of her distemper," according to the author.   Among her symptoms were nightmares, manic episodes and listlessness.   The devil is blamed for her misfortune.

428A [Head, Richard.] The Life and Death of Mother Shipton. London, Printed for B. Harris, 1677. 50 pages. H 1257*. EEB Reels 103:1, 1385:33 and 1656:11.

Head describes the life and prophecies of the fictitious Mother Shipton. Although a witch, she was widely respected. Head claims the devil visited her in various forms, and spirits played pranks on her. He also speaks of her legendary intelligence. Her prophecies concerned many rulers including Henry VIII, Edward VI, Queens Mary and Elizabeth, Charles I and II and Cromwell. She also supposedly predicted the great fire and plague. See also 730A and 833A.

429A [Heale, William.]   The Great Advocate and Oratour for Women. Or, The Arraignment...of...Husbands...who hold it lawfull to beate their Wives. London, 1682. 154 pages. H 1300B.

First published in 1609 as Apologie for Women, this book strongly condemns men who strike their wives. The author criticizes the Jacobean "custome so common to undervalue the worth of that sexe." He stresses the positive qualities of relations between the sexes and questions wife abuse as a test of manhood. Heale maintains the sexes are interdependent and men should not act as judge, jury and executioner of their wives.

430A Heers, Henry.   The most true and wonderful Narration of two women bewitched in Yorkshire...as it is attested under the hand of that most famous Physician Doctor Henry Heers. London, Printed for Thomas Vere and W. Gilbertson, 1658. H 1368. EEB Reel 601:18.

Two women gave evidence against an alleged witch at the Assizes at York. One of the bewitched made a terrifying noise, then vomited pins, wool and pieces of knives. Another vomited things she had supposedly seen in the witch's basket. Heers includes a recipe for a potion he used to cure her. The story is part of testimony from the attending physician.

431A A Hellish Murder Committed by a French Midwife, On the Body of her Husband. London, Printed for R. Sare and Randal Taylor, 1688. 39 pages. H 1384. EEB Reel 1060:8.

The author says he wishes to dispel rumors circulating about this bizarre murder case. He includes testimony claiming a midwife, Marie Hobry (also known as Mary Aubry), called her husband a dog and a drunken villain, then threatened to kill him. Her son testified she was in constant fear for her life. Hobry claimed her husband beat her for three months and refused a separation. In desperation she choked and dismembered the body to dispose of it and prevent identification. See also 8A, 793A, and 940A.

432A Herard, Claude. The Arguments of Monsieur Herard for Monsieur the Duke of Mazarine, against Madam the Dutchess...and the Factum for Madam the

Dutchess. London, Printed for C. Broom, 1699. 160 pages. H 1490. EEB Reel 1551:18.

These arguments (the duke's side taken by M. Herard and the duchess defended by M. St. Evremont) document a celebrated divorce case. The duke charged abandonment and desertion, threatening to withhold alimony and dowry. In turn, his behavior was characterized as outrageous, tyrannical and irresponsible. The Folger Shakespeare Library offers a variant spelling of the author's name: "Erard."

433A Herbert, Mr. Three Elegies upon the Much Lamented Loss of our Late Most Gracious Queen Mary. London, Printed by J. Heptinstall for Henry Playford, 1695. [18] pages. B 3356/H 1494. EEB Reels 1309:15 and 1398:5.

These three elegies, written on the death of Mary II, were set to music by John Blow and Henry Purcell. Two are in Latin and one in English. Both music and bucolic lyrics, complete with classical references, are included. Excerpt: "Panthea's Eye was over all the land;/She succour'd many Tender Lambs."

434A Herbert, William. Herberts Childbearing Woman From the Conception to the Weaning of the Child. Made in a devotion. London, Printed by R. A.and J. M. and are to be sold by John Hancock and Humphrey Tuckey, 1648. 132 pages. H 1540. EEB Reel 147:6 and TT Reel 251:E.1172(2).

These meditations and devotions are to be recited by women before, during and after childbirth. The volume includes occasional prayers for periods before and after birth, baptism and weaning; during labor and visits by friends; and to mark conditions of the child: "stirres," "angrie," "proud," "sicke," "stands alone," etc.

435A An Heroick Poem, Most Humbly Dedicated to the Sacred Majesty of Catherine Queen Dowager. London, Printed for Nathaniel Thompson, 1685. 6 pages. H 1586. EEB Reel 72:18.

This poem expresses sympathy for the recent death of Charles II, noting contributions of Catherine of Braganza: She placed English armies on African shores (presumably a reference to the acquisition of Tangiers) and held important ties to the Lancastrian line. The author praises her heroic qualities.

436A An Heroick Poem on her Highness The Lady Ann's Voyage into Scotland. London, Printed for R. Bentley, 1681. 4 pages. H 1587. EEB Reel 496:12.

On Princess Anne's return to her homeland in Scotland, the author calls her "the bright Daughter of his Highness" [James, Duke of York]. The piece is critical of the antagonism of the English, who were entertaining exclusion of James from the throne.

437A Hey Hoe for a Husband, Or, The Parliament of Maids: Their Desires, Decrees and Determinations. [London], 1647. 6 pages. H 1659. TT Reel 64:E.408(19).

This satire names members of Parliament, e.g., Sarah Sale-Woman, Dorothy Doe Well, Priscilla Prick-Song, and describes their primary concerns: to make men more flexible, to force every tenth man to marry every tenth maid, so unattractive women are not left as spinsters; to pronounce "cracked maids" virgins again, to render men more amorous, to force men to support their illegitimate children, and to stifle the advances of widows toward young men.

438A [Heydon, John.]   Advice to a Daughter. In opposition to the Advice to a Sonne. By Eugenius Theodidactus. London, Printed by J. Moxon for Francis Cossinet, 1658. [208] pages. H 1664. EEB Reel 147:7.

Sections about studies, love and marriage, travel, government and religion are included in this book.   Much is for men, who are warned against marrying for beauty and condemning women too quickly for boldness.   Heydon also discusses jointure, labor pain, poor marriages, and the desirability of children. Only the section about marriage is primarily for women.

439A Heyrick, Richard.   Queen Esthers Resolves: or A Princely Pattern of Heaven-born resolution, For all the Lovers of God and their Country: opened in a Sermon preached before the House of Commons. London, Printed for Luke Fawne and are to be sold by Thomas Smith, 1646. 32 pages. H 1749*. EEB Reel 1505:7.

Heyrick explores the bravery, virtue, wisdom and resolution of the biblical Queen Esther. He compares her situation to contemporary England--noting there are still Hamans (common enemies) to destroy, religion to establish in the land, peace to secure and government officials to honor.

440A Heywood, Thomas. Englands Elizabeth: Her Life and troubles. Cambridge, Printed by Roger Daniel and sold by J. Sweeting, 1641. 201 pages. H 1779.

This book discusses the early life of Queen Elizabeth and the difficulties she encountered during the reigns of Henry VIII, Edward VI and Queen Mary. Some of her own writing is included, but this is more a narrative of Elizabeth's public life.

441A [Heywood, Thomas.] The Generall History of Women, Containing the Lives of the most Holy and Prophane. London, Printed by W. H. for W. H., 1657.   651 pages. H 1784. EEB Reel 147:11.

This massive text commemorates great women of the past. Its nine books discuss goddesses, muses, prophets, queens, famous wives and mothers, as well as incestuous and adulterous women, chaste and wanton women, and, finally, the Amazons. Materials are drawn from biblical and ancient sources with few references to contemporary women.   The last chapter posits general principles for female behavior.

442A [Hickes, George.] Speculum Beatae Virginis. A discourse of the due praise and honour of the Virgin Mary. London, Printed and sold by Randal Taylor, 1686. 39 pages. H 1869. EEB Reel 496:33.

As Dean of Worcester and a nonjuror, Hickes held High Church principles and opposed the Roman Catholicism of James II. This volume, containing Catholic prayers to Mary, is meant to encourage a reunion of Anglican and Catholic faiths. Hickes' commentary on the prayers stresses the importance of Mary and her counsel. He relates her role as queen of heaven to human queens; thus, he supports the participation of women in government. He suggests that by denigrating the role of Mary, the Protestants have degraded the religious importance of women in general.

443A H[ilder], T[homas]. Conjugal Counsell: or, Seasonable Advice, both to Unmarried and Married Persons. London, Printed for John Stafford, 1653. 176 pages. H 1974. EEB Reel 942:6.

Hilder says the primary purpose of marriage is the propagation of God's church, so children should be viewed as blessings. The secondary purpose is to subdue base lusts. Hilder proposes basic qualifications of wives (sweet disposition, good Christian family, "competent outward estate," good "huswifery") as well as duties (cohabitation, submission, helpfulness, furtherance of the family fortune, indulgence of the husband's estate).

444A [Hill, William.] A New-Years Gift for Women. Being a True Looking Glass wherein they may see their duties. London, Printed by T. N. for the Author, 1660. 52 pages. H 2035. TT Reel 241:E.2114(1).

Hill claims his looking-glass reveals women's duties, "both towards God, and their own Husbands," irrespective of social rank. He says women lack humility and listen to the devil more often than to God. He names three types: the good and virtuous, the practical (instructed in attaining salvation), and the evil and vicious, whom he would condemn to hell.

445A Histoire Secrette de la Duchesse de Portsmouth. Londres: Chez Richard Baldwin, 1690. 192 pages. H 2092.

This colloquial account of involved romances at Charles II's court centers on the intrigues of one of his more famous mistresses, the Duchess of Portsmouth, Louise Renee de Keroualle; however, it also includes accounts of the affairs of other courtesans and courtiers.

446A An Historical Narrative of the German Princess, Containing All Material Passages...Not yet Published. London, Printed for Charles Moulton, 1663. 22 pages. H 2106. EEB Reel 1795:6.

This compilation of material by the defenders of accused bigamist Mary Carleton argues her husband's dishonesty and greed. It claims she fears charges against her will harm other women and "...a Dissolute Life in Men, is not held to be such a Vice as in Women." Some testimony by Carleton herself is included. A final poem refers to Amazons and suggests history has ignored most women. There were many publications about her during the period.

The History of Mademoiselle de St. Phale. See 777A.

447A The History of Mrs. Jane Shore. Concubine to K. Edward the Fourth, who was Wife to...a Goldsmith in London. [London], Printed for J. Clarke, W. Thackeray and T. Passinger, [1688]. [10 pages.] H 2125*. EEB Reel 1720:6.

Jane Shore was allegedly forced to marry Matthew, who rejected her after she became Edward's mistress. This tale reports her life as miserable and her end as tragic--she died in a ditch and was eaten by dogs. She should be an example to wives who would be unfaithful. Also included: "The History of Mr. Matthew Shore, wherein is shewed his sorrowful lamentation."

448A The History of Pope Joan and the Whores of Rome. Second Edition. London, 1687. 23 pages. H 2132. EEB Reel 3:46.

The author says the story of the legendary Pope Joan is a fable and refutes details of her life. He also discusses treatment of prostitutes in Rome by the pontiffs. See also 939A.

449A The History of the Life, Bloody Reign and Death of Queen Mary, Eldest Daughter to Henry VIII. London, Printed for D. Browne and T. Benskin, 1682. 179 pages. H 2168.

This blatantly anti-royalist, anti-papist tract describes atrocities committed by her sister Mary and recounts the beheading of Lady Jane Grey. It also tells of the confinement of Queen Elizabeth and "an account of the Martyrs that suffr'd Death during her most Cruel Reign."

450A The History of the Most Renowned Queen Elizabeth. London, Printed by W. O. and sold by C. Bates, [1700]. H 2173*.

This item is the same as 791A.

451A Hodges, Thomas. The Hoary Head Crowned. A Sermon Preached...at the Funerall of Fran. Walbank, A Very Aged and Religious Matron. Oxford, Printed by Leon Lichfield for Tho. Robinson, 1652. 32 pages. H 2320. EEB Reel 383:25.

Hodges was the Rector of Souldern and past senior fellow at St. Johns College, Cambridge. He focuses on the honorific status of the elderly. He speaks specifically of men, although the deceased was a woman. He maintains death for an aged man is a blessing and in their wisdom, the elderly act as God's deputies. No reference is made to the deceased.

452A Hodges, Thomas. Two Consolatory Letters Written to the Right Honourable the Countess of Westmoreland...The Second upon the Death of Mrs. Anne Cartwright, Her Honour's Children by Sir Roger Townshend, Bart., her Former Husband. London, Printed by A. Maxwell for Samuel Gellibrand, 1669. 32 pages. H 2324B.

Hodges was tutor to the countess' son and a neighbor of her daughter. The first letter consoles her on the death of her son, who died in his prime in a foreign land. The second concerns her daughter, who, dying in childbirth, left two small children. After eight of the countess' children predeceased her, she said: "I had rather have children without land, than land without children."

453A Holland, Samuel. On the untimely and much lamented death of Mrs. Anne Gray, the daughter of the Learnedly Accomplisht Doctor Nicholas Gray of Tunbridge in Kent, who dyed of the Small Pox. [London, 1657.] Broadside. H 2440. TT Reel 247:669.f.20(51).

This dramatic elegy was written for a young woman of eighteen. Excerpt: "Rich in her Sexes Value, good mens praise/And full of all could be desir'd, but dayes."

454A Holland, Samuel.   The Phaenix [sic] her Arrival and Welcome to England...Marriage of the Kind's Most Excellent Majesty with the Most Royal and Most Illustrious Donna Katharina of Portugal. London, Printed for the author, 1662. 7 pages. H 2442. EEB Reel 919:15.

This piece celebrates the marriage of Charles II and Catherine of Braganza in Portsmouth. Excerpt: "Now like two glorious Lamps may their Flames rise/Pure, and erect, until they touch the Skies."

455A Holles, Denzil. Mr. Denzell Hollis [sic], his Speech to the Lords, Concerning the setling of the Queen of Bohemia, and her Electoral Family, in their Right and Inheritance, with Restitution for their Sufferings.   London, Printed for Francis Constable, 1641. 6 pages. H 2477. TT Reel 35:E.198(39).

Holles says the Commons is considering the king's proposal for support of his sister, Elizabeth, her son (the Prince Palatine) and their family. Holles favors continued support because of their royal blood and his belief that their presence on the continent will further resistance to the spread of Catholicism there.

456A Hopkins, Charles. Boadicea Queen of Britain. London, Printed for Jacob Tonson, 1697. 56 pages. H 2719. EEB Reel 358:2.

Dedicated to the playwright William Congreve, this drama is based on an historical incident. It takes place in the city of Verulanium, one of several which were sacked when Boadicea (Boudicca, d. 62), Queen of Iceni, led a rebellion in East Anglia against the Romans. After her troops were routed by Suetonius, she poisoned herself. See also 86A.

457A Hopkins, John. The Victory of Death, or, the fall of beauty, a Visionary Pindarick Poem, Occasion'd by the...Death of...Lady Cutts. London, Printed by B. M. and are to be sold by Sam. Buckley and Rich. Wellington, 1698. 80 pages. H 2750.

The deceased was the second wife of John Cutts, Commander in Chief of the King's Forces in Ireland and Colonel in the Coldstream Guards. She died in childbirth at eighteen. This lengthy eulogistic poem utilizes much natural imagery. A substantial part lauds Lady Cutts' physical attributes. See also 51A, 733A, 851A, and 955A.

458A Hopkins, Matthew. The Discovery of Witches: in Answer to severall Queries, lately Delivered to the Judges of Assize for the County of Norfolk. London, Printed for R. Royston, 1647. 10 pages. H 2751. TT Reel 62:E.388(2).

This pamphlet, written by a self-described witch finder, presents questions and answers about identifying witches. For example, many people, especially the elderly, develop warts or extra teats: How can certitude of witchcraft be established in such cases? Hopkins replies the examining judges are very skillful.

459A [Horneck, Anthony.] A Letter from a Protestant Gentleman to a Lady Revolted to the Church of Rome. London, Printed for James Collins, 1678. 145 pages. H 2845. EEB Reel 568:1.

Horneck says the young woman he addresses has been deceived, is weak, and has made an important decision without due consideration. He guesses her reasons for converting to Catholicism in a lengthy discussion of doctrinal matters, including transubstantiation, idolatry and the Virgin Mary.   The book is signed by "N. N."

460A Horneck, Philip. A Sermon Occasioned by the Death of the Rt. Honourable, the Lady Guilford. London, Printed for Edmund Rumball, 1699. 31 pages. H 2854.

Horneck was chaplain to Lord Guilford. The deceased was likely the first wife of Francis, the second Baron Guilford. He says Lady Guilford's eternal life is assured because she perfectly performed the good works required of a married woman. The entire sermon is about her life and works of Christian charity.

461A [Howard, Thomas.]   The History of the Seven Wise Mistresses of Rome. London, Printed for M. Wotton and G. Conyers, 1686. [173] pages. H 3009*. EEB Reel 107:20.

Stories about Halicuja, Mardula, Circe, Boadicea, Penthifilla, Debora and Dejanara comprise this text.

462A Howe, John. A Discourse Relating to the Much-lamented Death, and Solemn Funeral, of our Incomparable and most Gracious Queen Mary. London, Printed for Brabazon Aylmer, 1695. 43 pages. H 3023.

Dedicated to Rachel, Lady Russell, this religious essay lauds the recently deceased Mary II, although it is not her official funeral sermon. Howe says she serves as the model by which all should take their measure.

463A Howe, John. A Funeral Sermon for Mrs. Esther Sampson, the late Wife of Henry Sampson, Doctor of Physick. London, Printed for Th. Parkhurst, 1690. 28 pages. H 3026.

Howe's sermon is an exemplum directed to those with "painful and chronical Diseases." The protagonist, Esther Sampson, is depicted as happy to be released at her death from illness and an unstable mental state. Only four pages are biographical; they describe her patience in sickness and desire to learn from her affliction.

464A Howe, John. A Funeral Sermon on the Death of that Pious Gentlewoman Mrs. Judith Hammond. London, Printed for Tho. Parkhurst, 1696. 31 pages. H 3029.

The deceased was the wife of the Rev. Henry Hammond, to whom the sermon is dedicated. Howe, an old friend, tries to assuage Hammond's grief. Speaking of Mrs. Hammond's piety and tender care of her children, he advises the congregation that contemplation of life everlasting helps to ease earthly woes.

465A Howe, John. A Funeral Sermon on the Decease of that Worthy Gentlewoman, Mrs. Margaret Baxter. London, Printed for Brabazon Aylmer, 1681. 42 pages. H 3030. EEB Reel 1334:4.

This sermon is dedicated to Baxter's husband, Richard, who was extremely distraught at his wife's death. Howe speaks of the need for confidence and complacency in the face of death. He mentions Margaret Charlton Baxter infrequently, rather concentrating on the preoccupation of humanity with worldly things.

466A Hubberthorn, Richard. A True Testimony of the zeal of Oxford Professors and University-men, who persecute the servants of the living God...Also the lewdness of those two great Mothers discovered. London, Printed for Giles Calvert, 1654. 14 pages. H 3240. TT Reel 123:E.806(8).

Two Quaker women, Elizabeth Heavens and Elizabeth Fletcher, were taken to the maximum security Buckerdo Prison for speaking in the streets. A high official of Oxford University interrogated them and recommended to the mayor that they be expelled from town. He refused to do so, but the justices said they could be whipped and caged. Citing the biblical "vagabonds" Christ and Paul, the author accuses them and the official of being "lyers, dissemblers, and deceivers of the world."

467A A Hue and Cry after Beauty and Virtue. [London? 1685.] 4 pages. H 3269*. EEB Reels 188:14 and 742:33.

This lewd, anti-papist pamphlet utilizes a scathing description of a woman, Madame Pandora, to mock the Church. She is followed by disease, calls herself a widow, but was never married, and conjures up her husband's ghost, who supposedly died at sea. A reward of 1000 pounds is offered for her return to the pope's palace, along with a free cure of venereal disease. Excerpt: "[She is] Pig-ey'd, Beetle-Brow'd, Horse-teeth'd, Woodcock'd nos'd, as crooked in body as in mind."

468A The Humble Petition of Many Thousands of Wives and Matrons of the City of London...for the Cessation of these Civill Wars. London, Printed for John Cookson, 1643. 8 pages. H 3475. EEB Reel 242:E.88(13) and TT Reel 15:E.88(13).

Ostensibly a petition to Parliament for a quick end to the Civil War, this is actually one of many semi-pornographic tracts supposedly written by lustful women who miss their absent husbands. They are anxious for their return because only "decrepid [sic] old men, that cannot life [sic] up any part about us" remain.

469A An Humble Remonstrance of the Batchelors, in and about London, to the Honourable House, in answer to a late paper, intitled "A Petition of the ladies for husbands". London, Printed for and sold by the Bookselling Batchelors in St. Paul's Church-yard, 1693. 4 pages. H 3616. EEB Reel 919:28.

This reply answers a humorous petition supposedly written by the women of London to the Commons requesting greater respect for marriage. The author proposes virgins be taxed on their maidenheads; that vintners and aledrapers, rather than matrons, determine measures; and suggests only married women appear at the theatre, at Whitehall and in the park.   Finally, he defends prostitution.   See also 632A, 695A and 697A, probably by the same author.

470A H[ume], P[atrick].   A Poem Dedicated to the Memory of...Queen Mary. London, Printed for Jacob Tonson, 1695.   16 pages.   H 3663A.

In this effusive expression of grief over the death of Mary II, Hume praises not only her leadership, but also her womanly qualities: "The Pillar of the Church, the partner of the throne; The Queen, the wife, the bosom friend in one." He represents Mary as a maternal figure throughout, to wit, "the tender nursing mother of the poor."

471A I., H. An heroick Elegie Upon the...Death of...Isabella Buggs. London, 1681. Broadside.   I 5A.   EEB Reel 1594:19.

A brief elegy to a recently departed woman, this broadside centers on her present and past husbands, father and genealogy.   The author praises her piety and role as mother of a large family, primarily daughters, of whom she had "enough to teach the Sexe of Woman-kind."

472A I., W.   A Sermon preached at the funeral of Mrs. Alice Bray, wife to Francis Bray of Farthingo...Northampton.   London, Printed for Matthew Walbancke, 1646. 28 pages.   I 19.   TT Reel 56:E.345(6).

The theme of this funeral sermon is the end of the godly and their blessed estate in death.   There is no biographical information about Bray.

473A Idem Iterum: Or, the history of Queen Mary's Big-belly.   [n.p., 1688?]   8 pages.   I 33.   EEB Reels 422:8 and 1632:65.

This volume offers one of several versions of a rumor surrounding the birth of James Francis Edward Stuart by Mary of Modena--that she was never pregnant, and a common child was smuggled into her room in a warming pan.   This piece includes a letter from the Council to the Bishop of London upon hearing she was "quick with child," the text of an act of Parliament concerning succession, and a prayer supposedly recited daily by the Dean of Westminster, for a "Male-child, well-favoured and witty."

474A Imitation and Caution for Christian Women: or, The Life and death of that Excellent Gentlewoman, Mrs. Mary Bewley.   London, Printed by E. M. for George Calvert, 1659.   18 pages.   I 55.

This superior funeral sermon preached by the Rev. Dr. Reynolds, is intended as a guide for Christian women.   It contains information about Bewley's life, family, friends and acquaintances.

475A The Impeachment of the Duke and Dutchess of Lauderdale, With their Brother My Lord Hatton.   [Edinburgh? 1676.]   4 pages.   I 98*.   EEB Reel 869:12.

The Duke and his brother are accused of exploiting their powerful governmental positions to their own financial advantage.   The duchess is charged with soliciting bribes from local magistrates.

476A In obitum et Exequis Illustrissimae Mariae. [London], Sold by John Whitlock, 1695. Broadside. I 119B. EEB Reel 1740:23.

This elegy appears in both Latin and English. It expresses England's grief at the death of Mary II, calling her the "best of queens" and "vertue's kind nurse." The author wishes King William well and hopes he will be the "happy instrument of lasting peace."

477A Ireland. By the Lords Justices of Ireland. Sydney, Thomas Coningsby. Whereas the Wives, Children and Familys, of severall persons...holde correspondence with, their majestys said Enemys. Dublin, Printed by Andrew Crook, Asignee of Benjamin Tooke, 1690. Broadside. I 942.

This proclamation was issued at their majesties castle in Dublin and signed by Jon Davis. It orders families of persons perceived as rebels and spies against William and Mary to be escorted beyond the river Shannon and the control of English authorities. They were permitted provisions for the journey.

478A Ivie, Thomas. Alimony Arraign'd: or the Remonstrance and Humble Appeal of Thomas Ivie, Esq. From the High Court of Chancery. London, 1654. 52 pages. I 1108.

In a legal squabble a man's possessions are claimed by his second wife and her relatives. He appeals directly to Cromwell because he cannot afford a decision in Chancery. Ivie, attacking the actions of "Lewd and Defamed Women, in Order to Separate Man and Wife," claims nonpartisanship, but says most of his estate has gone to a wife "whom I never denied or refused any thing whatsoever."

479A J., H. The History of the Life and Death of Pope Joan: Who was Elected to the Papacy, An. 855 Under the name of Johannes Anglus of Mentz [sic] in Germany. Published as an Advertisement to all Papists. London, Printed for F. Coles, 1663. 16 pages. J 14. EEB Reel 1740:39.

The subject of this anti-papist tract is the mythical Pope Joan, who allegedly ascended to the papacy under false pretences, became pregnant by an administrative officer and gave birth. The author argues the Catholic Church has lost its credibility because of her brief reign.

480A J., H. To the most Excellent Princesse the Duchess of Newcastle. London, Printed by Sarah Griffin, 1667. Broadside. J 17.

This panegyric tells of the duchess' great poetic talent. See also entries under Newcastle, Margaret Cavendish, Duchess of, in Part B.

481A J., T. A Brief Representation and Discovery of the notorious Falsehood and Dissimulation...free Confessions of Anne...taken before Brampton Gurdon, Esquire, Justice of the Peace. London, Printed by J. L. for Philemon Stephens, 1649. 10 pages. J 35. EEB Reel 459:6.

The author offers a brief unsympathetic biography of Anne Wells Hall, an Anabaptist depicted as suicidal and intermittently disturbed. Claiming she was possessed, she had convulsions and said she heard voices. Villagers alleged she tempted Nicholas Ware to commit adultery whereupon her husband left her. The author compares Hall to historical female figures who beguiled others into heresy.

482A J., T. Satan deluding by feigned miracles. discovered by the notorious falsehood and dissimulation of Nicholas Ware, and Matthew Hall...confessions of Anne...and others. [Edited by T. J.] London, Printed by R. I. for Philemon Stephens, 1655. 10 pages. J 45A.

This pamphlet is the same as 481A.

483A [Jeamson, Thomas.] Artificiall Embellishments. Or Arts Best Directions How to Preserve Beauty or Procure it. Oxford, Printed for William Hall, 1665. 192 pages. J 503. EEB Reel 816:20.

This guide for the use of cosmetics and medicinal remedies includes sections for improvement of the complexion, figure, teeth and breath, and beautification of various parts of the body. Pregnant women are advised how to insure that their children will be handsome.

484A Jenny, John. A Funeral Sermon preached at the Funeral of the Right Honourable The Lady Frances Paget. London, Printed by J. D. for Nevil Simmons, 1673. 26 pages. J 673A. EEB Reel 1779:25.

Paget was married to the Earl of Holland, who was executed for his allegiance to Charles I. The text stresses her piety, charity and maternal role.

485A Jessey, H[enry]. The Exceeding Riches of Grace advanced by the Spirit of Grace to an empty nothing creature, viz, Mrs. Sarah Wight, lately hopeless and restless: her soul now hopeful and joyful in the Lord. London, Printed by Matthew Simmons for Henry Overton and Hannah Allen, 1647. 160 pages. J 687*. TT Reel 175:E.1307(2). EEB Reels 985:21 and 1035:13.

During a trance Wight was unable to eat and could barely drink for seventy days. Jessey claims divine intervention enabled her to begin eating. He chronicles Wight's physical state, notes her conversations with visitors and describes her spiritual turmoil. He includes descriptions of her episodes of anger, head-banging and attempted suicide by drowning. See also 621B.

486A John Clayton, Executor of Dame Mary Clayton, Appellant. Prudence Clayton, Respondent. The Respondent's Case in the House of Peers. [London, 1699.] Broadside. C 4614.

Prudence Clayton claimed one-third of the property left by her father and 300 pounds explicitly left to her in his will. Her portion represented her share if the estate were divided equally among three children. Clayton's thirty-year effort to procure her share from her mother is related.

487A Jurieu, Pierre. The Reflections of the Rev. and Learned M. Jurieu, Upon the strange and Miraculous Exstasies of Isabel Vincent. London, Printed for Richard Baldwin, 1689. 68 pages. J 1212. EEB Reel 460:1.

A young shepherd girl of about sixteen went into a trance. Although she was illiterate when it began, and spoke only her local dialect, she allegedly spoke French fluently during the trance and was also able to recite unfamiliar psalms.

488A K., T. The Kitchin-Physician: A Guide for Good-Housewives in maintaining their Families in Health. London, Printed for Samuel Lee, 1680. 134 pages. K 20. EEB Reel 213:1.

This book is for nurses, housewives and midwives to use rather than rely on physicians, described as overly specialized. Emphasis is on bodily cleanliness. The volume includes remedies for skin problems, hair loss, headache, apoplexy, cough, and other common ailments. The recipes contain natural ingredients.

489A [Keeling, Josias.] The Queenes Proceedings in Holland. Being The Copie of a Letter sent from the Staple at Middleborough to Mr. Vanrode a Dutch Marchant [sic] in London. London, Printed by T. F. for I. M., 1642. [6] pages. K 124. EEB Reel 242:E.83(33) and TT Reel 14:E.83(33).

This document contains details about the Danish ambassador's visit to Henrietta Maria at The Hague and his message to the Low Countries. It also addresses money raised by priests and Jesuits in provincial cloisters for the Irish Rebellion and discusses the death of Bishop Cullen.

490A Keith, George. The Woman-Preacher of Samaria. [London], 1674. 25 pages. K 236. EEB Reel 1703:11.

This Quaker defense of women's preaching claims the "Woman-Preacher of Samaria" was "a better preacher, and more sufficiently qualified to preach than any of the men-preachers of the Man-made Ministry in these three Nations." She supposedly learned the truth directly from Christ and was thus better qualified than university-trained ministers. Keith says women need not ask their husbands for permission to speak when they are inspired by Christ.

491A Ken, Thomas. A Sermon preached at the funeral of...Lady Margaret Mainard, at Little Easton in Essex. London, Printed by M. Fletcher for Joanna Brome and Wm. Clarke in Winchester, 1682. 40 pages. K 279. EEB Reel 717:28.

This eulogy is dedicated to the widower, Lord William Mainard. Ken says his wife was over forty and had spent nine years at court. Her personal attributes included verbal felicity, piety, purity, innocence, industry, charity, and humility. She is called a dutiful daughter, avid reader, devoted mother and transcriber of favorite sermons.

492A [Kendrick, William.] The Whole Duty of a Woman: Or a Guide to the Female Sex. Written by a lady. Third Edition. London, Printed for J. Guillium, 1701. 184 pages. N.I.W.

Addressing the duties of daughter, wife and mother, Kendrick favors a traditional submissive role and its attendant attributes: modesty, chastity, humility, compassion, temperance, piety and affability. There is a section about medical preparations, beauty aids, candying and preserving. Although authorship is is question, Kendrick is a likely candidate. Records of earlier editions are unavailable.

493A Kettlewell, John. A Funeral Sermon for the Right Honourable, the Lady Frances Digby. London, Printed for Robert Kettlewell, 1684. 33 pages. K 368. EEB Reel 717:35.

Written for a woman who died suddenly at twenty-three, this sermon is dedicated to her husband, Lord Simon, Baron Digby of Geashill. The second half is a "portraiture," which claims to be sincere and understated. The Lady Frances is characterized as kind, pleasing, good-natured, pious, generous, humble, unpretentious and candid. She is also called a wise and careful mother.

494A A kind congratulation between Queen Elizabeth, and the late Queen Mary II of ever glorious memory. London, Printed for R. Smith, 1695. Broadside. K 479A.

This poetic dialogue between the two queens takes place in heaven. They discuss events of their respective reigns and allude to their officers and problems with the Church. Excerpt: "Since Fate's all-ruling Hand has then remov'd/Us Two from England, we so dearly lov'd:/For her Prosperity our Prayers we'll Joyn/ May England Flourish, and may Rome Decline."

495A L., A. A Question deeply concerning Married Persons, and such as intend to marry: Propounded and resolved according to the Scriptures. London, Printed for Tho. Underhill, 1653. 7 pages. L 5. EEB Reel 1723:2.

The author argues against female control of property a woman owns before marriage because: the husband is the household head; women's subservience dates from original sin; women must submit to men for their own "safety" and "God's honour"; and women can be easily "deceived in judgment and perverted in affection." The piece contains many biblical references.

496A [La Chappelle, Jean de.] The Unequal Match: Or, The Life of Mary of Anjou Queen of Majorca. An Historical Novel. Two Vols. London, Printed for Chas. Blount and Richard Butt, 1681. L 133 and L 134. EEB Reels 944:13 and 604:8.

La Chappelle's historical novel is about Mary, daughter of the king of Naples and Sicily, married to the king of Majorca, an old man with two other wives. It was a marriage dictated by the exigencies of diplomacy, and it doubtless brought her little happiness.

497A The Ladies Answer to the Busie-body, Who Wrote the Life and Death of DuVall. London, 1670. Broadside. C 1660.

Erroneously attributed to Elizabeth Cellier in the Wing STC because the preface is signed El. C., this broadside was clearly written by a man accusing the biographer of DuVall for attacking his honor. He criticizes him for maligning "Weak Women" and adds "I to thy Cost would soon defend their Fame." Cellier did not achieve notoriety until a decade after publication of this broadside.

498A The Ladies Behaviour. A Dialogue. Written, Originally in Italian, above an hundred and fifty years agoe. London, Printed and are to be sold by Randall Taylor, 1693. 154 pages. L 150. EEB Reel 638:3.

The author says he cares for women greatly and therefore is always in a passion. The text is comprised of advice supposedly offered by an older Italian woman to a young married woman whose husband is rarely at home. She encourages extramarital affairs, purchase of expensive clothing and a gay social life. Her primary message is a woman should exploit her beauty while young. It is doubtful the text was written by a woman.

499A The Ladies Champion. Confounding the Author of the Wandring Whore, by Eugenius Theodidactus...Powder-monkey, Universal Mountebank...and Scribler of that infamous Piece of Non-sense Advice to a Daughter, against Advice to a Son. London, 1660. 14 pages. L 151. TT Reel 156:E.1053(10).

In a coarse rejoinder to The Wandring Whore, a lewd serial, the author cynically argues the best prevention for prostitution is legalization of polygamy. Excerpt: "...is not using a handsom Girl wholsome, pleasurable, and tolerable?...I conceive...it is less criminal for a man to go and lie with a wench (I will not say another man's wife) than to lie with his wife when she is big with childe."

500A The Ladies Losse at the Adventures, of Five Hours: or, the Shifting of the Vaile. [London], 1663. 8 pages. L 156. EEB Reel 1062:16.

This lewd and humorous poem is about a woman who loses her pubic merkin ("muff") to a thief.

501A The Ladies Preparation to the Monthly Sacrament. Consisting of Prayers, Meditations, and Ejaculations, before, at and after Receiving the Lords Supper. London, Printed for Simon Neale, 1691. 152 pages. L 158.

Anglican prayers and meditations for the "Private Life of a Devout Lady" comprise this volume.

502A A Lady's Religion. London, Printed by Tho. Warren for Richard Baldwin, 1697. 71 pages. L 159.

The author encourages female piety without requiring the comprehension of scripture. Mary Astell's The Christian Religion as Profess'd by a Daughter of the Church of England (1705), a response to this book, argues against faith without understanding by women.

503A The Ladies Remonstrance: Or, A Declaration of the Waiting- Gentlewomen, Chamber-Maids, and Servant-Maids, of the City of London. Imprinted at London for Virgin Want, to be sold by John Satisfie, [1659]. 5 pages. L 160.

This bawdy pseudo-petition was supposedly written by the serving-women of London who, sexually unfulfilled, desire mature sexual partners, not masters who refuse to accept responsibility for their illegitimate children.

The Lady Bark. See 353A.

504A The Lady Dacre's case. [London? 1690.] Broadside. L 164.

The widow of M. P. Chaloner Chute and her grandson had a dispute over inheritance monies. See also 200A, 201A and 202A.

505A The Lady Gray Vindicated: Being an Answer to a Popish Pamphlet, entituled A true relation, of a strange apparition that appeared to Lady Gray, commanding her to deliver a message to His Grace the Duke of Monmouth. [London], 1681. Broadside. L 165. EEB Reels 519:38 and 718:19.

This broadside rebuts a pamphlet describing an apparition appearing to Lady [Mary] Grey telling her to deliver a message to the Duke of Monmouth. The author defends her character and the duke's claims for succession to the throne. Monmouth was the illegitimate son of Charles II by Lucy Walter. See also Addendum 164.

506A A Law against Cuckoldom. Or, the Tryal of Adultery. London, 1700. 7 pages. L 632. EEB Reel 1062:21.

This poem tells of Philipia of Prato, where the penalty for adultery was death. She was discovered fornicating by her husband, Rinaldo. At her trial she appeared gay and, in her own defense, noted women weren't allowed to vote on the adultery law (which applied only to wives). Philipia also persuaded her husband to testify that she was able to satisfy him. Her husband sneaked away as she was acquitted before a cheering crowd.

507A Le Moyne, Pierre. The Gallery of Heroick Women. London, Printed by R. Norton for Henry Seile, 1652. 181 pages. L 1045. EEB Reel 110:8.

Le Moyne, a Jesuit, describes the lives of great women of the past. Arrangement is by religious orientation: Jewish, barbarian/Roman, and Christian. He includes Deborah, Judith, Zenobia, Portia, Eleanor of Castile, Joan of Arc, and Mary, Queen of Scots. Each section addresses a moral issue as well as an individual. Examples: Are women capable of understanding philosophy? Can they cultivate qualities necessary for serving in the military?

508A [Leslie, William Lewis.] The Idea of a perfect Princesse, in the Life of St. Margaret Queen of Scotland. Paris, 1661. 101 pages. L 1173.

This French biography emphasizes moral values. St. Margaret (d.1093) was known for her piety, charitable works, and attempts to reform the church and refine domestic arts. Leslie includes a eulogy for Matilda, her daughter. The author wished to set an example for women "to improve the comliness of your Soules."

509A [Leti, Gregorio.] Il Puttanismo Di Roma, or the History of the Whores and Whoredoms of the Popes, Cardinals, and Clergy of Rome. Translated by I. D. London, 1670. 136 pages. L 1340A*. EEB Reel 1425:21.

This anti-Catholic satire was originally published pseudonymously in 1669 in Italian. Leti claims immorality was discovered by "a conclave of Ladies convened for the election of a new Pope"; this expose was commissioned by a Vatican courtesan. The fictive council of women speak for the several cardinals supposedly under their control. The meeting is followed by a dialogue between two men about the evil power of prostitutes within a system based on nepotism.

510A [Leti, Gregorio.] The Life of Donna Olimpia Maldachini, Who Governed the Church, during the time of Innocent the X. Written in Italian by Abbot Gualdi and Rendered into English. London, Printed by W. G. and to be sold by Robert Littlebury, 1666. 214 pages. L 1332*. EEB Reel 111:5.

Maldacini was the alleged power behind Innocent X. This Italian tale describes how she neglected her family to assist her brother-in-law until he was eventually elected pope. Leti claims they were lovers, even though Innocent was horribly ugly; their intimacy supports his contention that women desire to dominate at any cost.

511A "Letter concerning the manner of the Queen of Swedens renouncing her Religion." In A Book of the Continuation of Forreign [sic] Passages. London, Printed by M. S. for Thomas Jenner, 1657. 6 pages. Item: N.I.W. Collection: B 3716.

This letter describes Christina's public commitment to Catholicism, an event that took place at Innsbruck on October 26, 1655. The Archduke of Tirol attended, along with his brother, an archbishop, and his wife, sister to the Duke of Florence. The document says the queen accepted the apostolic and ecclesiastical traditions of the Church, the seven sacraments and their approved rites, the edicts of the Council of Trent, and so on.

512A A Letter from the Lady Cresswell to Madam C. the Midwife. On The Publishing her late Vindication, etc. Also A Whip for Impudence: or, A Lashing Repartee to the Snarling Midwifes Matchless Rogue: Being an Answer to that Rayling Libel. n.p., 1680. 4 pages. L 1529. EEB Reel 426:10.

This satirical "letter," supposedly by a notorious madam, accuses Elizabeth Cellier of seeking fame. Cellier was a midwife involved in the Meal-tub Plot. The author assumes the persona of an old friend, then becomes malicious. Excerpt: "She smells rank of Rome, and stinks of Plots and Conspiracies--/All her railing is her Barking and Howling against the Moon, the employ of an Irrational Animal." See also 137B, 138B, 260A, 603A, 787A and 880A.

513A A Letter of Advice to a Young Lady, Being Motives and Directions to Establish Her in the Protestant Religion. London, Printed and sold by Richard Baldwin, 1688. 48 pages. L 1567. EEB Reel 3:46.

This defense of Anglicanism against Catholicism is addressed to a young married woman who, with her family, has just left London. The author says her family is both her greatest treasure and greatest responsibility. He tries to convince her to be loyal to the Church of England and reject the unjustified arrogance of the Catholic Church.

514A Letter to a Gentlewoman Concerning Government. London, Printed and Sold by E. Whitlocke, 1697. 32 pages. L 1663. EEB Reel 1725:39.

This defense of William and Mary also supports oaths given to kings and the hereditary monarchy. The author discusses male versus female succession and criticizes women's meddling in government, a sphere supposedly beyond their "capacity and reach."

515A A Letter to a Virtuous Lady, To Disswade her from her Resolution of being a Nun. London, Printed for John Harris, 1686. Broadside. L 1697. EEB Reel 1152:35.

Written in the carpe diem tradition, this poem argues humans should be fruitful. The young woman is entreated not to "waste" her beauty by becoming a "Vestal Sacrifice" as a nun. Although she supposedly wishes to join a convent to avoid the temptation of sin, he advises, "Not all your Walls, nor Bars, can keep out Thought."

516A Letters and Poems in Honour of the Incomparable Princess, Margaret, Dutchess of Newcastle. [London] in the Savoy, Printed by Tho. Newcombe, 1676. 182 pages. L 1774. EEB Reel 1507:14.

Laudatory, often fawning, letters from scholars thank the duchess for contributing her works to various Cambridge colleges. The book includes some items from unaffiliated learned men like Thomas Glanville. See also entries under Newcastle, Margaret Cavendish, Duchess of in Part B.

517A Levingston, Thomas. Some Considerations humbly proposed to the worthy members of Parliament by Thomas Levingston, Esq. and Anne his wife, and William Powell. London, n.d. Broadside. L 1825A.

This case concerns title to the estate of the late Lady Powell, an aunt of Anne Levingston. John Blount and his wife Mary, Countess of Sterling (and others) claimed the Levingstons forced Powell to leave the property to Anne and cause a fine "to be antedated for the perfecting of the said settlement." The Levingstons wish to procure the deeds. See also 817A, 869A and Addendum 29.

518A Leycester, Peter. An answer to Sir Thomas Mainwaring's Book, Intituled, An Admonition to the Reader of Sir Peter Leycester's Books. [London], 1677. 44 pages. L 1941A.

This volume is Leycester's final printed statement in a debate with Mainwaring (apparently begun in 561A) about the legitimacy of his grandmother, Amicia. His focus is on local history and geography rather than the primary question of bastardy. Leycester angrily attacks his foe for warning readers not to read his work. See also entries under Thomas Mainwaring.

519A Leycester, Peter. An Answer to the Book of Sir Thomas Mainwaringe. [London], 1673. 90 pages. L 1942. EEB Reel 462:21.

An argument about the legitimacy of Leycester's grandmother Amicia (daughter of the Earl of Chester and wife of Ralph Mainwaring) is continued in this document.

520A Leycester, Peter. A Reply to Sr. Thomas Mainwaring's Answer to My Two Books. 103 pages. London, 1676. L 1944.

Leycester addresses whether Glanvil said women could deed property in which they hold a controlling interest. He defends his earlier criticism of Mainwaring and refutes his discussion of Leycester's errors. He includes new historical evidence for the charge that Amicia was a bastard.

521A Leycester, Peter.   Two books: The First being Styled A Reply to Mainwaring's...An Answer to Sir Peter Leycester's Addenda. [London], 1674. 96 pages. L 1944A.

Leycester answers Mainwaring's reply to his addenda point by point, citing historical precedent and logic. In a section entitled "The Law-Cases Mistaken" he argues his grandmother's legitimacy based on the principles of ancient law and historical records.

522A The Life and Character of Mrs. Mary Moders, alias Mary Stedman, alias Mary Carleton...The Famous German Princess. London, Printed for J. Cooke , [1678]. 76 pages. L 1990. EEB Reel 1595:93.

The author presents materials surrounding Moders' disguise as a German princess and her subsequent trial and execution. He includes a defense allegedly written by her against charges brought by her second husband John Carleton, whom she supposedly bigamously married. This is one of several pieces about the subject of much gossip during this period.

523A The Life and Death of Mrs. Margaret Andrews, the only child of Sir Henry Andrews, Baronet, And the Lady Elizabeth his wife of Lathbury, who died May 4th 1680. In the 14th Year of her Age. London, Printed for Nath. Ponder, 1680. 102 pages. L 2004. EEB Reel 111:8.

Andrews is called charitable, virtuous, pious and indifferent to wealth. The author notes her reading, prayers and acts of self-denial. See also 267A.

524A The Life and Death of Mrs. M. F., Commonly Called Mal Cutpurse. London, Printed for W. Gilbertson, 1662. 173 pages. L 2005.

Mary Frith, alias "Moll Cutpurse," was born sometime before 1590. The daughter of a shoemaker, she disliked housework and child care. She was an undisciplined youth and eventually took to forgery, dressing as a man, picking pockets and telling fortunes. Usually accompanied by a dog, she was thought to command a gang of thieves.

525A The Life and Death of Henrietta Maria. London, Printed for Dorman Newman, 1685. 108 pages. L 1995*.

This item is the same as 586A.

526A The Life and Death of that matchless Mirrour of Magnanimity. London, Printed for S. Speed, 1669. 108 pages. L 2012.

This item is the same as 586A.

527A The Life of that Incomparable Princess, Mary, Our Late Sovereign Lady, of ever blessed memory, who departed this Life, at her Royal Pallace at Kensington, the 28th of December, 1694. [London], Printed for Daniel Dring, 1695. 108 pages. L 2036. EEB Reel 154:5.

This somewhat maudlin tribute to Mary II, who died suddenly of smallpox, includes an idealized account of her life. The last section is in verse. The royalist author bemoans the beheading of Charles which preceded "the Harrows and Calamities of a Twelve Years Anarchy and Confusion." The book is dedicated to the Countess of Darby.

528A Lips, Joest. Miracles of the B. Virgin, or, an Historical Account of the Original, and Stupendous Performances of the Image, entituled, Our Blessed Lady of Halle. London, 1688. 36 pages. L 2361. EEB Reel 921:25.

Lips wishes to expose Catholic stories ("pretended miracles") about the Blessed Virgin. Such tales typically portray Mary reviving the dead or healing the sick. Examples: an innocent man rescued from the gallows in his final hour, a tailor saved after swallowing a needle, dispossession from bedevilment.

529A A List of the Parliament of Women. London, Printed for T. N., 1679. Broadside. L 2481. EEB Reel 1152:49.

The author satirizes the political rights of women, saying some women believe they should determine their own education and even serve in the army. Women are deemed equal only in their ability to talk. In response the women contend they have ruled in the past and can again. The parliament meets on London Bridge and includes "Mrs. Stink-ill," "Mrs. Cold-well," etc. See also 655A and entries by Henry Neville.

530A Littleton, Adam. A Sermon at the Funeral of the right honourable the Lady Jane, Eldest daughter to his Grace William, Duke of Newcastle and Wife to...Charles Cheyne, Esq; at Chelsea. London, Printed by John Macock, 1669. 56 [6] pages. L 2568. EEB Reel 767:6.

Littleton discusses the qualities of a good woman in some detail. She is characterized by conjugal fidelity, constancy of affection, domestic skills, diligence, thrift, discretion, a fine reputation, etc. He says women can acquire the same education afforded men, but admits they are confined to the domestic sphere by custom. The Lady Jane, daughter of the duke's first wife, Elizabeth Basset, is described as candid, even-tempered, generous, large-spirited, humble, charitable and modest.

531A The Lives of Sundry notorious Villains. London, Printed for the author and sold by Samuel Crouch, 1678. 167 pages. B 1739. EEB Reel 167:7.

This work is listed under Aphra Behn in the Wing STC, but it is neither attributed to her by the British Library nor signed by her. (In English Prose Fiction, 1660-1700 Mish states it has been wrongly attributed to her.)

532A A Living Epitaph upon the Crown'd Women, or the Lovely Granadeers. [London? 1700.] Broadside. L 2598.

This poem is about a contemporary hair style (the "cucko") which the author fears is being adopted by the middle class. Much sexual innuendo and word-play emphasize the connection between heads and tails. (Women are alleged to wear the breeches of late.)

533A L[ivingstone], W[illiam.] The Conflict in conscience of a dear Christian, named Bessie Clerkson in the Parish of Lanerk. Edinburgh, Printed for Andrew Anderson, 1664. 35 pages. L 2610*.

Clerkson was a young woman who died at the end of a lengthy exchange with her minister. Attempting to soothe her unsettled soul, he explained that God teaches by testing his "flock." The lesson: One should live a good and sinless life, inwardly as well as outwardly pure. This document was originally published in 1630.

534A Loftus, Dudley. Digamias Adikia; Or, The First Marriage of Katherine Fitzgerald, (Now Lady Decies) [sic]. London, 1677. 26 pages. L 2821. EEB Reel 1507:20.

Loftus bases his "modest and sober Treatise" on a verse from Deuteronomy encouraging the stoning of adulteresses. He presents the Lord Dacies' case against his wife, apparently married against her will at twelve. She tried to annul the union two years later and married another man. The legal argument centers on her rights and obligations.

535A London. [Moore, Sir John.] Lord Mayor. By the Mayor. To the Ward of----. Whereas the last Lords Day. London, Printed by Samuel Roycroft, 1681. Broadside. L 2884D.

This proclamation addresses London prostitutes, whom the mayor wishes to "punish and suppress." His concern is "a strange sort of Women (called nightwalkers) who go about the Streets in the Evening, tempting and inticeing Apprentices and others to Lewdness." He tells parish leaders they should warn tavern keepers not to serve alcohol on the sabbath or their licenses will be revoked.

536A The London Jilt: or, The politick Whore. Shewing, All the Artifices and Strategems which the Ladies of Pleasure make use of for the Intreaguing and Decoying of Men. Two Parts. London, Printed for Henry Rhodes, 1683. 129, 133 pages. L 2897B and C. EEB Reels 1619:17 and 18.

This typical bawdy tale of a prostitute contains more realistic detail than many of its genre. The protagonist worries about pregnancy and abuse by customers, uses a prophylactic and feigns orgasm to expedite business. The author emphasizes the narrative more than prurience.

537A L[onge], J. An Epitaph on the late deceased, that truely-Noble and Renowned Lady Elizabeth Cromwel...who lived to the age of 89. London, Printed for James Cottrel, 1655. Broadside. L 2994. TT Reel 246:669.f.19(41).

Lady Elizabeth is cited for a long life full of love for creatures in distress and for having given birth to the Protector, who "...freed us from Chains of Tyrants great." The broadside is primarily about her son.

538A A Looking Glass for Maids. Or, The Downfall of two most Desperate Lovers. Henry Hartlove and William Martin. [London], Printed for P. Coles, T. Vere, J. Wright, J. Clarke, W. Thackeray, and T. Passinger, [167-?]. Broadside. L 3022*.

This broadside, supposedly written by Ann Scarborow, tells of a young, beautiful virgin who, although promised to one man, takes a piece of gold from another. They duel for her hand and kill each other. The message, that women are deceptive and untrustworthy, is not likely a female author's.

539A A Looking-Glass for Wanton Women By the Example and Expiation of Mary Higgs who was executed on Wednesday the 18th of July, 1677 for committing the odious sin of Buggery, with her Dog. London, Printed for P. Brooksby, [1680?]. Broadside. L 3035.

Mary Higgs supposedly pursued evil and shunned modesty. She repented for her sin, but her soul could not be saved. The dog in question was hanged following her execution.

540A The Lords and Commons...taking into their consideration the great distress and calamity...Relief of Widows. [London, 1644.] Broadside. N.I.W. TT Reel 245:669.f.9(26).

This document authorizes collection of funds for the relief of widows in Plymouth, Melcomb Regis and Weymouth. It also authorizes assistance to soldiers and other destitute persons.

541A The Lost Maidenhead: Or Sylvia's Farewell to love. A New Satyr against MAN. London, Printed for H. Smith, 1691. 19 pages. L 3081.

The epistle dedicatory is directed to "All the Beaus, and Fortune-Hunters" of London. The satire relates the loss of Sylvia's innocence, her shame and revenge. It attacks male pride, immorality, mendacity and abuse of women. Excerpt: "What Males were born, Wee'd Eunuchs make, or else,/With care crush the young Vipers in their shells."

542A Love Letters between Polydorus, the Gothick King and Messalina, Late Queen of Albion. Paris, Printed for J. Lyford, 1689. 44 pages. B 1743. EEB Reel 1396:12.

This volume, also published as The Royal Wanton, contains letters supposedly transcribed by a confidante of the queen. It is one in a series of novels allegedly written by a woman, although there is no indication of authorship within the text, and this attribution remains dubious. The Wing STC credits only this volume to Aphra Behn. The British Library characterizes the series as a libel of Mary of Modena, so it is unlikely that Behn, a royalist, wrote it. The Library of Congress suggests Gregorio Leti as the possible author. See also 31A.

543A Lower, William. A Funeral Elegy on Her Illustrious Highnesse the Princesse Royal of Orange. [London? 1661.] Broadside. L 3317. EEB Reel 1574:14.

This elegy honors Mary, a sister of Charles II. Described as a saintly, religious woman, she is proposed as a model for "vertuous Ladies" and a "mirrour of perfection."

544A Lusts dominion; or, The Lascivious Queen. London, Printed for Francis Kirkman and are to be sold by Robert Pollard, 1657. [150] pages. L 3504A*. EEB Reel 36:2.

This tragedy, possibly based on The Spanish Moor's Tragedy by Thomas Dekker, is about Isabella and Ferdinand of Spain. The primary characters are Eleazar the Moor (former lover to the queen mother), his wife Maria (tragically beloved by Fernando), Isabella, the dying King Philip (father to Fernando), Hortenzo (lover to Isabella) and the queen mother, the "lascivious queen."

545A Lye, Thomas. The King of Terrors Metamorphosis. Or Death Transform'd into Sleep. A Sermon Preached at the Funeral of Mrs. Eliz. Nicoll, Daughter to...Mr. John Walker deceased, and late Wife of Mr. William Nicholl of London Draper. London, Printed by M. S. for Henry Cripps, 1660. 25 pages. L 3538. TT Reel 156:E.1053(4).

This sermon contains no biographical information about the deceased. Rather it explores Thessalonians 1.4, 13 and 14.

546A [Lygon, Richard.] Several Circircumstances [sic] to prove that Mrs. Jane Berkeley and Sir William Killigrew have combined together to defraud me of an estate. [London, 1654.] 115 pages. L 3560. TT Reel 113:E.732(1).

Lygon gives an interesting description of a woman who allegedly conspired to send him to prison because she was denied her share of an estate.

547A M., A. A Rich closet of Physical Secrets. London, Printed by Gartrude Dawson and to be sold by William Nealand, 1652. 52 pages. M 7. TT Reel 103:E.670(1).

This domestic guide includes material about preservatives against the plague and pox and a section on childbirth. The usual gynecological information is listed for the midwife--breakage of waters, removal of a dead fetus, the treatment of pain during nursing, etc. Subtitled "Physical experiments presented to our late Queen Elizabeth's own hands," the text is likely similar to Queen Elizabeth's Closet of Physical Secrets, apparently by the same author. See also 551A and Addendum 61.

548A M., J. On The never too much lamented Death of the most Illustrious Princess Henrietta Maria, Dutchess of Orleans. London, 1670. Broadside. M 44. EEB Reel 1574:20.

The poet mourns the queen with no mention of her late husband Charles I. He says with her death neither France nor England can claim true strength. Excerpt: "Her fall hath laid all the World's Wonders flat;/There's nothing in it now worth wondring at."

549A [M., M.] Good News to the Good Women, and to the Bad Women too that Will Grow Better. London, Printed for S. Darker and at John Gouges and at Elizabeth Degrate's, 1700. 16 pages. M 55. EEB Reel 640:4.

This religious tract, including many biblical references, is devoted mostly to the good deeds of women. The author blames Eve's sin for women's subjection and labor pain. He says it is also the reason for men's power within the churches. But since men possess the power, they should account for their failings and justify the poor example they have set for women.

550A M., W. The Compleat Cook...For dressing of Flesh and Fish, Ordering of Sauces, or making of Pastry. London, Printed for Nath. Brook, 1655. 123 pages. M 88. TT Reel 195:E.1531(1).

This simple book of recipes has no introductory remarks or specified audience. There is an index of recipes at the end.

551A M., W. The Queens Closet opened: Incomparable Secrets in Physick, Chirurgery, Preserving. London, Printed for Christian Eccleston, 1662. 300 pages. M 100*. EEB Reels 224:6, 640:5, 9 and 10; 673:5, 696:25, 1312:2 and 1619:36. TT Reel 194: E.1519(1).

This corrected and revised version of an earlier edition contains medicinal remedies. Many are recommended recipes suggested by physicians and prominent ladies. A later edition is entitled The Queen's Delight. See also 547A and Addendum 61.

Machiavelli, Niccolo, pseud. A Caveat for Wives to love their Husbands, or Pleasant News from Hell. See 184A.

Machiavelli, Niccolo, pseud. The Divell a Married Man. See 274A.

552A McMath, James. The Expert Mid-Wife: A Treatise of the Diseases of Women with Child. Edinburgh, Printed by George Mosman, [1694]. 394 pages. M 222.

McMath says midwives are fit to deliver children only through natural birth, "being only to sit and attend Nature's pace and progress." They should also accept work "which physicians give mid-wifes to do, as unnecessary and indecent for them." He includes sections about pathology in pregnant women, fertility and sterility, the nature and purpose of menstruation, stages of childbirth, difficult deliveries and infant illnesses.

553A Maddam Celliers Answer to the Popes Letter, dated from the Vatican the 1st of August, 1680, wherein she declared her Fidelity and Firmness to the Catholic Cause. London, Printed for D. Mallet, 1680. 4 pages. C 1659. EEB Reel 58:15.

Although credited to Elizabeth Cellier in the Wing STC, a midwife who figured prominently in the infamous Meal-tub Plot, this satirical item was not written by her.

554A Madam Gwins answer to the Dutchess of Portsmouths letter. London, Printed for J. Johnson, [1682]. Broadside. M 243.

This broadside reproduces a satirical fictitious correspondence between two mistresses of Charles II, actress Nell Gwynne, and Louise Renee de Keroualle, an extravagant and universally disliked Frenchwoman. Gwynne says the duchess is too loyal to France and claims she is attacking all English ladies. The text, which makes much of their alleged lustiness, is full of sexual innuendo.

555A The Maidens Best Adorning. A Directory for the Female-Sex: Being A Fathers Advice to his Daughter. London, Printed by George Larkin, 1687. Broadside. M 266.

This broadside advises young women to avoid idleness, overcome pride, practice temperance and select a husband for his fear of God rather than his wealth. Excerpt: "The Grace of Meekness is a Womans Crown!/Be Loving, Patient, Courteous and Kind."

556A The Maidens Plea: Or, Her Defence, and Vindication Of her Self, Against all Objections; Notwithstanding Mr. Harris's Dying in Bed with Her, July the 26th, 1684. London, Printed by G. Croom for the author, 1684. 6 pages. M 271A.

This political satire depends largely on the sexual double standard for its humor. In a self-defense before a jury the maiden claims she is not a prostitute, and Harris was drunk, so she kept him in bed for his own protection. She asks if she did not "act like a Parliament, more than like a Bawdy-House, in endeavoring so far to provide for the Good and Welfare of the Meanest Subject?"

557A The Maids Petition. London, Printed for A. L., 1647. 6 pages. M 280. EEB Reel 63:E.401(26).

This satire was ostensibly written on behalf of unmarried women who claim they'd have sexual intercourse with apprentices, but the men are occupied serving their masters. The young women ask to have alternate Tuesdays reserved for sexual recreation.

558A The Maids Prophecies or Englands Looking-glasse Dedicated to both Houses of Parliament, Sir Thomas Fairfax, and the Lord-Mayor of the city of LONDON. [London, 1648.] [8] pages. M 281. TT Reel 66:E.422(13).

In this anti-sectarian, anti-Puritan, anti-Revolutionary document, the author acknowledges the anomaly of female writing; however, calling herself Cassandra, she claims "this is the last age of the world," and the unusual is now commonplace. Among her prophecies: revenge against the plunderers of Ireland, sundering of the families who caused the dissolution of the royal family, widespread pestilence and famine, new converts to Judaism, and terrible revelations for the Shakers and Quakers. Female authorship is doubtful.

559A M[ainwaring], T[homas]. An Answer to Sir Peter Leicester's Addenda, or, Some things to be added in his Answer to Sir Thomas Mainwaring's Book. London, Printed for Samuel Lowndes, 1673/4. 53 pages. M 298. EEB Reel 673:9.

This book continues the dispute over Amicia Cyvelick's legitimacy, begun in 1673 (see 561A). Mainwaring argues Hugh Cyvelick, a twelfth-century ancestor, had a wife before he married Betred, by whom he fathered Amicia.

560A M[ainwaring], T[homas]. An Answer to Two Books. London, Printed for Sam. Lowndes, [1675.] 63 pages. M 299. EEB Reel 673:10.

Mainwaring continues the debate over the legitimacy of Amicia Cyvelick. He centers on women's inheritance of property, i.e., land given in marriage for which no service is done versus that for which homage is to be paid. In the latter case, the land could apparently revert to the donor.

561A M[ainwaring], T[homas.] A defence of Amicia, Daughter of Hugh Cyvelick Wherein it is proved that Sir Peter Leycester Hath without any just Grounds declared the said Amicia to be a Bastard. London, Printed for Samuel Lowndes, 1673. 80 pages. M 300. EEB Reel 465:16.

Mainwaring vindicates Amicia, daughter of the Earl of Chester and wife of Ralph Mainwaring, the grandmother of Leycester. Amicia's legitimacy was questioned by him. The author cites common law and traces the family history. See also other publications by Mainwaring and Leycester.

562A M[ainwaring], T[homas.] The Legitimacy of Amicia...clearly proved. London, Printed for Sam. Lowndes, 1679. 169 pages. M 301. EEB Reel 673:11.

This is a later document by Mainwaring in his debate with Sir Peter Leycester over the legitimacy of Leycester's grandmother. In this long and thorough defense, Mainwaring uses legal documentation and language taken from deeds in which her father, Hugh Cyvelick, made clear she was his lawful daughter.

563A M[ainwaring], T[homas.] A Reply to an Answer to the Defence of Amicia. London, Printed for S. Lowndes, 1673. 105 pages. M 303. EEB Reel 744:46.

This publication adds to the debate between Sir Peter Leycester and Mainwaring about the legitimacy of Leycester's deceased grandmother. Mainwaring implies Leycester's motives for debating are less than noble.

564A [Manley, Thomas.] A Short view of the Lives of those Illustrious Princes, Henry Duke of Glouster [sic], and Mary. London, Printed for a Society of Stationers, 1661. 114 pages. M 446*.

Henry and Mary were the brother and daughter of Charles I. In this biography, most of the material about Mary's character appears near the end. Its apparent rationale is establishing the duo's political and dynastic importance. Henry died at eighteen, and Mary went on to marry William III, Prince of Orange.

565A Manning, Francis. A Pastoral Essay, lamenting...Queen Mary. London, Printed for J. Weld and are to be sold by J. Whitlock, 1695. 10 pages. M 488.

Nymphs Damon and Melampus lament the death of Mary II in a typical stylized elegy. Excerpt: "Mourn British woods; let every Swain deplore/ Lament each Nymph: Sylvania is no more."

566A Manningham, Thomas. A Sermon preach'd...on the...Death of Queen Mary. London, Printed for Sam. Smith, Benj. Walford and Eliz. Crooke, 1695. 24 pages. M 504*.

Manningham says Mary's death has saddened and confused her people as would darkness at noon (quote from Amos 13.9-10). He speaks of Mary's character from primary knowledge--he was "Chaplain in Ordinary to His Majesty." She is lauded for her sweet disposition, personal devotion and interest in spreading the gospel.

567A Manton, Thomas. <u>Advice to Mourners Under the Loss of Dear Relations. In a funeral Sermon...on the...death of Mrs. Ann Terry...With an account of her Life, and Papers left under her own Hand</u>. London, Printed by J. D. for Jonathan Robinson, 1694. 34 pages. M 517. EEB Reel 1026:17.

Terry is remembered "as a Wife, a Mother, and a Mistress." About eighteen pages are devoted to her household management and maternal devotion, along with nine pages of elegiac material. Thirteen of her religious papers follow. Manton's daughter, Mrs. Terry apparently died at thirty-six after an extended illness.

568A Manzini, Giovanni Battista. <u>The Loving Husband, and Prudent Wife; Represented in the persons of St. Eustachius and Theopista, Martyrs</u>. London, Printed for J. Martin and J. Allestrye, 1657. 203 pages. M 556. EEB Reel 1425:31.

This Italian work, supposedly confirmed by Greek and Latin texts, depicts Eustachius as a courageous soldier and a generous husband. He and his wife Theopista were baptized, saw visions and were ultimately sacrificed as Christian martyrs. Theopista is depicted as a secondary figure.

569A [Markham, Gervase.] <u>The English House-Wife containing The inward and outward Vertues which ought to be in a Compleat Woman</u>. Fifth Edition. London, Printed for B. Alsop for John Harrison, 1649. 252 pages. M 629*. EEB Reels 1530:13, 1727:2 and 1782:4.

This typical household guide contains medicinal remedies, recipes, instructions for the dyeing and care of wool, and so on. Markham includes information about etiquette, weaving, sewing and brewing. The initial pages discuss the subordinate role of women and the dangers of extreme religious zeal. According to the Folger Shakespeare Library, Washington, D.C., this is the second part of Markham's earlier <u>Country Contentment</u>.

570A Marnette, M. <u>The Perfect Cook. Being the most exact directions...French and English</u>. London, Printed for Nath. Brooks, 1656. 346 pages. M 706. TT Reel 211:E.1695(1).

Marnette includes French recipes for pies, pastry, tarts, biscuits and egg dishes. A lengthy appendix offers English recipes for meat pies, fish, tarts, sauces and the like.

571A <u>Marriage Asserted: In Answer to a Book Entituled Conjugium Conjurgium</u>. London, Henry Herringman, 1674. 97 pages. M 709. EEB Reel 1657:10.

The author attacks a tract by William Ramsey that discourages men from marrying and criticizes women. He supports marriage as responsible for the "continuation of the species of mankind" and the fortitude "to avoid fornication." He defends women and criticizes Ramsey's arrogant anti-female views. See also 752A.

572A Marriott, Robert. <u>A Sermon in commemoration of...Mris. Elizabeth Dering, wife of Mr. Charles Dering...Pluckley in Kent</u>. London, Printed by E. P. for N. Bourne, 1641. 40 pages. M 715. EEB Reel 1406:4.

Inspired by Psalm 90.12, this eulogy is dedicated to Charles Dering. Material about his wife concerns her integrity, lingering consumption and lapse of faith. Marriott claims Dering called upon him during her vacillation; he was with her when she died.

573A [Massard, Jacques.] Remarks upon the Dream of the late Abdicated Queen of England. And upon that of Madam the dutchess of La Valiere, late mistress to the French King, and now Nun of the Order of Bare-Footed-Carmelites at Paris. London, Printed for Tho. Salusbury and are to be sold by R. Baldwin, 1690. 26 pages. M 1027. EEB Reel 945:14.

This anti-Catholic pamphlet, written by a divine, relates supposed bizarre dreams of Mary of Modena, wife of James II, and the Duchesse de la Valiere, a favorite of Louise XIV who died in a Carmelite convent in 1710. Massard interprets the dreams as predictive of the Church's future demise, the failure of the French king's invasion of Britain and the success of King William.

574A [Massarius, Alexander de Markis.] De Morbis Foemineis, The Womans Counsellour: or, The Feminine Physitian [sic]. London, Printed for John Streater, 1657. 211 pages. M 1028.

Massarius' general guide to women's health was translated from Latin. It contains references to Aristotle, Hippocrates, Galen and other ancients. Topics include flux of the menses, the fallen womb, barrenness, stillborn children, the nursing mother's milk supply, etc. He provides descriptions of maladies as well as remedies.

575A Master, Thomas. The Virgin Mary. A Sermon preached in St. Maries College. London, Printed by Robert White for Octavian Pullen Junior, 1665. 22 pages. M 1058. EEB Reel 1706:8.

Preached two decades (1641) before publication, this sermon elaborates on the lesser character of women, as exemplified by Mary: Females are only an image of a copy of God [man] and seldom attain the state of angels. Mary's rank was even lower because she was a virgin and married a carpenter. Classical references support the author's position.

576A Match me these two; or the Conviction and Arraignment of Britannicus and Lilburne with an answer to a Pamphlet, entitled, The Parliament of Ladies. London, 1647. M 1077. TT Reel 63:E.400(9).

This political satire is about an imaginary parliament of scholars and jurists who cross-examine Leveller John Lilburne and the author of A Parliament of Ladies [Henry Neville] under the charge of disturbing the peace and security of the kingdom. During the procedure Neville is placed among a group of women he had allegedly libelled in his pamphlet.

577A Mather, Cotton. Late Memorable Providences relating to Witchcraft and Possessions. London, Printed for Tho. Parkhurst, 1691. [144] pages. M 1118.

Mather claims witches can cut short the lives of "good men." He includes anecdotes about alleged witches and a discourse on the "Power and Malice of the Devils." They are called "an army in our air" which has its own leader and the Devils." They are called "an army in our air" which has its own leader and government. He advises resistance through avoiding discontent, idleness, and bad company while emphasizing faith. There is no identification of the gender of witches. Mather denounces the Quakers as possessed.

578A Mather, Cotton. Ornaments for the daughters of Zion. Cambridge [Massachusetts], Printed by S. G. and B. G. for Samuel Phillips, 1691[2]. M 1134*. EEB Reels 1487:41 and 1639:11.

The theme of this sermon is the desirability of modesty and piety in women. Mather points to illustrative biblical figures, advising women to pray, be fearful of God, suspicious of those who try to seduce them from the Lord, to keep silent, to shun artifice and maintain their faith in Christ. Maidenly virtues cited include constancy, efficiency and religiosity.

579A [Mather, Increase] et al. The Answer of Several Ministers in and near Boston...Whether it is Lawful for a Man to marry his Wives own Sister. Boston [Mass.], Printed for Bartholomew Green, 1695. 8 pages. M 1182. EEB Reel 283:12.

The authors argue strongly against marriage to a deceased wife's sister based on scriptural passages like Leviticus 18.6: "None shall approach to any that is near akin to him." This pamphlet, citing natural law and legal restrictions, was signed by eight ministers, including both Cotton and Increase Mather.

580A Mather, Increase. Cases of Conscience Concerning Evil Spirits Personating Men; Witches, Infallible Proofs of Guilt in such as are accused with that Crime. All considered according to the Scriptures, History, Experience, and the judgment of many Learned Men. Boston, Printed by Benjamin Harris, 1693. 44 pages. M 1193*. EEB Reel 154:17.

This tract is appended to A Further Account of the Tryals of the New England Witches, a two-page description of the charges brought against sixty-odd persons accused of witchcraft in Salem. In the more lengthy piece, Mather answers questions about the nature of witchcraft with reference to particular cases. He presents six scripture-based arguments which justify the existence of witches.

581A Mather, William. A Novelty: Or, A Government of Women distinct from Men Erected amongst some of the People called Quakers. London, Printed for Sarah Howkins, [1694?] 23 pages. M 1284C.

Mather's indignation stems from the Quaker practice of allowing the women's meeting to judge couples' fitness for marriage. He describes the women as "rustling in gaudy flower'd Stuffs, or Silks." Responding to [George Fox's] charge that his opinions of women render him unfit for a wife, he replies, "...we love our Wives as true Christians ought to do...Nor are we against Women's Declaring in a Religious Meeting...Nor are we against Women meeting by themselves...but not monthly for Government."

582A Mauriceau, Francois. The Accomplisht Midwife, Treating of the Diseases of Women with Child, and in Child-bed. London, Printed for John Darby and are to be sold by Benjamin Billingsley, 1673. 437 pages. M 1371A*. EEB Reel 1335:22.

Originally dedicated to the master surgeons of Paris, this work was translated by English gynecologist Hugh Chamberlen, senior. Mauriceau was a prominent French obstetrician, and this volume established obstetrics as a science. Its divisions are typical of gynecological texts: anatomy of women sexual organs, diseases of expectant mothers, natural and unnatural deliveries, etc. Chamberlen alludes to his family's secret (obstetrical forceps), but refuses to reveal it.

583A Mauriceau, Francois. The Diseases of Women with Child, And in Childbed. Translated by Hugh Chamberlen. "Second" Edition. London, Printed by J. D. and to be sold by Andrew Bell, 1696. M 1372A*. EEB Reel 1335:22.

This work is essentially the same as 582A.

584A [Mello, Francisco Manuel de.] The Government of a Wife: or, Wholsom and Pleasant Advice for Married Men. London, Printed for Jacob Tonson and R. Knaplock, 1697. 240 pages. M 1648A. EEB Reel 1670:11.

Published originally in Portuguese, this text is addressed to a young man contemplating marriage, advising how to choose and treat a wife. Mello encourages him to love her "but not so that the Husband be lessen'd or brought into danger." Viewed solely from the male perspective, marriage is described as a well-governed, controlled affair.

585A Memoirs of Queen Mary's Days; wherein the Church of England, and all the Inhabitants, may plainly see...the sad Effects which follow a Popish Successor enjoying the Crown of England. [London, 1679.] 4 pages. M 1669. EEB Reel 898:30.

This anti-papist tract about Mary, Queen of Scots includes a chronology of her reign, demonstrating how she established the "Pope's authority." The author claims Mary promised she would not alter religion and proposes that if a popish successor wins the throne, Protestant heirs will be in danger. Elizabeth's reign is lauded as peaceful, happy, glorious and plentiful.

586A Memoires of the Life and Death of that matchless Mirrour of Magnanimity and Heroick Virtues Henrietta Maria. London, 1671. 108 pages. M 1669A.

In this biography of the queen, dedicated to her son, Charles II, the author traces Henrietta Maria's childhood at the French court, her marriage to Charles I and involvement in public affairs, the growing royal family, early events of the Civil War, the queen's flight to France and her life in exile. The author was apparently a member of Henrietta Maria's court. Some primary documents are included.

587A Memoires of the Life of the Famous Madam Charlton Commonly Stiled the German Princess. London, Printed for Philip Brooksby, 1673. 16 pages. M 1670.

This is a rather negative description of the notorious Mary Carleton, who allegedly tricked a wealthy Kentish grazier's son by claiming to be of royal German blood. After their marriage was contracted, he discovered she had deceived him. Some accounts say she was finally hanged. This is one of several pieces about her.

588A The Mens Answer to the Womens Petition Against Coffee, Vindicating Their own Performances. London, 1674. 7 pages. M 1721. EEB Reel 1466:11.

This humorous reply answers a charge, allegedly written by women, that consumption of large quantities of coffee leads to lack of sexual interest and impotence. It argues men are as lusty as ever, and coffee, in fact, enhances lovemaking--it "makes the erection more Vigorous, the Ejaculation more full." See also 967A.

589A [Middleton, Thomas.] The Counterfeit Bridegroom. London, Printed for Langley Curtiss, 1677. 58 pages. M 1983. EEB Reel 642:23.

This play is attributed to Aphra Behn by John Genest. Others have ascribed it to her or to Thomas Betterton. It is an adaptation of Middleton's No Wit, No Help like a Woman's and is listed under Middleton in the Wing STC and under title in the British Library catalog.

590A The Midwife unmask'd: or, the Popish Design of Mrs. Cellier's Meal-Tub plainly made known. London, Printed for T. Davies, 1680. 4 pages. M 2002. EEB Reel 720:28.

Widespread rumors charged that an heir of James II and Mary of Modena was really a common child. Midwife Elizabeth Cellier was accused of conspiring with the Catholic party to substitute the false prince. This anti-papist diatribe attacks Cellier's self-defense against the charge that she deceived the public by finding the changeling. The author characterizes reputed Cellier writings as bold and libelous.

591A The Mid-wives just Complaint. London, 1646. 6 pages. M 2004. TT Reel 57:E.355(20).

This petition is identical to 592A except for the final paragraph.

592A The Mid-wives just Petition: or, A complaint of divers good Gentlewomen of that faculty. Shewing...their just cause of their sufferings in these distracted Times, for their want of TRADING. London, 1643. 6 pages. M 2005. EEB Reel 242:E.86(14) and TT Reel 15:E.86(14).

This mock petition, supposedly presented to the House of Commons, claims men away at war are unable to impregnate their wives; thus, midwives will lose their livelihood. A plea for peace holds that weapons and conditions of war are cruel; men should instead pursue their trades; internecine strife is more shameful than international battle; and war will upset the sexual balance of the population.

593A Milner, William. A Sermon at the Funeral of Mrs. Elizabeth Fisher, Sister to the Honourable Sir William Davis...And Wife to the Rev. Dr. Peter Fisher. London, Printed for Thomas Spred, 1698. 23 pages. M 2084. EEB Reel 720:33.

Milner calls Fisher's death premature and much lamented. He says she died
in a state of grace and is ready for immediate admission to heaven. The final
part deals with Fisher's life and how the women in her family took responsibility
for her religious training.

594A Milton, John. The Doctrine and Discipline of Divorce: Restor'd to the Good
of Both Sexes. London, Printed by T. P.and M. S., 1643. 48 pages. M 2108*.
EEB Reels 155:8 and 239:E.62(17); TT Reels 6:E.31(5) and 11:E.62(17).

Milton's famous tract argues for divorce. Marriage, he contends, should not
exist simply to discourage lust outside of wedlock; it should also be a loving
and helping relationship. A woman must operate as a "helpmeet," and if she
is not her husband's spiritual and intellectual equal, the marriage will not
succeed. Primary emphasis, however, is on the husband's needs. See also
33A.

595A Mistress Cellier's Lamentation for the Loss of her Liberty. London, Printed for
S. J., 1681. Broadside. C 1660A. EEB Reel 1183:28.

This satirical anti-Catholic piece is about Elizabeth Cellier, a principal in the
celebrated Meal-tub Plot. She calls herself an unfortunate, unhappy woman and
complains about her imprisonment and stint in the pillory, saying she must be
her own midwife and deliver herself from her troubles. Excerpt: "No Woman
would have been so much Priest-Ridd as I have been, few of My sex would
have carried their heavy Cross half so long and to no purpose."

596A Mr. De Labadie's letter to his daughter. [London], 1696. 46 pages. M
2261A. EEB Reel 1729:19.

This item contains letters written to Mary Anne De Labadie when she attended
Mary of Modena's delivery of the "false" Prince of Wales (James Francis Edward
Stuart). She was the wife, not the daughter of James de Labadie, valet to
James II. The Library of Congress suggests this publication was written by
William Fuller.

597A Mrs. Abigail; or, A Female Skirmish Between the Wife of a Country Squire,
And the Wife of a Doctor. London, Printed for A. Baldwin, 1700. 20 pages. M
2280. EEB Reel 1707:11.

An altercation between two women at a dinner party serves as a vehicle for
attacking contemporary clerical education. The author emphasizes the higher
status of gentlemen relative to parish priests. The humorous tale about an
ambitious clergyman was supposedly written in a letter to a friend.

598A Mistris Parliament Brought to Bed of a Monstrous Childe of Reformation. By
Mercurius Melancholicus, pseud. [London], 1648. [6] pages. M 2281. TT Reel
69:E.437(24).

In this religious/political satire in dialogue form, birth imagery is utilized
throughout. It describes the delivery by Mistris Parliament of a deformed
monster without a head and with the feet of a bear. Excerpt: "Oh 'tis Blood,
innocent blood, that hath lain in clodds congealed at my stomack this full 7
yeers."

599A Mistris Parliament her gossipping. Full of mirth, merry tales. By Mercurius Melancholicus, pseud. [London], 1647. 8 pages. M 2282. TT Reel 70:E.443(28).

This royalist satire utilizes the imagery of witchcraft. England is "bewitch'd" by Mistris Parliament, charged with attempting to change the laws of the kingdom and "root out" the king. The gossips who speak the dialogue search her for witch's marks.

600A Mistris Parliament Her Invitation of Mrs. London, to a T--giving Dinner. For the great and mighty Victorie, which Mr. Horton obtained over Major Powell in Wales. By Mercurius Melancholicus, pseud. [London], 1648. 8 pages. M 2283. TT Reel 70:E.446(7).

In a satire lampooning Parliament, female characters include Mrs. London, Mrs. Militia, Mrs. Truth and Mrs. Parliament. The immediate occasion for the piece was the engagement of Cromwell's forces (led by Thomas Horton) in South Wales near Carmarthen by Powell, who slipped away with few losses.

601A Mistris Parliament Presented in her Bed, after the sure travaile and hard labour which she endured last week, in the Birth of her Monstrous Offspring, the Childe of Deformation [sic]. By Mercurius Melancholicus, pseud. [London], 1648. [5] pages. M 2284. TT Reel 69:E.441(21).

In this satire, a discourse ensues among Mrs. Sedition, Mrs. Jealousie, Mrs. Synod and various gossips. The publication continues 598A.

602A Mris. Rump Brought to Bed of a Monster, with her Terrible Pangs, Bitter Teeming, Hard Labour, and Lamentable Travel from Portsmouth to Westminster. [London], Printed by Portcullis Damgate for Theod. Microcosmus, 1660. Broadside. M 2285.

This political satire employs the image of a Portsmouth prostitute in labor who cannot deliver her child. She spits up gold ("For love of which I sold my God, murdered my king, gave away my Soul, and pulld down the gates"). The attendants are all female--Mrs. Ordinance, Mrs. Schisme, Mrs. Sedition, etc. She finally gives birth to a monster without a head. See also 346A, another version of this item.

603A Modesty Triumphing over Impudence. Or, Some Notes upon a late romance published by E. Cellier, Midwife. London, Printed for Johnathan Wilkins, 1680. 19 pages. M 2379. EEB Reel 429:1.

Cellier was implicated in the Meal-tub Plot. This lengthy textual critique of her self-defense quotes extensively from her work, extracting phrases and words for special examination. It is strongly anti-papist in tone, claiming Cellier's writing has brought dishonor to England and her kings. See also 137B, 138B, 260A, 512A, 787A and 880A.

604A A Monstrous Birth: or, a True relation of three strange things like young cats, all speckled, which came from a woman dwelling at Wetwan in Yorkshire and how the devil kept her company. London, Printed for Livewel Chapman, 1657. 5 pages. M 2467.

This tale concerns the slightly daft wife of a laborer, thought to be pregnant, who was given a potion by a stranger. She gave birth to three monstrous feline beings that died despite her attempts to suckle them. The author notes such strange phenomena are typical of recent events in the North.

605A Morgan, Matthew. Eugenia: or an Elegy upon the Death of the honourable Madame. Oxford, Printed by Leonard Lichfield, 1694. 34 pages. M 2734. EEB Reel 1406:23.

In this typical elegy, with bucolic setting and characters, Morgan extols the wit, learning, modesty, humor, and beauty of the deceased. She is celebrated for her sweet but commanding mien, wide travels, large library, great estate, appreciation of art and command of Greek. Although Eugenia was also the pen name of Mary Chudleigh, this elegy was apparently written for another woman. (Chudleigh died in 1710.)

606A [Morgan, Matthew.] A Poem to the Queen, upon the King's Victory in Ireland, and his Voyage to Holland. Oxford, Printed by Leonard Lichfield for John Wilmot, 1691. 38 pages. M 2735. EEB Reel 643:11.

Although dedicated to Mary II, this poem is primarily about King William. He is compared with ancient warriors and various historical figures.

607A [Morgan, Thomas, of Oxford.] Allegations in Behalf of the High and Mighty Princess the Lady Mary, now Queen of Scots. London, Printed for J. D., 1690. 19 pages. M 2754.

In a lengthy, convoluted argument Morgan supports Mary's claim to the Scottish crown against Catherine Grey, granddaughter of Charles Brandon. Brandon's marriage to Mary (sister to Henry VIII) is deemed illegal because his first wife, Margaret Mortimer, was still living. Any offspring of the union would thus be illegitimate and unable to ascend to the throne. See also 723A.

608A Morgue, Matthieu de. Les Deux Faces de la vie et de la mort de Marie de Medicis Royne de France, vefve [sic] de Henry IV. Mere de Loys [sic] XIII. Anvers, [1643]. 56 pages. N.I.W. TT Reel 119:E.783(1).

This French funeral sermon honors the second wife of Henry IV, also a granddaughter of Duke Cosimo of Italy. She represented the final days of the great Medici family.

609A [Morley, George.] Several Treatises...A Letter Written by the Bishop of Winchester to Her Highness the Duchess of York Some Months before Her Death. London, Printed for Joanna Brome, 1683. 23 pages. M 2796. EEB Reel 542:4.

The sixth item in this volume is a letter criticizing Anne's Catholic inclinations. Morley (Bishop of Winchester) says rumors about her alleged papist sympathies are based on her avoidance of the Anglican communion. Morley alludes to Eve's temptation by analogy and suggests Anne make a public declaration of allegiance to the Church of England. See also 638B.

610A A Most Certain, Strange, and true Discovery of a Witch. [London], Printed for John Hammond, 1643. [5] pages. M 2870. TT Reel 12:E.69(9). EEB Reel 240:E.69(9).

A tall, slender woman was seen dancing on the river at Newbury by Parliamentary soldiers. They fired at her, but she caught their bullets in her hands and chewed them. When her devilish power left her, she began to cry, but the soldiers killed her. The author claims the story shows "weake women" are capable of witchcraft caused by "inveterate malice" and "revengefull wrath."

611A A Most Strange and Wonderfull Apperation...also The true relation of a miraculous and prodigious birth. London, Printed for I. H., [1645]. 8 pages. M 2921. TT Reel 50:E.303(22).

Mistress Browne, a London cutler's wife, gave birth to a stillborn monster with no head or feet. Rather, it had a hollow between its shoulders from which a perfect, though tiny, child emerged. There is brief mention only of the event on the final two pages of this document.

612A The Mother's Blessing, Being Several Godley Admonitions Given by a Mother unto her Children upon her Death-bed. [London], Printed by I. M. for I. Clarke, W. Thackeray and T. Passinger, 1685. [12] pages. M 2937. EEB Reel 1747:37.

In this guide for virtuous living, the author encourages attention to spiritual matters and discourages commerce with nonreligious persons. The style is quite formal with little affect or personal concern evident; thus, it is questionable that it was written by a mother for her children.

613A Motteux, Peter. Maria. A Poem Occasioned by the Death of Her Majesty. London, Printed for Peter Buck, 1695. 12 pages. M 2956. EEB Reel 769:12.

This eulogy is a romanticization of death and grief rather than a description of the characteristics of Mary II. Excerpt: "At least the Centre of our Dust is there,/Our Fire, the Soul, springs to its native skies,/And there Maria claim'd the loftiest Sphere;/That sun set here, more gloriously to rise."

614A The Mourning Poets: or, An account of the Poems on the death of the Queen. In a letter to a friend. London, Printed for J. Whitlock, 1695. 12 pages. M 2993. EEB Reel 769:14.

This poet ridicules colleagues for their pathetic memorials to Mary II. Calling them pedantic and bombastic, he claims "Beaux, Lawyers, Merchants, Prentices, Musicians" and the like have all gone "mad with Elegy." Some poets are praised for their work, however; among them are Tate, Cowley, Waller, Dennis and Motteux.

615A The Mournful Widows Garland. In Three Parts. London, Printed for J. Blare, 1700. 8 pages. N.I.W.

This lengthy song tells of a widow with five children whose eldest son worked so hard to support his family that he perished at fifteen. When the queen learned of the family's poverty, she offered twenty pieces of gold, then a pension to the widow. Though realistic, the tale is probably apocryphal.

616A Murther, Murther. Or, A bloody Relation how Anne Hamton, dwelling in Westminster nigh London, by poyson murthered her deare husband...assisted and counselled thereunto by Margaret Harwood. London, Printed for Tho. Bates, 1641. 6 pages. M 3084. EEB Reel 255:E.172(7) and TT Reel 30:E.172(7).

A woman conspired with her female landlord to poison her husband. She is portrayed as a person of "contrary disposition" who gossiped, wasted money and made merry when her husband experienced misfortune. Her loving and conciliatory husband died a grotesque death. The two women were in prison awaiting trial.

617A Murther Upon Murther: Being a Full Relation of a Horrid and Bloody Murther committed Upon...S[arah] Hodges...E. Smith. London, Printed for G. Croom, 1691. Broadside. M 3088. EEB Reel 1210:20.

This broadside tells of the bloody murders of three women in a coffee-house, two of whom were robbed and found nude.

618A Murther will out, or a True and Faithful relation of an Horrible Murther commited Thirty-Three years ago, by an unnatural Mother, upon the body of her own Child. [London], Printed for C. Passinger, [1675]. 6 pages. M 3093.

A woman's infant became sickly and cried incessantly. When its medical care depleted her funds, she was supposedly visited by Satan who encouraged its murder. She placed the infant under a tub where it died. Although she became deathly ill herself, she was removed to prison "where she remains very penitent."

619A Mysogynus: or, A Satyr upon Women. London, Printed for John Langly, 1682. 7 pages. M 3178. EEB Reel 1336:16.

This is a strongly anti-female satire arguing women abuse men and are responsible for evil: "She'll kill, as does a Basilisk, or worse if it can/Insensibly she blinds, and burns the Man./Her outsides fair and pleasing, when the while she kills as craftily as the Crocodile/Usurps his right, raigns [sic] o're her fellow slaves."

620A N., T. A Poem on the Queen. London, Printed for Richard Baldwin, 1695. 5 pages. N 78. EEB Reel 1489:23.

Mourning Mary II the poet writes a simple memorial, tracing her life from birth. Excerpt: "She knew it must be sod, and was content./No struggles sought to violate/That Law that from the first Creation took its date,/And Salique must remain to the Conlusive Stroke of Fate."

621A A Narrative and Testimony concerning Grace Watson, Daughter of Samuel and Mary Watson. London, Printed for Thomas Northcott, 1690. 19 pages. N 167.

A pious young woman who died at nineteen had been well educated, knew scripture thoroughly and dedicated herself to things spiritual. The text makes interesting use of marital imagery: She "entered into the Bride-Chamber of

Immortal Joy, Glory, and Immutable Satisfaction." Her final words and the testimony of her parents are included.

622A A Narrative of the Late Extraordinary Cure Wrought in an Instant upon Mrs. Eliz. Savage (lame from birth) without the Using of any Natural Means. London, Printed for John Dunton and John Harris, 1694. 46 pages. N 193. EEB Reel 746:36.

The wife of a schoolmaster afflicted with palsy claimed it was cured as a result of her husband's prayers. Affidavits of her husband and several neighbors are included. The author defends cure through divine intervention and claims those who don't believe in it must be atheists.

623A A Narrative of the Process against Madam Brinvilliers; And of her Condemnation and Execution for Having Poisoned her Father and two Brothers. London, Roger L'Estrange, Printed for Jonathan Edwyn, 1676. 24 pages. N 220. EEB Reel 872:20.

This French story tells of the prosecution of Mme. Brinvilliers by Mme. D'Aubray, her sister-in-law. Brinvilliers was apparently encouraged by her lover, St. Croix, to commit murder. When she refused to confess, she was put to the rack. After she relented and confessed, she was beheaded.

624A Naunton, Robert. Fragments Regalia: Or, Observations on the Late Queen Elizabeth. London, Printed by G. Dawson, for William Sheares, 1653. 87 pages. N 253. EEB Reel 37:3.

These "fragments" comprise a brief biography of Elizabeth that includes commentary about her character, aides and affairs of state. It also contains some original correspondence. Naunton was secretary of state to James I and later Master of the Court of Wards. This volume was written early in his career but published posthumously.

625A [Neville, Henry.] An Exact Diurnall of the severall passages in the Parliament of Ladyes. [London], 1647. 8 pages. N 504. TT Reel 61:E.386(4).

Neville was a leading seventeenth-century Platonist and a member of Cromwell's council. This political satire is directed at Prince Rupert, Lord Digby, Lord Cottington and others. Charges against each are levelled with sentences specified. Among the female judges is Moll Cutpurse, an infamous pickpocket.

626A [Neville, Henry.] The Ladies, A Second Time, Assembled in Parliament. [London], 1647. 12 pages. N 507. TT Reel 64:E.406(23).

This pamphlet continues 630A, a semi-pornographic satire of a women's government. Here the women allow bishops to continue to hold their sees, for they have sexually pleased the women. They debate meanings of simple words while preoccupied with sexual fulfillment.

627A [Neville, Henry.] The Ladies Parliament. [London, 1647.] N 508. TT Reel 164:E.1143(1).

This publication is another edition of 629A with satirical verses appended.

628A [Neville, Henry.] Newes from the New-Exchange, or the Commonwealth of Ladies, Drawn to Life. London, Printed in the Yeare, of Women without Grace, 1650. 22 pages. N 510. TT Reel 90:E.590(10).

In this satire of both women and cavalier morality, Neville contends men earlier denied women their liberty. Women were confined to "their Homes and Closets," and had access only to footmen or ushers for sexual gratification. Here women have their own governing body and militia to guarantee sexual freedom and availability of young cavaliers. Neville asserts women are now "a part of the Free-People of this Nation." A list of prominent women is appended with their sexual exploits. See also 633A.

629A [Neville, Henry.] The Parliament of Ladies. Or divers Remarkable Passages of Ladies in Spring-garden. London, 1647. 15 pages. N 511*.

This variant edition of Neville's original satire (630A) is corrected and supplemented.

630A [Neville, Henry.] A Parliament of Ladies. With Their Lawes newly Enacted. [London], 1647. 16 pages. N 512A. EEB Reel 643:21 and TT Reels 61:E.384(9) and 62:E.388(4).

When a young Roman boy tells his mother the senators have passed a law permitting bigamy, she convenes a parliament of women to abrogate the law. Among the laws passed by the fictitious body: Women may have two husbands, fondle men's sexual organs, feast and banquet as they wish, and vex and torment their husbands.

631A [Neville, Henry.] The Parliament of Women. With the Merrie Lawes by them newly enacted, to live in more ease, pompe, pride and wantonnesse. London, Printed for W. Wilson, 1646. [20] pages. P 505*. EEB Reel 573:6; TT Reels 165:E.1150(5) and 206:E.1636(2).

These publications are 1646 and 1656 editions of 630A.

632A A New Bill, drawn up by a Committee of Grievances, in Reply to the Ladies and Batchelors Petition and Remonstrances. n.p., [1693] 4 pages. N 580B.

This satire responds to previous petitions by "virgins" and "bachelors." The bachelors allege the virgins make courtship difficult and fear matrimony. The women maintain there are too many virgins and wine is an unfair competitor. Women are likened to instruments to be played and nuts to be shelled. See also 469A, 695A and 697A, probably by the same author.

633A New Newes from the Old Exchange: or, The Commonwealth of Vertuous Laides [sic] lively deciphered: Being a modest Answer to an immodest scurrilous Phamphlet [sic]. [London], Not Printed in the Yeare of Women without Grace, but in that yeare when the Author of it with thousands more manifestly have showed themselves to be almost gracelesse, [1650]. 8 pages. N 687. TT Reel 91:E.595(6).

This pamphlet answers 628A. The author laments the passing of lashing as punishment for satire. He claims [Neville] has libelled the reputations of virtuous, pious and charitable persons--including the Countesses of Kent, Exeter, Carlisle, Bath and Newport; and the Ladies Savill and Marchionesse of Winchester.

634A The New Popish Sham-plot discovered; or, the cursed contrivance of the Earl of Danby, Mrs. Celier, with the popish lords, and priests. London, Printed for T. Davies, 1681. Broadside. N 718*. EEB Reel 966:44.

This anti-papist document charges the Earl of Danby, Elizabeth Cellier, and the popish lords and priests in the Tower and at Newgate with conspiracy. They allegedly suborned witnesses to testify that Sir Edmund Bury-Godfrey committed suicide. The author also notes a man named Macgarff confessed to lying about taking Cellier's advice (a midwife involved in the infamous Meal-tub Plot).

635A A New Song Sung in Abdelazer. [London? 1695.] Broadside. B 1747.

This song appears in Aphra Behn's play Abdelazer, or the Moor's Revenge. It relates the sad experience of two lovers: "But my poor heart alone is harm'd/Whilst thine the Victor is, and free." Although the Wing STC attributes it to Behn, she probably did not write it.

636A A New Vision of the Lady Gr--s [Grey] concerning her Sister, the Lady Henrietta Berkley. London, Printed for J. Smith, 1682. Broadside. N 791. EEB Reel 1640:17.

In a letter addressed to Madame Fan[shaw?], a current scandal is satirized. During 1682 Forde Grey, the Earl of Tankerville, left his wife Mary and eloped with his sister-in-law, the Lady Henrietta Berkeley.

637A The New Wife of Beath [sic] Much Better Reformed, Enlarged, and Corrected. Glasgow, Printed by Robert Sanders, One of his Majesties Printers, 1700. 23 pages. N 796. EEB Reel 1783:15.

This publication is an expurgated version of Chaucer's famous tale with nothing to "offend the wise and judicious." Whatever was considered "papal or heretic" is excised from this edition.

Newey, Charles. Captain Charles Newey's wonder Discovery. See 148A.

638A Newcome, Henry. The Compleat Mother. Or An Earnest Persuasive to all Mothers...to Nurse their own Children. London, Printed for J. Wyat, 1695. 112 pages. N 893. EEB Reel 156:6.

The author labels the reluctance of women to breastfeed a disgrace, even a "sin." He is especially critical of wealthy women and of the allegedly deleterious effects of wet-nursing. Newcome was the rector of Tattenhall in Chester, and he employs scriptural allusions and religious commentary to support his case.

639A The Newgate Salutation: or, A Dialogue between Sir W[illiam] W[aller] and Mrs. Cellier. London, Printed for the use of Students in Whittington's Colledge, [1681?]. Broadside. N 918A. EEB Reel 542:13.

This ballad comments on the threat of papists and Puritans to political stability. Cellier was a protagonist in the infamous Meal-tub Plot, and Waller was the Parliamentarian who found evidence implicating her in the anti-Protestant conspiracy.

640A News from Basing-Stoak, of one Mrs. Blunden A Masters Wife, who was Buried Alive. Relating how she was over-heard by the School-Boys, that were playing near her Grave. [London, Printed for John Millet, 1680?] 8 pages. N 947.

Mrs. Blunden was discovered buried alive by a group of schoolboys playing near her grave. They heard moaning, but when they reported the incident to their master, he doubted them. It was some time before they were believed and she was disinterred, still alive.

641A Newes from Holland: of the Entertainment of the Queenes Majestie [and] the Princesse Marie...May the 20th, 1642. London, Printed for Ed. Blackmore, 1642. 6 pages. N 967. EEB Reel 252:E.148(10) and TT Reel 26:E.148(10).

This document describes the welcome regatta and reception for Henrietta Maria and Princess Mary on their visit to Holland. The queen's barge was drawn by swans rather than oars into Amsterdam. Pageants and displays accompanied their every movement. The Prince and Princess of Orange were also present. The second half concerns operations of the Dutch military and the Prince.

642A News from New-England: or A most strange and prodigious birth. London, Printed for John G. Smith, 1642. 5 pages. N 984. EEB Reel 251:E.144(22) and TT Reel 26:E.144(22).

Several "monstrous births" which allegedly took place in Boston, Savoy, Ravenna, Paris and in other cities and times are described in this pamphlet.

643A News from Newgate: or, The Female Muggleton...a certain Fanatical Woman...speaking...Blasphemous Words. London, Printed for P. B., 1678. 6 pages. N 987. EEB Reel 700:1.

The "Female Muggleton" of the title was a Ranter, a servant noted for her skill, diligence and honesty who was also a "great exclaimer against the establisht churches." She attended many different services and, like Muggleton, claimed divine insight. She presented her radical views in a churchyard at Stepney and was accused of blasphemy. She remained unrepentant in prison. The author's conclusion: Weak minds should follow the precepts of the established Church.

644A Newton, John, of St. Martin's. The Penitent Recognition of Joseph's Brethren: A Sermon Occasion'd by Elizabeth Ridgeway, Who for the Petit Treason of Poysoning her Husband was...Burnt at Leicester. London, Printed for Richard Chiswell, 1684. 34 pages. N 1073*. EEB Reel 393:21.

The preface to the sermon relates the story of Elizabeth Ridgeway. Married for three weeks to a tailor who died suddenly, she was convicted of poisoning him. Although she produced many character witnesses and asserted her innocence, the judge would not reverse the decision. The sermon concerns the importance of confessing guilt.

645A Nicholetts, Charles. A Burning yet Unconsumed Bush, Exemplified. In the Dolorous Life, and Glorious Death, Of that Young Convert, And Most Excellent Saint, Mrs. Mary Harrison, Who Departed this life June 21st, in the 23rd Year of her Age. London, Printed and Sold by B. Harris, 1700. 167 pages. N 1084. EEB Reel 393:22.

This sermon was written by the minister of Harrison's church at Chichester. She was apparently sickly, but bright and courteous with a sweet nature. Before her conversion, she was obsessed with fashion, "a meer lump of Pride and Vanity;" she was transformed into a pious individual.

646A The Night-bell-man of Pickadilly to the Princess of Denmark. [London, 1693.] Broadside. N 1153A.

This broadside satirizes Queen Mary's alienation from her sister Anne.

647A The Night-Walker: Or, Evening Rambles in Search After Lewd Women, With the Conferences Held with Them. Two Vols. London, Printed for James Orme, 1696-97. N.I.W.

Sometimes attributed to John Dunton, this series was published between September of 1696 and March of 1697. Dedicating it to "the Whore-Masters of London and Westminster," the author claims the strumpets are condemned by God. He says prostitution was encouraged by Charles II and James II "so we might become an easier Conquest to Popery and Slavery." The author includes gossip and anecdotes (many seemingly apocryphal) about men and women of London.

648A The Night-walkers Declaration: Or, the Distressed Whores Advice to all their Sisters in City and Country. London, Printed for D. M., 1676. 8 pages. N 1156. EEB Reel 1748:33.

This confession, supposedly stemming from recent "tribulations," describes reasons for becoming a prostitute--high breeding, pride and idleness. The "whores" admit thievery of clients and lament indignities of the profession: pawing in taverns, disrobing by apprentices. Their purpose is supposedly to warn sisters to be careful--don't traffic with strangers, ply in town, beg ale or openly solicit. Although this piece was probably written by a man, it is remarkably sympathetic to the plight of prostitutes.

649A Norfolk, Henry Howard, Seventh Duke of. His Grace the Duke of Norfolk's Charge against the Dutchess, and the Dutchesses Answer. London, 1692. 22 pages. N 1231. EEB Reel 1407:17.

This document concerns the divorce case of the Duke and Duchess of Norfolk. He brought charges of adultery, naming a Mr. Germaine (her future husband) as correspondent. Servants testified they saw Germaine in the duchess' bedchamber. The duchess pointed to their many years of marital happiness and her fine reputation. She also attempted to discredit eyewitness testimony, noting Mr. Germaine wore a blonde wig, whereas the servants claimed they saw a dark-haired man. See also 35A, 164A, 886A and 920A.

650A Norfolk, Henry Howard, Seventh Duke of. The Duke of Norfolk's Order about the Habit the Ladies are to be in that attend the Queen at her Coronation. [London], Printed for Nat. Thompson, 1685. Broadside. N 1232. EEB Reel 503:4.

This official royal document specifies standards for clothing of women of different ranks attending the coronation of Queen Mary of Modena, wife to James II. Excerpt: "A Dutchess' Train to be Two Yards upon the Ground, the Cape Poudred with Four Rows of Ermin, the Mantle Edg'd with Five Inches of Ermin."

651A Norfolk, Henry Howard, Seventh Duke of. The Earl Marshal's Order Touching the Habits of the Peeresses at the Coronation of...William and...Mary. London, Printed for Edward Jones, 1688. Broadside. N 1232B.

This broadside is similar to 650A but was issued for the coronation of William and Mary.

652A [Norris, James.] Haec and Hic: or, The Feminine Gender More Worthy than the Masculine. London, Printed by Joseph Harefinch for James Norris, 1683. 165 pages. N 1242A.

Norris defends women against "the Virulent Tongues and Pens of Malevolent Men," whom he calls unmanly and disgraceful to their mothers. On theological grounds, he says Eve was not the originator of sin, and women were created in God's image. He claims women are a sweet, lonely, innocent sex, no more vain than many men. Norris concludes with a list of chaste virgins, good wives and educated women (all flourishing before the early sixteenth century).

653A [Norris, James.] The Accomplished Lady. London, Printed for James Norris, 1684. 165 pages. N 1242B.

This item is the same as 652A.

Norris, John. Letters concerning the Love of God. See 12B.

654A Norris, John. Reflections upon the Conduct of Human Life: With Reference to the Study of Learning and Knowledge. In a Letter to the Excellent Lady, the Lady Masham. Second Edition. London, Printed for S. Marship, 1691. 187 pages. N 1268*. EEB Reels 363:14 and 723:1.

In this essay, inscribed to theologian and writer Damaris Masham, Norris explores the intellectual conduct of human life. He discusses the method, desire and "prosecution" of learning. In a postscript he addresses the Quaker notion of divine light. A sermon preached in the Abbey Church of Bath is appended. See also 441B.

655A Now or Never: Or, A New Parliament of Women Assembled. London, Printed for George Horton, 1656. [6] pages. N 1434. TT Reel 133:E.885(9).

This satirical pamphlet proposes women should rule their husbands, no man should call his wife a prostitute or beat her, adulterous women should be flogged with "pudding-pyes," and young men should have to marry by twenty-four or be fined. Men are called self-interested and tyrannical, while women are deemed fit to rule because of their superior moral nature and beauty. See also 529A.

656A Observations on the Lady Wentworth's Proposal. [London, 1677.] Broadside. O 103A. EEB Reel 1750:16.

This item appears to be the first page of a longer document. It discusses a legal dispute among the Lady Wentworth, the Lady Poole (her sister), and the Countess of Newburgh over the Earl of Cleaveland's property. Wentworth claims the court cannot act until the minor whose interest is at stake reaches majority. She says the 6000-pound debt allegedly owed by the Earl to the two other women can be paid only through a Parliamentary act. She says he joined the army to avoid his creditors, and his property is in trusteeship. Henrietta Maria Wentworth was the mistress of James, Duke of Monmouth. See also 176A amd 177A.

657A [Ockland, Christopher.] The Pope's Farewel; Or, Queen Ann's Dream containing a true Prognostick of her own Death, Together with the extirpation of Popery out of these Realms. [London], Printed by J. M. for T. W., [1680]. 8 pages. O 128A. EEB Reel 393:33.

Ockland wrote this piece in Latin in 1582 during the reign of Elizabeth. It is a poetic prophecy about various events including the expulsion of Catholics under Edward VI. There is a dialogue between Elizabeth and Anne about the predictions, but the verse is primarily anti-papist with a final section focusing on Charles II and the threat from his brother James.

658A An Ode on Her Royal Highness the Princess of Orange. [London, 1688/9.] Broadside. O 133. EEB Reel 1766:20.

This song was written in the Hague by "a person of Quality." Mary (Urania) is depicted as the union of earth and heaven, the "Princess of Conquering Charms." William is called the "Hero of Conquering Arms."

659A Officium B. Mariae Virg. nuper reformatum. London, Typis Henrici Hills, [1687]. 476 pages. O 154. EEB Reel 1750:24.

This compilation of official Catholic texts in Latin includes songs, psalms, papal orations, hymns, and other material relating to the Virgin Mary and promulgated by Pope Urban III.

660A O[gden], S[amuel]. Epicedium, or, a Funeral Elegy on the Death of our Late Gracious Sovereign. London, Printed for John Everingham, 1695. 8 pages. O 161A.

Written on the death of Mary II, this elegy employs typical pastoral conventions. Ogden begins with a description of the grief of the queen's subjects, then notes her qualities as a wise and worthy monarch and wife.

661A [Oldham, John.] "A Satyr upon a Woman, who by her Falshood and Scorn was the Death of a Friend." In Satyrs Upon the Jesuits: Written in the Year 1679. Second Edition. London, Printed for Joseph Hindmarsh, 1681. [10 pages.] Item: N.I.W. Collection: O 245*. EEB Reel 614:3.

This misogynistic piece blames beautiful women for capitalizing on men's lust by inciting them to crime. Excerpt: "Vilest of that viler Sex, who damn'd us all/ Ordain'd to cause, and plague us, for our fall."

662A [Oldham, John.] Upon the Marriage of the Prince of Orange With the Lady Mary. [London], Printed by T. N. for Henry Herringman, 1677. 4 pages. O 250. EEB Reel 1766:25.

This poem honors William and Mary who under "equal Majesty did Wed." Oldham praises the prince's great valor and prays Mary will deliver children painlessly.

663A Oldisworth, Giles. The Illustrious Wife. London, 1673. O 253. 48 pages. EEB Reel 1766:26.

This item is the same as 673A. Oldisworth, the nephew of Sir Thomas Overbury, is the illustrator.

664A Oliver, John. A Present for Teeming Women. Or, Scripture- Directions for Women with Child, how to prepare for the Houre of Travel. London, Printed by Sarah Griffin for Mary Rothwell, 1663. 144 pages. O 276*. EEB Reel 1447:16.

This book includes prayers for pregnant women. Oliver entreats them to be patient in the midst of pain and to try not to cry out and moan, as they "discourage" passers-by. He also mentions those who have already suffered pain in labor as inspirational examples to those about to give birth.

665A On the Death of her Illustrious Grace Anne Dutchess Dowager of Albemarle. London, 1669. Broadside. O 304.

This eulogy was written for a woman who died within twenty days of her husband. She is called a loyal royalist, a careful domestic and a modest and charitable woman. Termed an old-fashioned woman, she was true to her husband and graced her high social position.

666A On the Death of Mris. Mary Soame, Wife of Mr. Edmund Soame of Hackney. [London, 1669.] Broadside. O 305B. EEB Reel 1576:5.

Soame died at twenty-five, leaving two small children. She was afflicted for many months with pain and "strange fits." The conceit of this elegy is death as enemy. "Death" defends its role as a necessary link in the life cycle, noting those who have eternal life taste death only briefly.

667A On the Death of the Queen, a Poem. London, Printed and sold by John Whitlock, 1695. 10 pages. O 311. EEB Reel 1407:25.

This poem marks the passing of Mary II. The poet mentions her pursuit by several European princes and characterizes her reign as merciful, bold and wise. The grief of the country and Mary's servants, in particular, is described.

668A On the Death of the Queen An Ode. [London, 1695?] O 311A. 8 pages. EEB Reel 1750:37.

The poet encourages the open expression of grief for Mary II, noting her virtue outstripped human wit. He expresses a positive view of marriage, emphasizing the support of a good, kind and wise woman. He also tries to distinguish between love and lust. Excerpt: "God form'd her so, that to her Husband she/Like Eve, should all the world of Woman be."

669A On the untimely death of Mrs. Anne Gray, the daughter of the Learnedly accomplisht doctor Nicholas Gray of Tunbridge in Kent. [London], Printed for Samuel Holland, 1657. Broadside. N.I.W. TT Reel 247:669.f.20(51).

This broadside memorializes a young woman who died of smallpox at eighteen.

670A The Oppressed Prisoners Complaint. Of Their Great Oppression: With a loud call to Englands Magistrates. [London? 1662.] Broadside. B 3064A.

Attributed to Quaker Sarah Blackborow in the Wing STC, this appeal for religious liberty was presented during a trial at the Old Bailey. Internal evidence suggests it may have been written by a man. He speaks of himself and his compatriots as "free-born Englishmen." Excerpt: "Most Poor, and from our Wives and Children rended/And here abus'd, when we should be defended."

671A The Origine of Atheism. By Dorotheus Sicurus, pseud. London, Printed for William Kettilby, 1684. C 7431A. EEB Reel 823:24.

The British Library indicates this book was pseudonymously written by Thomas Theodorus Crisius.

672A Ouriana: The High and Mighty Lady the Princess Royal of Aurange congratulated. London, Printed for W. Godbid, 1660. Broadside. O 593. TT Reel 247: 669.f.26(12).

This publication marks the arrival in England of Princess Mary, queen consort to William II, Prince of Orange, and sister of Charles II, who died later in the year.

673A Overbury, Thomas, Elder. The Illustrious Wife: Viz. That Excellent Poem, Sir Thomas Overburie's Wife Illustrated by Giles Oldisworth. London, 1673. O 608A. 48 pages. EEB Reel 1784:20.

Overbury's often reprinted poem is inspired by Proverbs 12.4: "A Virtuous Woman is a crown unto her Husband." Each woman is called "a Brief of Woman-kind" who represents Eve as helpmate. As "shells" for male posterity, women should be wise but not formally educated. Valued wifely attributes are domesticity, obedience, thoughtfulness and piety.

674A Overbury, Thomas, Elder. Sir Thomas Overbury. His wife. With additions of New Characters, and many other Witty Conceits never before Printed. London, Printed for William Shears, 1655. 255 pages. O 610*. EEB Reel 1784:21.

Introductory material laments Overbury's untimely death through poisoning in the Tower. Laudatory material precedes and follows the poem. Also included are humorous items about current news, the university, stereotypical characters (the puritan, the hypocrite, the dunce) and a list of paradoxes. The poem itself is a reprinted piece about Overbury's wife.

675A [Overbury, Thomas, Younger.] A True and Perfect Account of the Examination, Confession, Tryall, Condemnation, and Execution of Joan Perry and her two sons, John and Richard Perry, for the supposed Murder of William Harrison, Gent. London, Printed for F. and B. Sprint, G. Conyers and T. Ballard, 1676. 46 pages. O 614*. EEB Reels 1621:5 and 1784:22.

Perry and her two sons of Gloucestershire were executed for the murder of their employer, William Harrison. Although he was supposedly killed while collecting rents, he was actually abducted and taken to Turkey for two years; thus, his innocent servants were hanged for a murder which hadn't taken place.

676A The Oxford-Act: A Poem. London, Printed for Randal Taylor, 1693. 22 pages. O 847*. EEB Reel 1024:8.

This work is incorrectly attributed to Alicia D'Anvers by the British Library and the Library of Congress. Internal evidence indicates it was written by a man. For example, focusing on sexual advances toward women, the author offers sexually suggestive advice, referring to his sex as male.

677A Oxford, University of. Epicedia academiae Oxoniensis...Mariae principis Arausionensis. Oxoniae, typis Lichfieldianis, 1660. [87] pages. O 877. EEB Reel 1675:11.

This collection of poems by Oxford dons commemorates the death of Mary of Orange, sister to Charles II.

678A Oxford, University of. Epicedia...In obitum Henriettae Mariae. Oxonii, e typographia Sheldoniana, 1669. [no pagination] O 879.

This item is the same as 679A.

679A Oxford, University of. Epicedia Universitatis Oxoniensis in Obitum Illustrissime Principis Henriettae Mariae Ducisse Aurelianensis. Oxonii, e Theatro Sheldoniano, 1670. 58 pages. O 881. EEB Reel 1640:30.

This volume honors the late Queen Henrietta Maria. Poems by dons of the Oxford colleges laud her, praise her loyalty to Charles I and note the talents of her son, Charles II.

680A Oxford, University of. Musarum Oxoniensium. Ettibathpia Serenissimae Reginarum Mariae ex Batavia Feliciter Reduci Publico Voto D. D. D. Oxford, Leonardus Lichfield, 1643. 62 pages. O 903. EEB Reel 239:E.62(14) and TT Reel 11:E.62(14.)

These brief poems and letters, offered in the midst of the Civil War, offer respect and loyalty to Henrietta Maria and Charles I. Many of the pieces are in Latin. A lengthy speech by the University orator is included.

681A Oxford, University of. Pietas Universitatis Oxoniensis in Obitum...Reginae Mariae. Oxonii, E Theatro Sheldoniano, 1695. 130 pages. O 937. EEB Reel 747:22.

Oxford dons wrote these Latin, Hebrew, Arabic, English and Greek eulogistic verses on the death of Mary II.

682A Oxford, University of. Vota Oxoniensia pro Guilhelmo rege et Maria Regina. [Oxford], E Theatro Sheldoniano, 1689. [30] and [105] pages. O 992. EEB Reel 725:7.

These formal effusive verses by dons of Oxford colleges honor William and Mary on their ascension to the throne. They are in Latin as well as English, Arabic, Hebrew and Greek.

683A P., D. Madame Semphronia's Farewell, Or an Elegy. [London, 1681.] Broadside. P 12. EEB Reel 469:10.

This sorrowful lament was supposedly written by a woman who attracted many men when she first came to London, although she was especially interested in only one prince. After she relinquished her virtue to him, they were blissful until he began to show interest in other women. The address is directed to the Thames River, to which the speaker says she is herewith adding her tears. This is possibly a satire of a court figure. Female authorship is doubtful.

684A P., T. A Relation of the Diabolical Practices of above Twenty Wizards and Witches of the Sheriffdom of Renfrew in the Kingdom of Scotland, contain'd in their Tryalls, Examinations, and Confessions. London, Printed for Hugh Newman, [1698]. 24 pages. P 118 A. EEB Reel 508:9.

This document reports on a commission of enquiry after trials during which the alleged witches were pricked with needles to see if they would bleed or cry out in pain. The accused were Katherine Campbell, Elizabeth Anderson, Margaret Lang, Agnes Nesmith, Agnes Foster, Margaret Fulton and two men, John and James Lindsay. All were sentenced to be burned.

685A [Pallavicino, Ferrante.] The Whore's Rhetorick, calculated to the Meridian of London and conformed to the Rules of Art. In Two Dialogues. [By Philo Puttanus, pseud.] London, Printed for George Shell, 1683. 222 pages. P 213. EEB Reel 893:19.

This adaptation of Pallavicino's La Retorica delle Puttane (1642) capitalizes on the recent conviction of a famous bawd, Mrs. Cresswell. In these fictitious dialogues she offers amusing advice to a young aspiring prostitute. Secondary themes are anti-Puritanism and avarice. Excerpt: "It is not enough to have a charming person, killing looks, and a graceful meen [sic]; cunning, art, and good fortune do the work, all the rest are but mere bubbles."

686A The Parable of the Puppies: or the Top-Knots Vindicated. London, Printed for T. Burdet, 1691. 4 pages. P 325. EEB Reel 747:40.

This satire on men's fashions replies to 306A. Here a bitch named Phancey whelps male puppies ("Tory-Rory," "Amorous," "Drunkard," etc.). One is sent to

Paris to learn French tricks. The foppish pups are compared to men who "First taught us, and now exceed us in all manner of Effeminacy." The author mocks men's manners, interactions, coffee-house banter, and so on. Although he pretends to be female, the author is likely a male. See also 912A.

687A Parker, Thomas. The Copy of a Letter Written by Thomas Parker, pastor of the Church of Newbury in New England, to his Sister, Mrs. Elizabeth Avery... Touching Sundry Opinions by her Professed and Maintained. London, Printed by John Field for Edmund Paxton, 1650. 20 pages. P 475. TT Reel 89:E.584(3).

In this letter of 1648, Parker attacks the "heretical" opinions of his sister, Fifth Monarchist Elizabeth Avery. He also criticizes her refusal to join her husband in religious observances. (Her actions could be construed as defiant of patriarchal rule.) He calls her arrogant and asks her to repent for "your printing of a Book, beyond the custom of your Sex." Although Parker claims there are "horrid things" in Avery's book, he admits he has not actually seen it. See also 24B.

A Parliament of Ladies. See 630A.

The Parliament of Women. See 631A.

688A A Pastoral Upon the Death of Her Grace the Dutchess of Ormond. [London], Printed for N. Thompson, 1684. 4 pages. P 678. EEB Reel 748:1.

This elegy is a dialogue between two nymphs, Myrtillo and Alexis, who mourn Pyrrha (Ormond). The duchess was married for fifty years and had five children. Little about her personal life is included.

689A [Patrick, John.] The Virgin Mary misrepresented by the Roman Church. Part I. London, Printed for Richard Chiswell, [1688]. 155 pages. P 736. EEB Reel 395:6.

The author considers the conception and the nativity of Mary in his criticism of the Catholic Church. Excerpt: "They have put a Sceptre into the hands of this Handmaid of the Lord, as she calls her self...they have advanced her into a Throne by God himself; and, without asking his leave, call her the Queen of Heaven." This book has been erroneously attributed to both Lynn and Simon Patrick.

690A Payne, William. A Sermon upon the Death of the Queen. London, Printed by J. R. for B. Aylmer, S. Smith, B. Walford, 1695. 32 pages. P 909*. EEB Reel 701:13.

This eulogy is typical in its use of biblical allusions, but is unusual because it is quite personal. It includes descriptions of Mary's charity, piety and devotion (her "last and greatest" virtues). She is also praised for paying little heed to fashion.

Pechey, John, ed. The Compleat Midwife's Practice Enlarged. See 227A.

691A Pechey, John. A General Treatise of the Diseases of Maids, Bigbellied Women, Child-bed-Women, and Widows. London, Printed for Henry Bonwick, 1696. 256 pages. P 1024*. EEB Reel 327:10.

Pechey bases his guide to women's diseases on work by Rodericus e Castro and "others." He describes and discusses treatments for ailments from abscesses, barrenness and madness through womb worms.

692A Penn, William. An Account of the Blessed End of Guilema Maria Penn, and of Springet Penn, the beloved Wife and Eldest Son of William Penn. [London], Printed for the Benefit of His Family, Relations... Friends, [1699]. 18 pages. P 1243.

This material is about Penn's wife and his eldest son, Springet Penn, who had both recently died. It includes anecdotes about his wife, focusing on her religiosity and her bravery in the face of death.

693A A Perfect Relation Of the Cause and Manner of Apprehending William Needle and Mistris Phillips, Both dwelling in the Town of Banbury in Oxfordshire. [London, 1643.] 6 pages. P 1509. TT Reel 42:E.247(13).

Phillips, the wife of a magistrate, dispatched Needle as a messenger to Bister, where troops were quartered. Needle was apprehended and interrogated, then imprisoned. Phillips was also consigned to jail. (She had ten children, one nursing.) Both were sentenced to death. Although Needle was executed, Phillips was made to stand with a noose around her neck surrounded by her children, then paraded in the marketplace and returned to prison.

694A The Petition of the Ladies at Court Intended to be Presented to the House of Lords: Against the Pride and Luxury of the City Dames. [London], Printed and sold by R. J., 1681. Broadside. P 1811.

This "petition" complains that fashionable city women are ignoring class boundaries in surpassing court ladies in finery. Their "bold Usurpations and insolent practices" are forcing aristocratic women to complete, resulting in an increase in bankruptcy and cuckoldry in the court.

695A The Petition of the Ladies of London and Westminster to the Honourable House of Husbands. London, Printed for Mary Want-man, the Fore-maid of the Petitioners and sold by A. Roper, 1693. 4 pages. P 1812. EEB Reel 872:58.

This semi-pornographic satire focuses on women's political rights and sexual insatiability. The author cites wine-drinking as the cause of male carousing. He likens women to fields to be plowed and cultivated. The petition demands men of quality marry by age twenty-one, single men refrain from visiting taverns, and so on. See also 469A, 632A and 697A, probably by the same author.

696A The Petition of the Weamen of Middlesex...with the Apprentices of Londons Petition. London, Printed for William Bowden, 1641. [3] pages. P 1838. EEB Reel 256:E.180(17) and TT Reel 31:E.180(17).

In this satirical anti-religious petition, the author addresses subjects like the Book of Common Prayer, bishops' miters and divorce. The "petitioners" ask that anthems be banned from cathedrals because the voices of the boys put women "in mind of a bawdy-house." An allusion to the mythical Pope Joan and her "great belly" is included. The subtitle states the document will not be presented to Parliament "until it should please God to endue [sic] [women] with more wit, and lesse Non-sence."

697A The Petition of the Widows, in and about London and Westminster, for a Redress of their Grievances. London, Printed for the Use of the Wide-o's, 1693. 4 pages. P 1839. EEB Reel 1292:4.

This parody of the social importance of virginity answers 695A, presenting demands of widows. The primary metaphors are woman as horse and man as rider, woman as rock and man as shipwreck upon it, and woman as a walled city and a fired gun. See also 469A, 632A and 695A, probably by the same author.

698A Phillips, John. In Memory Of Our Late Most Gracious Lady, Mary Queen of Great Britain, France and Ireland. London, Printed for John Harris, 1695. 10 pages. P 2086. EEB Reel 505:8.

This poem is typical of the eulogies for Mary II: It is solemn and straightforward with little emphasis on her personal qualities. Excerpt: "She, the Indulgent Mistress, all the while/At home kept all in Order, all in peace./And the vast Household liv'd releas'd from Fear/O'reshadow'd by her Providential Care."

699A Philogynes. The Freedom of the Fair Sex Asserted: or, Woman the Crown of the Creation. In a Letter to a Young Lady. London, Printed by J. Nutt, 1700. [No pagination.] F 2125B.

The author says a woman's obligation to a man should be exercised in "such a manner as will prove much more easie and Natural to herself, as well as more Useful and Advantageous to us." He cites the Fall as the source of women's subservience and, although he thinks women are better natured and more religious than men, he says learned females lack native ability.

700A Piety promoted by Faithfulness, Manifested by Several Testimonies Concerning that True Servant of God Ann[e] Whitehead. [London?], 1686. 124 pages. P 2217A.

Testimonies by Quaker Whitehead's husband and friends lament her death and honor her piety and good works. Women speak about her great contributions to the women's meeting. A list of female Friends who note her fine character concludes the document.

701A A Pindarick Ode on the Death of the Queen. By a young gentleman. London, Printed and are to be sold by John Whitlock, 1695. 6 pages. P 2253. EEB Reel 396:2.

These dramatic verses honor Mary II, who died suddenly of smallpox. The author describes a dream sequence in which her spirit visits him: "She stood clad all in white/Thick Purple Spots bedeckt her Heavenly Face./But with such Majesty, with such a Grace:/She looked so innocent, and yet so bright/Her Glory expell'd the darkness of the Night."

702A Pitt, Moses. <u>An Account of one Ann Jeffries, now living in the County of Cornwall</u>. London, Printed for Richard Cumberland 1696. 23 pages. P 2301. EEB Reel 505:14.

This description of a woman supposedly fed by fairies for six months is contained in a letter from Pitt to the Bishop of Gloucester. She learned how to make effective salves from them and never charged her patients. Jeffries refused to discuss her experience and wanted no books or ballads written about it.

703A Plat, Sir Hugh. <u>Delights for Ladies. To Adorn their Persons, Tables, Closets and Distillatories: with Beauties, Banquets, Perfumes and Waters</u>. London, Printed by William Dugard, 1651. 130 pages. P 2381*.

This cookbook includes sections about preserving, candying, conserving, distillation, cookery, "huswifery," powders, ointments, herbal salves, etc.

704A <u>A Pleasant Dialogue betwixt Two Wanton Ladies of Pleasure...The Dutchess of Portsmouth...to her former Felicity</u>. London, Printed for John Millet, 1685. Broadside. P 2543A.

In this ballad about two mistresses of Charles II, the Duchess of Portsmouth longs to return to France, while Nell Gwynne bemoans her situation and asks for instruction in French romance. The duchess refers obliquely to her covered [pock-marked] face. They both gloat over the profit they've made from the English treasury. Gwynne says she can always ply her trade in France.

705A <u>The Pleasures of Matrimony, Intermix'd with a Variety of Merry and Delightful Stories</u>. London, Printed by A. G. for Henry Rhodes, 1688. 228 pages. P 2565. EEB Reel 221:12.

This interesting negative description of marriage notes the unfair status of women in English society. It argues men have the advantages, including the right to attend universities. It continues: "...nor are the men ignorant of this Advantage of theirs...and Partiality to themselves as if they were Saints, and the Women Devils."

706A <u>A Poem Occasion's by the Death of her Late Majesty of Ever Happy and Sacred Memory</u>. London, Printed and sold by J. Whitlock, 1695. 4 pages. P 2678A. EEB Reel 1641:10.

The poet seeks solace to mourn Mary, who, he says, has left earth for a celestial throne. He emphasizes her fine character and her subjects' great loss. Excerpt: "What Vertues scatter'd through the Sex appear/In Her, a glorious Constellation were."

707A <u>A Poem On and To Her Gracious Majesty Upon the Day of Her Happy Coronation</u>. [London], Printed for Nathaniel Thompson, 1685. 5 pages. P 2683. EEB Reel 819:9.

This flattering poem was written for the coronation of Mary II. Excerpt: "Yet in defence of her Religious Faith/Sh' appeas'd the King's and wav'd the people's wrath./And being with Her Gods Decrees content/She Calm'd a Mis-informed Parliament."

708A A Poem on the Coronation of King William and Queen Mary. London, Printed and are to be sold by Randal Taylor, 1689. 16 pages. P 2690.

This poem expresses support for the royal couple and attacks James II as a tyrant. The poet lauds William for his accomplishments in the Low Countries, emphasizes the importance of the Protestant succession and praises Mary for her virtue and strength.

709A A Poem on the Death of Queen Hester. London, Printed for William Leech, [1680]. 17 pages. P 2696. EEB Reel 847:5.

This poem, included in a collection of anonymous poetry, is a narrative of the biblical story of Queen Esther, describing her match with the king. Her humble birth is noted.

710A A Poem on the Italian Woman Lately come into England; who Sings at the Musick House in York-Buildings. London, Printed for Randal Taylor, 1692. Broadside. P 2697. EEB Reel 1554:8.

This poem praises an unnamed singer's ability. The author argues musical instruments should now remain silent, for her voice shames them. He thanks her for bringing beauty to the new year and says she should stay through the spring.

711A A Poem to Her Royal highness upon the Birth of her Daughter. London, Printed for J. Smeetman, 1682. Broadside. P 2706. EEB Reel 819:12.

This jocular anti-woman poem expresses disappointment at the birth of a female heir (Princess Charlotte Margaret) to James and Mary, perhaps in reference to rumors that substitution of a male child was entertained. The poet speaks of celebrations planned for a male heir which must be cancelled and of women's failings. Excerpt: "A Girl, though fair, yet is the bane of Bliss,/'Tis Gloomy Woman Darkens Paradice."

712A A Poem to the Charming Fair One. [London, 1679?] 2 pages. P 2708. EEB Reel 847:7.

The poet praises a French heroine who resembles Joan of Arc, but who is probably fictitious. She supposedly saved France from a stronger England; however, she sought wealth and honor and was motivated by pride.

713A A Poem upon the Death of the Queen. [London, 1695.] Broadside. P 2714A. EEB Reel 1576:41.

This elegy written in iambic pentameter honors Mary II. She is described as a caring monarch with "comely sweetness in Her Smile." Excerpt: "Such Majesty sat on Her Brow,/She made the stubborn sex to bow./All but Her conq'ring William she/Did make to bow and bend the knee."

714A A Poetical Essay devoted to the Glorious Memory of our Late Queen. London, 1695. 12 pages. P 2736. EEB Reel 287:5.

This poem written for Mary II alludes to other such eulogies: "Poets, and Priests, alike aspire to Fame/In paying Tribute to Maria's Name;/And with sev'ral Crown adorn'd each Head;/To Man and Wife did equal right proclaim,/A Right which from the Choice of Heav'n, and Nations, came." There is praise of Mary's piety and wisdom with strong anti-clerical overtones.

715A [Pomfret, Thomas.] The Life of the Right Honourable and Religious lady Christian Late Countess dowager of Devonshire.   London, Printed by William Rawlins for the author, 1685. 98 pages. P 2799. EEB Reel 506:12.

Pomfret wrote this piece out of affection and admiration for the mother of the Earl of Devonshire. He directs it to satirists of women who write "invectives against the whole Sex." Although the biography praises the Countess, it is valuable primarily for information about her management of household affairs, the family and its lawsuits, and the political and social milieu of the period.

716A The Poor Whores Complaint to the Apprentices of London. London, 1672. Broadside. P 2895A.

In this satire London prostitutes complain of rising rents and few customers. Most soldiers and sailors have gone off to the Dutch wars; those remaining shun brothels for fear of impression into the Navy. The whores encourage the apprentices to rob their masters and blame innocent persons; in return for their services, the prostitutes would be entitled to half the booty. See also 204A, 724A and 952A.

717A The Poor-Whores Petition. To the most splendid Illustrious, Serene and Eminent Lady of Pleasure, the Countess of Castlemayne. The Humble Petition of the Undone Company of poore distressed Whores, Bawds, Pimps, and Panders, etc. [London], 1668. 4 pages. P 2897.

This satirical petition, supposedly signed by notorious bawds Damaris Page and Mrs. Cresswell, sets forth the plight of homeless prostitutes with venereal disease. They petition the countess, said to have reached her position plying their trade. Castlemaine was an early mistress to Charles II. See also 405A.

718A The Pope's Letter to Madame Cellier, in Relation to her Great Sufferings for the Catholic Cause, and likewise Maddam Celliers Lamentation standing on the Pillory. London, D. Mallet, 1680. 4 pages. P 2935. EEB Reel 1042:8.

This anti-papist attack satirizes Elizabeth Cellier, prominent in the Meal-tub Plot. It depicts the pope honoring her along with the greatest saints of the Church. Cellier offers a rueful lamentation while shackled in the pillory, and the pope praises her contributions to the Catholic cause.

719A Portsmouth's Lamentation Or, a Dialogue between Two Amorous Ladies, E. G. and D. P. [London, Printed for C. Dennison, 1685.] Broadside. P 3008.

This ballad reports a supposed conversation between two mistresses of Charles II. Nell Gwynne asks the Duchess of Portsmouth when she will return to

France, now that her salad days have passed. The duchess replies she is sad because her profligate ways have brought her little gain and much fatigue. She says if she could reach her native land with her gold, "there would I briskly sing, and dance,/And Riot beyond measure."

720A [Poulain de la Barre, Francois.] The Woman as Good as the Man: or, the Equality of Both Sexes. London, Printed by T. M. for N. Brooks, 1677. 185 pages. P 3038. EEB Reel 1192:5.

This lengthy essay by a seventeenth-century French feminist, employs a Cartesian model to argue the intellectual equality of the sexes. de la Barre says the people who degrade women in the worst ways are the vulgar and "almost all the learned," He explains the evolution of sex roles and argues education is necessary for women to debunk misconceptions about their sex and assume their rightful places in government and the military.

721A Prance, Miles. Mr. Prance's Answer to Mrs. Cellier's Libel. London, Printed for L. Curtis, 1680. 18 pages. P 3171. EEB Reel 574:20.

This anti-papist tract focuses on Elizabeth Cellier's role in the Meal-tub Plot. Prance attacks her   personally and professionally, commenting on her "bulk" and her influence on children, possibly in her role as a midwife or in reference to her plan for the care of foundling children (139B).

722A [Pratt, Daniel.] The Life of the Blessed St. Agnes Virgin and Martyr, In Prose and Verse. By L. Sherling, pseud. London, Printed by T. H. for G. K., 1677. 127 pages. P 3179.

According to this romantic biography, Agnes was of unknown parentage, born during the reign of Diocletian in Rome. She decided to remain a virgin in childhood, but attracted a young man who tried to force marriage. She was finally sent to the stake for her religious views and refusal to wed.

723A Prechac, Jean de. The Illustrious Lovers, or Princely adventures in the courts of England and France...being an historical account of the famous loves of Mary, sometimes Queen of France (daughter to Henry the 7th) and Charles Brandon, the renown'd Duke of Suffolk. London, Printed for William Whitwood, 1686. 243[8] pages. P 3207aA.

This fictionalized biography concerns Mary, the young queen (1496-1533) of Louis XII. When he died soon after their marriage, she met Brandon in Greenwich. Her daughter Frances eventually became the mother of Lady Jane Grey. See also 607A.

724A The Prentices Answer to the Whores Petition. London, 1668. Broadside. A 3584.

Apprentices deny an accusation by prostitutes that they attacked a brothel, claiming they do not patronize bawdy houses. They call prostitutes a temptation to the young and carriers of venereal disease. See also 204A, 716A and 952A.

725A A present for a Papist: or the Life and Death of Pope Joan, Plainly Proving...that a Woman called Joan, was really Pope of Rome. [By Alexander Cooke.] London, Printed for T. D., 1675. 165 pages. P 3244. EEB Reel 1512:4.

A German woman who concealed her sex and studied in Athens supposedly became pope on the death of Leo IV. She allegedly became pregnant and gave birth in the streets where she died. This volume includes Church histories which refer to her infamous tenure and other clerical corruption. Other publications of the period focused on the fictitious Pope Joan as well.

726A Price, Lawrence. Bloody actions performed. Or, A brief and true Relation of three Notorious Murthers, committed by three Bloud-Thirsty men, 2. upon their own Wives. [London], Printed for W. Gilbertson, 1653. 16 pages. P 3355.

Two crazed husbands allegedly murdered their virtuous wives--one hacked her to death with a cleaver, and one stabbed his wife thirty times without provocation.

727A P[rice], L[aurence.] The Vertuous Wife is the Glory of her Husband. London, Printed for T. Passenger, 1667. 21 pages. P 3387*.

This work defends "vertuous" women, while establishing guidelines for wifely conduct. Characteristics of a good wife include humility, patience, fear of God and love of and subjection to the husband.

728A Prideaux, John. Euchologia: Or, The Doctrine of Practical Praying By the Right Reverend...Late Bishops of Worcester. Being a Legacy Left to his Daughters. London, Printed for Richard Marriot, 1655. 285 pages. P 3424. TT Reel 193:E.1515(1).

Prideaux's legacy is bequeathed to his daughters, Sarah Hodges and Elizabeth Sutton, both married to ministers and sole survivors of nine children. It consists primarily of an encouragement to pray based on the Book of Common Prayer. He also warns them to beware of unbridled reformers and avoid becoming silly women who are easily led astray.

729A The Prince of Orange...his Royall Entertainment to the Queen of England...at the Hague, and Her Majesties gracious Answer unto the same. London, Printed for Henrie Barwicke, 1641. [6] pages. P 3485. EEB Reel 250:E.138(17) and TT Reel 25:E.138(17).

The author purports to paraphrase the words of Henrietta Maria and Prince William during her visit to the Hague. Her twin motive was apparently to marry the prince to her daughter Mary and win financial support for the royal cause. She compares William to Cicero and Vergil, and makes flattering comments about his person: "Your Aromatick smelling-breath is so odiferous, that it exceeds the Arabian Odours, and seems rather celestial." The expansive language renders authenticity doubtful.

730A The Prophesie of Mother Shipton in the raigne of King Henry the Eighth. London, Printed for Richard Lownds, 1641. 6 pages. S 3445*. EEB Reels 1295:4, 1732:10 and 257:E.181(15); TT Reels 25:E.141(2), 32:E.181(15) and 81:E.522(34).

The mythical Mother Shipton was a witch able to predict the future. She supposedly foretold the deaths of Wolsey and Lord Percy, among others. Publications about her powers probably incorporated tales commonly told in the environs of York. See Wing STC numbers S 3442 through 3456 for additional items about her. See also 428A and 833A.

731A A Prospective for King and Subjects. By Wendy Oxford, pseud. London, Printed to [sic] Leyden by John Pricton, 1652. 32 pages. O 844. EEB Reel 1769:3.

The Wing STC lists this item under Wendy Oxford, but it was apparently written by the same man who wrote The Unexpected Life and Vincit Qui Partur.

732A Provost, John. Instructions to a Nobleman's Daughter concerning Religion. London, Printed by W. R. for D. Brown and L. Stokey, 1700. 120 pages. P 3877. EEB Reel 1192:12.

This Anglican document is a sensitive guide to spirituality. Provost, apparently a local prelate, is "exhorting, advising, intreating your Ladyship to continue and improve your Piety." He reminds her to be cheerful, value prayer, take the sacrament and remember the duties incumbent upon one of her station.

733A Provost, John. A Sermon on the Occasion of the Death of...Elizabeth, Lady Cutts. [London], Printed by E. J. for S. Lowndes, 1698. 36 pages. P 3878. EEB Reel 875:42.

This sermon is dedicated to Lord Cutts, Colonel in the Coldstream Guards. Its theme is threefold: Take note of the upright, remember their works and in particular the peaceful final days of the deceased. Lady Cutts is described as a devout, reverent, modest, sincere and innocent woman. She died childless at eighteen. See also 51A, 457A, 851A and 955A.

734A Prude, John. A Sermon at the Funeral of the Learned and Ingenious Mrs. Ann Baynard, Daughter and only child of Dr. Edward Baynard. London, Printed for Daniel Brown, 1697. 32 pages. P 3881.

Baynard's father was a fellow of the College of Physicians. Prude calls her "that most Pious and Learned young Gentlewoman" and a "subtle Disputant" in the "hard and knotty argument of metaphysical Learning." He also refers to her knowledge of languages and philosophy, her great modesty, friendship and charity.

735A [Puccini, Vincentio.] The life of Saint Mary Magdalene of Pazzi, A Carmelate Nunn. London, Printed for Randal Taylor, 1687. 134 pages. P 4158*. EEB Reel 1512:16.

Translated from the Italian in Paris where it was originally published in 1670, this work is an enquiry into the nature of "ecstasies," defined as the suspension of ordinary acts of reason and understanding caused by holy or evil spirits or natural causes. Saint Mary, given to raptures and bouts of melancholy, was austere, charitable and physically weak.

736A Pym, John. <u>The Reasons of the House of Commons to Stay the Queenes</u> <u>going to Holland. Delivered to the Lords, at a Conference the 14 July, by John</u> <u>Pym</u>. [London], 1641. 8 pages. P 4273. TT Reel 29:E.164(3).

Pym thinks the papists have a plan that touches on Henrietta Maria's journey to The Hague because they have been raising cash and gold. The House of Commons has heard the queen has packed money, jewels and plate--acts that may potentially impoverish the State. The MPs think it will dishonor the nation if the queen leaves because she is unhappy in England, so they offer to oblige her.

737A <u>Queene Eleanor's Confession: Shewing how King Henry...came to her</u>. London, Printed for C. Bates, [1670?] Broadside. Q 151.

In an imaginary scene, the queen, fearful of dying, sends for two friars. They are really Henry II and the Earl Martial in disguise. She confesses an adulterous liaison, a plot to poison the king, and a greater fondness for her eldest son over Henry's (her second).

738A <u>The Queene Leying in state who departed this life the 28 day of December</u> <u>1694</u>. [London], Printed and sould [sic] by Joh: [sic] Overton without Newbate, [1694?]. Broadside. Q 153.

This broadside depicts Mary II lying in state, mourned by five figures, probably women. An epitaph concludes: "...as having lost the sweetest Queen,/as ever in the Realm was seen."

739A <u>The Queen of England's Prophecie concerning Prince Charles</u>.   London, Printed for R. W., 1649. 6 pages. Q 154. TT Reel 85:E.552(13).

Henrietta Maria supposedly wrote to Prince Charles requesting a meeting at Amiens and describing her dream that all would be lost if he alienated Ireland and "cast himself" upon Scotland. His letter to her contains a prophecy delivered to Cromwell by some Yorkshire women. It describes a divine proclamation decreeing Parliament must reform the clergy, aid the poor, and resolve differences at home. The queen's authorship is doubtful.

<u>The Queen's Delight</u>. See 551A.

740A <u>A Queens Delight; Or, The Art of Preserving, Conserving and Candying</u>. [London], Printed by J. Winter, for Nat. Brook, 1668. 101 pages. Q 156B*.

This cookbook emphasizes instructions for making ale, sweets, preserved fruits, and medicinal herbs and fruit. Its "Table" refers to pages not included in the examined volume.

741A <u>The Queenes Letter to the Kings most Excellent Majesty; expressing her royal</u> <u>inclination to His Sacred Majesty...Sept. 7, 1647</u>. [London], 1647. 5 pages. Q 157E. TT Reel 64:E.407(11).

Henrietta Maria tells Charles I she regrets the new civil war. She advises him to "grant your Parliament and people whatsoever with a good Conscience and honour, you may." She warns he cannot lessen the Church's patrimony and but grant London and other strongholds the right to raise armies for the present. This item is suppositious.

742A The Queens Majesties Declaration and Desires to the States of Holland. [London], Printed for J. Tompson and A. Coe, 1642. 6 pages. Q 157F.

This document includes Henrietta Maria's message about the king's "levying" of forces and names of the lords who are to come to England. Both houses of Parliament received letters from Holland indicating ships were moving northward, but the English navy refused them entry. The queen laments civil unrest in Britain as well as reputed anti-royalist activities and warns of potential bloodshed. Henrietta Maria probably did not issue this declaration.

743A The Queens Majesties Letter to the Parliament of England, concerning Her Dread Soveraign Lord the King, and Her Proposals and Desires, touching his Royall Person, With the Resolution of the Parlilment [sic] concerning the said Letter. London, Printed for L. White, [1649]. 6 pages. H 1461. TT Reel 83:E.537(9).

This document is actually a discussion of Parliament's decision to try Charles I for treason. There is mention of a letter from the queen concerning the king, but apparently Parliament set it aside. It is neither included nor described.

744A The Queens Majesties Propositions to to [sic] the Kings Most Excellent Majesty. London, Printed for E. Cotton, 1647. Q 157G. TT Reel 64:E.407(40).

This Puritan military document requests that Lord Thomas Fairfax control the troops in London. It closes with the signature "The General's Declaration."

745A The Queens Proceedings in Yorkshire. [London], Printed for T. Wright, 1643. 4 pages. Q 158. EEB Reel 243:E.93(2) and TT Reel 16:E.93(2).

This report concerns Henrietta Maria's projected arrival in either York, with the Earl of Newcastle's army, or in London. It includes three resolutions passed by the House of Commons about the queen's raising of forces and circumstances surrounding her return to England.

746A The Queenes Speech as it was delivered to the House of Commons by Sir Thomas Jermyn. [London], 1641. Broadside. H 1467. EEB Reel 1760:18.

This broadside concerns reasons of the House of Commons to stay Henrietta Maria's voyage to Holland.

747A R., J. L.   An Elegy on the Death of her Late Sacred Majesty Mary the Second, Queen of England. York, Printed by John White for Francis Hildyard, 1695. 12 pages. R 39. EEB Reel 1534:5.

The poet laments his inadequate muse, given the importance of his subject. He stresses Mary's contributions to the Crown, the depth of her love for William and her legacy. He urges William to protect the values the monarchs shared. Excerpt: "In her a perfect Scheme of heav'n we see,/Beauty without, within all pietye."

748A [Rabisha, William.] <u>The Whole Body of Cookery Dissected...for Ladies and Gentlewomen</u>. London, Printed by R. W. for Giles Calvert, 1661. 260[4] pages. R 114*. EEB Reel 289:9.

This book includes menus and recipes for seasons of the year. Sections address candying, conserving, pickling, pastes and syrups. The dedication is to the Duchesses of Richmond and Buckingham, Lady Jane Lane, Lady Mary Tufton, and Lady Agnes Walker. Rabisha claims he has served as a master cook in several households.

749A Rainbowe, Edward. <u>A Sermon Preached at Walden in Essex...at the Interring of...Susanna, Countess of Suffolke</u>. London, Printed by W. Wilson for Gabriell Bedell, M. M. and T. C., 1649. 34 pages. R 141. TT Reel 83:E.532(40).

Rainbowe's sermon is primarily about the meaning of a good name. Material on the countess begins on page eleven. She is credited with a sharp wit, sound judgment, divine fancy, a good memory and a methodical mind. At twenty-two she left two children.

750A Rainbowe, Edward. <u>A Sermon Preached at the Funeral of the Rt. Hon. Anne, Countess of Pembroke, Dorset and Montgomery</u>. London, Printed for R. Royston and H. Broom, 1677. 68 pages. R 142. EEB Reel 397:14.

This typically effusive funeral sermon describes the deceased, Anne Herbert, Lady Clifford, as "a great Pattern of Vertue, and an eminent Benefactor to her Generation." Rainbowe discusses the proper roles of men and women in his commentary and includes biographical information about the countess.

751A [Raleigh, Carew.] <u>Observations upon Some particular Persons ... Compleat History of the Lives and Reignes of Mary, Queen of Scotland, and of Her son James</u>. London, Printed for Ga. Bedell and Tho. Collins, 1656. 21 pages. R 149. TT Reel 78:E.490(2).

Raleigh criticizes a book by William Sanderson (784A) that he alleges is by other people. He claims it is illogical, disjointed and unintelligible. Raleigh offers some biographical information about Sanderson, but says very little about his treatment of Mary.

752A [Ramsey, William.] <u>Conjugium Conjurgium: or, Some serious considerations on Marriage</u>. By William Seymar, pseud. London, Printed for John Amery, 1675. 92 pages. R 229*. EEB Reels 774:6 and 1429:8.

Ramsey argues against marriage and deprecates women in general. He calls children "certain cares" and "uncertain comforts," mentioning sons who betrayed their fathers. Ramsey encourages virginity and cautions especially against nonspiritual values in married life. Excerpt: "If thou be wise, since there is such hazard, such deceit in the Female Sex, keep thy self as thou art, 'tis best to be free." See also 571A.

753A <u>The Ranters Monster: Being a true Relation of one Mary Adams</u>. London, Printed for George Horton, 1652. 8 pages. A 488. TT Reel 101:E.658(6).

This anti-Ranter tract alleges that Mary Adams, a free love advocate, claimed she was the Virgin Mary about to give birth to Christ and that the Church's teachings were false because the messiah had not yet been born. The local minister imprisoned her. While in jail, after a nine-day labor, she supposedly had a toad-like stillborn monster with claws. She is said to have been covered with boils and blotches before her death in jail. The story is confirmed by the minister and ten other officials.

754A A Rare Example of a Vertuous Maid[en] in Paris who was...put in Prison...to compell her to Popery. [London, 1700?] Broadside. R 279C*.

A young Protestant woman was jailed by her mother and relations in an effort to force her conversion to Catholicism. She resisted and was allegedly burned at the stake. The author praises her courage in refusing the mass.

755A Rawson, Joseph. Poems on the Lamented Death of...Queen Mary. London, Printed for Thomas Bennet, 1695. 4 pages. R 378. EEB Reel 398:10.

Mary II is honored in this poem. The author expresses the country's grief but says little about her personal or leadership qualities. Excerpt: "Oh! She was innocent as Angels are/Chast, as those happy beings, and as fair:/Adorn'd with Princely Virtues as with blood;/As great as Heav'n could make her and as good."

756A Reasons for Crowning the Prince and Princess of Orange King and Queen Joyntly, and for placing Executive Power in the Prince alone.   n.p., 1689. Broadside. R 489. EEB Reel 775:18.

The author says James II has forfeited the crown by trying to "subvert the constitution of the Kingdom" through adherence to poor advice offered by Jesuits, foreigners and others. Thus his power has reverted to the people. The author supports a replacement who is not in the line of direct succession to avoid a dispute over a claim by the Prince of Wales and to meet the challenge presented by the present political situation in Europe. The author also considers a "Vigorous and masculine administration" to be "more capable to govern than a woman." The princely status of William is also invoked.

757A Reasons for the Reversal of the Decree against Mrs. Bertie, and her sons. [1690?] 3 pages. N.I.W.

This case concerns conditions placed on Eleanora Bertie's inheritance from her uncle. The original will contained none, but another required marriage to Lord Guildford within three years. She was removed from London against her will and controlled by others. The legal question turns on whether the case should be tried in equity, under civil law, or "whether that very Court which thus restrain'd her should judge her to have fail'd in her Duty." Bertie was the Countess of Abingdon.

758A Reasons Humbly Offer'd for Placing his Highness the Prince of Orange Singly, on the Throne, during Life. [London, 1689.] Broadside. R 538. EEB Reel 507:22.

The author offers four reasons to support the rule of William without Mary: It would prevent his return to Holland if Mary were to predecease him; dividing power would weaken the throne; disagreement between the two sovereigns would result in inefficiency and further weakness; and, finally, Mary would share in the glory without "the trouble of it," safe from "Solicitations on the behalf of papists," if William were king alone.

759A A Relation of the Miraculous Cure of Mrs. Lydia Hills.   Second Edition. London, Printed by W. Wilde, 1696. 16 pages. R 854*.

The author claims Mrs. Hills was cured of an old lameness. Her deposition to the Lord Mayor about it is included. She attributes her cure to prayer.

760A A Remonstrance of the Shee-citizens of London, And of Many Thousands of other freeborne Women of England. [London], 1647. 6 pages. R 1014. TT Reel 64:E.404(2).

This risque satire was supposedly written by women who complain their husbands are too "undernourished and tired from warres and hard times" to satisfy their wives sexually. They request license to copulate freely with the king's courtiers.

761A "The Resolution of the House of Commons touching the Queene of Bohemia and the Prince Elector Palatine." In The Articles or Charge exhibited in Parliament, against Matthew Wren. [London, 1641]. [1] page. Item: N.I.W. Collection: A 3882. TT Reel 29:E.165(4).

This resolution, appearing on page five, states the House of Commons "doth approve of his Majesties pious intentions in the behalfe of his...Sister" for advice and assistance. It may have angered Charles I who did not seek Parliament's approval for financial aid to his sister.

762A The Resolution of the Women of London to the Parliament. [London], Printed for William Watson, 1642. [6] pages. R 1159. EEB Reel 247:E.114(14) and TT Reel 20:E.114(14).

This satire proposes that, in war-time, married women scold their husbands so much they'll volunteer for the military. Then the wives can carouse and take lovers. The piece also mocks the king's "withdrawal" from the government. Blame for the king's disaffection is attributed to a "malignant party who hath perswaded [him] to raise this Army."

763A The Restor'd Maiden-head. A New Satyr against Woman: Occasion'd By an Infant, who was the cause of the Death of my Friend. Dondon [sic], Printed for H. Smith, 1691. 19 pages. R 1177. EEB Reel 799:6.

The relations of the sexes is the subject of this humorous poem. Misogynistic, sometimes caustic in tone, it reviews famous historical incidents like the ravishing of Helen and Leda.

764A Reyner, Edward. Considerations Concerning Marriage, the Honour, Duties, Benefits, Troubles of it. London, Printed by J. T. for Thomas Newberry, 1657. 87 pages. R 1221. EEB Reel 474:9.

This religious tract contains many biblical references and, while it purports to focus on marriage, it simultaneously develops the dogma of the inferiority of women. Reyner attends to the mutual duties of partners and the sanctity of marriage. The problems children bring are addressed under "Troubles."

765A Reynolds, Edward. Mary Magdalens Love to Christ. Opened In a Sermon Preached at the Funeral of Mistris Elizabeth Thomason. London, 1659. 68 pages. R 1264. TT Reel 227:E.1820(1).

Reynolds speaks of Mary's love as stronger than the learning of theologians and capable of immediate knowledge of Christ. Only the final five pages contain information about Thomason. She is called young, solemn, meek-spirited and industrious. During a year spent with his family, she showed great interest in the moral development of his children. She loved privacy, reading and prayer.

766A Reynolds, Lancelot. A Panegyrick on her most Excellent Majestie, Katherine, Queen of England. London, Printed by R. Vaughan, [1661]. 8 Pages. R 1320. EEB Reel 290:9.

This poem honors the arrival of Catherine of Braganza, who came from a Portuguese cloister in 1662 to marry Charles II. The poem says little about Catherine; it is formulaic in its praise of the union.

767A The Rising Sun: or, Verses upon the Queen's Birth-Day. London, 1690. 20 pages. R 1538A. EEB Reel 799:23.

In this occasional poem, Mary II is compared both to Queen Elizabeth and, ironically because of her barren marriage, to a nursing mother. Her qualities of piety and judgment are celebrated, and there is mention of her refusal to receive from Parliament a subsidy separate from her husband, William.

768A Robinson, Ralph. Safe Conduct...A Sermon Preached at Dunstans in the East London...at the Funerall of Mrs. Thomasin Barnardiston, late Wife of Mr. Samuel Barnardiston, Merchant. London, Printed by R. I. for Stephen Bowtell, 1654. 93 pages. R 1711. TT Reel 125:E.823(7).

This sermon is dedicated to the widower, who requested its publication. Biographical information about his wife begins in the final few pages. From a wealthy family, she had a religious education and proved a loving wife and good companion. She is called humble, meek and modest. After a brief illness during which she sustained head pains, she died at twenty.

769A [Rochester, John Wilmot, Earl of.] Female Excellence: Or Woman Displayed, In Several Satyrick Poems. London, Printed for Norman Nelson, 1679. 8 pages. R 1749. EEB Reel 777:9.

Women are accused of witchcraft and sorcery in this satire: they are born into slavery, while men are born to rule. The author laments his victimization by feminine beauty despite women's imperfections. The Houghton Library, Harvard University, suggests this work has been erroneously attributed to the Earl of Rochester. Robert Gould has also been credited with authoship.

770A [Rochester, John Wilmot, Earl of.] A Satyr against Marriage. [London, 1680.] Broadside. S 710A.

More virulent than the typical anti-marriage work, this brief poem is "Directed to that In-considerable animal, called HUSBAND." It satirizes the allegedly horrid life of husbands. The author is noted for his bitter melancholy view. The Houghton Library, Harvard University, attributes this work to Rochester and notes it should not be confused with an anonymous work of the same title published in 1700.

771A [Roesslin, Eucharius.] The Birth of Mankynde, otherwise named The Womans Booke. Fourth Edition. London, Printed for J. L., Henry Hood, Abel Roper and Richard Tomlins, 1654. 193 pages. R 1782B*.

This classic gynecological text, originally published in England in 1545, is based on Roesslin's Latin De Partu Hominis. The translator, physician Thomas Raynalde, says the illustrations will elucidate the text for female nonpractitioners. Nine parts address conception, childbirth, nursing, miscarriages and the fetus. This edition follows modern medical principles and corrects earlier inaccurate information.

772A R[ogers], D[aniel.] Matrimonial Honour: or, The Mutual Crowne and Comfort of godly, loyall, and chaste Marriage. London, Printed by Th. Harper for Philip Nevil, 1642. 387 pages. R 1797. EEB Reel 925:3.

This massive treatise discusses societal and religious benefits of marriage, holding that a disciplined family insures an orderly household and commonwealth. Rogers delineates the duties of each family member and defends traditional marriage as a buttress to church and state. He reiterates women's duty to nurse, be helpful and subordinate to husbands. He also alleges that if both spouses are bad, the woman is usually worse.

773A Rogers, Timothy. The Character of a Good Woman, Both in a Single and Married State...Funeral Discourse...of Mrs. Elizabeth Dunton. London, For John Harris, 1697. 174 pages. R 1846. EEB Reel 509:4.

This funeral sermon is most interesting, both because of its content and its subject, Elizabeth Dunton. She was the wife of John Dunton, publisher of The Athenian Mercury, and a supporter of women's education. The essay shows strong support for women's learning and mentions feminists such as Mary Astell. See also 305A.

774A [Rowlands, Samuel.] A Crew of kind London Gossips, All met to be Merry. Complaining of their Husbands. With their Husbands Answers in their own Defence. London, 1663. 144 pages. R 2078. EEB Reel 437:9.

Dedicated to "Mayds of London" who are entreated not to abuse their husbands when they marry, women humorously enumerate male shortcomings--stinginess, physical abuse ("If he strike me, Ile match him blow for blow"), drunkenness, gambling, filthiness, adultery, and so on. The husbands answer in turn, complaining of their domineering, gossiping wives.

775A <u>The Royall Virgin. Or, The Declaration of Sevfral [sic] Maydens In and About the once Honourable City of London</u>. [London], Printed for Virgin Hope-well, and are to be sold at the Maiden-Starre, 1660 (in hand, Feb. 9, 1659). Broadside. R 2156. TT Reel 247:669.f.23(36).

This political satire is a call for the restoration of Charles II and a denunciation of the Rump Parliament.

<u>The Royal Wanton</u>. See 31A.

776A Rymer, Thomas. <u>A Poem on the Arrival of Queen Mary. Feb. the 12th 1689</u>. London, Printed for Awnsham Churchil, 1689. R 2427. EEB Reel 1156:10.

This laudatory poem honors Mary, Princess of Orange, who had just arrived at Whitehall from The Hague to accept the crown.

777A [S., B.] <u>The History of Mademoiselle de St. Phale, Giving a Full Account of the Miraculous Conversion of a Noble French Lady and her Daughter, to the Reformed Religion</u>. London, Printed by J. A. for J. Hancock, 1691. 202 pages. H 2124. EEB Reel 73:6.

This volume is supposedly a translated biography of a young Burgundian woman raised as a Catholic. Her mother urges her to convert her brother, who mocks her religion. There is much discussion of religious dogma. The heroine finally decides to convert. Although the story may be true, female authorship is doubtful.

778A S., J. <u>A Brief History of the Pious and Glorious Life and Actions of the Most Illustrious Princess, Mary Queen of England</u>. Second Edition. London, Printed for John Gwillim, 1695. 136 pages. S 46*. EEB Reel 990:11.

This narrative of Queen Mary's life concerns how she and William assumed the throne and the events leading to her death.

779A S., M. <u>The Great Birth of Man: or, the Excellency of Man's Creation and Endowments Above the Original of Woman</u>. Second Edition. London, Printed for J. M. and Sold by John Taylor, 1688. 24 pages. S 114A*. EEB Reel 1046:4.

This lengthy poem about the creation contains a description of women's allegedly base nature and the "wiser brain" of men, which renders them immune to temptation by Satan. The author describes men as "the great Object of Omnipotence,/Made like a God, both Masculine and Brave,/Design'd the Empire of the World to have." As creatures of a lower order, women are supposedly meant to serve.

780A S., T. <u>An Account of Queen Mary's Methods for Introducing Popery</u>. London, Printed for John Gay, 1681. 12 pages. S 150. EEB Reel 509:29.

Dedicated to the Earl of Shaftesbury, the work describes the introduction of Catholicism into Scotland by Mary, Queen of Scots as a model of a possible scenario for 1681. It chronicles how her council encouraged her, how she gradually allowed the Catholic Church to gain dominance and how, finally, she persecuted Protestants.

781A [Saint-Real, Caesar Viscard de.] Underline: The Memoires of the Dutchess of Mazarine. London, Printed and are to be sold by William Cademan, 1676. 130 pages. S 355*. EEB Reel 1366:13.

This romantic account of political intrigues and courtly dalliances is based on biographical information about the duchess, Hortense Mancini, but apparently was not written by her. It is attributed to Saint-Real by the Folger Shakespeare Library, Washington, D.C., although the title page lists de la Porte as author and P. Porter as translator.

782A The Saints Testimony finishing through Sufferings: Or, The Proceedings of the Court against the servants of Jesus at the Assizes in Banbury. Also a relation of Margaret Vivers. London, Printed for Giles Calvert, 1655. 44 pages. S 365. TT Reel 130:E.857(7).

Short pieces describe the bases for prison sentences given to Quakers Anne Audland, Jane Waugh and Sarah Tims; and defend Margaret Vivers, detained for no apparent cause but speaking out in church. A religious tract by Anne Audland, "A Warning from the Spirit of the Lord," is included.

783A Sanderson, William.   An Answer to a scurrilous pamphlet intituled, Observations upon a Compleat History of...Mary. London, Printed for the Author and are to be Sold by George Sawbridge and Richard Tomlins, 1656. 32 pages. S 644. EEB Reel 226:7.

The author defends his biography of Mary, Queen of Scots (784A), refuting the allegedly libelous statements of his critic, Carew Raleigh (see 751A).

784A Sanderson, William. A Complete History of the Lives and Reigns of Mary Queen of Scotland. London, Printed for Humphrey Mosely, Richard Tomlins and George Sawbridge, 1656. 599 pages. S 647. EEB Reel 226:9.

This work is about James I, as well as the political, religious and military history of Scotland. Material about Mary centers on her disputes and relations with the Scottish lords and Elizabeth, commerce with John Knox and details of her execution.

785A A Satyr against Whoring. In Answer to a Satyr against Marriage. London, Printed for J. Green, 1682. Broadside. S 716*. EEB Reel 1293:30 and 31.

This broadside attacks lustful men who frequent prostitutes, contract venereal disease and infect their wives, wreaking havoc on their families and society. The author says they should be condemned to continue until they "unpittied on a Dunghil die." The author implies their actions can be understood, for being a husband is difficult, and the demands of a wife and marriage are many.

786A A Satyr [in verse, on Judge Jeffreys and the Duchess of Portsmouth]. [London, 1680.] Broadside. S 707*. EEB Reel 1293:28.

This anti-papist satire characterizes Jeffreys, the judge who exonerated prospective royal assassin Wakeman, as a friend of the pope. Portsmouth, a mistress of Charles II, is the only person named specifically: "Portsmouth, that

Pocky-Bitch,/A Damn'd Papistical-Drab,/An ugly deformed Witch,/Eaten up with the Mange and Scab."

787A The Scarlet Beast Stript Naked, being the mistery of the Meal-tub the second time unravelled; or a brief answer to the Popish-midwives scandalous narrative, intituled Malice Defeated. London, Printed for D. Mallet, [1680]. 4 pages. S 826. EEB Reel 822:14.

This short piece is an anti-papist attack against Elizabeth Cellier, a midwife involved in the infamous Meal-tub Plot and her self-defense, Malice Defeated. The author contends Cellier is the most talented defender of Roman Catholicism; her ability to deceive surpasses the notorious Pope Joan. See also 137B, 138B, D 184, 512A, 603A and 880A.

788A Scot, Reginald. The Discovery of Witchcraft: Proving, That the Compacts and contracts of witches with Devils...are but Erroneous Novelties and imaginary Conceptions. In Sixteen Books. London, Printed for A. Clark, and sold by Dixy Page, 1665. 292 pages. S 945*. EEB Reels 159:5, 578:3, 822:21 and 1129:18.

Scot's book is similar to 15A. Scot singles out witch hunters who supposedly transform the spirits of devils into animate beings. He says it is generally poor old women who are accused of witchcraft, harming neighbors' animals or possessions. He dismisses simpleminded people who accept stories about witches, and analyzes scripture to show it does not support a broad interpretation of the powers of witches.

789A Scott, John. A Sermon Preached at the funeral of the Lady Newland. London, 1690. 19 pages. S 2075.

This sermon is primarily about the afterlife, but it contains some commentary on the deceased, whom the author did not know. He characterizes her as devout and self-critical, possessing many womanly virtues.

The Second Part of the Amours of Messalina. See 31A.

790A The Second Part of The boy of Bilson: or, a True...Relation of the Impostor, Susanna Fowles. London, Printed and are to be sold by E. Whitlock, [1698]. 24 pages. S 2300. EEB Reel 1557:27.

Susanna Fowles repeatedly argued with her husband about her dowry, finally claiming possession so she could leave him. When two bishops discovered her ruse, she confessed the deception. Perry thinks she was easily convicted because of her poor reputation, "being of a testy froward Temper, a Temper incident to Old Age." See also 368A.

791A The Secret History of the Most Renowned Queen Elizabeth and the E[arl] of Essex. Cologne [London], Printed for Will with the Wisp [R. Bentley?], 1680. 115 pages. S 2342*. EEB Reels 293:5 and 1752:24.

This popular fictionalized account of the "affair" between Queen Elizabeth and Robert Devereux, Earl of Essex contains a number of flagrant historical errors.

792A Sermon, William. <u>The Ladies Companion, or, the English Midwife</u>. London, Printed for Edward Thomas, 1671. 206 pages. S 2628. EEB Reel 334:3.

Like other gynecological texts, this describes how pregnant women should behave, special problems arising from a difficult labor, advice for midwives and lay information for childbirth preparation.

793A [Settle, Elkanah.] <u>An Epilogue to the French Midwife's Tragedy, who was burnt in Leicester-fields, March 2, 1687 for the barbarous murder of her husband Denis Hobry</u>. London, Printed for Randal Taylor, 1688. Broadside. S 2680A.

In this poem about the controversial murder of a husband by his abused wife, French midwife Mary Hobry is compared to Medea and called deserving of death. See also 8A, 431A and 940A.

794A Settle, Elkanah. <u>The Female Prelate: Being the History of the Life and Death of Pope Joan</u>. London, Printed for W. Cademan, 1680. 72 pages. S 2684*. EEB Reel 877:7.

This tragedy portrays Pope Joan, a female prelate who, disguised as a man, supposedly served as pope until her death soon after assuming office. She allegedly gave birth during her tenure. This tale was the subject of many publications throughout the century.

795A Sewall, Samuel. <u>Mrs. Judith Hull, of Boston, in N[ew] E[ngland]...late wife of John Hull Esq</u>. [Boston, (Mass.), Printed for Bartholomew Green, 1695.] Broadside. S 2819.

Sewall includes a brief obituary and epitaph emphasizing Hull's religious zeal and resemblance to her namesake, the biblical Judith. Excerpt: "An Humble Soul, Trim'd with an High Neglect/Of Gay Things, but with Ancient Glories deck't."

796A Sewall, Samuel. <u>Mrs. Mehetabel Holt...A Person of Early Piety</u>. [Boston, 1689/90.] Broadside. S 2820.

This broadside apparently reproduces the grave-site epitaph of an American woman of thirty-eight who died in 1677 at Bishop-Stoke. Excerpt: "America afforded me my Birth,/And Friendly Europe grants me Whit'ning Earth...Quietly rest then let my hopeful Dust/Until the Resurrection of the Just."

797A Sh[b], Jo. <u>A Funeral Elegy on the Right Honourable the Lady Viscountesse Castleton</u>. [London, 1667?] Broadside. S 2831. EEB Reel 1315:14.

The deceased was born in Yorkshire, died in London and was married to a member of the House of Commons. She is described as a good Christian, charitable and properly modest. Excerpt: "Able she was with Learned men to reason,/Nimbly confuting Heresy and Treason."

798A Shadwell, Thomas. <u>A Congratulatory Poem to the most illustrious Queen Mary upon her arrival in England</u>. London, Printed for James Knapton, 1689. 7 pages. S 2840. EEB Reel 368:9.

This flattering poem avers England enthusiastically awaits the ascension of William and Mary. Excerpt: "She comes, she comes, the Fair, the Good, the Wise,/With loudest Acclaimations rend the skies."

799A Shannon, Francis Boyle, Viscount. Discourses and Essays Useful for the Vain Modish Ladies and their Gallants. Two Parts. Second Edition. [London], Printed for John Taylor, 1696. S 2963*. EEB Reel 1678:5.

This massive tome, encouraging women to be virtuous and control their vanity, is dedicated to Elizabeth, Countess of Northumberland. Shannon complains that with encouragement from men, contemporary women have departed from Eve's role as helpmate. He suggests much bad social change stems from the preoccupation of parents with matching estates rather than individuals.

800A [Shannon, Francis Boyle, Viscount.]   Several Discourses and Characters Address'd to the ladies of the Age. Wherein the vanities of the modish women are discovered, written at the request of a lady, by a person of honour.   London, Printed for Christopher Wilkinson, 1689. 199 pages. S 2965B. EEB Reel 297:44.

In this epistle directed to fashionable ladies, Shannon says although he has formerly encouraged women to expand their experience, he now wishes to dissuade them from worldly endeavors and to return to innocence.   He suggests they leave London to pursue a simpler life in the countryside. This generally anti-female tract criticizes society women.

801A Shaw, John.   Mistress Shaw's Tomb-stone. Or, The Saints Remains... Remarkable passages in the holy life and happy death of...Mrs. Dorothy Shaw. London, Printed for Nathaniel Brooks, 1658. 104 pages. S 3029.

Shaw was a minister in Hull and, describing himself as his wife's dearest friend, he presents some of her religious writings for himself and his six daughters. The Shaws were married twenty-five years. Emphasis is on her charity, piety and duties as a minister's wife.

802A The She Wedding: Or A Marriage, between Mary A. Seamans Mistress, and Margaret a Carpenters Wife at Deptford. London, George Croom, 1684. 7 pages. S 3055. EEB Reel 339:10.

A misogynistic prologue discusses female cunning and presents a remarkably coarse fictionalized conversation among some women. The story tells of two women who married--one single and pregnant, the other disguised as a man. Their union insured that the pregnant woman could gain support from her lover's mother by showing a false marriage certificate. Both were jailed for disgracing "the honest state of matrimony."

803A Shinkin ap Shone Her Prognostication for the Ensuing Year 1654. By Shinkin ap Shone, pseud. [London], Printed for the Author and to be sold at His Shop, [1654]. 8 pages. A 2385. TT Reel 112:E.731(5).

This almanac foretells worldwide events. It also offers a story about Welsh origins. Female authorship is doubtful because of the book's humorous style and its imprint. Excerpt: "Her duz humbly conceive, that this Star duz portend (if any thing at all) either peace or war, or both, but which her do not very well know...because her library was burnt at the destruction of Sodom and Gomorah."

804A [Shirley, John.] The Accomplished Ladies Rich Closet of Rarities: or, the Ingenious Gentlewoman and Servant maids Delightful Companion. London, Printed by W. W. for Nicholas Boddington and Josiah Blare, 1687. 231 pages. S 3498*.

This household guide is intended for women "from infancy to extremity of Age" and "from the Lady, to the inferiour Servant- Maid." It contains recipes, cooking techniques, beauty aids, rules of etiquette, etc. The second section, directed to young gentlewomen, concerns their behavior towards their parents and servants and establishes rules for selection of a husband.

805A [Shirley, John.] The Illustrious History of Women, or, A compendium of the many Virtues that Adorn the Fair Sex. London, Printed by John Harris, 1686. 158 pages. S 3508. EEB Reel 1315:18.

Shirley describes renowned women, especially classical and biblical figures. They are typically heroic, wise and beautiful. He discusses women who represent chaste love, piety, patience, temperance and courage, concluding with principles that supposedly govern a woman's spiritual and rational capacities, including determinants of the soul's immortality. Shirley closes with a litany of the characteristics preferred in a wife or widow.

806A A Short Testimony concerning the Death and Finishing of Judieth [sic] Fell. London, Printed and sold by Andrew Sowle, 1682. 7 pages. S 3633. EEB Reel 1536:37.

The deceased, who died at twenty-four, was a good Quaker, the daughter of Thomas and Anne Fell. She was possibly a relation of Margaret Fell Fox. Throughout an illness marked by violent fits, she demonstrated great courage. Commentaries by relatives are appended; notably, her uncle raised her for ten years while her father was incarcerated for failure to pay tithes.

807A [Shower, John.] A Sermon Preacht upon the Death of Mrs. Anne Barnardiston. London, Printed by J. A. for Benjamin Alsop and John Dunton, 1682. 38 pages. S 3690. EEB Reel 728:19.

Shower's funeral sermon was written for a woman who died at seventeen, having learned modesty and virtue from her older sisters. His primary emphasis is on her piety with a lengthy description of her final days.

808A Signes and Wonders from Heaven. With a true Relation of a Monster borne in Ratcliffe Highway. London, Printed for T. Forcet, 1646. 5 pages. S 3777. TT Reel 49:E.295(2).

This pamphlet discusses several events, including alleged witchcraft in Stepney Parish and the execution of others accused in Suffolke. Most of the text is about a monster born near London to Mistris Hart, a courteous and religious woman. The child was a noseless, legless, handless hermaphrodite whose single ear was attached to its neck. It succumbed soon after birth.

809A The Sisters of the Scabards holiday: or, A dialogue between...Mrs. Bloomesbury, and Mrs. Long-acre. [London], 1641. 5 pages. S 3909. EEB Reel 255:E.168(8) and TT Reel 29:E.168(8).

"Prostitutes" discuss the ramifications for their profession of the civil law in this attack on the lasciviousness and venery of lawyers. Law clerks allegedly visit the proprietors of brothels between court sessions, trying to blackmail them. The prostitutes are concerned with lodgings and medical care for their older sisters. A typical device is employed--criticism of a group (lawyers) through its alleged connection with immoral women. The Brothers of the Blade is a rejoinder.

810A The Snare of the Devill discovered; or, A true relation of the sad condition of Lydia the wife of John Rogers in Wapping. London, Printed for Edward Thomas, 1658. 10 [2] pages. S 4388. TT Reel 228:E.1833(2).

Lydia, the wife of a carpenter, made a contract with the devil for money. Her confession to a minister is paraphrased here. Although formerly religious, she became an Anabaptist and a follower of astrology. She claimed the devil appeared to her in the form of a man who asked for her blood because he had no ink; she obliged him by cutting her vein. The tale is presented as a warning to Christians to beware of heretics and seducers.

811A Some things memorably considered in the Conditions, Life, and Death of the ever blessed and now eternally happy, Mris. Anne Bowes. [London, 1641?] Broadside. S 4624. TT Reel 245: 669.f.4(29).

Bowes died at forty-one after a lengthy illness--perhaps a brain tumor--marked by intense pain and protracted insomnia. She was pious, modest, obedient, bashful and industrious. This eulogy focuses on her courage, selflessness and strong faith.

812A [Sowersby, Leonard.]   The Ladies Dispensatory, containing the Natures, Vertues and Qualities of all Herbs. London, Printed for R. Ibitson and are to be sold by George Calvert, 1652. 317 [21] pages. S 4781. TT Reel 172:E.1258(1).

This work contains long lists of medical recipes for diseases, not just those of women. They constitute an attempt to organize "Simples useful in Physick." Sowersby says no such systematic account has yet been published in English.

813A [Spagnuoli, Battista Mantuanus.]   Mantuan English'd...or The character of a Bad Woman. [London? 1680?] 4 pages. S 4792.

Spagnuoli claims he does not wish to offend, but merely to describe the archetypal bad woman. She is characterized as the source of all torment, as lustful ("While to allay, not quench her wanton [lust]/ Sometimes she Dildoes, Sometimes Fires, Stalion hires"), unfeeling, odiferous and arrogant. Spagnuoli invites someone else to write about the good woman.

814A Spencer, Benjamin. A Dumb Speech. Or A Sermon made, but no Sermon preached, at the Funerall of the Right Vertuous, Mrs. Mary Overman, Wife to Mr. Thomas Overman, the younger...Southwarke. London, Printed for John Clark, 1646. 75 pages. S 4942. TT Reel 167:E.1180(3).

This sermon, dedicated to the widower, is based on Philip 1.21. Biographical material is rather vague. Overman's family, named Breton, was ancient. Her industry, piety and courage in the face of death are noted. An appendix by Thomas Overman mentions his wife's humility, righteousness and quotidian reading and writing devotions. Overman calls himself her "passionate admirer."

815A A Spirit Moving in the Women-Preachers: or, Certaine Quaeres vented and put forth unto this affronted, Brazen-faced, Strange, New Feminine Brood. London, Printed for Henry Shepheard, and William Ley, 1646. [10] pages. S 4990. TT Reel 53:E.324(10).

The author criticizes women preachers' "foolish, proud, vain-glorious insolencies...transgressing the rules of Nature, Modesty, Divinities, Discretion," etc. He accuses them of enchanting and dominating men and of speaking to mixed congregations. Calling them the weaker vessel, he says the spirit of wisdom and understanding in Christ is not meant for women.

816A Sprint, John. The Bride-Womans Counselor. Being a Sermon Preach'd at a Wedding. May the 11th, 1699. London, Printed by H. Hills, 1700? 16 pages. S 5084. EEB Reel 298:16.

This sermon addresses the duties of women "to content and please their husbands." Sprint says a woman's lot is "harder and more difficult than man['s]." This fact, coupled with their alleged inferior intelligence, accounts for their rule-governed lives. Women who are disobedient, stubborn, or foolish are responsible for corrupting men and causing marital discord. He entreats men to abide women for their spiritual welfare. See response by Mary Chudleigh, 149B.

817A The State of the Case in Brief, Between the Countess of Sterlin [sic] and others by petition in Parliament. London, 1654. Broadside. L 1824. TT Reel 246:669.f.19(43).

Servants and heirs of Lady Powell complain her niece Anne Levingston and her husband tried to usurp Powell's estate by firing servants and denying visitation rights to relatives. The couple allegedly extorted 40,000 pounds from Powell, and Levingston endeared herself to Powell through sorcery, love-power and other "wicked practices." This case is interesting because of references to Levingston's childlessness--presumably a reason why she should not inherit--and false claims of motherhood. See also 517A, 869A and Addendum 29.

818A Stearne, John, of Lawshall. A Confirmation and Discovery of Witch-craft. London, Printed for William Wilson, 1648. 67 pages. S 5365. EEB Reel 1390:14.

Stearne cites scripture extensively to support his belief in evil, Satan and witches. He describes the techniques of witchcraft, noting female witches outnumber males, "especially of the hurting witches." He speculates about the predominance of women, naming indicted individuals and charges against them.

819A Stepney, George. A Poem dedicated to the Blessed Memory of her late gracious majesty Queen Mary. London, Printed for Jacob Tonson, 1695. 8 pages. S 5468. EEB Reel 515:24.

Stepney's eulogy honors Mary II. He says the sword, represented by William, and the justice and care that characterized Mary, will both devolve upon William. Excerpt: "All that was Charming in the Fairer Kind,/With Manly Sense, and Resolution joyned;/A Mein compos'd of Mildness and of State,/Not by Constraint, or Affection Great."

820A Stevenson, Matthew. The Low Estate of the Low-Countrey Countess of Holland on her Deathbed. London, Printed for M. Stevenson, 1672. Broadside. S 5502.

Stevenson attacks Holland as a woman who "Fancy'd herself Sole Sovereign of the Main." He uses female sexual imagery to comment on her domination of the seas, suggesting she has become emotional and unrestrained.

Stiff, Mary. [pseud.] The Good Womens Cryes against the excise of all their Commodities. See 397A.

821A Stockden, John. The seven women confessors...which lived...in Coven-Garden [sic]. London, Printed for John Smith, [1642]. [5] pages. S 5695. EEB Reel 249:E.134(15) and TT Reel 24:E.134(15).

Stockden's anti-Catholic satire portrays church missionaries quartered in a Covent Garden brothel. The prostitutes offer their services--"not only for absolution, but distraction." Their patrons vow never to confess to a man again.

822A Stockton, Owen. Consolation in Life and Death...of Mrs. Ellen Asty. [London], Printed by J. R. for Tho. Parkhurst, 1681. [139] pages. S 5697. EEB Reel 1072:11.

This lengthy sermon is an expanded version of one Stockton had preached before his death; it was later published posthumously. The final pages, paginated separately, describe Asty's life. Although emphasis is on religious duty, her private life is treated briefly.

823A Strafford, Thomas Wentworth, Earl of. A Letter sent from the Earl of Strafford to his Lady in Ireland. [London], 1641. 4 pages. S 5786*. EEB Reel 261:E.208(14).

This letter was written by a leading advisor to Charles I shortly before his execution. In a moving, loving letter, he asks his wife not to mourn for long. He apologizes for leaving a meager estate, notes his debtors and debts, and encourages her to re-marry quickly, but to be chary of fortune hunters.

824A A Strange and Horrible Relation of a Bloody and Inhumane Murther committed on the body of a Jewish Woman...Shropshire. London, 1674. 6 pages. S 5818A.

This tale, recounted also in 835A, is about a young pregnant Jewish woman who was burned in a fireplace after secretly giving birth. Most of the document tell of John Adams, a servant who murdered his master's wife and daughter after robbing them and igniting their house. See also 247A.

825A A Strange and Lamentable Accident that happened lately at Mears Ashby in Northamptonshire. London, Printed for Rich. Harper and Thomas Wine, 1642. 5 pages. S 5819. EEB Reel 246:E.113(15) and TT Reel 20:E.113(15).

Mary Wilmore, the wife of a rough mason, delivered a headless child with a cross upon its breast. She had said she would rather have a child with no head than to have its head signed with a cross in baptism. The account is signed by John Locke, a cleric.

826A Strange and Miraculous Newes from Turkie...Of a Woman which was seene in the Firmament...at...Mahomets Tombe. London, Printed for Perrey, 1642. 5 pages. S 5824. EEB Reel 252:E.151(2) and TT Reel 27:E.151(2).

A vision of an ethereal woman was seen in the sky near Mohammed's tomb in Medina. She was surrounded by Arabian armies which fled when she opened a volume revealing the Moslem religion to be false and Christ to be the true savior. The English ambassador at Constantinople received this information.

827A Strange and Terrible Newes from Cambridge, Being a true Relation of the Quakers bewitching of Mary Philips out of the Bed from her Husband in the Night, and transformed her into the shape of a bay mare. London, Printed for C. Brooks, 1659. [8] pages. S 5827. EEB Reels 515:41.

A woman, supposedly enchanted, was transformed into a horse. After returning to human form, she accused a couple of the bewitching, but they denied the charge and were acquitted in court. The author cites other tales as proof of witchcraft and magic, claiming both witches and magicians are sent by the "Prince of Darkness." The Quakers are accused of "tampering about futurities," predicting London and Southwark would "[desolve] and [extinguish] in smoak." See also 828A.

828A The Strange and Terrible news from Cambridge proved false. In [Blackley, James.] A Lying Wonder Discovered. London, Printed for Thos. Simmons, 1659. 8 pages. Item: N.I.W. Collection: B 3075. EEB Reel 809:7.

The second item in this pamphlet answers 827A wherein Quakers were accused of witchcraft by Mary Pryor, known as a lewd alcoholic. (Apparently money to prosecute the case came from local Anglican priests.) The author includes an interesting argument against witchcraft, basing his incredulity on God's omnipotence: He claims Satan cannot create or alter life.

829A Strange and Terrible News from Ireland, or a full and true relation of a maid at Dublin. [London, 1673?]. 5 pages. S 5829.

A young woman accused of a crime, "solemnly wished the Divel might burn her if she did it." The following night she was found with her skin lying by her, "black like burnt leather." The author bemoans the spread of filthy curses, profane oaths and atheism.

830A Strange and Terrible news from the Queene in Holland Shewing plainely the intelligence of the king of His intention to raise Armes. London, Printed for Thomas Baker, 1642. 5 pages. S 5832. EEB Reel 515:42.

Henrietta Maria, in residence at The Hague, allegedly heard of the king's quarrels with Parliament and his preparations for battle. She received weekly intelligence reports and was asked to raise arms to support him, but resolved not to return until there was peace at home. The Dutch preferred that "no ammunition be conveyed to this kingdome under pretence of his Majesties service."

831A A Strange and True Conference between Two Notorious Bawds, Damarose Page and Pris Fotheringham. By Megg Spenser. [London?], 1660. 8 pages. S 5833A.

In this imaginary conversation, two prostitutes in Newgate trade anecdotes about their families and professional experiences. They posit rules to control stealing amongst their colleagues and customers. Fotheringham wishes to "reduce this Price-office of my Chuck-Office." The Guildhall Library notes Megg Spenser is the pseudonymous "over-seer of the whores" on the Bank-Side.

832A Strange and True Newes from Jack-a-Newberries Six Windmills: or the Crafty, impudent, common-whore (turn'd Bawd) Anatomised. By Peter Aretine Cardinall of Rome. [London?], Printed for Rodericus and Castro, 1660. 6 pages. S 5835.

This scatological story tells of Pris Fotheringham, a notorious prostitute who supposedly went to Newgate and caught the pox before returning to her husband. Rules for pick-pocketing are included as well as details of the prostitute's "chuck-office" trick--wherein she is said to have stood on her head while men tossed a half-crown toward her breechless bottom.

833A The Strange and Wonderful History of Mother Shipton. [London], Printed for W. H. and sold by J. Conyers, 1686. 24 pages. S 5848. EEB Reel 1733:4.

The father of the mythical Mother Shipton, supposedly from Yorkshire, was a necromancer. This volume describes her birth, life, death, burial and prophecies--about Henry VIII, Edward VI, Mary, Elizabeth, James I, Charles I and II, and so on. See also 428A and 730A.

834A Strange and Wonderful News from Durham. Or The Virgins Caveat Against Infant-Murther. London, 1679. 5 pages. N.I.W.

A lovely and virtuous young woman became pregnant and, attempting to conceal her sin, secretly murdered the infant upon its birth. The child's ghost revealed its grave, and the "beautiful Unfortunate" was arrested.

835A Strange and Wonderful News from Warwick-shire...And also a true Relation of a horrible Murther committed on the Body of a Jewish Woman. London, Printed for J. Coniers and Charles Passenger, [1680?]. 5 pages. S 5869AB.

A rabbi's daughter of questionable morals conceived a child and was thrown into a fire, as allegedly prescribed by Jewish law. The story was reported by a midwife who heard her screams as she left the delivery site. The tale follows the first item in the collection, a ghost story. See also 824A.

836A Strange and Wonderful News from Yowel in Surrey; Giving a True and Just Account of One Elizabeth Burgiss. West Smithfield, Printed for J. Clarke, 1681. 6 pages. S 5869B. EEB Reel 1558:8.

Burgiss was a servant who, after a visit by Joan Buts (suspected of witchcraft), experienced strange occurrences: books flew about the house, items came sailing toward her, and she had lumps of clay pulled from her back, full of pins and thorns. Later her mother attacked Buts at a local fair. See also 11A.

837A Strange and Wonderful Relation of a Barbarous Murder Committed by James Robison, a Brick-layer, upon the body of his own wife. London, 1679. [8] pages. S 5874A.

Robison, the son of lower-class industrious parents, was influenced by his unsavory companions. He married at his parents' request to settle down; however, he was not content and apparently murdered his wife. The second tale concerns a wayward priest accused of murdering a child begotten of his affair with a young gentlewoman.

838A A Strange and Wonderful Relation of the Burying alive of Joan Bridges of Rochester in the County of Kent. London, Printed for E. G., 1646. 6 pages. S 5878.

In a drunken stupor, Joan Bridges was mistaken for dead and buried. The women of the town took up a collection for her disinterment. The author claims she was seen after burial by over 500 persons trying to escape the coffin.

839A A Strange but True Account of the Barbarous Usage of Three Young Ladies in France for being Protestants. London, Printed for E. Brooks, 1681. Broadside. S 5881. EEB Reel 1131:6.

This allegedly true tale was meant to expose mistreatment of Protestants in France. Three sisters lost their brothers in battle and were orphaned when their parents died from grief. A Jesuit priest attempted to place them in a convent, but they were saved by a Protestant who helped them escape to England.

840A Strange News from Arpington near Bexly in Kent: Being a True Narrative of a young maid who was possest with several Devils. London, Printed for R. G., 1679. 6 pages. S 5884C*.

A young possessed woman supposedly became a snake and wrapped her body around a praying doctor. One spirit spoke through her clenched teeth, saying "weaker and weaker and weaker..." The events are corroborated by several spectators and a reliable woman of quality.

841A Strange News from Bartholomew-Fair, or, the Wandering-Whore Discovered...in Whore and Bacon-Lane. By Peter Aretine. London, Printed for Theodorus Microcosmus, 1661. 6 pages. S 5886.

Three prostitutes, Bonny Besse of Whore and Bacon Lane, Merry Moll of Duck Street and pretty Peg of Py-corner discuss ways to pick pockets at a fair and increase their income. This publication responds to The Wandring Whore, a serial (935A). See also 499A and 936A.

842A Strange News from Scotland, Or, A strange Relation of a terrible and prodigious Monster, borne to the amazement of all those that were spectators. [London, Printed by E. P. for W. Lee, 1647.] 5 pages. S 5900. TT Reel 64:E.408(14).

In Hadensworth near Edinburgh an hermaphrodite was born with two heads (seemingly male and female), cloven feet, and hands at its knees. The mother died after confessing "...to see the utter ruine and subversion of all Church and State-Government."

843A A Strange Witch at Greenwich. With a discussion of Walking Spirits and Spectars of Dead Men. By Hieronymus Magomastix. London, Printed by Thomas Harper for John Saywell, 1650. 28 pages. S 5920. TT Reel 92:E.600(15).

The pranks of a mischievous witch are said to be attributable, perhaps, to a servant removed from her grave when her death was suspected as unnatural. The pamphlet includes a general discussion of witchcraft with historical references.

844A Strickland, Robert. The Queenes Resolution discovered by some Letters in the House of Commons. London, Printed for Richard Butler, 1642. 8 pages. S 5974. EEB Reel 248:E.122(25) and TT Reel 21:E.122(25).

This document is one of several purporting to expose a cache of arms aboard Henrietta Maria's ships.

845A Strode, S. A Poem on the Death of Her Most Sacred Majesty. London, Printed and are to be sold by J. Whitlock, 1695. 4 pages. S 5979. EEB Reel 1537:20.

This eulogy for Mary II refers to Britain's grief and sadness at her passing. Strode notes the poor will miss her charity, but those in heaven will be enriched by her. Excerpt: "Great William lives; let us not always grieve,/Under his Wings securely we may live."

846A Strong, James. Joanereidos: or, Feminine Valour; Eminently discovered in western women, at the siege of Lyme. n.p., Re-printed A.D. 1674 (with additions) for the satisfaction of his Friends. [24] pages. S 5990*. EEB Reel 948:19 and TT Reel 47:E.287(1).

Originally printed in 1645, this piece concerns the participation of women in the defense of Lyme in Dorset (1643) during a royalist siege led by Prince Maurice. Although Strong praised their valour, his depiction of the women was later satirized, particularly in "Tobie Trundle," included in this edition. The mocking prologue and epilogue are by others.

847A Stubbes, Phillip, Senior. A Crystal glasse for Christian Women. London, Printed for John Wright, 1646. [20] pages. S 6074*.

This funeral sermon honors Katherine Stubbes, called "a mirrour of women-hood and now being dead, is a perfect pattern of true Christianity." Married at fifteen, Stubbes died of puerperal fever by twenty. This sixteenth-century piece went through twenty editions by 1664.

848A Swetnam, Joseph. The Arraignment of Lewd, Idle, Forward, and Unconstant Women: Or, The Vanity of Them. London, Printed for F. Grove, 1660. S 6251.

One of the most important misogynistic works of the Jacobean period, this coarse 1615 piece attacks women, emphasizing their alleged untrustworthiness and insatiable lust. Swetnam tells men to avoid women at all costs. His anti-female statements cite biblical passages.

849A T., R. A Character of a Female-Cockney, Brought upon the publicke Theater. To be Judged, censored...by...the late revived work of Laborer-in-Vain. London, Printed for John Harrison, 1656. [7] pages. T 45A. EEB Reel 1342:17.

A greedy, coquettish, simian-like prostitute, lewdly described, is called a true descendent of Eve. The author claims she has taken her act from a theatrical stage to a bawdy-house.

850A Talbot, James. Instructions to a Painter, upon the Death and Funeral of her late Majesty Queen Mary of blessed memory. London, Printed for Jacob Tonson, 1695. 14 pages. T 113. EEB Reel 298:28.

Talbot's poetic eulogy for Mary II is dedicated to Charles, Duke of Somerset. The painting is a rhetorical device for communicating grief, i.e., various virtues are personified pictorially, each figure mourning the queen.

851A Tate, Nahun. A Consolatory Poem to the Right Honourable John Lord Cutts, upon the Death of his Most Accomplish'd Lady. London, Printed by R. R. for Henry Playford, 1698. 9 pages. T 179. EEB Reel 803:4.

Classical figures dramatize the grief of Lord Cutts for Lady Elizabeth Cutts, who died at eighteen in childbirth. He was Commander in Chief of the King's Forces in Ireland and Colonel in the Coldstream Guards. A romanticized description of Lady Cutts is included, but there is no biographical material. Example: "Her temper'd Mirth was like a Morning-Ray/All Mildly Bright, and Innocently Gay." See also 51A, 457A, 733A and 955A.

852A Tate, Nahum. Elegies on Her late Majesty...[and] the Countess of Dorset. London, Printed for J. Wild, 1699. 125 pages. T 183. EEB Reel 516:18.

This book contains elegies for four prominent persons, including Mary II and the Countess of Dorset. Tate calls the countess a "gen'rous Patroness," and notes she gave comfort to those in distress. He calls her daughter, Lady Mary Sackville, a "living relique...of the Fair Deceased." Material about Mary is similar to that in other elegies for her.

853A Tate, N[ahum.] The Mausolaeum. A Funeral Poem On our late Gracious Sovereign Queen Mary, of Blessed Memory. London, Printed for B. Aylmer, W. Rogers, and B. Baldwin, 1695. 19 pages. T 194. EEB Reel 516:22.

This pastoral elegy was written on the sudden death of Mary II by England's poet laureate. Tate describes the grief of the queen's family and friends, the pageantry of the funeral and the importance of maintaining a strong country in the wake of the tragedy. Excerpt: "Bereav'd of ev'ry Blessing I Enjoy'd,/My Temples Sack'd, my Votaries Destroy'd."

854A Tate, N[ahum.]   A Present for the Ladies: Being an Historical Account of Several Illustrious Persons of the Female Sex. Second Edition. London, Printed for Francis Saunders, 1693. 148 pages. T 212*. EEB Reels 1579:35 and 1662:9.

This defense of women derives from Agrippa's The Excellency of the Female Sex. It argues women's worth from a symbolic model, e.g., Eve signifying life and Adam, earth. Tate presents a lengthy list of the accomplishments of great women possessed of "feminine" virtues like constancy, modesty and fortitude. He thinks women are more forgiving, temperate, mild and meek than men.

855A Taylor, Jeremy. A Copy of a Letter to a Gentlewoman Newly Seduced to the Church of Rome. London, Printed for Richard Chiswell, 1687. 21 pages. T 306. EEB Reel 516:30.

The woman addressed has apparently left the Church of England (her husband's and family's church) for the Catholic faith. Taylor defends Anglican doctrine, liturgy and discipline and says he awaits her return "from when you are fallen."

856A Taylor, Jeremy. A Funeral Sermon, Preached at the Obsequies of...the Lady Frances, Countesse of Carbery. London, Printed by F. F. for R. Royston, 1650. 36 pages. T 335. EEB Reel 804:2.

This vivid and compelling funeral speech focuses on the inevitability of death. Some biographical information reveals the innocence and piety of the deceased. Excerpt: "Then we must lay our heads down upon a turfe and entertain creeping things in the cells and little chambers of our eyes, and dwell with worms till time and death shall be no more."

857A Taylor, Nathanael. A Funeral Sermon Occasioned by the Death of the Lady Lane (late Wife of the Right Worshipful Sir Thomas Lane, Knight and Alderman of the City of London); who Died Nov. the 29th, 1698. London, Printed for Thomas Cockerill, 1699. 42 pages. T 641.

Taylor wishes to remind listeners of their own mortality and lack of free will. He also speaks against obsession with the flesh and epicurianism.

858A The Ten Pleasures of Marriage, and the Second Part, The Confession of the New Married Couple. London, Privately Printed for the Navarre Society and Harry F. Marks, 1923. 280 pages. N.I.W.

This volume is credited to a typographer named Marsh by both the British Library and the Library of Congress, even though John Harvey, who wrote the introduction, attributes it to Aphra Behn. The bases for Harvey's conclusion are the appearance of "A. B." after the first part, Behn's Dutch associations (the book was thought to have been printed in Holland), and Behn's knowledge of

London and medicine (both evident in the book). Given the author's cynical view of marriage and caustic remarks about women, this attribution seems tenuous when considered within Behn's canon. Excerpt: "...all the venomous Creatures in the World, have not so much poison spread or contained in their whole bodies; as one devillish-natured woman alone hath in her tongue."

859A Tenison, Thomas. A sermon preached at the funeral of Her late Majesty Queen Mary of ever blessed memory in the Abbey-Church in Westminster. London, Printed for Ri. Chiswell, 1695. 34 pages. T 720*. EEB Reels 704:7 and 949:5.

This sermon was delivered at a special ceremony held over two months after the death of Mary in December. Tenison, the Archbishop of Canterbury, describes events precipitating her death and discusses Mary's excellent memory as well as her piety, charity, humility, learning, books and administrative ability. He lists the main points of the eulogy as the greatness of the loss, its cause, the good that tempered the evil of the loss, and the duty of all to cease mourning.

860A The Third Advice to a Painter, how to draw the Effigies of the Whore of Rome. Whose Character is lively represented by a bad Woman. [London? 1679.] 4 pages. T 898. EEB Reel 517:16.

This antipapist verse utilizes much derogatory female imagery.

The Third Part of the Amours of Messalina. See 31A.

861A Thompson, Robert. Sponsa...The Marriage Between the Lady Katharine Fitz-Gerald and Edward Villiers Esq. London, Printed for Benjamin Tooke, [1677]. 35 pages. T 1007. EEB Reel 900:2.

This legal argument concerns the case of the Lady Katharine, victim of an arranged marriage at twelve to a boy of eight. Twenty-one months later she "disagreed to the same" and married Edward Villiers. Thompson claims the first marriage was "de futuro," or promised, and a promise to marry cannot be construed as a marriage. He maintains the boy had to have been fourteen to contract marriage legally.

862A Thorowgood, George. Pray Be Not Angry; or, The Women's New Law. London, Printed for George Horton, 1656. 5 pages. T 1064. TT Reel 133:E.885(7).

Thorowgood's misogynistic instructions for choosing a good wife or virtuous mistress tell how to distinguish between "an enticing and dissembling Whore" and an honest woman. He claims women hate being denied things they want, but will reject unsolicited gifts and flatter potential gift-givers. The moral: Avoid a wicked woman or she will eventually control you.

863A Three Speeches, Being speeches such as the like were never Spoken in the City...the second by Mistris Warden...the third by Mistris Wardens Chamber-maid. London, Printed for S. R., 1642. 8 pages. T 1118. TT Reel 41:E.240(31).

This satire purports to be a transcription of speeches by a man and two women to a female audience. The first two speakers seem incoherent, if not inebriated.

Their topics are Ireland, the Anabaptists, liturgical language, papists and religion in general. The second speech was published separately as 63A. It is apparently a mockery of public speaking by women.

864A The Tickler Tickled: or the Observator Upon, the Late Tryals of Sir Geo. Wakeman. By Margery Mason, Spinster, pseud. London, Printed for A. Brewster, 1679. 8 pages. T 1159. EEB Reel 401:10.

This humorous work has been falsely attributed to a cunning women who criticizes the Popish Plot defendants. It is a satire of the free-living urban woman, both mistress and servant.

865A To His Excellency General Monck. The Humble Petition of the Lady Lambert, Sheweth. London, Printed for Henry James, [1659]. Broadside. N.I.W. TT Reel 247:669.f.23(6).

In this sexual satire of Commonwealth leaders, the wife of commander John Lambert is accused of familiarity with Oliver Cromwell..."out of whose breeches she had the Instrument of Government." Monck's deception of Lambert following their treaty underlies the burlesque.

866A To The General Council of Officers. The Representation of divers Citizens of London. London, 1659. F 638B. TT Reel 247: 669.f.22(17).

Although the Wing STC credits this item to Margaret Askew Fell Fox, her name does not appear in the piece.

867A To the Praise of Mrs. Cellier the Popish Midwife: on Her Incomparable Book. London, Printed for Walter Davis, [1680]. Broadside. T 1596.

This is one of several critical pieces about midwife Elizabeth Cellier and the Meal-tub Plot. Mocking her as the "brightest Glory of your Sex, and age," more fair and sage than even "Popess Joan," it combines anti-Catholic and anti-female views.

868A To the Queens Majesty on her Happy Arrival. London, Printed for Henry Herringham, 1662. Broadside. T 1598A. EEB Reel 1580:5.

Catherine of Braganza, a Spanish princess who became queen to Charles II, is honored upon her arrival at Portsmouth. The poem emphasizes her beauty, chastity and political value to England.

869A To the Right Honourable, the Parliament of the Common-wealth of England, Scotland and Ireland. The Humble Petition of Mary C. of Sterling, and John Blount her husband, Sir Robert Croke...[and many others]. [London, 1654.] Broadside. T 1706C. TT Reel 246:669.f.19(31).

This case concerns the estate of Sir Peter Vanlore the older, who had left his castle and parks in Wiltshire to his daughter Lady Powell and her heirs. Because she died without issue, Sir Peter's heirs attempted to gain access to the estate. There are details about Lady Powell and her estranged husband, and attempts to seize her property by her relatives. See also 571A, 817A and Addendum 29.

870A [Toland, John.] Amyntor: or, A defence of Milton's life...and to the exceptions made against my Lord Angelesey's Memorandum, Dr. Walhe's Book, or Mrs. Gauden's Narrative, which last piece is now the first time published at large. London, [1699]. 172 pages. T 1760. EEB Reel 299:4.

The authorship of "Icon Basilike," originally attributed to Charles I, was questioned by John Milton in his "Iconoclastes." Mrs. Gauden contended her late husband wrote it and sent his manuscript for approval to the king during his imprisonment at Carisbrook. Based on Gauden's alleged authorship, his wife applied for remission of claims upon his estate. This narrative, found after her death in 1671, was first published here. Toland had attributed authorship to Gauden in his 1698 edition of Milton's prose works.

871A Toll, Thomas. The Female Duel, or the Ladies Lookinglass Representing a Scripture Combate. London, Printed by H. Bell, and P. Lilicrap, 1661. 248 pages. T 1776. TT Reel 226: E.1813(2).

Toll presents a debate "between a Roman Catholic Lady and the Wife of a Dignified Person in the Church of England." After airing their differences, they presented a defense of orthodox religion and Anabaptist views. Toll praises the "masculine vigour" of the two, although he cannot identify them.

872A Torshell, Samuel. The Womans Glorie. A Treatise, Asserting the due Honour of that Sexe, And Directing wherein that Honour consists. London, Printed by G. M. for John Bellamie, 1645. 232 pages. T 1941*. EEB Reels 617:8 and 900:24.

This lengthy guide for female behavior was dedicated to and written for Princess Elizabeth, daughter of Charles I. Torshell says a woman is optimally pious, calm, watchful and composed. He counsels modesty and humility as well. Along with material about classical and biblical figures, Torshell cites Jane Grey and Anna Maria van Schurman as models.

873A Toy, John. A Sermon Preached in the Cathedrall Church of Worcester the Second of Febr. last being Candlemas day, at the funerall of Mris. Alice Tomkins. London, 1642. 21 pages. T 1996. TT Reel 27:E.154(47).

Toy focuses on the theme of Job 14--the misery and brevity of life. He also speaks of the appointed hour of judgment day. Finally he calls Tomkins a good housewife and Christian who was charitable and beloved.

874A Treason Discovered from Holland: or, A Discoverie of a most damnable and divellish attempt of two Jesuites, and three other Catholiques, against the life and person of the Ladie Elisabeth. London, Printed for I. Tompson, 1642. 6 pages. T 2074. TT Reel 25:E.138(14).

This anti-papist document claims while Henrietta Maria was in Paris, the Catholics had a paper delivered to Princess Elizabeth by two priests. As she was examining it, one drew a pistol, but it wouldn't fire. She fled to her chamber. The two visitors were put on the rack, confessed and were sent to the dungeon. Three others are also named in the complicity.

875A The Tryal and Condemnation of Mervin Lord Audley, Earl of Castlehaven at Westminster, April the 5th, 1631. London, 1699. 31 pages. T 2144. TT Reel 14:E.84(2).

This transcript supports charges that the Earl of Castlehaven committed sodomy, conspired in raping his wife, and abetted the sexual molestation of his step-daughter. The celebrated trial is significant for the admittance of testimony by the Earl's wife against her husband and for the broad definition of rape that was placed into the record. A nearly identical document was published in 1642: The Arraignment and Conviction of Mervin Lord Audley. See also 201B and 247B.

876A The Tryal and Conviction of John Tasborough and Ann Price for Subordination [sic] of Perjury, in Endeavoring to perswade Mr. Stephen Dugdale To retract and deny his Evidence about the Horrid Popish Plot. London, Printed for Robert Pawlett, 1679/80. 59 pages. T 2161. EEB Reel 585:11.

This transcript reports the attempted bribery of Dugdale by Price to convince him to retract testimony he had given against persons accused in the Popish Plot. He was offered both money and assistance in escaping. Although Price pleaded not guilty, she was convicted. When she asked to be returned to the Gatehouse, the justices balked: "No, we must have no favour for you that would destroy us all."

877A The Tryal and Conviction of Mary Butler, alias Strickland...for Counterfeiting a Bond of 40,000 [Pounds]. London, Printed for F. C., 1700. 28 pages. T 2162.

A widow accused of defrauding an alderman supposedly counterfeited a bond requiring payment of 40,000 pounds by his heirs after his death. She maintained an attorney wrote the bond because he wished to avoid raising the suspicions of his wife about liens against his estate. He was allegedly prepared to offer his wife a different bond. (It seems it was acceptable for men to deceive their wives in such matters.) Strickland was ordered to pay 500 pounds to the Crown and was sent to prison until payment was made.

878A The Tryall and Examination of Mrs. Joan Peterson, before...the Old Bayley...for her supposed Witchcraft...and poysoning of the Lady Powel at Chelsey: Together with her Confession at the Bar. London, Printed for G. Morton, 1652. 8 pages. T 2167. TT Reel 101:E.659(15).

Peterson, tried for witchcraft in the poisoning of Lady Powell, was supposedly "a practitioner in physick, but suspected to be a witch." She denied the charge and claimed she had given only nourishing medicines to Lady Powell. Several witnesses said Powell died a natural death at eighty. A verdict had not been reached when this account went to press. Another tale about Giles Fenderlin, who allegedly made a pact with the devil, is also included. See also 961A.

879A The Trial of Edmund Audley for the Murder of Mrs. Hannah Bullevant [sic]. London, Printed by John Darby, 1698. Broadside. T 2184A.

In the trial of a man for shooting a woman in Aldersgate, one witness saw him emerging from a shop declaring "he had killed Queen Mary, who had been there incognito." The alleged murderer talks about a conspiracy to place the late king on the throne. He was found guilty of willful murder. See also 238A.

880A The Tryall of Elizabeth Cellier, the Popish Midwife, at the Old Baily. London, Printed by A. Godbid for L. C., 1680. 4 pages. T 2187*. EEB Reels 519:2 and 648:5.

This sham trial concerns a claim of libel against Cellier for publishing Malice Defeated in which she defended herself against a charge of high treason. The transcript is replete with sexual allusions and attacks Cellier's Catholicism as well as her midwifery. This is one of several criticisms of Cellier for her alleged role in the Meal-tub Plot. See also 137B, 138B, 260A, 512A, 603A and 787A.

881A The Trial of Henry Care, Gent...also the tryal of Elizabeth Cellier. London, Printed by I. G. for R. Taylor, 1681. 26 pages. T 2190. EEB Reel 519:3.

The transcript of Cellier's trial is not included in the copy examined.

882A The Tryal of Spencer Cowper, Esq. London, Printed for Isaac Cleave, Matt. Wotton, and John Bullord, [1699]. 46 pages. T 2224. EEB Reel 677:14.

Sarah Stout, sole executrix of her father's estate, was murdered. The alleged killers included Cowper, a family friend who had offered investment advice. After gaining the trust and funds of Sarah and her mother Mary, Cowper allegedly recruited others to help drown her. The conspirators claimed she committed suicide because she was pregnant. Several physicians testified she had been bludgeoned to death. Upon exhumation of the body, they found her uterus "perfectly free and empty, and of the natural figure and magnitude, as usually in virgins." See also 168A, 258A and 280A.

883A A Tryal of Witches, at the Assizes held at...the County of Suffolk...Before Sir Matthew Hale. London, Printed for William Shrewsbury, 1682. 59 pages. T 2240. EEB Reel 1160:26.

This 1664 transcript, based on an eyewitness account, tells of two widows who became angry with their neighbors and bewitched their five children. One mother claimed her child's resultant lameness coincided with the onset of menstruation. Those in attendance were pleased with the guilty verdict.

884A The Tryals of H. Cornish, Esq.; For conspiring...and Elizabeth Gaunt...for Harbouring and Maintaining Rebels. London, Printed for George Croom, 1685. 42 pages. T 2250.

This complicated transcript is primarily a report of Cornish's trial; however, Anabaptist Gaunt's indictment for harboring traitors is included. At first she pled ignorance of legalities, then claimed she was not guilty. Gaunt was the last woman political prisoner sentenced to die. She was burnt at the stake. See also Addendum 14 and 73.

885A A True Account of the late Most doleful, and lamentable Tragedy of old Madam Gwinn. [London, 1679]. 4 pages. T 2384.

This tale about actress Nell Gwynne's mother's death had considerable currency during the period. It tells of her alleged drowning in a fish pond and the pomposity of her funeral. The author calls her end a proper epitaph for a madam. He says women are a threat to society because of their tongues, their only weapons, and claims Gwynne possessed the worst, and most typically female traits. See also 321A.

886A A True Account of the Proceedings before the House of Lords...Between the Duke and Dutchess of Norfolk. London, [1692]. 44 pages. T 2393A.

This pamphlet answers "two scandalous Pamphlets." It includes statements of witnesses and judgments about their credibility. The issue is the duke's desire to divorce his wife on grounds of adultery so he could have heirs. The duchess claimed she had never been accused of wrongdoing before the court. See also 35A, 164A, 649A and 920A.

887A A True and Wonderful Account of a cure of the King's-evil, by Mrs. F., sister to His Grace the Duke of Monmouth. London, 1681. Broadside. T 2584. EEB Reel 1296:54.

In this political attack on the Duke of Monmouth, an illegitimate son of Charles II, his sister Mary Fanshawe, daughter of Lucy Walter, supposedly laid hands on a sickly young man and cured him. The author also claims Monmouth brought a lion into his cell in the Tower to prove his invincibility and thus, his claim to royalty. "Kings-Evil" is a double-entendre: The ability to cure it--a form of scrofula--was the sole province of royalty. The term is also a mockery of Monmouth, who allegedly aspired to the throne. See also 37A.

888A A True and Wonderful Relation of a Murther committed in the Parish of Newington...by a Maid. London, Printed for T. Benskin, 1681. 2 pages. T 2586. EEB Reel 519:36.

Charity Philpot, a servant to seamstress Mrs. Mathews, threatened to murder her mistress and her child and burn down their house. While the woman went for help, the servant slit the child's throat. She then took poison while awaiting the constable. This brief description is meant to discourage criminality and encourage piety.

889A A True Copy of a Letter of Consolation. London, Printed for W. Johnson, 1681. Broadside. C 1663A.

This anti-papist diatribe was not written by Elizabeth Cellier, although it is attributed to her in the Wing STC. In an alleged conversation with a co-conspirator in the Meal-tub Plot, she claims the two worked for the Catholic Church in the "publick calling [of lying]." Her colleague is told to "curse and Ruin Thy Native Country if Thou Canst."

890A A True Copie of a Letter of Special Consequence from Rotterdam respecting Arms and Ammunition collected by Queen Henrietta Maria for shipment to England. London, Imprinted for Henry Overton, 1642. Broadside. T 2619. TT Reel 245:f.669.f.6(110).

This letter describes ships laden with ammunition intended for the queen and claims she has arms for 15,000 men. The varieties of powder and guns are elaborated, and Holland is named as her base of support.

891A A True Relation of the taking of a great Ship at Yarmouth...also Her Majesties letter to the King. London, Printed for H. Blake, 1642. [6 pages.] T 2567. EEB Reel 248:E.121(21) and TT Reel 21: E.121(21).

A letter allegedly from Henrietta Maria was found aboard a ship carrying ammunition and weapons. It was tossed overboard but retrieved by a local fisherman. This document summarizes the incident as reported to Parliament, stating the queen was expected with fourteen Dutch ships for protection. The ship was eventually seized at Yarmouth.

892A A True Relation of Mary Jenkinson, who was killed by one of the Lyons in the Tower. [London], Printed for George Croom, 1685/86. Broadside. T 2911A. EEB Reel 1391:5.

Jenkinson, a young woman from Norfolk, lived with the lion-keeper in the Tower. During a tour of the den a lion ripped off her arm, and she died. The moral: "...every good Christian [ought] to consider their...end before they go hence and be no more seen."

893A A True Relation of the most Horrid and Barbarous murders committed by Abigail Hill of St. Olaves Southwark, on the persons of four Infants. London, Printed for F. Coles, 1658. 14 pages. T 3008. TT Reel 243:E.1881(2).

Hill was convicted for the deaths of four parish children for whom she was wet nurse. At her demise, she supposedly jeered at her executioners and refused to confess to the crimes.

894A The True Relation of the Queenes departure from Falmouth into Brest. London, Printed for Matthew Walbancke, 1644. [6 pages.] T 3030. EEB Reel 228:E.2(29) and TT Reel 1:E.2(29).

This document describes Henrietta Maria's departure from England with the Lord Admiral in pursuit. He sent his ships to overtake hers, and three of the strongest fired over 100 shots. Nevertheless, she had the advantage of the wind and a galley of sixteen oars: "It is thought that all the ships in the world could not overtake her." She was unsuccessfully pursued to Brest in France.

895A A True Relation of the sad and Deplorable Condition of a Poor Woman in Rosemary-Lane near Tower-hill. London, Printed for R. G., 1680. 8 pages. T 3041. EEB Reel 440:16.

A number of strange or horrible events occurred in 1680: A woman's feet rotted and were burned so she was left with maggot-infested stumps; some women were saved by a man on shore when their boat capsized; and a huge hail storm raised the water so high in parts of London that animals were carried off. The collection is typical of contemporary descriptions of unusual or bizarre events.

896A <u>A True Relation of the Treaty and Ratification of the Marriage concluded and agreed upon between our Soveraigne Lord Charles...and the Lady Henrietta Maria</u>. n.p., 1642. 8 pages. T 3062. EEB Reel 247:E.118(35) and TT Reel 21:E.118(35).

This reprint of the 1625 marital agreement between the principals emphasizes the importance of binding the two royal houses. It stipulates the ceremonial procedures, the parties responsible for payments with amounts due, and the respective sums and lands to be exchanged as part of the marital contract.

897A <u>The True Relation of the Tryals at the Sessions of Oyer and Terminer...as [sic] particularly of Elizabeth Wigenton</u>. [London, 1695.] 4 pages. T 3063.

Wigenton, a coat-maker, was charged with murdering her thirteen-year-old female apprentice. The girl had done some work improperly, and Wigenton beat her with rods until she died. She claimed she had not meant to kill her. She was found guilty of "wilful murder."

898A <u>A true relation of the Wonderful cure of Mary Maillard, (lame almost ever since she was born) on Sunday the 26th of Nov. 1693. With the affidavits and certificates of the girl, and several other credible and worthy persons</u>. London, Printed for Richard Baldwin, 1694. 48 pages. T 3073*. EEB Reel 554:12.

This version corrects <u>An account of the wonderful cure of Mary Maillard</u>, repudiated by [the printer] Edward Cooke. The first part expresses skepticism about most "magical" healing, but requests objectivity for this particular case. Maillard's supposedly "supernatural" healing of lameness had taken place without human intervention. See also 416A.

899A <u>A True Relation of two wonderfull Sleepers. The one...Elizabeth Jenkins</u>. London, Printed for Thomas Bates, 1646. 8 pages. T 3076. TT Reel 56:E.349(8).

A woman slept very deeply for six days. Her temperature dropped, her pulse slowed, and her breathing started to fade. Eventually she awakened. The author thinks the incident was God's work. A short description of a similar event in a man is included.

900A <u>The Truest Account of Mr. Fuller's Discovery of the true mother of the pretended Prince of Wales, Born the 10th of June, 1688</u>. London, Printed for the Author, 1696. 31 pages. T 3131. EEB Reel 853:77.

This document includes eyewitness testimonials about the birth of a child to Queen Mary, wife of James II, from gentlewomen of the bed-chamber, the laundress, the attending physicians, the drynurse, and the apothecary. They refute a rumor that the baby, James Francis Edward Stuart, was smuggled into the queen's room in a warming pan. Skepticism about the birth was based partially on the fact that Mary had already given birth to five children, all of whom died.

901A Tryon, Thomas. <u>The good Housewife Made a Doctor</u>. Second Edition. London, Printed for H. N. and T. S., 1692. 285 pages. T 3181*.

Tryon includes recipes for preparing broths, candy, pies, etc. and describes properties and uses of foods. He offers medical advice, such as methods to prevent scurvy and make poultices for burns, boils and scalded limbs. This is one of many guides combining culinary and medical advice.

902A Tryon, Thomas. Health's Grand Preservative: or the Womens best Doctor. London, Printed for the author and sold by Thomas Benskin, 1682. 22 pages. T 3182A.

Tryon offers advice to women about improving their health. He warns against eating too much meat, recommends herbal remedies, and so on. He says drinking spirits is "against the Feminine Nature," and contends the female diet is crucial because the preservation of mankind depends on women's "Temperance and Government."

903A Tub-preachers overturned or Independency to be abandoned and abhor'd as destructive to the...Church and Common-wealth of England. London, Printed for George Lindsey, 1647. 16 pages. T 3207. TT Reel 61:E.384(7).

The author criticizes "independents," i.e., preachers who usurp the ministry and spread heresies among the weak. He says they use women just as the devil used Eve: "Ye act the devil's part of a strong man and take possession." Implying sexual seduction, the author claims married women are especially vulnerable. Mrs. Attaway, a preacher who attacked infant baptism and argued for women's freedom of speech, was apparently a special target of this pamphlet.

904A Two most Strange Wonders:...a most fearful judgement which befell Dorothy Matley of Ashover in the County of Derby. London, Printed for W. Gilbertson, 1661. 16 pages. T 3490. TT Reel 233:E.1874(4).

Only a few pages are devoted to Matley's story. She denied a charge of cheating a boy of two pence, and vowed the earth could swallow her whole if she were lying. Shortly thereafter this event occurred. Apparently Matley was frequently accused of cheating her neighbors and had often uttered the vow. The moral of the tale: One should not commit a sin and follow it with a dare to Providence.

905A Two New Novels...II. The Fatal Beauty of Agnes de Castro. P[eter] Bellon, trans. Two Parts. London, London [sic] Printed for R. Bentley, 1688. 102 pages. A 3793/T 3491. EEB Reel 371:3.

This novel, supposedly written by a French woman, was likely by Jean de Brilhac. Based on the story of Ines de Castro, daughter of Pedro Fernandez de Castro, it was translated by others, including Aphra Behn (40B).

906A The Unfortunate maid cheated being a true and very pleasant relation of one Jone Fletcher, of High-Holbourne...married a Woman in Man's Apparel, who went by the Name of Black Richard, alias John Hilliard. London, Printed for J. Smith, 1699. 4 pages. U 57B.

A humorous risque dialogue tells of a female who worked for six years in men's clothing as a laborer while she courted women. Her gender was discovered when an acquaintance learned she had two children through the pretext of seeing if she "were capable of Family-Duty."

907A The Unfortunate Quaker. An Account of the Strange and Wonderful Manner How one Mrs. Cockbil...was found miserably Scorch'd and parch'd to Death. London, Printed by J. W., 1697. Broadside. U 58A. EEB Reel 1296:72.

Cockbill, the Quaker wife of a Holborn glover, was found by a washer-woman with burns about her neck and head. She was accused of imbibing brandy and committing "vilest Iniquities" while wearing "Puritanical Garb."

908A The Unnatural Grand Mother, Or a true Relation of a most barbarous Murther Commited [sic] by Elizabeth Howard. London, Printed for Thomas Higgins, 1659. [6] pages. U 86. EEB Reel 441:4.

A woman who sold fruit in Cheapside allegedly drowned her grandchild. Her daughter, also a peddler, had to seek child care outside of London because of poor financial resources. The author maintains the woman did not deny her crime.

909A V. A Mappe of Mischief, or a Dialogue Between V. and E. concerning the going of Qu. M. into V. V. much lamenteth therefore, and if [sic] not comforted by E. n. p., 1641. 6 pages. V 1. EEB Reel 255:E.169(5) and TT Reel 30:E.169(5).

This anti-royalist tract reproduces a fictitious dialogue between an English and a French woman. There is much feminine imagery, especially relating to childbirth. The point is to express England's relief at the departure of Henrietta Maria: "I am suddenly to be rid of a plague...I have a long time been in labour with this same piece which hath made choice of thee, and now even now I am to be deliver'd."

910A V., W. The Ladie's Blush: The History of Susanna, the Great Example of Conjugal Chastity. London, Printed by James Cotterel for Robert Robinson, 1673. 40 pages. V 15. EEB Reel 402:11.

This work is a paean to Susanna, who chose public execution rather than submit to the advances of two elders. Statements argue against women's usurpation of their husbands' authority. The author is especially critical of women who, during the Civil War, tried to lead their families toward unorthodox religious views.

911A [Vanel, Charles.] The Royal Mistresses of France, or, the Secret History of the Amours of all the French Kings. London, Printed for Henry Rhodes and John Harris, 1659. 260 pages. V 90. EEB Reel 585:6.

This romance characterizes reigns of the French kings by the ascendancy of their mistresses. It is basically a fictionalized portrayal of the French court.

912A The Vanity of Female Pride. A True Relation of a Sow that Pig'd Seven Monstrous Pigs. London, Printed by G. C., 1691. Broadside. V 93A. EEB Reel 901:68.

The author says the top-knot, a popular female hairdo, exemplifies wickedness wrought through the pride of women. The central allegory tells of a sow in

Wiltshire that gave birth to seven swine, each with a differently colored topknot. The lesson for women: Bedeck yourselves with "Humility, Vertue and Modesty," especially because worthy men are repelled by such artifices as fashionable hairdos. See also 686A.

913A [Varet, Alexandre Louis.] The Nunns Complaint against the Fryars. London, Printed by E. H. for Robt. Pawlett, 1676. 186 pages. V 110. EEB Reel 1076:26.

Varet catalogs incidents of debauchery at the French cloister of St. Clare near Provins which allegedly occurred between 1663 and 1667. The nuns accused the Cordeliers (their Franciscan confessors) of corrupting the morals of novices and newly professed nuns and of intervening in the election of abbesses.

914A [Vaumoriere, Pierre d'Ortigue de.] Amours of the Count de Dunois. Made English. London, Printed for William Cademan, 1675. 154 pages. D 1187 EEB Reel 140:14.

The British Library attributes this work to Vaumoriere, even though it is listed under Marie Catherine Hortense Desjardins in the Wing STC. The epistle to the reader by the English printer suggests male authorship.

915A Vauts, Mones A. The Husband's Authority Unvail'd; wherein it is moderately discussed whether it be fit or lawfull for a good man, to beat his bad wife. London, Printed by T. N. for Robt. Bostock, 1650. 100 pages. V 163. TT Reel 93:E.608(19).

Vauts maintains this document is humble, though rambling and annotated with biblical references. A husband's authority is held to be self-evident; thus, his focus is the relation of subjection to command. In return for obedience, wives can expect honor. Good women with cruel or churlish husbands will reap their rewards in the hereafter, while drunken or profane men are warned against abusing their wives.

916A [Vernon, Samuel.] The Trepan: Being a True Relation, full of stupendious [sic] variety, of the Strange practices of Mehetabel, the Wife of Edward Jones, and Elizabeth, wife of Lt. John Pigeon. [London], 1656. 38 pages. V 253A. TT Reel 133:E.884(1)

This item is nearly identical to 917A.

917A [Vernon, Samuel.] A Brief Relation of the Strange and Unnatural Practices of Wessel Goodwin, Mehetabel Jones the wife of Edward Jones, and Elizabeth Pigeon, the wife of John Pigeon. [London], 1654. 33 pages. V 253B*. EEB Reel 16:23 and TT Reel 124:E.818(19).

Goodwin was compulsively enamored of music. When his wife died, neighbors tried to marry him to Mehetabel Jones, sister of Elizabeth Pigeon. The two connived to deprive his heirs before they were finally brought to court; the case was dismissed on a technicality. Vernon calls them wicked "sirens" and invokes biblical verses to describe their sinfulness. Excerpt: "Here behold seducing women cunning in wickedness, creeping into a silly man's house, and leading him captive to their wicked purposes."

918A Verses to Mrs. Mary More. [London], 1674. Broadside. V 264.

This broadside is identical to Addendum 169.

919A A Vindication of a Distressed Lady. In Answer to a pernitious [sic], scandalous, Libellous pamphlet. London, 1663. 7 pages. V 463B. EEB Reel 1538:16.

In answer to The Lawyers Clarke Trappan'd by the Crafty Whore of Canterbury this pamphlet defends Mary Carleton, the notorious "German Princess," accused of falsely assuming the identity of a German noblewoman and committing bigamy. It defends her character and denies the accusations against her. See also Addendum 115.

920A A Vindication of Her Grace, Mary, Dutchess of Norfolk. London, 1693. 45 pages. V 477A. EEB Reel 1602:14.

This defense presents the duchess' side of an infamous and acrimonious divorce case. Her husband's charges of adultery are disputed either by the facts or by questions about the character of his witnesses (mostly servants). The duke's divorce bill was rejected twice by the House of Lords, although his claim for damages against his wife's alleged lover was rewarded at the King's Bench. Also included are correspondence, a chronology of the case and several supporting documents. See also 35A, 164A, 649A and 886A.

921A The Virgin-Mother: A Divine Poem which may properly serve for a Christmas Carol. London, 1665. 6 pages. V 634A. EEB Reel 1297:8.

This joyful poem urges both virgins and matrons to visit Bethlehem. Mary's virginity is celebrated and her preeminence secured in the pantheon of female biblical figures--Sarah, Judith, Rebecca, Rachel.

922A The Virgins Complaint for the losse of their Sweet-hearts, by these Present Wars, and their Virginities against their wills. London, Printed for Henry Wilson, [1643]. [6] pages. V 640*. TT Reel 15:E.86(38).

This anti-military satire blames war for the loss of virile young men. The author says only through copulation is population increased, thus providing soldiers for defense. He blames war for the decay of trade and the cornuting of absent husbands and recalls the divine prohibition against the taking of life.

923A The Virtuous Wife. A Poem. In Answer to the Choice, That would have no Wife. London, Printed and are to be sold by J. Nutt, 1700. 7 pages. V 652. EEB Reel 1558:55.

The poet describes the ideal wife--her character, talents, religion, temper, conduct and conversation. Desirable traits include modesty, humor, devotion and gracefulness. Her occupations should be primarily reading good books and doing needlework.

924A Vliet, Jan van. In Mortem Serenissimae Principis Mariae ad Regen Elegia. London, 1660. Broadside. V 672. EEB Reel 1485:29 and TT Reel 247:669.f.26(42).

This broadside is an elegy in Latin for Princess Mary, daughter of Charles I and Henrietta Maria.

925A [Voiture, Vincent de.] Zelinda: An Excellent new Romance. London, Printed by T. R. and N. T. for James Magnes and Richard Bentley, 1676. 127 pages. S 2164. EEB Reel 616:5.

The authorship of this novel is in dispute. The title page lists "T. D., Gent." as author and "Monsieur de Scudery" (Madeline de Scudery) as translator. There is additional support for male authorship, possibly de Voiture, in the preface. The romance is set in Spain and revolves around the love of Zelinda, an orphan, for Alcidalis, a prince. The plot contains intrigues and battles in Sardinia as well as the separation and reunion of the lovers.

926A W[hitehall], R[obert]. Lines to the...Ingenious Mrs. Mary More; upon her sending Sir Thomas More's picture. [Oxford], 1674. Broadside. W 97.

This brief poem extends thanks for Mary More's portrait of Sir Thomas More, apparently a gift to the Long Gallery "at the Public Schools in Oxon." The author was a don at Merton College, Oxford. This item is the same as 918A.

927A Wagstaffe, John. The Question of Witchcraft Debated. A Discourse against their Opinion that affirm Witches. Second Edition. London, Printed for Edw. Millington, 1671. 128 pages. W 199*. EEB Reel 829:29.

Wagstaffe's book is an expanded version of an earlier work attacking the "absurd opinion of Witchcraft." He denies it is blasphemous to question the existence of witches and defends his efforts to challenge belief in witches, saying his purpose is to aid "the saving of innocent persons, from torture and death itself." He concludes with a long justification for his opinions based on biblical passages and historical sources.

928A [Wake, William.] Preparation for death. Being a letter sent to a young Gentlewoman in France. London, Printed for Richard Chiswell, 1687. 155 pages. W 253. EEB Reel 881:11.

This private letter was published only after distribution of copies by relatives following the death of the young woman. Its primary message is the futility of concentrating on worldly things, while ignoring the hereafter. Wake entreats his correspondent to avoid the weakness of many ill persons: peevishness.

929A Walker, Anthony. [Eureka, Eureka], The Virtuous Woman. Found her losses Bewailed, and Character Exemplified in a Sermon...at the Funeral of Mary, Countess Dowager of Warwick. London, Printed for Nathanael Ranew, 1678. 224 pages. W 301. EEB Reel 1243:11.

This sermon is dedicated to Catherine, Viscountess Ranleagh and her brother Robert Boyle, executors of the countess' will. Discussion of the deceased is limited almost entirely to the Countess' religious activities. It includes her "Rules for Holy Living" as well as her occasional meditations upon scriptures. See also 381A and material by Warwick in Part B.

930A Walker, Anthony. The Holy Life of Mrs. Elizabeth Walker, Late Wife of A. W. Rector of Fyfield in Essex. London, Printed by John Leake for the Author, 1690. 296 pages. W 305. EEB Reel 854:9.

Walker's biography honors his recently deceased wife. Letters and papers by her are included (mostly religious documents admonishing others to lead a godly life). Walker tells of their eleven children, three of whom died. Elizabeth Walker taught her maidservants to read, and was known for her piety, charitable works, culinary skills and business acumen.

931A Waller, Edmund.   Of the Lady Mary.   [London],   Printed for Henry Herringman, 1677. 4 pages. W 503. EEB Reel 904:3.

Waller's romantic poem about the marriage of William of Orange and Mary II gives special thanks to Charles II for improving relations with Holland through their union.

932A W[aller], E[dmund.] To the Queen upon Her Majesties birth-day. [London], Printed for Henry Herringman, [1663]. W 530A.

Waller's birthday wish for Mary II offers thanks for her recovery and mentions the women who lamented her recent illness.

933A [Walsh, William.] A Dialogue concerning Women, being a Defence of the Sex. Written to Eugenia [Lady Mary Chudleigh]. London, Printed for R. Bentley and F. Tonson, 1691. 134 pages. W 645. EEB Reel 442:8.

Walsh's book is a criticism of misogynistic writings, ubiquitous during this period. It presents a conversation between two ancients over the question of women's worth and includes accounts of women drawn from biblical and classical sources.

934A [Walsh, William.] A Funeral Elegy upon the death of the Queen. London, Printed for Jacob Tonson, 1695. 11 pages. W 646. EEB Reel 904:28.

This poem is addressed to the Marquis of Normandy. Walsh points to various constituencies of Mary II and offers reasons for their grief, e.g., women are "now divested of their pride" and must learn not to dwell on "Beauty, Wit, and Youth." A supporter of women, Walsh thinks mourning may be easier for men because of the distractions of their public activity.

935A The Wandring Whore. A Dialogue between Magdalena a Crafty Bawd, Julietta an Exquisite Whore, Francion a Lascivious Gall And Gusman a Pimping Hector. Numbers 1-6. London, [Printed for John Garfield], 1660-1663. N.I.W. EEB Reel 276:14 (F 888); TT Reels 156:E.1053(3) and (8); 248:E.1054(4).

This series of bawdy pamphlets is modelled on Pietro Aretino's La Puttante Errante.   Two prostitutes relate anecdotes about reputed debauchery and knavery, utilizing puns, innuendo and military slang. Lists of allegedly real brothels and practicing whores and pimps are included. At least two names of prostitutes are corroborated elsewhere--Damaris Page and Madame Cresswell. The popularity of coffee-houses and the increase in self-employed prostitutes are blamed for sluggish business. John Garfield is sometimes suggested as the author of this series. See also 499A, 841A and 936A.

936A The Wandring Whores Complaint for Want of Trading. Wherein The Cabinet of her iniquity is unlockt and all her secrets laid open. London, Printed for J. Jones, 1663. 6 pages. W 705.

This bawdy dialogue between two prostitutes describes much farcical sexual activity. The women blame the proliferation of coffee-houses and private prostitutes for their slow business. A concluding poem lists clients who are sexual or financial failures. See also 499A, 841A and 935A.

937A W[ard], E[dward.] Female Policy Detected: Or, The Arts of a Designing Woman Laid Open. London, Printed for John Willis and Joseph Boddington, [1693]. 140 pages. W 734.

Ward proposes to expose the deceptive ways of women for the young. He describes women as vain, inconstant, revengeful, proud and ungrateful. The second part defends married men against "peevish, fretful, scolding wives." It includes a separately titled work, "The Batchelor's Estimate," a single man's reckoning of the costs of married life.

938A Ward, Edward. The Insinuating Bawd and the Repenting Harlot. Written by a whore at Tunbridge and dedicated to a bawd at the Bath. London, [1700?]. 12 pages. W 738A*. EEB Reel 904:39.

This humorous poem is about erosion of beauty through debauchery and the cleansing of sin in the baths. The harlot of the title regrets her earlier wicked ways, taught by the bawd. She supposedly writes the poem to caution the naive and describe how she was led astray through "verbal witchcraft." Excerpt: "Her Limbs that, with such Air and Freedom mov'd,/Are Lazy Grown, unfit to be Belov'd."

939A [Ware, Robert.] Pope Joan: or, an Account Collected out of the Romish Authors, Proved to be of the Clergy and Members of that Church. London, Printed for Wm. Miller, 1689. 24 pages. W 850. EEB Reel 1135:7.

This document attempts to prove the existence of Pope Joan, a mythical figure who supposedly studied in Athens, ascended to the papacy, became pregnant and delivered a child. Many church histories are cited, including commentaries by Theodorus de Niem and Laonicus Calcocondila. Ware criticizes 448A, a piece that calls the story a fable.

940A A Warning-piece to all married men and women. Being the full confession of Mary Hobry, the French midwife Who Murdered her Husband...for which she receiv'd Sentence to be Burnt alive. [London, Printed for George Croom, 1688]. Broadside. W 935.

This broadside tells the allegedly true story of a midwife whose husband regularly abused her. After he drunkenly beat her, she strangled him while he slept. Because Hobry could not afford to flee the country, she dismembered and disposed of his body piecemeal so it couldn't be identified. The song suggests her case demonstrates murderers should not go free. See also 8A, 431A and 793A.

941A Warning for Servants: And a caution to Protestants. Or, the case of Margaret Clark, lately executed for firing her masters house in Southwark. London, Printed for Tho. Parkhurst, 1680. 32 pages. C 4483. EEB Reel 87:7.

Clark is praised for confessing to arson, for meekness and friendliness to visitors who came to see her in prison, and for forthrightness with ministers; however, she was convicted and executed for her crime. Her co-conspirator, a male, was freed. This is an interesting comparison between his behavior and her courageous dignity. See also 152B.

942A Waters, James. A sermon preach'd at the funeral of the Right Honourable Anne Baroness Holles of Ifeild in Sussex. London, Printed by J. R. for Johnathan Greenwood, 1682. 35 pages. W 1057. EEB Reel 780:13.

Holles was the wife of Francis Lord Holles. Most of the sermon addresses avoiding the desire for worldly goods. The final few pages discuss the baroness' anonymous charitable contributions, her religious instruction to her servants, her humility, and her exemplary relationship with her son, statesman Denzil Holles.

943A [Watkins, Richard.] Newes from the Dead. Or, a True and Exact Narration of the Miraculous deliverance of Anne Greene, who being Executed at Oxford... afterwards revived. Oxford, Printed by Leonard Lichfield for Tho. Robinson, 1651. 10 pages. W 1072*. TT Reel 96: E.625(14).

This fascinating narrative is preceded by fourteen pages of poetry by Oxford scholars about the incident. Greene, a young servant impregnated by her master's grandson, was charged with the murder of their infant. She was hanged and placed in a coffin; her miraculous recovery prompted discussion of her guilt, the state of the fetus and the female menstrual cycle. See also 129A.

944A W[atkinson], P[eter.] Mary's Choice Declared in a Sermon Preached at the Funeral of the Rt. Hon. Lady Mary Wharton, late wife of the Hon. Sir Thomas Wharton, Knight of the Bath. London, Printed by Robert White for Henry Mortlock, 1674. 46 pages.   W 1079. EEB Reel 1107:21.

The first part of this eulogy is a sermon; material about the deceased begins on page twenty-seven. The Lady Wharton was born in 1615 and married at thirty. She is praised for her modesty in behavior and dress, her sensible diet, comportment, reading, charity, good nature and exemplary relationship with her husband. Some excerpts from her letters are included.

945A Webster, John. The Displaying of Supposed Witchcraft...a corporeal League... betwixt the Devil and the Witch. London, Printed by J. M., 1677. 346 pages. W 1230. EEB Reel 44:7.

Webster was a nonconformist physician who served as chaplain and surgeon to the parliamentary army. He advocated reform of grammar schools away from classical training and toward a more practical education. In this treatise, he invokes the scientific method in criticizing the existence of witchcraft. He maintains ignorance is responsible for the current mania.

946A [Wecker, Hans Jacobi]. <u>Arts Masterpiece: or, The Beautifying Part of Physick. Whereby all Defects of Nature in both Sexes are amended, Age renewed, Youth continued and all imperfections fairly remedied</u>. London, Printed for Nath. Brook, 1660. 140 pages. W 1234*. TT Reels 242:E.2124(3) and 243:E.2140(3).

Dedicated to the ladies and signed "L. D.," this prescriptive guide offers formulae for depilatories, ointments, pomanders and powders. It also gives remedies for burns, bites, baldness, eye maladies, skin and dental problems and the like.

947A Wenlock, John. <u>Upon our royal Queens Majesties most happy arrivall, the most illustrious Donna Catherina sole sister to the high and mighty King of Portugal</u>. London, Printed for Thomas Child and Leonard Parry, 1662. Broadside. W 1351.

This poem welcomes Catherine of Braganza, who had recently arrived in England to wed Charles II.

948A Wesley, Samuel. <u>Elegies on the Queen and Archbishop</u>. London, Printed by B. Motte for C. Harper, 1695. 29 pages. W 1368.

These formal verses praise the recently deceased Mary II and the Archbishop of Canterbury, Thomas Tenison.

949A Weston, John. <u>The Amazon Queen, or, the Amours of Thalestris to Alexander the Great</u>. London, Printed for Henry Herringman, 1667. 56 pages. W 1479. EEB Reel 1452:6.

This play revolves around the Amazon queen's efforts to encourage her daughter to develop a romantic interest in men and fall in love with Alexander the Great. It is a typical Restoration comedy with romantic intrigues, but the mysteries and powers traditionally attributed to the Amazons provide material for a unique perspective of women.

950A Whatman, Edward. <u>Funerall Obsequies, To the Rt. Hon. the Lady Elizabeth Hopton</u>. London, 1647. 5 pages. W 1591. TT Reel 61:E.384(14).

This poem honoring a beloved woman, recently deceased, is filled with fond praise. It is a lamentation over the poet's great loss.

951A White, George. <u>An Advertisement anent the Reading of the Books of Antonia Borignion [sic]</u>. Aberdeen, Printed for John Forbes, 1700. 96 pages. W 1767.

White, a minister in Aberdeen, published this volume to discourage the reading of Bourignon's writings. He claims several young gentlemen experienced increased melancholy following the perusal of her work. White, who maintains Bourignon was an ignorant enthusiast, attempts to expose her vanity and substantiate his claim that she knew little scripture. See also material by Bourignon in Part B.

952A <u>The Whores Petition. To the London Prentices</u>. London, 1668. 6 pages. W 2069.

This humorous petition, supposedly written by a group of prostitutes whose brothel was ransacked by rowdy apprentices, was published after an actual attack occurred. The women seek to remain in their lodgings and request that the young men control their behavior in the future. They claim the men's theft of their china and linen is at least as morally questionable as prostitution. They ask for a truce of mutual non-belligerence. See also 204A, 716A and 724A.

953A Whyte, Humphrey. A sermon Peach'd at the Funeral of Anne Lady Burgoyne. London, Printed for Tho. Hodgkin and are to be sold by Randal Taylor, 1694. 27 pages. W 2075. EEB Reel 1821:13.

The Lady Anne was the widow of Sir Roger Burgoyne, knight and baronet of the county of Warwick. The sermon is based on Psalms 112.6: "The Righteous shall be in everlasting remembrance." Whyte praises the widow's charity, piety and intelligence at some length, calling her "a person of as refined a Wit, and of as true a Judgment as any woman this age has produced."

954A The Widowes Lamentation for the Absence of their deare Children and Suitors. London, Printed for John Robinson, 1643. 8 pages. W 2093. EEB Reel 242:E.88(26) and TT Reel 15:E.88(26).

This humorous piece petitions for new husbands. The "widows" claim their husbands have died violent deaths far away in the cause of the "civill warres." They lament the lack of lusty young men to marry: "...we being growne meere toothlesse mumping things, having no body to warme our frosty constitutions."

955A Wigan, William. A Funeral Sermon Preached on the decease of the hon. The Lady Eliz. Cutts, late wife of the Rt. Hon. The Lord Cutts. London, Printed for Walter Kettilby, 1697. 30 pages. W 2098. EEB Reel 950:30.

The Lady Elizabeth Pickering Cutts was the second wife of Lord Cutts, a lieutenant general. She died after giving birth to a stillborn child at eighteen. The theme is Lady Cutts' desire to die a righteous person. There is little personal material in it. See also 51A, 457A, 733A and 851A.

956A [Wilkinson, Richard.] A True and Perfect Relation of Elizabeth Freeman. London, Printed for J. B., 1680. Broadside. W 2248. EEB Reel 1081:11.

Wilkinson describes a vision seen by Freeman and recorded by a local gentleman, the rector and schoolmaster. A ghost holding a child warned her the king was to be poisoned; it appeared four times telling her to warn him of imminent danger.

957A [Wilkinson, Robert of Southwark.] The Merchant Royal. A Sermon Preached at White-Hall before the Kings Majestie at the Nuptials of Lord Hay and his Lady. London, Printed by Thomas James for John Lawrence, 1682. 39 pages. W 2251A.

Wilkinson's text, taken from Proverbs 31: "Shee is like a merchant shippe, shee bringeth her food from a farre," presents a nautical analogy for the exemplary wife. She is responsible for her husband's success and serves as a vessel for his goods. Although he possesses her, like a ship, he is to govern her with love "tempered with equality." This sermon was originally published in 1607.

958A Willes, Samuel. A Sermon preach'd at the funeral of...Lady Mary, daughter to Ferdinando late Earl of Huntingdon, and wife to William Joliffe...in Stafford. London, Printed by J. D. for John Baker, 1679. 36 pages. W 2305. EEB Reel 301:7.

This sermon focuses on the characteristics of the saved; however, some biographical material describes the Lady Mary as kind, pious and charitable. On her deathbed she lamented that she was distracted from the love of God by her great attention to her only child.

959A Wills, Daniel. A Relation in part of What passed through a True and Faithful Servant and Handmaid of the Lord, Mary Page. [London, 1665]. 8 pages. W 2865.

This religious tract relates the story of a woman who died after speaking spontaneously and with great fervor in an outpouring of faith. Her monologue, witnessed by four women, occurred while she lay in a sick bed.

960A The Wise-womans saving the city. [London, 1647.] [21] pages. W 3103. EEB Reel 1244:23.

This anti-royalist, pro-military document compares Charles I, in exile at Oxford, to the biblical Sheba, "a Traytor to the Kingdom of Israel." (Sheba, a male, revolted against David and fled to Abel-Beth-Maacah, whose inhabitants offered his head to save themselves.) Brave Hebrew women are cited as models for Londoners, who are encouraged to treat traitors harshly.

961A The Witch of Wapping, or An Exact and Perfect Relation, of the Life and Devilish Practices of Joan Peterson...hanged at Tyburn on Monday the 11th of April, 1652. London, Printed for Thomas Spring, 1652. 8 pages. W 3137. TT Reel 101:E.659(18).

Peterson allegedly bewitched a child, frightened a baker, and fornicated with the devil, who assumed the form of a dog or squirrel. There is little evidence cited. The confession and admonishment to women of Prudence Lee, a woman convicted of murdering her husband, are omitted from the copy examined. See also 878A.

962A The Woeful Lamentation of Mrs. Jane Shore, a Gold-smith's Wife...sometime King Edward the Fourth's concubine. [London], Printed for F. Coles, T. Vere and W. Gilbertson, [1658-64]. Broadside. W 3244B*.

Shore, renowned for her beauty and forced to marry against her will, attracted the attention of the king. When she became his mistress, her husband left for the continent. After the king died, her popularity at court waned. Her later years are described as lonely and disgraced.

963A Woman Turn'd Bully. London, Printed by J. C. for Thomas Dring, 1685. 83 pages. W 3322. TT Reel 246:669.f.16(30).

Although this play is attributed to Aphra Behn by some sources, her authorship is doubtful. It was performed by the Duke's company in 1675.

964A The Woman Warrier [sic]: Being an Account of a Young Woman...who changing her Apparel Entered her self on Board, in quality of a Soldier. [London], Printed for Charles Bates, [1690]. Broadside. W 3323.

A woman supposedly disguised herself as a man so she could follow her soldier-husband to battle. She remained undetected both on board ship and on the battlefield. During the battle she fought valiantly and was wounded. She died during her return trip to London.

965A Women will Have their Will: or, Give Christmas his Due. In a Dialogue between Mrs. Custome, a Victuallers wife...and Mrs. Newcome, a Captains wife. London, Printed by E. P. for W. G., 1648. 16 pages. W 3327. TT Reel 167:E.1182(12).

This satire alleges the Reformation has prompted Parliament to outlaw Christmas because it is Romish. The women of the title are vehicles for this message.

966A The Womens Complaint against Tobacco Or, an excellent help to Multiplication. London, Printed in the Year, 1675. 6 pages. W 3328A.

This pamphlet is typical of misogynistic semi-pornographic satires which focus on women's alleged uncontrollable lust. Here tobacco renders their husbands impotent. The women hold a meeting at Gossip's Hall and attempt to outlaw the use of tobacco. They contend its hot and dry nature evaporates the moisture reserves in the body. Because they all want to speak simultaneously, the meeting proves fruitless.

967A The Women's Petition against Coffee...Grand Inconveniences accrusing [sic] to their Sex from the Excessive Use of that Drying, Enfeebling Liquour. London, 1674. 6 pages. W 3331. EEB Reel 829:44.

Charging insatiable female lust, this piece argues men are now impotent because of the effects of coffee ("boiled soot"). Also, by patronizing coffee houses, not ale houses, men have become more loquacious than women. Excerpt: "Never did Men wear greater Breeches, or carry less in them of any mettle whatsoever." See also 588A.

968A Wonderful News from Wales; or, a True Narrative of an Old Woman living near Lanselin in Denbighshire, whose Memory serves her truly and perfectly to relate what she hath seen and done one-hundred and thirty Years ago. London, Printed for C. L., 1677. 8 pages. W 3369B.

Jane Morgan was reputed to be a centenarian who did not use a walking stick or spectacles and possessed keen senses of sight and smell. This pamphlet presents a brief history of her family, including her birth to a mother alleged to be over sixty. Additional details of her remarkable physical state are offered.

969A The Wonderful Works of God, declared by a strange Prophecie of a Maid that lately lived neere Worsop in Nottingham-shire. London, Printed for John Thomas, 1641. 6 pages. W 3377. TT Reel 32:E.181(18).

A young woman died on the sixteenth of November, only to rise after twenty hours and live for another five days. She apparently predicted war and fear would befall Great Britain because of its pride, visions and strange signs would be seen, and the millennium would take place.

970A [Wood, Hugh.] A Brief Treatise of Religious womens meetings services and testimonies. [London], Printed and sold by Andrew Sowle, 1684. 47 pages. W 3393.

Wood's document supports the Quaker women's meetings. He cites the Bible as a source for his position; however, his approval is contingent on female adherence to Christian principles of modesty and humility. Wood criticizes priests who permit women to preach or prophesy only if they are "approved and licensed by themselves." This stricture, he claims, presents a deliberate obstacle to women preachers.

971A Worden, Thomas. An Account of Some of the Dying Sayings of Susannah Yeats, Late Wife of Samuel Yeats...in Gloucestershire. London, Printed for William Marshall, 1688. 32 pages. W 3577. EEB Reel 1516:16.

Worden excerpts some of Yeats' final religious ruminations and describes apparitions she saw as death approached. His Puritanical sermon, about Christ's response to his own death and the prevalence of sin, comprises most of the text.

972A Wortley, Francis. The Dutie of Sir Francis Wortley; delineated in his pious pity, and Christian Commiseration of the sorrowes and Sufferings of the most vertuous, yet unfortunate Lady Elisabeth Queene of Bohemia. London, Printed by R. O. for F. W., 1651. 8 pages. W 3636. TT Reel 29:E.165(16).

Wortley's serious poetic tribute relates the story of the sister of Charles II, whose husband was banished, whose first son died and whose third was taken prisoner. It is primarily about her male relatives.

973A Y[eokney], W[alter]. The Entertainment of the Lady Monk, at Fishers-Folly. Together with an Addresse made to her by a member of the Colledge of Bedlam at her Visiting those Phanatiques. [London], 1660. Broadside. Y 31. EEB Reel 729:21.

This humorous political broadside is directed at Monck, a Parliamentary general who attempted to return Charles II to the throne. His new loyalty to the king is mocked through Lady Monck, who is only indirectly mentioned as the wife of "so wise, go great, so good a mate."

Addendum

WORKS BY WOMEN

1 [Aulnoy, Marie Catherine Jumelle de Berneville, Comtesse d'.] <u>Mother Bunch's Closet Newly Broke Open</u>. London, Printed by A. M. for P. Brooksby, 1685. M 2936A.

2 Behn, Aphra. <u>Three Histories. Viz., Oroonoko...The Fair Jilt...Agnes de Castro</u>. London, Printed for W. Canning, 1688. B 1766A.

3 [Behn, Aphra.] <u>To poet Bavius</u>. London, Printed for the author, 1688. B 1767.

4 Behn, Aphra. <u>The Town Raves. A Song</u>. [London?, 1696.] B 1770A.

5 [Bettris, Jeane.] <u>Spiritual Discoveries</u>. Second Edition. [n.p.], 1657. B 2086.
6 Boulbie, Judith. <u>A Warning and lamentation over England</u>. [London], 1679. B 3828B.

7 [Carleton, Mary.] <u>The Case of Mary Carleton</u>. London, Printed for Sam: Speed and Hen: Marsh, 1663. C 586A.

8 [Cheevers, Sarah.] <u>To Xelos...or, A Brief Narration of the mysteries of state carried on by the Spanish faction in England</u>. The Hague, Printed for S. Brown, 1651. C 3777.

9 Crisp, Stephen. <u>A Backslider Reproved...unto which is added, a Brief Answer [by Anne Travers and Elizabeth Coleman] to a pamphlet [by Elizabeth Atkinson]</u>. [London], 1669. C 6925.

10 <u>The Diary of the Lady Anne Clifford</u>. With an introductory note by Victoria Sackville-West. New York: G. H. Doran, c1923.

11 [Douglas, Eleanor Touchet Davies, Lady.] <u>Prophetia de die</u>. n.p., Exedebat Tho. Paine, 1644. D 2005.

12 Dowdall, Katherine. <u>To the Honourable the Knights</u>. Dublin, 1695. D 2055B.

13 <u>Four Letters from the Queen in France</u>. [London, 1651.] F 1661A.

14 Friends, Society of. <u>York Yearly Meeting of Women Friends</u>. [London, 1700.] F 2240.

15 [Gaunt, Elizabeth.] <u>Mrs. E. Gaunt's last Speech, who was burnt at London...as it was written by her own hand</u>. [Amsterdam?, 1685.] G 381A.

16 Gilman, Anne. <u>To the Inhabitants of the Earth</u>. [London], 1669.
G 768A.

17 James, Elinor. <u>Mrs. Jame's (sic) Apology</u>. [London, 1694.] J 415A.

18 James, Elinor. <u>Mrs. James's application to the...Commons</u>. [London?, 1695.]
J 415B.

19 James, Elinor. <u>Dear Soveraign</u>. [London, 1687.] J 416A.

20 James, Elinor. <u>Mrs. James's humble letter</u>. [London?, 1699.] J 417aA.

21 James, Elinor. <u>I can assure your honours</u>. East India Company. [London, 1699?] [India office] J 417bA.

22 James, Elinor. <u>May it please your honours</u>. East India Company. [London, 1699?] [India office] J 417AB.

23 James, Elinor. <u>My Lords, I did not think</u>. [London?, 1690.] J 419A.

24 James, Elinor. <u>To the honourable House of Commons</u>. [payment of King's debts] [London?, 1685.] J 421B.

25 James, Elinor. <u>To the honourable House of Commons</u>. [East India Company] [London?, 1699.] J 421C.

26 Jinner, Sarah. <u>An Almanack or prognostication for...1658</u>. n.p., 1658. A 1844.

27 Jinner, Sarah. <u>An Almanack or prognostication for...1659</u>. London, Printed by J. S. for the Company of Stationers, [1659]. A 1845.

28 Jinner, Sarah. <u>An Almanack or prognostication for...1660</u>. n.p., [1660.] A 1846.

29 Jinner, Sarah. <u>An Almanack or prognostication for...1664</u>. n.p., 1664. A 1847.

30 [Levingston, Anne.] <u>A True Narrative of the Case</u>. [London?, 1646.] L 1825.

31 [Pix, Mary (Griffith).] <u>The Inhumane Cardinal; or, Innocence Betray'd</u>. A Novel, Written by a Gentlewoman. London, 1696. P 2329A.

32 Pix, Mary. <u>Alass When Charming Silvia's son</u>. [London], Printed for Thomas Cross, [1697.] P 2325.

33 [Pix, Mary.] <u>To the Right Honourable the Earl of Kent...this poem</u>. [London, 1700?] P 2332A.

34 Polwhele, Elizabeth. <u>The Frolicks, or, The Lawyer Cheated</u>. Judith Milhous and Robert D. Hume, eds. Ithaca: Cornell University Press, 1977.

35 Poole, Elizabeth. <u>A Prophecie touching the Death of King Charles</u>. London, Printed for J. H., 1649. P 2809A.

36 Rone, Elizabeth. <u>The Description of the Singers of Israel</u>. [London, 1680.] R 1914aA.

37 Rone, Elizabeth. <u>Elizabeth Rone's short answer to Ellinor James' long preamble</u>. [London], Printed for D. K., 1687. R 1914B.

38 [Scudery, Madeline de.] <u>The History of Philoxypes and Polycrite</u>. London, Printed for Humphrey Moseley, 1652. S 2159A.

39 [Scudery, Madeline de.] <u>Severall Witty Discourses</u>. London, Printed for Henry Herringman, 1661. S 2161A.

40 Sutton, Katherine. <u>A Christian woman's experience</u>. Rotterdam, 1668. S 6212.

41 Walker, Mary. <u>The Case of Mrs. M. W. the wife of Clement Walker, Esq</u>. [London, 1650.] W 395*.

42 Wentworth, Anne. <u>The Revelation of Jesus Christ</u>. [London], 1679. W 1355A.

43 Wentworth, Lady Henrietta Maria. <u>An Answer made by...in behalf of her daughters</u>. [London, 1675.] W 1356A.

44 White, Dorothy. <u>An Alarum sounded forth from</u>. London, 1662. W 1744.

45 White, Dorothy. <u>The voice of the Lord</u>. London, 1662. W 1761.

46 Whitrow, Joan. <u>To the King and both Houses of Parliament: Say unto them, Thus saith the Lord</u>. London, Printed for E. Whitlock, 1696. W 2038.

47 [Winchelsea, Anne (Kingsmill) Finch, Countess of.] <u>The prerogatives of love</u>. [London, 1695.] W 2966.

48 York, Anne Hyde, Duchess of. <u>Reasons for her leaving the Communion</u>. [London, 1670.] Y 47.

WORKS FOR AND ABOUT WOMEN

49 A., S. <u>The Virgin Saint</u>. London, Printed for Jonathan Robinson, 1673. A 28A.

50 <u>An account of the fund for the relief of widows</u>. London, 1673. A 293.

51 <u>An account of the solemn funeral...Countess of Arran</u>. [London], Printed for Thomas Newcombe, 1668. A 390.

52 <u>Animadversions on the Lady Marquess</u>. London, Printed for J. Jordan, 1680? A 3196.

53 A[ylett], R[obert]. <u>Devotions, viz. A Good Womans...Prayer</u>. London, Printed by T. M. for Abel Roper, 1655.

54 B., C. <u>A Congratulatory Poem to her Royal Highness</u>. London, Printed for Nat. Thompson, 1682. N.I.W.

55 B., W. <u>The Ladies Milk-House: or, The Oppressed Man's Complaint</u>. [London], 1684. B 215.

56 <u>The Bawds Tryal and Execution: Also, A Short Account of her whole Life and Travels</u>. By Misomastropus, pseud. London, Printed for L. C., 1679. B 1166.

57 [Bell, John.] <u>Witchcraft Proven</u>. Glasgow, Printed by Robert Sanders, 1697. B 1801.

58 Boules, Dr. <u>The Queens royal closet newly opened</u>. London, Printed for Francis Cole, T. Vere, I. Wright, and J. Clark, 1675. B 3828C.

59 <u>A Brief Relation of the Order and Institute of the English Religious Women at Liege</u>. [Liege, 1652.] B 4627.

60 <u>Bloody Newes from Dover, Being a True Relation of the great and bloudy Murder, committed by Mary Champion (an Anabaptist) who cut off her Childs head</u>. London, 1646. B 3267.

61 [Buckingham, John Sheffield, Duke of.] <u>An ode in memory of...Queen Mary</u>. [London, 1695.] B 5342.

62 <u>The C----'s petition to the Parliament of Women</u>. London, Printed for A. Chamberlain, 1684. C 175.

63 <u>The Cabinet Open'd, or the Secret History of the Amours of Madam de Maintenon, with the French King</u>. London, 1690. In Modern Novels, Vol. XI. London, 1690. N.I.W.

64 Carleton, John. <u>The Ultimate Vale of J. Carleton...being a true description of the passages of that grand impostor, late a pretended Germane-Lady</u>. London, Printed for J. Jones, 1663. C 586.

65 <u>The Case of Mrs. Arabella Thompson, Widow</u>. [London, 1680?] Broadside. C 960.

66 <u>The Case of Dame Margaret Areskine</u>. Edinburgh, 1690. C 901B.

67 <u>The Case of Katherine Harris</u>. [n.p., 1695.] C 938.

68 <u>The Case of Richard and Ann Ashfield</u>. [London, 1698?] C 967B.

69 <u>The Case of Spencer Cowper</u>. [London? 1700.] C 1005.

70 <u>A Catalogue of Jilts</u>. London, Printed for R. W., 1691. C 1340.

71 Chamberlain, T[homas]. <u>A Full Supply of such most usefull and admirable Secrets, which Mr. Nicholas Culpeper...in the art of Midwifry, have hitherto wilfully passed by</u>. London, Printed for N. Brooke, 1659. C 1817B.

72 Charles, King, James, Duke, Katherine, Queen, Mary, Dutchess. London, Printed by G. Croom on the ice, 1684. C 3661.

73 The Confession, Profession and Conversion of...young Gentlewoman. [London], Printed for B. Aylmer, 1684. C 5802.

74 Constance of Cleveland: A...sonnet of the most fair Lady...and her disloyall knight. [London], Printed for F. Coles, T. Vere, J. W[right], and W. Gilbertson, [1660?]. C 5937.

75 Cornish, Henry. A True Account of the Behaviour and Manner of the Execution of Elizabeth Gaunt. London, 1685. C 6325.

76 The Country Lass, who left her Spinning-Wheel for a more pleasant Employment. London, 1690. C 6540.

77 [Crouch, Nathaniel.] The kingdom of darkness: Or, The History of daemons, spectors, witches, apparitions, possessions, disturbances, and other wonderful and supernatural delusions, mischievous feats, and malicious impostures of the devil. By R. B. (pseud.) London, Printed for Nath. Crouch, 1688. C 7342.

78 Dands, John. A light to Lilie. Second Edition. London, Printed for W. H., 1643. D 169*.

79 Dangerfield, Thomas. The Case of Tho. Dangerfield: with some remarkable passages that happened at the tryals of Elizabeth Cellier. London, Printed for the author, 1680. C 1181.

80 D[eloney], T[homas]. The most rare and excellent history of the Dutches of Suffokls (sic) calamity. [London], Printed for W. Thackeray, J. M. and A. M., [1685]. D 959.

81 The Deplorable Case of Many Poor Widows. [London, 1692?] D 1069.

82 Deplorable News from Southwark. [London], Printed for Tho. Vere, [1655?]. D 1075.

83 Dreadful News from Southwark. London, [1679?]. D 2153.

84 The Dutchess of Portsmouths Farewel. London, Printed for J. Clarke, W. Thackeray, and T. Passinger, [1685]. D 2426A.

85 The Duke's Daughter's cruelty. London, Printed for J. Deacon, [1688-95]. D 2516.

86 [Elizabeth of Bohemia, Consort of Frederick I, King of Bohemia.] The Declaration of... concerning her [Elizabeth of Bohemia] coming. December 14, 1642. London, Printed for H. Blundell, 1642. E 526A.

87 [England. Parliament.] An Act to prevent the destroying and murthering of Bastard Children. London, Printed for S. Roycroft, 1680. E 1154A.

88 An Epicaedium on the Death of her Most Serene Majesty Henrietta Maria. [London, 1669.] E 3143.

89 An Exact Relation of the Barbarous Murder committed on Lawrence Corddel A Butcher. London, Printed for J. Jones, 1661. E 3682.

90 The Examination, Confession and Execution of Ursula Corabet. London, Printed for John Andrews, [1660/1]. E 3711.

91 F., S. Death in a New Dress: Or sportive funeral elegies. London, Printed for Isaac Pridmore, 1656. F 54.

92 Falconer, David. Information for my Lord and Lady Nairn. London, 1690. F 295.

93 The Female-Triumph or Mistris White Asserted. London, 1647. F 670.

94 The Female's Frolick. London, Printed by and for W. O., for T. Norris [1680-90]. F 672.

95 Fifteen Real Comforts of Matrimony, Being in requital of the late Fifteen Sham-Comforts. With Satyrical Reflections on Whoring, And the Debauchery of this Age. London, Printed for Benjamin Alsop and Th. Malthus, 1683. F 887.

96 F[ord], E[dward]. Wine and Women: Or a briefe Description of the common courtesie of a Curtezan. London, Printed for John Hammond, 1647. F 1462.

97 Fore-Warn'd, Fore-Arm'd: Or, A Caveat to Batchelors, In The character of a Bad Woman. London, Printed for T. Snowden, 1684. F 1556.

98 Fox, George. For the Holy Women that trust in God. [London, 1686.] F 1820.

99 The Friendly Society for Widows. London, Printed for F. C., 1696. F 2226.

100 A Full and True account of a most Barbarous Murther...on...Mrs. Johannah Williams. London, Printed for T. Lightbody, 1699. F 2293G.

101 Furly, John. The Substance of a Letter...paper put forth by a...deceitful woman, that subscribes herself Sarah Hayward. n.p., 1666. N.I.W.

102 Furly, John. A Testimony to the True Light...Elizabeth [Furly]. [London], 1670. F 2541A*.

103 God's Strange and terrible Judgment in Oxfordshire. London, Printed for D. M., 1677. G 962.

104 Golborne, John. A Friendly Apology in the Behalf of the womans excellency. London, Printed for H. Mortlocke, 1674. G 1009.

105 The Gossips Braule, or The Women wear the Breeches. A Mock Comedy. London, 1655. G 1315.

106 The Gossips Feast or, Morrall Tales. London, 1647. G 1316.

107 Great Britains lamentation: or, The Funeral Obsequies. London, Printed for John Whitlock, 1694/5. G 1668.

108 History of the Amours of the French Court, viz. of Madam de la Valliere, Madam de Olonne, Madam de Chastillion, Madam de Sivigny. In Four Parts. [London, Printed for Richard Bentley?], 1684. H 2143A.

109 The Honourable state of Matrimony. [By D. B.] London, Printed for Francis Pearse, 1685. H 2601.

110 Horrid News from St. Martins...A true Relation how a Girl not full 16...Murdered her own Mother. London, Printed for D. M., 1677. H 2864.

111 Humphreys, John. The Womans priviledges above the man. London, Printed for Henry Million, 1680. H 3724.

112 K[irkman], F[rancis]. The Counterfeit Lady Unveiled...Mary Carleton. London, Printed for Peter Parker, 1673. K 630A*.

113 The Ladies of London's Petition. [London], Printed for Josiah Blare, [1684-88]. L 157.

114 The Ladyes Vindication. London, Printed for William Gilbertson, [1662]. L 162.

115 The Lambs Defence against Lyes. London, Printed for Giles Calvert, 1656. L 249.

116 The Lawyers Clarke trappand by the crafty Whore of Canterbury... Mary Mauders. London, Printed for J. Johnson, 1663. L 739F.

117 The Life and Pranks of Long Meg of Westminster. London, c1680. L 2020A.

118 Lilburne, John. L. Col. John Lilburne his letter to his...wife. [Amsterdam, Printed for L. I., 1652]. L 2136.

119 The London Bawd, with her Character and Life. Fourth Edition. London, Printed for John Gwillim, 1711. N.I.W.

120 The Merry Dutch Miller: And New Invented Windmill. Wherewith he undertaketh to graint all Sorts of Women. London, Printed by E. Crowch for F. Coles, T. Vere and J. Wright, 1672. M 1863.

121 Mr. Thomas Dangerfeild's Particular Narrative. London, Printed for Henry Hills, 1679. N.I.W.

122 Mrs. Page's complaint for causing her husband to be murdered. [London], Printed by and for W. D., [1670?]. M 2280B.

123 A Monstrous Birth...Wetwan in Yorke-shire. London, Printed for Livewel Chapman, 1657. M 2467.

124 [Morley, George.] Several Treatises...Letter to Ann, Duchess of York. London, Printed for Joanna Brome, 1683. M 2796.

125 The Murderous Midwife, with her Roasted Punishment. London, 1673. M 3097.

126 News from Old Gravel-lane: Or, a True and Perfect Relation of a Woman That is Tormented with the Devil. [London], 1675. N 987A.

127 On the death of a Queen. [London, 1695.] O 303aA.

128 Overbury, Thomas, Younger. Truth Brought to light by Time. The Proceedings touching on the Divorce between the Lady Frances Howard and Robert, Earl of Essex...His Majesties gracious pardon and favour to the Countess. London, Printed by R. C. for Michael Spark, 1651. [No pagination.] N.I.W.

129 Paterson, Ninian. On the lamentable death of the Lady Lee, Younger. Edinburough?, 1686. P 701.

130 P[ecke], T]homas]. Advice to Balaam's Ass; or, Momus catechised. London, Printed by E. B. for Henry Marsh, 1658. P 1039.

131 The Petition of the Company of Silk-throwsters. [n.p.], 1641. P 1792.

132 Petition to the Houses of Parliament from distressed Sea-men's (sic) wives. [London, 1667.] P 1857.

133 The Picture of the Princesse Henrietta. [London], 1660. N.I.W.

134 [Prechac, Jean de.] The Princess of Fess. London, Printed for R. Bently and M. Magnes, 1682. P 3207B.

135 The Queen of the milk-women...Mrs. E. G. [n.p., 1698.] Q 154A.

136 The Queen's Birth-day song. April 30. 1691. [London], Printed and are to be sold by Randal Taylor, 1691. Q 156A.

137 The Queens Lamentation. London, Printed for Charles Tyus, [1660]. Q 157C.

138 Relation of Mary Jenkinson. London, 1685/6. R 806.

139 Relation of the design of Mrs. [Mary] Hampson. [London, 1685.] R 822.

140 A Relation of the true funerals of...Marquesse of Montrose. London, 1661. R 882.

141 A Reply to the Hertford letter: Mris. Stout's Death. London, Printed by M. Fabian, 1699. R 1074.

142 [Rochester, John Wilmot, Earl of.] Artemisa to Cloe. A Letter from a Lady in the Town to a Lady in the Country. London, Printed for William Leach, 1679. R 1740A.

143 <u>A Sad and Sorrowful Relation of Laurence Cauthorn, Butcher</u>.   [London], Printed for Austin Rice, 1661.   S 244E.

144 <u>Sir T. J.'s speech to his wife</u>.   [London, 1685.]   S 3888.

145 Skinner, John.   <u>A Strange and Wonderful relation of Margaret Gurr</u>.   [London], Printed for I. W., I. C., W. T. and T. P., 168?   S 3944.

146 <u>The Snare of the Devill Discovered: or, A True and perfect Relation of the sad and deplorable Condition of Lydia the wife of John Rogers House-Carpenter</u>. London, Printed for Edward Thomas, 1658.   S 4388.

147 <u>Some Luck, Some Wit...sonnet...M. Carleton, commonly called The German Princess</u>.   London, Printed for Phillip Brooksby, [1673].   S 4536.

148 Stafford, Richard.   <u>To the present Queen Mary</u>.   [London, 1692.]   S 5147.

149 <u>Strange and Dreadful News from the town of Deptford, in the county of Kent, being the full, true, and sad relation of one Anne Arthur who, according to her own report, had divers discourses with the devil</u>.   [London, Printed for D. W., 1684/5.] S 5815AB.

150 <u>Strange and Terrible News from Shorditch of a Woman that hath sold her self to the divil</u>.   London, Printed for D. M., 1674.   S 5831A.

151 <u>Strange and Terrible News from Gloucester...Death of the Clark's Daughter of Brokington</u>.   London, Printed by J. C. for N. T., 1660.   S 5834.

152 <u>Strange and Wonderful Relation from Shadwell...Mrs. Moon</u>.   London, Printed for W. Smith, 1674.   S 5874bA.

153 <u>A Strange and Wonderful Relation of an old woman that was drowned at Ratcliff Highway</u>.   Two Vols. in One.   Stratford upon Avon, Printed for T. Pasham, [c1680].   S 5876*.

154 <u>The Strange Monster or true news from Nottinghamshire</u>.   [London], Printed for Peter Lillierap (sic), 1668.   S 5884A.

155 <u>Strange News from Shadwell...the death of Alice Fowler</u>.   London, Printed for E. Mallet, 1684?   S 5903.

156 <u>The Strange Witch at Greenwich.</u>   By Hieronymus Magomastin, pseud. London, Printed for Thomas Harper and sold by John Saywell, 1650.   S 5920.

157 [Stuckley, Lewis.]   <u>Manifest Trust or an Inversion...Mary Allein</u>.   London, Printed by D. M. for M. Keinton, 1658.   S 6090.

158 Tate, Nahum.   <u>Ode upon her Majesty's birth day</u>.   London, Printed for Richard Baldwin, 1693.   T 197.

159 Tenison, Thomas, Archbishop of Canterbury.   <u>Oraison funebre de...Maria Reine</u>. A Londres, se vend chez la veufue Maret et Henry Ribotteau, 1695.   T 706B.

160 Tenison, Thomas, Archbishop of Canterbury. <u>Sermon prononce aux funerailles de la reine Marie II</u>. [London], se vend par C. Lucas, 1695. T 722A.

161 <u>Three Inhumane Murthers, Committed By one Bloudy Person, upon His Father, his Mother, and his Wife</u>. London, Printed for H. E., 1675. T 1093E.

162 [Tilbury, Samuel.] <u>Bloudy Newes from the North, and the Ranting Adamites Declaration</u>. London, 1650. T 1162.

163 <u>To the Pious and Sacred Memory of Our Late Dread (sic) Sovereign</u>. London, Printed for J. Littleton and sold by W. Bonny, 1695. T 1595.

164 <u>To the Queen on her Birthday</u>. [London], 1663. T 1598.

165 <u>Treason and Murther: Or, The Bloody Father-in-Law</u>. London, Printed for E. Miles, [1674]. T 2071.

166 <u>A Tryal of skill, performed by a poor decayed Gentlewoman, Who cheated a rich Grasier of Sevenscore pound, and left him a Child to keep</u>. [London], Printed for F. Coles, T. Vere, J. Wright and J. Clarke, [1674-79]. T 2221*.

167 <u>A true account of the behaviour and confession of Alice Millikin</u>. London, 1686. T 2343.

168 <u>A True Account of the Tryal of Mrs. Mary Carlton</u>. London, Printed for Charls [sic] Moulton, 1663. T 2406A.

169 <u>A True relation of a strange apparition which appear'd to the Lady Gray, commanding her to deliver a message to His Grace the Duke of Monmouth</u>. London, Printed for Benjamin Harris and are to be sold by Langley Curtis, 1681. T 2893.

170 <u>The Unfortunate Concubines: The History of Fair Rosamond, Mistress to Henry the Second; And Jane Shore, Concubine to Edward the fourth; Kings of England</u>. London, n.d. N.I.W.

171 <u>Uraniae Metamorphosis in Sydus: or, The Transfiguration of...Queen Mary</u>. London, Printed for John Graves, and are to be sold by John Whitlock, 1695. U 125.

172 <u>A Vindication of a Marriage life</u>. [London?], 1675. V 464A*.

173 Walker, Anthony. <u>The Vertuous Wife</u>. [London], Printed for N. R. and sold by J. Robinson and Churchill, J. Taylor and J. Wyat, 1694. W 311A.

174 <u>The Westminster Wedding: or, Trick for Trick</u>. [London], Printed for Josiah Blare, [1683-1700]. W 1472A.

175 [Whitaker, Edward.] <u>The Death, Burial, and Resurrection of the act of the 35th of Eliz</u>. [London, Printed for Nath. Thompson, 1681.] W 1701A.

176 Whitehall, Robert. <u>To the no less vertuous than ingenious Mris. Mary More</u>. [Oxford, Printed at the Sheldonian Theatre], 1674. Broadside. W 1877.

177 [Winnell, Thomas.] <u>The Best Portion...funeral of Mrs. Mary Steed</u>. Exon, Printed by Sam. Parker and Sam. Farley and...sold by H. Chaulkin and at Joshua Mechoe's, [1699?]. N.I.W.

178 <u>The Widows' and Orphans' Advocate</u>. [London], 1688. W 2092.

179 <u>Witchcraft discovered and punished</u>. [London, 1682.] W 3138.

180 <u>The Womens complaint against their bad husbands</u>. London, Printed for T. M., 1676. W 3328.

181 <u>The Women's Fegari[es]</u>. London, Printed for J. Clark, [1675]. W 3329.

182 <u>Wonderful News from Buckinghamshire. Or, A Perfect Relation How a young Maid hath been for Twelve years and upwards possest with the Devil</u>. London, Printed for D. M., 1677. W 3369.

183 <u>The Young Womans Complaint</u>. London, Printed for W. Gilbertson, [1655-65]. Y 134.

Women Printers,
Publishers and Booksellers

Allen, Hanna[h]
Alsop, Elizabeth
Andrews, Elizabeth
Avery, Mary
Baldwin, Ann[e]
Bell, J[e]ane
Bever, Elizabeth
Blageart, Mrs.
Blaiklock, Hannah
Boler, Anne
Bourn[e], Jane
Brewster, Ann[e]
Broad[e], Alice
Brome, Charlotte
Brome, Joanna
Brusey, Mary
Burton, Sarah
Button, Sarah
Calvert, Elizabeth
[Campbell, Agnes] (Andrew Anderson)
Christian, Antonie, widow of
Clark, Hannah
Clark, Maria
Clark[e], Mary
Clowes, Janes
Coe, Jane
Colledge, Elizabeth
Crabbaert, John, widow of
Cotes, Ellen
Crips, Mrs.
Crook[e], Mary
Crooke, Elizabeth
Curteyne, Alice

Davis, Mrs.
Daniel, Mary
Dawson, Gartrude
Dring, Dorothy
Dwight, Anne
Edwards, Mrs.
Fabian, Mary
Fairbeard, Sarah
Feltham, Mrs.
Flesher, Elizabeth
Forrester, Susanna
Godbid, Anne
Griffin, Sarah
Grover, Mrs.
Gurnel, Mary
Hally, Mrs.
Harris, Elizabeth
Harris, Mrs.
Harris, Sarah
Harris, Widow
Harrison, Martha
Hodgkinson, Elizabeth
Holt, Elizabeth
Hood, Anne
Hunt, Anne
Howell, Mary
Howell, Widow
Howkins, Sarah
Hurlock, Elizabeth
Islip, Susan
Leigh, Susanah
Lichfield, Anne
Magnes, Mary

Chronological Index

References are to page numbers. There may be more than one item per page.

General Index

References are to page numbers. Authors are omitted.

About the Compilers

HILDA L. SMITH is a Professor at The Center for Women's Studies at the University of Cincinnati. She is the author of *Reason's Disciples: Seventeenth-Century English Feminists* (1982).

SUSAN CARDINALE was previously a Reference Librarian and Rare Books Librarian at the University of Maryland. She is the author of *Anthologies by and About Women: An Analytical Index* (Greenwood Press, 1982).